P. 65 - A.B. waiting on new word
as we connect w "concrete universal" -
Hegel. With justice! - (Maoist?)
but Maoism was a bloody
totalitarianism! Still he lives
for justice in concrete terms -
not abstract - phil.
P. 333 - Good on Xn. forgiveness as
"universal concrete" - "focused infinity"

THE ADVENTURE OF
FRENCH PHILOSOPHY

THE ADVENTURE OF FRENCH PHILOSOPHY

ALAIN BADIOU

Edited and translated with an introduction by Bruno Bosteels

VERSO

London • New York

This edition first published by Verso 2012
© Alain Badiou 2012
Introduction and translation © Bruno Bosteels 2012

Verso would like to thank the following publications and publishers who
published earlier versions of the essays collected here: Albin Michel, *The
Bible and Critical Theory*, *Le Célibataire*, Columbia University Press, *Critique*,
Duke University Press, *Economy and Society*, Editions Horlieu, *Élucidations*,
Les Empêcheurs de penser en rond, François Maspero, *Galilée*, *Le Monde*,
New Left Review, *Po&sie*, *Polygraph*, re.press, Seuil, *Les Temps modernes*.

1 3 5 7 9 10 8 6 4 2

Verso
UK: 6 Meard Street, London W1F 0EG
US: 20 Jay Street, Suite 1010, Brooklyn, NY 11201
www.versobooks.com

Verso is the imprint of New Left Books

ISBN-13: 978-1-84467-793-1

British Library Cataloguing in Publication Data
A catalogue record for this book is available from the British Library

Library of Congress Cataloging-in-Publication Data

Badiou, Alain.
[Selections. English. 2012]
The adventure of French philosophy / Alain Badiou ; edited and translated
with an introduction by Bruno Bosteels.
  p. cm.
Includes bibliographical references and index.
ISBN 978-1-84467-793-1 (alk. paper)
1. Philosophy, French--20th century. I. Bosteels, Bruno. II. Title.
B2430.B272E5 2012
194--dc23

2012001110

Typeset in Fournier by Hewer UK Ltd, Edinburgh
Printed in the US by Maple Vail

Handwritten annotations (top):

✓ Translator-editor

Selected horrible pro-Maoist bits. So A.B. made a great political misjudgement in Maoism but let's see

Platonism's concrete universal — valued

Absolutes, not his fulfilled

Political judgement — which is abright to defend pro — but not as Mao did!

Contents

'93

Translator's Introduction

I

Alain Badiou certainly needs no introduction. Having risen sharply from the anonymity in which he tirelessly worked for decades, Badiou is now a central figure in that strange and shifting constellation called French theory or philosophy. The idea of gathering the texts in this volume, however, and the reasons behind their selection will merit a few words of explanation — not least because no such collection exists in French, and because Badiou himself never envisioned these pieces as providing a systematic overview of recent French philosophy. Rather, composed over a period of exactly forty years — between 1967 and 2007 — the texts collected here were written in response to the currents and events that made up the philosophical moments in which they then, most often polemically, sought to intervene.

First and foremost, *The Adventure of French Philosophy* stems from a desire to make available a series of texts that, while crucial for understanding Badiou's place and role in the tradition of French thought, have not been included in any of the available volumes of his miscellaneous writings. In some cases, these essays are very hard or even impossible to find in French — such as, for instance, the piece here on Michel Foucault or the previously unpublished articles on Monique David-Ménard and Guy Lardreau. The closest relative to and perfect companion for the present collection, in terms of a cross-generational portrait of French philosophy, is Badiou's recent *Pocket Pantheon*, which includes commemorative essays prompted by the death, or the anniversary of the passing, of some of the thinkers who are discussed here.[1] Figures who appear in both these volumes, though regarded from different angles and therefore without a substantive overlap in treatment, include Louis Althusser, Jean-Paul Sartre, Georges Canguilhem, Michel Foucault, Gilles Deleuze, Jean-François Lyotard and Françoise Proust. Other French thinkers less commonly associated with Badiou, but who are no less significant for his personal, professional, and institutional formation – as he discusses here – include Barbara Cassin, Paul Ricoeur and François Jullien.

In addition, *The Adventure of French Philosophy* will allow the reader to appreciate Badiou's artistry and skill in two underappreciated subgenres. Here we see not only a grand system-builder (as in *Being and Event* or *Logics of Worlds*), esoteric seminar leader (as in *Theory of the Subject*), seasoned pedagogue (as in *Ethics* or *Manifesto for Philosophy*), unforgiving and widely unforgiven polemicist (as in *Gilles Deleuze: The Clamor of Being*), or satirist of the political moment (most notoriously in *The Meaning of Sarkozy*). Here we see Badiou as a master of the philosophical lecture and the review essay. And these – the public lecture and the accomplished review – are the privileged formats in Parts I and II of this collection, followed in Part III by two short, circumstantial notices on Gilles Deleuze and François Jullien respectively.

To these subgenres, I could certainly have added that of the preface,

---

1   Alain Badiou, *Pocket Pantheon: Figures of Postwar Philosophy*, trans. David Macey (London: Verso, 2009). In 'A Note on the Texts' contained in this last volume, Badiou himself recommends the parallel reading of Elisabeth Roudinesco, *Philosophy in Turbulent Times: Canguilhem, Sartre, Foucault, Althusser, Deleuze, Derrida*, trans. Willliam McCuaig (New York: Columbia University Press, 2008). Badiou borrows the notion of 'moments' in French philosophy (specifically, the moment around 1900, the moment around World War II, and the moment of the 1960s to the present) from Frédéric Worms, *La Philosophie en France au XXe siècle: Moments* (Paris: Gallimard, 2009).

in which Badiou has written some gems. I am thinking in particular of the prefaces he composed for books by Danièle Moatti-Gornet, Danielle Eleb, and – in retrospect, perhaps regrettably – Mehdi Belhaj Kacem.[2] However, insofar as a preface's content and aim are typically subservient to the book for which it is written, I have decided not to include any of Badiou's prefatory essays. Also not included here are the early texts he wrote for *Cahiers pour l'analyse*, since a separate anthology is forthcoming from Verso with materials drawn from this important journal of the Cercle d'Epistémologie at the École Normale Supérieure.[3] And finally, for reasons of space, I have not included any of the ever-expanding number of interviews in which Badiou reminisces about, settles his accounts with, or pays his debts to the immensely rich yet internally divided tradition of French philosophy.[4]

II

A few recurrent lines of argumentation run through this collection as a whole. These produce what I would call the *constitutive polemical knots* that give Badiou's philosophy its distinctive orientation, tonality

---

2   Alain Badiou, 'Préface: De la femme comme catégorie de l'être', in Danièle Moatti-Gornet, *Qu'est-ce qu'une femme? Traité d'ontologie* (Paris: L'Harmattan, 1999), pp. 11–14; 'Préface: Destin des figures', in Danielle Eleb, *Figures du destin: Aristote, Freud et Lacan ou la rencontre du réel* (Paris: Erès, 2004), pp. 9–11; 'Un corsaire du concept', in Mehdi Belhaj Kacem, *Événement et répétition* (Auch: Tristram, 2004), pp. 11–17.
3   Alain Badiou's important early papers, 'La subversion infinitésimale' and 'Marque et manque: à propos du zéro', were first published in *Cahiers pour l'analyse* 9 (1968): 118–37; and 10 (1969): 150–73. The English translations, 'Infinitesimal Subversion' and 'Mark and Lack', will be included in the volume *Concept and Form: The* Cahiers pour l'analyse *and Contemporary French Thought* (London: Verso, forthcoming). The second of these essays, in particular, would have been a good fit for the present collection, insofar as it deals with Jacques-Alain Miller's contribution to the structuralist dialectic.
4   Plans are currently under way to collect all of these interviews in chronological order with the French publisher Nous. The first volume has appeared as Alain Badiou, *Entretiens, 1: 1981–1989* (Caen: Nous, 2011).

and feel. Indeed, one of this thinker's greatest virtues – which to others might seem to be a defect, especially in his writings on other philosophers – lies in giving thought a decisive orientation by leading readers to the point where they must take a stand in one way or another. Each of Badiou's knots, in this sense, begs to be cut. And the task of his thought – for example, in reviewing someone else's work – lies in facilitating these cuts and in elucidating the consequences of choosing one knot and one cut – one *act* – over another.

Some mean-spirited readers – and there is no shortage of them – will argue that Badiou always imports his own concepts into and violently imposes them onto the works he is in the process of discussing. But then again, even readers who passionately disagree with Badiou will be able, I think, to more pointedly circumscribe the specific sites of their disagreement with him and to more effectively account for this discord, once they take the chance these pieces give to them.

And who, in any event, can claim to be one of those 'innocent' or 'honest' readers who would not filter others' works through their own conceptual grid – which is to say, at bottom, through the peculiar ensemble of their own prior readings and efforts at articulation? In this regard, Badiou is not as different from other readers and writers as he may seem at first sight. 'I am being unfair', he admits at one point in his review of Françoise Proust's book on Kant, before adding, 'as one always is'.[5] Even before the invention of portable reading devices, we have always carried our libraries, so to speak, on our backs. In fact, whether justly or unjustly, we *are* our libraries – including the gaps that signal lost or lent-out books and the piles of books on our desk or crowded out of the shelves.

What we obtain in the pages that follow, then, is a snapshot of Badiou's personal library, or at least of one of its subsections – the

---

5   See below, p. 292.

one dealing with contemporary French thought.[6] Badiou only expects that, when one enters the fray and discusses this section of his library, one does so fully aware of the underlying systematicity of one's own framework and the set of commitments – whether theoretical or practical, conceptual or stylistic, formal or political – that this framework most often silently enables, if it does not render them hopelessly 'natural' and 'self-evident'. For example, in Badiou's review of Paul Ricoeur's book on memory and oblivion, his charge is not that there has been some conceptual failure or theoretical inconsistency, but rather that the author has failed to render explicit the presupposition *behind* his call for forgiveness, so that we find only at the last moment what was there from the beginning – namely, the notion of a subject who cannot *not* be Christian. Badiou writes,

> Fundamentally, my main criticism bears on what I consider to be not so much hypocrisy as a lack of civility, a lack of civility common to so many Christian proponents of phenomenology: the absurd concealment of the true source of conceptual constructions and philosophical polemics.[7]

Contrary to what his critics make of this brutal taste for explicitness, it is precisely such a lack of civility that Badiou seeks to avoid by constantly laying bare the principles – his own, as well as those of the authors he discusses – underpinning the defining choices

---

6   Other volumes will collect Badiou's writings on theatre, on poetry and prose, and on the antiphilosophies of Kierkegaard, Nietzsche and Lacan. See respectively Alain Badiou, *Writings on Theatre*, ed. and trans. Bruno Bosteels (London: Verso, forthcoming); *'The Age of the Poets' and Other Writings on Poetry and Prose*, ed. and trans. Bruno Bosteels with Emily Apter (London: Verso, forthcoming); and *What Is Antiphilosophy? Writings on Kierkegaard, Nietzsche, and Lacan*, ed. and trans. Bruno Bosteels (Durham, NC: Duke University Press, forthcoming). His writings on cinema have been collected in Alain Badiou, *Cinéma*, ed. Antoine de Baecque (Paris: Nova, 2010).

7   See below, p. 333.

within the so-called French moment of contemporary philosophy. From among these choices, I will limit myself to enumerating five basic categorial oppositions.

1. Life or Concept?   *Existentialism!*

This is no doubt the fundamental opposition, or the primary decision. Only on one side of the opposition, though, is this fact of decision acknowledged as such; the other, in contrast, will most often presuppose an underlying continuity of which the decision is then merely a secondary and inessential result or a superficial emanation.

The choice here is between conceiving of thought as fundamentally arising from within the depths of an all-encompassing life (vitalism), or conceiving of thought as a cut that interrupts or breaks with vital flux in favour of the strict assemblage of concepts (formalism). Ultimately, however, the issue is not so much which reading is the correct one – the vitalist or the formalist – but, rather, what the implications are of choosing one over the other. The interpretation of 'being' as a vast and living tissue surely produces an entirely different series of effects than the deduction of 'being' as a set of lifeless axioms and structures. In both cases, for example, the aim may well be to produce a concept of 'being' as multiple. Yet the age-old debate between the paradigms of the continuous and the discrete persists in this alternative between life and concept, between existence and axiom, or between the multiple as nature and the multiple as number.

In fact, well before Badiou utilized this division as a key organizing principle of his reading of French philosophy, Michel Foucault had drawn a similar line of demarcation.

Without ignoring the cleavages which, during these last years after the end of the war, were able to oppose Marxists and non-Marxists, Freudians and non-Freudians, specialists in a single discipline and

philosophers, academics and non-academics, theorists and politicians, it does seem to me that one could find another dividing line
which cuts through all these oppositions.

So Foucault writes in his 1978 introduction to the English translation of his mentor Georges Canguilhem's *On the Normal and the
Pathological*. He continues:

> It is the line that separates a philosophy of experience, of sense and
> of subject and a philosophy of knowledge, of rationality and of
> concept. On the one hand, one network is that of Sartre and
> Merleau-Ponty; and then another is that of Cavaillès, Bachelard and
> Canguilhem. In other words we are dealing with two modalities
> according to which phenomenology was taken up in France, when
> quite late – around 1930 – it finally began to be, if not known, at
> least recognized.[8]

For Foucault, this alternative between life and the concept, between
experience and knowledge, or between sense and form, for many
decades continued to put its stamp on the development of philosophy in France: 'Whatever they may have been after shifts,
ramifications, interactions, even rapprochements, these two forms
of thought in France have constituted two philosophical directions
which have remained profoundly heterogeneous.'[9]

Badiou generalizes this great dividing line, both by projecting it
back onto the origins of philosophy and by extending the references
to include a growing number of contemporary French thinkers.
Thus, he writes: 'In fact, there have never been but two schemes, or
paradigms, of the Multiple: the mathematic and the organicist, Plato

---

8 Michel Foucault, 'Introduction', in Georges Canguilhem, *On the Normal and
the Pathological*, trans. Carolyn R. Fawcett (Dordrecht: D. Reidel, 1978),
pp. ix–x.
9 Foucault, 'Introduction', p. x.

or Aristotle.'[10] Mathematics or organicism, geometry or biology, the set or the fold: such would be the forms taken by the recurrent alternative that now seems to traverse the entire history of thought, up to and including the contemporary moment. 'The animal or the number? This is the cross of metaphysics', Badiou also writes in his review of Deleuze's *The Fold: Leibniz and the Baroque*, 'and the greatness of Deleuze-Leibniz, metaphysician of the divergent world of modernity, is to choose without hesitation for the animal'.[11] This preferential option for the pole of nature or the animal usually involves some form or other of organicism, if not a strict biologism. As Deleuze says of Leibniz, at stake is not only an animal psychology but also an animal cosmology and – we might add – a whole animal ontology. Being itself, thus, is thought of as a living organism, as an all-embracing and respiring animal. The other pole, by contrast, conceives of being as an infinite mass of impassive entities, the generic 'stuffness' of which can be thought through only at the cost of an axiomatic formalisation that is diametrically opposed to a phenomenological description.

Even though his most recent major book, *Logics of Worlds*, ends with a section titled 'What Is It to Live?', Badiou obviously associates his own orientation with formalism, with concept or number, placing himself unapologetically in the lineage of Cavaillès and Lautman, while attributing prominent vitalisms in France to a lineage of life-philosophy that reaches from Bergson to Deleuze to the early Lyotard – the Lyotard who, in *Dérive à partir de Marx et Freud*, for example, embraces 'the great *Triebe*, the major flows that will change all visible dispositifs and that will change the very meaning of operationality'.[12] Even more intriguingly, Badiou finds similar traces of the notion of a quasi-vitalist 'dark backdrop' as supporting the transcendental receptivity towards the event in

---

10   See below, p. 247.
11   See below, p. 247.
12   Quoted in Badiou, *Pocket Pantheon*, p. 99.

Françoise Proust's original reading of Kant. This goes to show that, more so than the mere choice of a name for being – life or concept, fold or set, animal or number – what is at stake in this disquisition is the chain of philosophical consequences that can be derived from such a choice. 'In philosophy, assigning the name of being is a crucial decision. It expresses the very nature of thought', Badiou writes in one of his most lucid and concise statements on Deleuze. 'Even the name "being", if chosen as the name of being, harbours a decision that is by no means tautological, as can be readily seen in Heidegger. And of course any name of being conditions the further nominations that it induces.'[13]

For Badiou, ultimately, the choice of life as the name of being, or the reference to a dark backdrop as the ground for the subject's passive receptivity towards the event, leads to the postulate of an underlying continuity – no matter how tenuous or obscure – between being and event. Thus, for example, 'Deleuze constructs an immense, virtuosic, and ramified phenomenological apparatus in order to write the ontological equation: being = event', whereas Badiou claims 'that the pure multiple, the generic form of being, can never welcome the event within itself as its virtual component; but, on the contrary, that the event itself takes place by a rare and incalculable supplementation'.[14] Similarly, for all of Françoise Proust's insistence on the cut introduced by the event as a singular and unpredictable caesura, by locating a transcendental passivity at the

pause in poetry

13   Alain Badiou, 'Of Life as a Name of Being, or, Deleuze's Vitalist Ontology', trans. Alberto Toscano, *Pli: The Warwick Journal of Philosophy* 10 (2000): 193. This paper is also included, under the title 'Deleuze's Vitalist Ontology', as chapter 4 of Alain Badiou, *Briefings on Existence: A Short Transitory Ontology*, trans. Norman Madarasz (Buffalo: State University of New York Press, 2009), pp. 63–73. Beyond the horizon of French philosophy, Badiou also mobilizes the nature/number or poem/matheme oppositions as part of his proposal for an alternative history of philosophy over and against the Heideggerian lineage. See Meditation 11, 'Nature: Poem or Matheme?' in Alain Badiou, *Being and Event*, trans. Oliver Feltham (London: Continuum, 2005), pp. 123–9.
14   Badiou, 'Of Life as a Name of Being', p. 198.

heart of the subject, she nonetheless still seems to suggest that the event is somehow drawn from within the regular order of being as its invisible or inapparent reverse side. Thus, through this sombre ground or dark backdrop, being and event would ultimately fuse together for Françoise Proust: 'Basically, her whole project is to think being in such a way as to fuse in its constituent duplicity being in the true sense, or the being of being, and the event or the activation of counter-being', Badiou writes in *Pocket Pantheon*. 'I part company with Françoise Proust over the doctrine of being', he continues, 'which I believe to be undivided, and that of the event, which is not a counter-being or the structural double of being-as-state, but the hazardous suspension of one of the axioms of the multiple'.[15] The hazardous occurrence of an event presupposes an incalculable excess or separation; it is neither cut from the same cloth as the regulated order of objectivity nor spun out thereof as a latent potential. Thus, from the fundamental decision regarding the name of being we are led to the next categorial opposition, regarding the continuity or discontinuity between being and event.

2. Continuity or Discontinuity?

Citing Canguilhem's history of conceptual 'transformations' and 'displacements' as well as Bachelard's 'epistemological break', so crucial for Althusser, it is once again Foucault who gives us a precise summary of the underlying shift with regard to the themes of continuity and discontinuity in French thought. 'In short, the history of thought, of knowledge, of philosophy, of literature seems to be seeking, and discovering, more and more discontinuities, whereas history itself appears to be abandoning the irruption of events in favour of stable structures', Foucault writes in *The Archaeology of Knowledge*. In actual fact, though, it is the status of the discontinuous that is changing: 'Discontinuity was the stigma of temporal

---

15 Badiou, *Pocket Pantheon*, p. 187.

dislocation that it was the historian's task to remove from history. It has now become one of the basic elements of historical analysis.'[16]

Now, following Badiou, one could argue that if nature is the adopted paradigm, then to think the irruption of an event – in politics or in art, for instance – means to capture life as one vast and self-divergent process of becoming: life as a single plane of immanence folding back and forth upon itself, expanding and contracting. Nature, from such a perspective of immanence, neither makes any leaps nor allows any gaps to open up in the continuum of life, despite the possibility of constant changes, even catastrophic ones. 'The event is the ontological realization of the eternal truth of the One, of the infinite power of Life', as Badiou writes about Deleuze. 'It is by no means that which a void, or an astonishment, separates from what becomes. On the contrary, it is the concentration of the continuity of life, its intensification.'[17] If, by contrast, we adopt the paradigm of the lifeless number – of algebra and topology, or of set theory – then we have to account differently for the possibility of genuine change. No longer the result of a spontaneous process, change from this perspective also cannot be reduced to being a mere fold in the living tissue of an all-encompassing organicism. Instead, there must be a sharp break from the decrees of fate: the sudden apparition of a gap, a supplement, or at the very least a minimal difference, comparable to the *clinamen* – that is, the slight 'deviation' or 'swerve' by which ancient atomists understood motion to include novelty, change, and, indeed, free will wresting itself from the chains of necessity:

> An event is never the concentration of vital continuity or the imma-nent intensification of a becoming. It is never coextensive with becoming. On the contrary, it is a pure cut in becoming made by an

---

16   Michel Foucault, *The Archaeology of Knowledge*, trans. Alan M. Sheridan Smith (New York: Pantheon, 1972), pp. 6, 8.

17   Alain Badiou, 'The Event According to Deleuze', in *Logics of Worlds: Being and Event, 2*, trans. Alberto Toscano (London: Continuum, 2009), p. 382.

object of the world, through that object's auto-appearance; but it is also the supplementing of appearing through the upsurge of a trace: the old inexistent which has become an intense existence.[18]

Here, then, we are no longer dealing just with questions regarding the implied ontologies of the authors under discussion and whether their paradigm of being is natural or mathematical, but, rather, with the possibility of thinking, within either of these paradigms, that which is not being qua being – namely, the event.

In other words, at stake is the possibility of thinking the event as a moment of singular change within or beyond the order of being. Unless we adopt the model of organic growth, with novelty unfolding naturally or virtually out of one and the same order, the key is to understand how change is not just the effect of an element of chance or contingency added onto a pre-existing structure from the outside, in the way that traditionally freedom and necessity – the noumenal and the phenomenal – are opposed. Instead, the very structure of what is given continually revolves around a central void, which can be rendered visible and formalized only because its effects become apparent in the slight deviations and disturbances caused at the edges.

Again, if we adopt the paradigm of life or nature, this question does not even pose itself, since in principle all distance, including critical distance or the break between science and ideology, can be brought back into the multiple folds of immanence. Ideology, for instance, simply does not exist from this standpoint: 'We are no more familiar with scientificity than we are with ideology; all we know are assemblages.'[19] But, then, if there is no ideology, there is

---

18   Badiou, 'The Event According to Deleuze', p. 384.
19   Gilles Deleuze and Félix Guattari, *A Thousand Plateaus: Capitalism and Schizophrenia*, trans. Brian Massumi (Minneapolis: University of Minnesota Press, 1987), p. 22. Deleuze and Guattari are obviously arguing against the science/ideology break found in the tradition of orthodox Althusserianism, See also, earlier in the same text: 'There is no ideology and never has been' (p. 4).

also no hope – nor even any need – for a critique of ideology. The subject's task within this paradigm is never a question of raising consciousness from its blind and ignorant state, nor of importing a critical consciousness, whether individual or class-based, from the outside. It is instead a question of experiencing the extent to which the world as it is, with everything that takes place in it, already signals the becoming of a unique yet all-consuming event. This then requires neither an epistemological break between science and ideology nor a leap into some mystical or messianic beyond. Rather, to live life in immanence means to apprehend events where others see only stable identities and, conversely, to accept that everything that occurs can become the quasi-cause of an event. We might say that

> there is, in a certain respect, no change except a change of the will, a sort of leaping in place of the whole body which exchanges its organic will for a spiritual will. It wills now not exactly what occurs, but something *in* that which occurs, something yet to come which would be consistent with what occurs, in accordance with the laws of an obscure, humorous conformity: the Event.[20]

This also means that, seen from the perspective of life or nature's immanent power, nothing changes at all, even though in a different way everything changes – or rather, everything *is* change.

In any case, for this horizon of all-encompassing change to become effectuated, there seems to be no need for a subject in the conventional sense of the term. Rather, in an ascetic process of becoming-impersonal or becoming-imperceptible, an individual ceases to be a person with a stable identity, an inner will separate from the outside world, or a clear sense of the lines of demarcation that separate action and passion, form and matter, animate and

---

20   Gilles Deleuze, *The Logic of Sense*, ed. Constantin V. Boundas, trans. Mark Lester and Charles Stivale (New York: Columbia University Press, 1990), p. 149.

inanimate. This process requires, in a continuous and almost imperceptible conversion, to turn oneself into the site of an event, to participate in the struggle that makes individuals into passageways to be traversed by events.

> It would be necessary for the individual to grasp herself as event; and that she grasp the event actualized within her as another individual grafted onto her. In this case, she would not understand, want, or represent this event without also understanding and wanting all other events as individuals, and without representing all other individuals as events.[21]

From the perspective of pure immanence, in other words, grasping oneself as event, or letting oneself be grasped by events as they occur, also entails a dissipation of the subject. As immanence becomes absolute, the subject becomes imperceptible, vanishing, as it were, into the substance of life as immanence – life itself as a continuous, singular, and impersonal event.

Perhaps, though, the issue is not any more easily solved when we adopt the formalist or structural-axiomatic paradigm. Even when priority is given to the break over the continuum, to punctuality over organicity, and to the void over the holism of life as process, the subject risks being reduced to the stable function of responding to the call of the existing structure. This would still only serve to confirm the status quo, even while offering the subject the lure of an active role in the structure's smooth functioning. The event, finally, would become an invariant feature of every structure – the constitutive non-place of every set of assigned places – and thus, essentially, a non-event covered once again by a transcendental subject.

Here Badiou engages in a polemic that reaches from 'The (Re) commencement of Dialectical Materialism' to his first major work, *Theory of the Subject*, most notably in the sections that deal with the

---

21 Deleuze, *The Logic of Sense*, p. 178.

so-called 'structural dialectic' common to Althusser and Lacan. For the latter, every structure, far from constituting some homogeneous grid without holes, is built around a determinate lack that could be said to be its absent cause. Even while seeming to be a contingent obstacle to its completion, such a paradoxical element is actually essential to the structurality of the structure itself. Depending on the point of view, there is always a lack or excess, something that is missing or sticks out, which embodies the structure's inherent obstacle and that keeps it from constituting a self-contained totality. However, this could seem to suggest that the subject is still only the place-holder of a structural invariant – that is, the recurrent effect of the vanishing causality of a lack or excess in the structure. The structure would then include the subject, to be sure, but only by means of an ideological suturing operation which it would be the task of analysis to unravel by pinpointing

> the term with the double function, inasmuch as it determines the belonging of all other terms to the structure, while itself being excluded from it by the specific operation through which it figures in the structure only in the guise of its *representative* (its *lieu-tenant*, or place-holder, to use a concept from Lacan).[22]

For Badiou, by contrast, the subject is caused by the supplementation of an event that exceeds even the transcendental law of the structure with the pure chance of a singular and undecidable occurrence. Thus, the structurality of the structure itself undergoes the shock of transformation, to the point where 'there is truly found something the existence of which Lacan denies – an other of the Other, from which it follows that what functions as the first Other is no longer a disguised modality of the Same'.[23] Badiou's overall

---

22   See below, p. 157, note 45.
23   Alain Badiou, *Theory of the Subject*, trans. Bruno Bosteels (London: Continuum, 2009), p. 156.

wager is thus a bet on the transformative effects of a discontinuous event upon the continuum of what is given, by changing the old into the genuinely new.

Still, with regard to the decision over continuity and discontinuity, there remains to this day the sense of a lingering hesitation in Badiou. On the one hand, he writes for example in *Logics of Worlds*: 'It is necessary to think discontinuity *as such*, a discontinuity that cannot be reduced to any creative univocity, as indistinct or chaotic as the concept of such a univocity may be.'[24] In other words, the aim of philosophy would be to think being, event, truth, and subject in strict discontinuity, without folding them into the dark chaotic backdrop of life as pure immanence. And yet, on the other hand, there would seem to be no subject without some minimal compromise and equivocation between elements of the continuous and the discontinuous. Thus, we can also read in *Logics of Worlds*: 'A subject is a sequence involving continuities and discontinuities, openings and points. The "and" incarnates itself as subject.'[25] The reasons for this hesitation are not purely conceptual, insofar as they are directed, as always, at the political circumstances in which Badiou is working. In fact, throughout much of the 1980s and early 1990s, in the wake of the publication of *Being and Event*, Badiou can be said to have privileged an ultra-leftist insistence on radical discontinuity. 'One divides into two', the Maoist guideline that served him during the red years of 1966–1976, thus risks veering off in the direction of a mystical 'two times one', even in his work of the following decade.[26] And this mystical reading in fact became the dominant approach to Badiou's work once it was translated into English, so that Badiou

24 Badiou, *Logics of Worlds*, p. 362.
25 Badiou, *Logics of Worlds*, p. 83. For a more detailed discussion of this hesitation in Badiou's work, see chapter 6 in Bruno Bosteels, *Badiou and Politics* (Durham, NC: Duke University Press, 2011).
26 See chapter 12, 'An Angel Has Passed', for Badiou's rebuttal of this ultra-leftist, or Linbiaoist, deviation in his review of Guy Lardreau and Christian Jambet, a couple of ex-Maoists turned New Philosophers.

himself, partly in response to this reception, began revising such ultra-leftist excesses by insisting on the necessary 'worldly' and 'bodily' inscription of a truth, for instance, in *Logics of Worlds*. Finally, it seems that such an approach of self-critical correction – a turn to the right to counterbalance a previous ultra-leftism – will continue in the promised third volume of *Being and Event*, currently announced under the title *The Immanence of Truths*.

Perhaps the most concise summary of this ongoing polemic, then, would be to state that Badiou's philosophy seeks to engage in a battle on two fronts. He wishes neither to reduce the event empirically or genealogically to its enabling conditions in the situation at hand, nor to raise the event dogmatically or messianically into the heavens of a radical discontinuity. As he concludes one of his essays on Deleuze:

> To break with empiricism is to think the event as the advent of what subtracts itself from all experience: the ontologically un-founded and the transcendentally discontinuous. To break with dogmatism is to remove the event from the ascendancy of the One. It is to subtract it from Life in order to deliver it to the stars.[27]

This last reference to the starry sky should not be seen as a thinly veiled religious invocation; instead, it too alludes to the power of number to produce a constellation, as cold with neglect and disuse as a dice throw for Mallarmé.

3. Finitude or Infinity?

Another concentrated expression of the fundamental polemics running through Badiou's assessment of contemporary French thought concerns the struggle over finitude and infinity. Ever since Heidegger's reading of Kant, we could say that nearly all contemporary philosophy

---

27   Badiou, 'The Event According to Deleuze', p. 387.

conceives of itself in one way or another as an analytic of finitude, over and against the traditional metaphysics of infinity. The result of this change is that today it has become a tautology to speak of finite thinking. Thinking as such is nothing but the exposure of, and to, finitude. 'Not only is human intuition finite, but also, and perhaps in a far more original way, is thinking finite', Heidegger writes. Or again: '*Finite thinking* is a tautology, after the fashion of a round circle.'[28]

Instead of interpreting finitude primarily in terms of death and mortality, as in *Being and Time*, Heidegger's turn to the *Critique of Pure Reason* allows him to develop the view that finitude in fact involves an essential relation not to this one life, being or entity and their possible end, but to the very question of being qua being, which is and always has been the only question worthy of that which Heidegger at this point still calls a 'metaphysics' or 'fundamental ontology'.[29] Soon afterwards, starting in the 1930s, Heidegger abandons both of these terms in favour of a 'thinking' that is at once more generic and more enigmatic and that serves as a name for non-metaphysical ways of retrieving the question of being. In fact, it is precisely the notion of finitude, once the place of its inscription is moved from the mortal human being onto being itself – and ultimately, onto the event of being – which alone enables and subsequently continues to guarantee the radical possibility of a post-metaphysical mode of thinking.

If Heidegger inaugurates the paradigm of finitude through his repetition of Kant, within the tradition of French thought it belongs to Foucault, in the final section of *The Order of Things* on 'Man and His Doubles', to have demonstrated the wide-ranging impact of such a paradigm on modernity as a whole. What Foucault, following Heidegger, calls an 'analytic of finitude' marks for him the very

---

28 Martin Heidegger, *Phenomenological Interpretation of Kant's Critique of Pure Reason*, trans. Parvis Emad and Kenneth Maly (Bloomington: Indiana University Press, 1997), p. 106; and *Kant and the Problem of Metaphysics*, trans. Richard Taft (Bloomington: Indiana University Press, 1997), p. 175.

29 Heidegger, *Kant and the Problem of Metaphysics*, pp. 155, 161.

threshold between the classical age and modernity, or between our prehistory and the contemporary moment. 'Our culture crossed the threshold beyond which we recognize our modernity when finitude was conceived in an interminable cross-reference with itself', Foucault writes. 'Modern culture can conceive of man because it conceives of the finite on the basis of itself.'[30] The human sciences, in particular, are unthinkable without crossing such a threshold into an understanding of the finite without infinity – that is, of finitude outside of the metaphysical and frequently theological schemas that oppose the finite to the infinite, on the model of creatures and their Creator.

Among the many aspects worth highlighting in this widespread interpretation of the notion of finitude, we can single out a complete overthrow of the stubbornly pejorative connotations that cling to the notion wherever finitude is understood as defect or lack, hindrance or shortcoming. For Heidegger and Foucault, finitude is not merely a limitation of human knowledge, since it alone is what first opens up the possibility of asking the questions of being, of truth, or of knowing as such. Alphonse de Waelhens and Walter Biemel, the translators of the French version of Heidegger's *Kant and the Problem of Metaphysics* – which Foucault most certainly had before him when composing *The Order of Things* – write:

> Instead of thought and knowledge being considered as an accession to the absolute which, in man, finds itself accidentally hindered in delivering its full effects, instead of holding this hindrance to be an

---

30 Michel Foucault, *The Order of Things: An Archaeology of the Human Sciences* (London and New York: Routledge, 2002), p. 346. The thinker who most persistently develops this analytic of finitude in France today, often starting from Heidegger's *Kantbuch* as well, is Jean-Luc Nancy. See, above all, the title-essay in Nancy's collection *A Finite Thinking*, ed. Simon Sparks (Stanford: Stanford University Press, 2003), pp. 3–30. Badiou provides a detailed reading of this essay in chapter 6, 'The Reserved Offering'. For a different take on Kant's influence in this regard, see also the work of Badiou's ally Quentin Meillassoux, *After Finitude: An Essay on the Contingency of Necessity*, trans. Ray Brassier (London: Continuum, 2008).

extrinsic or purely negative limitation, now it is a question of
bringing to light finitude as the positive structure and the essence
itself of knowing.[31]

Foucault, for his part, discusses three dominant and vaguely successive modalities by which finitude doubles back upon itself so as to
uncover, in its apparent limitations, the positive conditions of possibility for knowledge and truth. These modalities are, respectively,
the redoubling of the empirical and the transcendental; the double of
the cogito and the unconscious, or of thinking and the un-thought;
and the retreat and the return of origin. In each of these three cases,
the thinking of the finite is severed from all references to the infinite:

> The experience taking form at the beginning of the nineteenth
> century situates the discovery of finitude not within the thought of
> the infinite, but at the very heart of those contents that are given, by
> the finite act of knowing, as the concrete forms of finite existence.
> Hence the interminable to and fro of a double system of reference:
> if man's knowledge is finite, it is because he is trapped, without
> possibility of liberation, within the positive contents of language,
> labour, and life; and inversely, if life, labour, and language may be
> posited in their positivity, it is because knowledge has finite forms.[32]

It is in this sense that the analytic of finitude, standing at the threshold of a modernity from which we would not yet have been able to
escape, breaks completely with the classical metaphysics of infinity
that preceded it.

A 'finite thinking' is also said to have critical and anti-dogmatic
or even anti-idealist leverage. To quote de Waelhens and Biemel

---

31   Alphonse de Waelhens and Walter Biemel, in Martin Heidegger, *Kant et le
problème de la métaphysique*, trans. Alphonse de Waelhens and Walter Biemel
(Paris: Gallimard, 1981), p. 19.
32   Foucault, *The Order of Things*, p. 345.

once more: 'To link the understanding of being and man's finitude, to write a metaphysics of finitude' – in the sense of the term 'metaphysics' that Heidegger would later abandon in favor of 'thinking' – 'this also means to forbid oneself to ever invert the roles by making this metaphysics, surreptitiously or not, into an absolute knowledge of the finite, proclaimed true in itself.'[33] Or, as Heidegger himself writes: 'All philosophizing, being a human activity, is incomplete, finite and restricted. Even philosophy as knowledge of the whole must be content and give up the idea of grasping the whole at a stroke.'[34] And it is this same anti-dogmatic potential that Foucault discovers in the modern analytic of finitude at work in human sciences such as biology, political economy and philology:

> Modern thought, then, will contest even its own metaphysical impulses, and show that reflections upon life, labour, and language, in so far as they have value as analytics of finitude, express the end of metaphysics: the philosophy of life denounces metaphysics as a veil of illusion, that of labour denounces it as an alienated form of thought and an ideology, that of language as a cultural episode.[35]

For Badiou, however, this is where we might want to sound a shrill, sharply dissonant note in the midst of this chorus singing finitude's praise, as if it contained the sole and lasting promise of post-metaphysical thought. While it once had the critical virtue of fending off the twin errors of blind dogmatism and empty empiricism, 'finitude' has today become a dogma that risks keeping the empirical from being internally transformed. And conversely, 'infinity' – which was once, in its virtual rather than its actual form, inseparable from the idealist vagaries of theology – is perhaps the

---

33 De Waelhens and Biemel, in Heidegger, *Kant et le problème de la métaphysique*, p. 49.
34 Quoted in Michael Inwoord, 'Finitude', *A Heidegger Dictionary* (Oxford: Blackwell, 1999), p. 70.
35 Foucault, *The Order of Things*, p. 346.

only materialist answer to the jargon of finitude today (provided, of course, that we understand what this implies for the definitions of 'materialism' and 'idealism').

When thinking can be no more than the exposure of and to finitude without falling into idealist, metaphysical or dogmatic illusion, any attempt to change that which finitude exposes is also blocked in advance. Thinking as finite thinking thus sustains its radicality only by showing that it does not make the mistake of having confidence in, let alone acting upon, some notion of actual infinity. Or to put it differently, for the analytic of finitude any appeal to the actual infinite must by definition be seen as disastrous – as signalling some impending violence that is often referred to in the moralizing language of 'the worst',[36] while genuine radicalism would consist in at least having avoided all that. In contrast, if we follow Badiou and define 'idealism' as a tendency to grant antecedence not to mind over matter so much as to law over the interruption of law, then the paradigm of finitude which we find in the critique or deconstruction of metaphysics, perhaps no less than in negative dialectics, has – by positing the finitude of truth and knowledge as a new and insuperable law – in fact become idealist. 'The indivisibility of the law of the place exempts it from the real. To link up this exception in the domain of theory amounts to stipulating the radical anteriority of the rule', writes Badiou. 'The position of this antecedence is elaborated in philosophy as idealism.'[37] Against this new idealism, what needs to be affirmed is the infinite neither as a virtual progression nor as an asymptotically approachable beyond, but as the name for the immanent excess of the finite over its own resources: 'It is this immanent creative power, this indestructible capacity to

36   On the frequent use of the expression 'the worst' (*le pire*) in deconstructive arguments, see for example Leonard Lawlor's entry on 'Jacques Derrida' in the *Stanford Encyclopedia of Philosophy*, open-access at plato.stanford.edu/entries/derrida/.

37   Badiou, *Theory of the Subject*, p. 184.

overstep boundaries, which is the infinite as *quality* of the finite.'[38] And finally, in contrast with the power of time to signal the analytic of finitude in the Heideggerian tradition, this affirmation could be interpreted as a call to consider the possibility that paradoxically 'eternity' and 'immortality' may contain the seeds for a secular and materialist return of the infinite as the power to break with the bounds of finitude.

In terms of this polemic against finitude, Badiou finds an unsuspected ally in Deleuze. Indeed, Deleuze's unrelenting defence of the powers of the infinite is one of the reasons why he should continue to be our contemporary, according to Badiou. All the lessons to be drawn from Deleuze, thus,

> can be summed up in one negative prescription: fight the spirit of finitude, fight the false innocence, the morality of defeat and resignation implicit in the word 'finitude' and tiresome 'modest' proclamations about the finite destiny of the human creature; and in one affirmative prescription: trust only in the infinite.[39]

Conversely, Badiou's objections to Lyotard, Lardreau or Françoise Proust, in his otherwise admiring reviews of their work, can be summed up in the fact that they concede too much to the spirit of finitude. 'Ultimately, this is a differend about infinity, I think. Or about its correlation with the finite', Badiou writes about Lyotard in *Pocket Pantheon*. 'I am both less inimical to Hegel than he is, and also less inclined to make concessions to Kant over the motif of the

---

38 Badiou, *The Century*, trans. Alberto Toscano (Cambridge: Polity, 2007), p. 158. In this passage, Badiou is reading the section 'Quantity' from Hegel's *Science of Logic*. Badiou concludes: 'The synthetic definition proposed by Hegel (I will borrow his vocabulary here) is that (the quantum's) infinity comes to be when the act of self-overcoming is once again taken up into itself. Hegel adds that in this moment the infinite exceeds the sphere of the quantitative and becomes qualitative' (p. 157).

39 Badiou, *Pocket Pantheon*, p. 118.

Law.'[40] Indeed, insofar as the motif of finitude typically involves some form of Kantianism, Badiou will sometimes phrase his plea for a laicization of the infinite as a bold defence of Hegel's dialectic over and against Kant's critical machinery.

4. Critique or Dialectic?

For better or for worse, Badiou clearly has but little patience for Kant:

> Kant is exemplarily an author with whom I cannot attain familiarity. Everything in him exasperates me, above all his legalism – always asking *Quid juris?* or 'Haven't you crossed the limit?' – combined, as in today's United States, with a religiosity that is all the more dismal in that it is both omnipresent and vague.[41]

Every 'return to Kant', as Badiou writes below in his review of Lardreau's *La Véracité*, should be interpreted as a sign of 'morbid and regressive times'.[42] For this reason, the opening of a properly materialist and dialectical philosophy of the event also demands a rebuttal of Kantianism.

If Kant is Badiou's most loyal enemy, then Hegel is without doubt – of all the canonical philosophers apart from Plato – his most constant interlocutor. At least in Badiou's published work, no other philosopher is read with the same fervour or with the same level of consistency as the author of *The Science of Logic*: 'I have never ceased measuring myself up to this book, almost as unreadable as Joyce's *Finnegans Wake*.'[43] Both *Being and Event* and *Logics of Worlds* thus contain important sections devoted to Hegel, and there are a sufficient number of occasional references to Hegel

---

40 Badiou, *Pocket Pantheon*, p. 111.
41 Badiou, *Logics of Worlds*, p. 537.
42 See below, p. 308. Badiou's original expression in French is '*des périodes repliées et funestes*'.
43 Badiou, *Logics of Worlds*, p. 531.

scattered throughout most of Badiou's recent publications to warrant the claim that he continues to see himself as a dialectical thinker who works in Hegel's shadow.

'You could almost say that my entire enterprise is one giant confrontation [*démêlé*] with the dialectic', Badiou states in an interview.

> That is why sometimes I declare myself a dialectician and write in defence of the great dialecticians (but I mean the French dialecticians, which is not exactly the same as the Hegelian dialectic), while at other times I declare myself an anti-dialectician.[44]

On one hand, Badiou slowly but surely seems to have moved from a dialectical to a mathematical outlook, to the point that we might be able to read the later writings in light of what he says about Hegel in *Being and Event*: 'Mathematics occurs here as discontinuity within the dialectic.'[45] On the other hand, though – as late as in *Peut-on penser la politique?* – all of Badiou's major philosophical concepts are still presented as the building blocks for a new dialectic:

> I hold that the concepts of event, structure, intervention, and fidelity are the very concepts of the dialectic, insofar as the latter is not reduced to the flat image, which was already inadequate for Hegel himself, of totalization and the labor of the negative.[46]

---

44 Alain Badiou, 'Beyond Formalisation: An Interview with Alain Badiou', *The One or the Other: French Philosophy Today*, ed. Peter Hallward, *Angelaki* 8.2 (2003): 122–3. By French dialecticians, Badiou somewhat idiosyncratically refers to two classical authors – Blaise Pascal and Jean-Jacques Rousseau – and two modern ones – Stéphane Mallarmé and Jacques Lacan. For the exact meaning of the dialectic in this context, see Alain Badiou, 'Généalogie de la dialectique', *Peut-on penser la politique?* (Paris: Seuil, 1985), pp. 84–91.

45 Badiou, *Being and Event*, p. 169.

46 Badiou, *Peut-on penser la politique?*, p. 84.

And, if anything, *Logics of Worlds* only further highlights this continuity, as Badiou now labels his entire philosophical project – or at least the ideological atmosphere surrounding it – a new 'materialist dialectic' as opposed to the dominant ideology of 'democratic materialism', which for its part thrives on the motifs of finitude and the critical postulation of unknowables:

> So it is important that by 'materialist dialectic' we understand the deployment of a critique of every critique. To have done, if possible, with the watered-down Kant of limits, rights and unknowables. To affirm, with Mao Tse-tung (why not?): 'We will come to know everything that we did not know before.'[47]

The sheer fact of this continued interest in Hegel in and of itself deserves some comment insofar as Badiou is formed in a school of thought dominated by the influence of Althusser for whom Hegel is the philosophical curse that weighs down Marx and Marxism, continuing to threaten both with the temptation to relapse into one form or another of idealism. Badiou's Hegelianism thus completely runs counter to the accepted wisdom of orthodox Althusserians. This is because Badiou is not convinced that the author of *For Marx* managed to be done with Hegel: 'It is not enough to *declare* oneself outside of Hegel in order effectively to exit an accursed reign in which, as we know, nothing is easier than endlessly to sing the song

---

47 Badiou, *Logics of Worlds*, p. 8. It is above all in Badiou's earlier works, most notably in the article 'Infinitesimal Subversion', in the prefatory remarks and footnotes to the translation of *The Rational Kernel of the Hegelian Dialectic*, and in the entire first part of *Theory of the Subject*, that Badiou argues in a detailed and painstaking way for the possibility of a materialist reading of Hegel's dialectic. See chapter 2 'Hegel in France'. Badiou's more recent invocations of Hegel, on the other hand, also have little to do with what we might describe as the counter-intuitive image of Hegel as a thinker not of the absolute but of finitude – an image of thought that runs the gamut from Theodor Adorno to Slavoj Žižek, by way of Jean-Luc Nancy and Catherine Malabou.

of departure while staying *in the same spot.*[48] And yet, we are also far removed from the image of Hegel popularized by Alexandre Kojève, whose introductory lectures on the *Phenomenology of Spirit*, particularly the section on the dialectic of lord and bondsman, heavily marked all of French thought from André Breton to Jean-Paul Sartre to Jacques Lacan.

This grandiose but also debilitating alternative is precisely what Badiou's retrieval of the Hegelian dialectic seeks to overcome. He will try to do so, moreover, with an eye on developing his philosophical loyalty to the two major referents of French Maoism. 'What the Cultural Revolution and May 1968 made clear on a massive scale was the need for something entirely different from an oscillation of national intellectual traditions (between the Descartes of the cogito, Sartre, and the Descartes of the machines, Althusser)', Badiou recalls: 'The Maoist aim is to break with this alternation, with this avoidance.'[49] Hegel's fate according to Badiou, then, is to be neither inverted nor discarded but internally divided. This division of Hegel, in fact, seems to be the only remedy against the temptation to submit his work to either an idealist or a positivist reductionism.

Hegel must be split in two. And in fact, the dialectic itself comes to be defined as a logic of scission, to the point that all its concepts are in turn internally divided between a dialectical and a non-dialectical side: 'The dialectic itself is so to speak dialectical, insofar as its conceptual operators, which reflect reality, are all equally split.'[50] This interpretive principle applies in the first place to Hegel:

> Thus, it is the style of transformation at work in Hegel that we must also question and divide: in a way, we must seize the Two of the Two, the dialecticity of the Hegelian dialectic, and see what in this movement finally leads back to the One.

---

48 See below, pp. 168–9.
49 See below, pp. 23–4.
50 Alain Badiou, *Théorie de la contradiction* (Paris: François Maspero, 1975), p. 81.

So Badiou concludes in the last synthetic footnote to *The Rational Kernel of the Hegelian Dialectic*, and later, in *Can Politics Be Thought?*, he seems to reiterate the same principle:

> The dialecticity of the dialectic consists precisely in having its conceptual history, and to divide the Hegelian matrix up to the point where it turns out to be in its very being a doctrine of the event, and not a regulated adventure of the spirit. A politics, rather than a history.[51]

This is much less the old story of a rational kernel hidden in an idealist shell than it is the entirely novel idea that this kernel must itself be split: 'It is the kernel itself that is cracked, as in those peaches that are furthermore so irritating to eat whose hard internal object quickly cracks between one's teeth into two pivoting halves.'[52] It is only by cracking the rational kernel of the Hegelian dialectic that we can begin to understand how this dialectic presents a doctrine of the event – one that precisely articulates a theory of the subject onto the fundamental crack or discontinuity in the edifice of being – that anticipates Badiou's own.

We are now in a better position to understand why it is that Badiou, in the closing text of the present volume, can define himself as 'a philosopher of the post-dialectical dialectic'.[53] This dialectic is *post*-dialectical insofar as it reiterates some of the more common, if not hackneyed criticisms thrown at Hegel. Badiou first of all claims on numerous occasions that Hegel's dialectic, at least when considered globally, tends to be circular – presupposing the end in the beginning and leading back in the conclusion to a speculative restating of its initial presupposition. This means that there is no genuine

---

51   Badiou, *Le noyau rationnel de la dialectique hégélienne*, p. 91; *Peut-on penser la politique?*, p. 84.
52   Badiou, *Theory of the Subject*, p. 3.
53   See below, p. 346.

novelty or change, only repetition and return. 'It would not be an exaggeration to say that all of Hegel can be found in the following: the "still-more" is immanent to the "already": everything that is, is already "still-more".'[54] For Badiou, the materialist answer to the dominance of this looping-back mechanism corresponds to the image of a periodization by way of breaks and leaps, followed by qualitatively new retroactions: 'Hegel, on this point, must be divided once again. He must be divided in terms of the procedures he proposes for looping back the whole process. To be brief, we will oppose (materialist) *periodization* to (idealist) *circularity*.'[55] The Hegelian circle is thus undone in favour of an image of the dialectical process as a spiral, combining the circle and the leap from quantity to quality in an ongoing series of symptomatic torsions.

In the second place, Badiou's dialectic is critical of Hegel's tendency to subordinate the logic of scission, especially when translated in the idealist or at best derivative terms of negation and the negation of negation, to the notion of the true as totality. 'Hegel is without the shadow of a doubt the philosopher who has pushed furthest the interiorization of Totality into even the slightest movement of thought', whereas Badiou's materialist dialectic − like Adorno's negative dialectics − starts from the principle that the Whole is the false. Or, rather, there is no Whole. So Badiou writes in *Logics of Worlds*,

> One could argue that whereas we launch a transcendental theory of worlds by saying 'There is no Whole', Hegel guarantees the inception of the dialectical odyssey by positing that 'There is nothing but the Whole'. It is immensely interesting to examine the consequences of an axiom so radically opposed to the inaugural axiom of this book.

54 Badiou, *Being and Event*, p. 162.
55 Badiou, *Theory of the Subject*, p. 18.

And Badiou continues, still in *Logics of Worlds*:

> Of course, we share with Hegel a conviction about the identity of being and thought. But for us this identity is a local occurrence and not a totalized result. We also share with Hegel the conviction regarding a universality of the True. But for us this universality is guaranteed by the singularity of truth-events, and not by the view that the Whole is the history of its immanent reflection.[56]

Thirdly, perhaps the most original criticism of the Hegelian dialectic appears in *Being and Event*, when Badiou shows how the condemnation of the 'bad infinity' of mathematics as opposed to the 'good infinity' of the subjective dialectic actually showcases the pre-Cantorian nature of the *Science of Logic*. This argument is a good example of the dialecticity of the dialectic.

> After all, the bad infinity is bad due to the very same thing which makes it good in Hegelian terms: it does not break the ontological immanence of the one; better still, it derives from the latter. Its limited or finite character originates in its being solely defined locally, by the still-more of this already that is determinateness.[57]

The infinite, thus, would be intrinsic to the finite – indeed, it can be wholly inferred or generated out of the latter, as its immanent passing over of itself into its opposite. For Badiou, this generative ontology, in which quantity and quality are said intrinsically to pass into one another, cannot hide the central disjunction or split between the two – a disjunction or split which the word 'infinity' merely seeks to cover up in the guise of a false homonymy. 'The "good quantitative infinity" is a properly Hegelian hallucination', Badiou concludes, before announcing for his part a subtractive ontology,

---

56   Badiou, *Logics of Worlds*, pp. 141 and 142–3.
57   Badiou, *Being and Event*, p. 165.

based on a Cantorian understanding of multiple infinities, to replace Hegel's generative ontology:

> It was on the basis of a completely different psychosis, in which God in-consists, that Cantor had to extract the means for legitimately naming the infinite multiplicities – at the price, however, of transferring to them the very proliferation that Hegel imagined one could reduce (it being bad) through the artifice of its differentiable indifference.[58]

While thus in many ways decisively *post*-dialectical, Badiou nonetheless remains at the same time a post-*dialectical* thinker writing in the wake of Hegel. This positive legacy, too, can be summarized in three main points. For Badiou, truth is first of all a process or a labour, rather than an act of revelation or a propositional attribute:

> At least in this regard I remain more profoundly Hegelian. That is, I am convinced that the new can only be thought as process. There surely is novelty in the event's upsurge, but this novelty is always evanescent. It is not there that we can pinpoint the new in its materiality, but that is precisely the point that interests me: the materiality of the new.[59]

The practice of philosophy, secondly, amounts to thinking the truths of one's time, truths that have already occurred before the arrival of the philosopher on the scene of the event. 'I have assigned philosophy the task of constructing thought's embrace of its own time, of refracting newborn truths through the unique prism of concepts', Badiou claims.

---

58 Badiou, *Being and Event*, pp. 169–70.
59 Badiou in Bruno Bosteels, 'Can Change Be Thought? A Dialogue with Alain Badiou', *Alain Badiou: Philosophy and Its Conditions*, ed. Gabriel Riera (Albany: State University of New York Press, 2005), p. 253.

In this aspect, too, I think that I am fairly Hegelian. In certain regards, philosophy would rather have a tendency always to arrive too late. Ultimately, the owl of Minerva only takes flight at dusk. I understand this fairly well, even though obviously not for the same reasons as Hegel. I understand that the major problem for the philosopher is to arrive early enough.[60]

For Badiou unlike Hegel, however, this thinking of the truths of one's time does not presuppose an intrinsic temporalization of the concept – or to put it the other way around, the concept is not the effectuation of history's immanent rationality. In fact, this is precisely the point where Badiou's notion of rupture, introduced by the discontinuity of a contingent event, breaks with the subjective immanence and circularity of the Hegelian dialectic. This also means that for a philosopher of the post-dialectical dialectic, such as Badiou sees himself, thinking must break with the Romantic paradigm of the historicity of thought in which philosophy is typically called upon to appear and – nowadays at least – to plead guilty in the tribunal of a world-historical reason whose blindfolded goddess seems to be at the beck and call of finitude. 'There is a very tenacious and profound link between the disentanglement of mathematics and philosophy and the preservation, in the inverted or diverted form of finitude, of a non-appropriable or unnameable horizon of immortal divinity', a tendency which can be overcome only through a radical secularization of the infinite:

> Only by relating the infinite back to a neutral banality, by inscribing eternity in the matheme alone, by simultaneously abandoning historicism and finitude, does it become possible to think within a radically deconsecrated realm. Henceforth, the finite, which

---

60   Alain Badiou, *Theoretical Writings*, ed. and trans. Ray Brassier and Alberto Toscano (London: Continuum, 2004), p. 14; and Badiou in Bosteels, 'Can Change Be Thought?', p. 254.

continues to be in thrall of an ethical *aura* and to be grasped in the pathos of mortal-being, must only be conceived of as a truth's differential incision within the banal fabric of infinity.[61]

Despite his pre-Cantorian deposing of the bad infinity of mathematics, Hegel's most precious gift to the twenty-first century according to Badiou – over and against the twentieth century's complete domination by Kant's analytic of finitude, as retrieved by almost every major philosopher from Heidegger and Foucault to Nancy and Malabou – might well have been the search for a secular or a-theological infinity.

In other words, Badiou's ongoing confrontation with the legacy of Hegel's dialectic once again announces a battle on two fronts – which sends us back to the previous discussion: Badiou resists the dogmatism of every metaphysics of theological infinity, on one hand, while he stands against the (perhaps no less theological) scepticism of the analytic of finitude, on the other.

> The decisive point here is that, for Hegel, mathematics and philosophical speculation share a fundamental concept: the concept of the infinite. More particularly, the destitution of the metaphysical concept of infinity – in other words, the destitution of classical theology – is initially undertaken through the determination of the mathematical concept of the infinite.[62]

As we saw before, however, the destitution of the traditional metaphysics of the infinite should not lead to an embrace of radical finitude but to a thorough immanentization of infinity. 'I think Hegel saw it before anyone else: ultimately, mathematics proposes

---

61 Badiou, *Theoretical Writings*, pp. 26–7. On the problem of historicism and the tribunal of history for philosophy, see also Alain Badiou, *Manifesto for Philosophy*, trans. Norman Madarasz (Albany: State University of New York Press, 1999), pp. 29–31, 113–38.
62 Badiou, *Theoretical Writings*, p. 10.

a new concept of the infinite', even if the real mathematical revolution was and perhaps is still to come. 'Nevertheless, we do know why mathematics teaches us that there is no reason whatsoever to confine thinking within the ambit of finitude. With mathematics we know that, as Hegel would have said, the infinite is nearby.'[63] This promise is actually not limited to mathematics but is also announced by certain art forms in the twentieth century. 'There is no separate or ideal infinite. The infinite is not captured *in* form; it *transits through form*. If it is an event – if it is *what happens* – finite form can be equivalent to an infinite opening', Badiou writes in *The Century*. And in an explicit return to the argument over bad infinity from Hegel's *Science of Logic*, previously criticized in *Being and Event*, he concludes this time with a word of praise for the immanent power of the infinite as displayed in art: 'The infinite as pure creation is thereby attained by taking hold of that which makes the obdurate activity of surpassing count "in itself", and not by virtue of subsequent repetitions.'[64]

Hegel against Kant; the dialectic of infinity against the analytic of finitude; the indestructible capacity to overstep boundaries against their obsessive-compulsive fixating – for Badiou, these points at once sum up and summon us to the philosophical battle of the twenty-first century against the dominant motifs of the twentieth.

5. Leftism or Maoism?

Yet the most surprising texts in the present collection are undoubtedly those that refuse to engage in a purely philosophical battle. I am referring to Badiou's shocking attacks on the 'potato fascism' of Deleuze and Guattari, or on the 'Manichaeism' of New Philosophers Guy Lardreau and Christian Jambet. These are obviously texts written in the heat of the moment, without the slightest concession

---

63 Badiou, *Theoretical Writings*, p. 18.
64 Badiou, *The Century*, pp. 155, 158.

to academic decorum and guided only by the perspective of political antagonism: 'The only lesson from which there is no turning
back is the lesson of antagonism.'[65] This then raises the question of
the degree to which Badiou would have subsequently modified not
just the tone of his polemics, but also their content.

When writing these polemics, Badiou was a militant leading
figure in a small Maoist organization, the Union des Communistes
de France Marxiste-Léniniste (UCFML). Founded in 1969/1970 as
an offshoot of the Parti Socialiste Unifié (PSU), in which Badiou
had tried in vain to propose to found a 'Marxist-Leninist party of
the new type', the UCFML would continue throughout the 1970s to
intervene in the political and cultural-artistic scene in France. The
group published a newspaper, *Le Marxiste-Léniniste*, numerous
pamphlets on Maoism and the international political situation, as
well as booklets in a series co-edited by Badiou and his friend
Sylvain Lazarus for the French publisher François Maspero.[66] It was
as part of this series that the UCFML's Yenan Philosophy Group,
clearly spearheaded by Badiou, published a collection of essays
titled *The Current Situation on the Philosophical Front*, including
analyses of Deleuze and Guattari's *Anti-Oedipus* and *A Thousand
Plateaus*, Jacques-Alain Miller's brand of Lacanianism as a structural pseudo-dialectic, Lardreau and Jambet's ultra-leftist Maoism,
and Dominique Lecourt's Althusserian take on the Lyssenko affair.
Of these texts, I have translated the ones signed by Badiou – as
Badiou, and under his pseudonym Georges Peyrol – as well as the
introduction collectively signed by the Yenan Philosophy Group.

What makes these texts so shocking is the fact that they go
completely against the grain of all the received wisdom about '1968
thought' (*la pensée '68*), as Luc Ferry and Alain Renaut call the

---

65   See below, p. 221, note 14.
66   For a complete bibliography of the UCFML as well as a representative
selection of texts, see the dossier *Alain Badiou and Cultural Revolution*, special
issue of the journal *positions: east asia cultures critique* 13.3 (2005); and for a more
detailed analysis of Badiou's Maoism, see chapter 3 in my *Badiou and Politics*.

philosophical tradition of Foucault, Derrida, Lacan, and the others that frequently get referred to as 'French theory'.[67] For Badiou, in fact, this tradition of thought is complicit with the posthumous betrayal of the events of May '68 and their aftermath in the first half of the 1970s. Whereas most readers of Foucault, Lyotard, or Deleuze and Guattari, for example, see their work as a continuation of the liberatory impulse of those events, Badiou and his cohorts of the UCFML see in them an anti-dialectical, anti-Marxist and ultimately anti-political form of ultra-leftism. Concretely, the well-known topics of power and resistance, mastery and rebellion, desire and flux, discourse and textuality would respond to a quest for a purified form of antagonism – a dualism that politically does not move beyond the external opposition of masses and the State, or the plebes and the State – without any class-based internal divisions: 'Everywhere to substitute the couple masses/State for the class struggle (that is, everywhere to substitute ideology for politics): that is all there is to it', the Yenan Philosophy Group writes. 'The hatred of the proletariat, combined with the abstract cult of the "masses" and the aesthetic despair. That is what public opinion is preparing for.'[68] This means that, contrary to what Ferry and Renaut claim in their attack on 'the thought of '68', French theory is actually incapable of representing an adequate balance sheet of the experience of political militancy during the so-called 'red years' of 1966 to 1972.

The immediate context of Badiou's polemics, in this sense, is the phenomenon of the Union de la Gauche (Union of the Left), which between 1972 and 1977 brought together the French Parti Socialiste

---

67   See Luc Ferry and Alain Renaut's *La Pensée 68* (Paris: Gallimard, 1985), translated as *French Philosophy of the Sixties: An Essay on Antihumanism*, trans. Mary H.S. Cattani (Amherst: University of Massachusetts Press, 1990). For a more sympathetic take, see François Cusset, *French Theory: How Foucault, Derrida, Deleuze & Co. Transformed the Intellectual Life of the United States*, trans. Jeff Fort (Minneapolis: University of Minnesota Press, 2008).
68   See below, p. 11.

(Socialist Party), the Parti Communiste Français (French Communist Party) and the Mouvement des Radicaux de Gauche (Movement of Left Radicals) on the basis of an electoral Programme Commun de Gouvernement (Common Programme for Governance). As stated in 'The Current Situation on the Philosophical Front', the year 1972 thus marks the moment of a great ideological reversal, which the Yenan Philosophy Group believed was merely confirmed in the misguided intellectual balance sheet drawn up by the leading intellectuals of the time. On the other hand, the year 1977, usually associated with the mediatic rise to fame of New Philosophers such as André Glucksmann or Bernard Henri-Lévy, is not a turning point but merely the continuation of one and the same ideological backlash. This explains why, in Badiou's booklets *Théorie de la contradiction* and *De l'idéologie*, which date from the same period, Glucksmann and Deleuze are similarly diagnosed as cases of left-wing deviation, to be contrasted with a properly Maoist-Hegelian understanding of the dialectics of scission. 'In this regard, the "massist" ideology that came out of 1968 excels in flattening out the dialectical analysis', Badiou remarks: 'Always the same exalted masses against the identical power, the invariable system.'[69] Cutting across this inoperative dualism, politics according to Badiou must be thought through the complete arsenal of concepts implied in the logic of scission that is most succinctly encapsulated in the Maoist formula 'One divides into two'. He explains:

> We are in favour of the increase by scission of the new. We want neither the sanctified and obscure, inoperative and repetitive, ultra-leftist masses nor the revisionist union, which is but the façade of a sinister dictatorship. What is proletarian, especially today, divides and combats the minute fractures that are internal to the 'movement', and makes them grow to the point where they become what is principal.[70]

---

69   Badiou, *Théorie de la contradiction*, p. 69.
70   Ibid.

Now, when terms such as 'revolution' or 'proletariat' gradually disappear from Badiou's lexicon in favour of 'emancipation' or 'subject', should we conclude that his 1977 analysis of 'the current situation on the philosophical front' has become obsolete? What happens when, towards the mid-1980s, Badiou suddenly devotes highly admiring and academically respectable reviews to books such as *The Fold* and *The Differend* by his one-time adversaries, Deleuze and Lyotard? Is this merely a change in form and protocol, leaving the underlying evaluations untouched? Or has Badiou undergone an in-depth transformation in his view of the relation between philosophy and politics?

Badiou himself seems to suggest the existence of a deeper continuity. 'During the militant fury of the red years between 1966 and 1980, that took the form of violent opposition', he writes in *Pocket Pantheon* about Deleuze's antithesis to his own stance. 'Much later, I learned to love Deleuze, but from within a controversy that would not die down. Platonism and anti-Platonism, basically.'[71] About Lyotard, similarly, Badiou writes in *Logics of Worlds*:

> I often dubbed him a modern sophist, and he regarded me as a Stalinist. One day, at the beginning of the 1980s, coming out of a philosophy department meeting at Paris VIII, we drove back from François Châtelet's home towards Montparnasse. It was pouring rain, so we stopped the car for a while by the sidewalk. A long conversation ensued, both abrupt and trusting, in the narrow confines of the vehicle. Later Lyotard compared it to a talk under a tent among warriors from the *Iliad*.[72]

---

71   Badiou, *Pocket Pantheon*, p. 194. See also Badiou's recollections in the 'Introduction: So Near! So Far!' to his *Deleuze: The Clamor of Being*, trans. Louise Burchill (Minneapolis: University of Minnesota Press, 2000), pp. 1–8.
72   Badiou, *Logics of Worlds*, p. 553.

In both of these cases, the reader who consults Badiou's reviews of *The Fold* and *The Differend* in this volume will be able to appreciate the extent to which we are dealing with sobered-up versions of the same polemics that roused his fury a decade earlier.

However, one major change in substance that does occur is the one that concerns the very relation between philosophy and politics. That is to say, whereas Badiou gladly subordinates all philosophy to the tasks of political antagonism throughout the 1970s and up to the publication of *Theory of the Subject* in 1982, his reviews of Lyotard and Deleuze in the mid-1980s begin to pave the way for a measured and systematic proposal in his 1988 opus *Being and Event*, in which philosophy receives autonomous validation as the eternal discourse of being, truth and the subject. Consider, for example, how the Yenan Philosophy Group views the role of philosophy:

> Philosophy thoroughly summoned by history. The servant not of the sciences but of weaponry. Not the reign of the eternal, much less of wisdom, but the trenchant figure of the actual, of the divided, of class. Not heaven and air, the place of contemplative transparency. Not at all the nocturnal waters of reconciliation. But the resilient earth of production, the weight of interestedness, the fire of the historical ordeal.[73]

A decade later, Badiou appears to argue the exact opposite of the Yenan Philosophy Group's declaration. In his *Deleuze: The Clamor of Being*, for instance, Badiou writes: 'Political sequences, bearing the stamp of the event, are one thing; philosophical eternity, even if, in its construction, it is conditioned by politics, is another.'[74]

I leave it to the reader to decide on the specific advantages and disadvantages of such opposed viewpoints. The fact of the matter is

---

73   See below, p. 1.
74   Badiou, *Deleuze: The Clamor of Being*, p. 4.

that Badiou now believes that his earlier philosophy was sutured onto politics and politics alone under the influence of Maoism, whereas a strict separation of philosophy and politics – with politics being just one of philosophy's four conditions, alongside science, art and love – would allow for a more nuanced and comprehensive (re)commencement of philosophy.

III

At this point, three final remarks are called for. The first concerns the exact nature of the categorial oppositions outlined above. We are obviously not dealing with simple choices among a plethora of options available in the marketplace of ideas. But neither is it a mere matter of theoretical consistency, whereby one option would be correct and the other incorrect. Rather, these are what we might call forced choices. Instead of merely choosing one option over another, we are in some way chosen by them – sometimes against our conscious knowledge and contrary to our natural inclination: 'Thinking is not the spontaneous effusion of a personal capacity. It is the power, won only with the greatest difficulty against oneself, of being constrained to the world's play.'[75] As subjects of thinking, we are nothing but force-fields traversed by the power of such categorial oppositions to affect and inflect the set of opinions, events, habits and prejudices that attune us to the task of our thinking.

Second, the appearance of binary oppositions is no less potentially misleading than the suggestion of a free rational choice between them. For Badiou, indeed, the point of philosophical thinking is always to trace a diagonal through and across established binaries:

The notion that thought should always establish itself beyond categorical oppositions, thereby delineating an unprecedented diagonal, is constitutive of philosophy of itself. The whole question consists

---

75   Badiou, *Deleuze: The Clamor of Being*, p. 12.

in knowing what value to ascribe to the operators of this diagonal trajectory, and in identifying the unknown resource to which they summon thought.[76]

More specifically, philosophy can be said to variously traverse the binary oppositions outlined above from the angle of ontology (or science of being), from the angle of the theory of the subject, and from the angle of an event-based doctrine of truth. In his reviews here of books by Lyotard, Deleuze, Proust and David-Ménard, especially, Badiou will thus introduce a recurrent set of questions (or 'punctuations') that concern their respective doctrines of being, subject, and event. It is by diagonally cutting across oppositions such as life and concept, continuity and discontinuity, finitude and the infinite, critique and dialectic, leftism and Marxism or Maoism, that the reader obtains the different understandings of being, subject, and event that map out the adventure of French philosophy according to Badiou.

This clearly leaves open the question of language as a significant lacuna in Badiou's philosophy, a fact that furthermore seems to be confirmed by the absence of anything resembling a sustained engagement with Derrida's deconstructive understanding of language and writing.[77] This is because Badiou considers the so-called linguistic turn to have had nothing but disastrous consequences for philosophy. For Badiou, subordinating the doctrine of being to the logic of the signifier or to a linguistic anthropology

---

76 Badiou, *Theoretical Writings*, p. 69.
77 Badiou has written only one short homage to Derrida, formulated in terms of the pursuit of (his own concept of) the inexistent, in *Pocket Pantheon*, pp. 125–44. The only other published exchange clearly represents a missed encounter between Badiou and Derrida, mediated by René Major, on the occasion of a philosophical conference on the legacy of Jacques Lacan. The correspondence from this polemic can be found in the appendix published in the conference proceedings. See 'Annexes (Correspondance et Post-scriptum)', in *Lacan avec les philosophes* (Paris: Albin Michel, 1991), pp. 421–52.

amounts to reducing philosophy to sophistics – ontology then becomes what Barbara Cassin, following Novalis, calls 'logology'. Aside from his polemics against the great modern sophists that would include everyone from the second Wittgenstein to the late Lyotard, the fact remains that there is a rather glaring absence of any theory of language in Badiou's philosophy of the event: 'Regarding the seizing of the truths of our times, there is, in the refusal to take into account the constitutive dimension of *language* for thought – and, therefore, for the subject as for truth – a preconceived bias that seems untenable.'[78]

Badiou also never indulges in play on etymologies and alleged un-translatables, nor does he in any way privilege the aura of the original, mostly Greek or German, texts of philosophy, as has become customary in much post-Heideggerian thinking. For Badiou, the French language would be utterly foreign to such auratic philosophical uses. As he boldly proclaims in his contribution to Barbara Cassin's ambitious *Vocabulaire européen des philosophies*:

> Against the fascination for the word and for etymology, that is, for the origin and for substance, the French language plays up the primacy of syntax, that is, of the relation and the assertion. And this is why, once more, philosophy in the French language is political: between axiom and sentence, against consensus and ambiguity, the French language imprints its certainty and its authority, which also make up its persuasive beauty.[79]

Again, with his affirmation that philosophical language in general and French philosophical language in particular is at once polemical and universal, Badiou's point is to avoid both the sophistic

---

78   François Wahl, 'Preface: The Subtractive', in Alain Badiou, *Conditions*, trans. Steven Corcoran (London: Continuum, 2008), p. xxxvii.

79   Alain Badiou, 'De la langue française comme évidement', in *Vocabulaire européen des philosophies: Dictionnaire des intraduisibles*, ed. Barbara Cassin (Paris: Le Robert/Seuil, 2004), p. 465.

relativism of a discursive anthropology and the auratic dogmatism of a silent act.

And finally, to justify taking the title of the volume's preface as that of the collection as a whole, I could invoke two useful precedents: Maurice Merleau-Ponty's *Adventures of the Dialectic* and Gianni Vattimo's *The Adventure of Difference*. Badiou's approach in the texts translated here can in fact be said to continue and extend both of these precursors. On the one hand, by targeting the Manichaean or Gnostic 'ultra-leftism' of the likes of Lardreau and Jambet, he somehow expands upon Merleau-Ponty's equally ferocious indictment of Sartre's 'ultra-Bolshevism'.[80] This rebuttal then takes the form of a reconsideration of the very nature of the dialectic. On the other hand, Badiou also implicitly seems to accept several of Vattimo's criticisms of the French philosophies of difference, from Derrida to Deleuze, which manage to escape the Hegelian dialectic only by positing a certain direct access to the play of difference as such.

> Even if only in a somewhat unusual sense, *différance* is in every respect an archstructure, diametrically opposed to Heideggerian ontological difference as an aspect of the eventuality and therefore also of the historicity of Being. *Différance* as archstructure is not in history, it never comes to pass, but then again constitutes a return to the most classic qualification of metaphysical Being, eternity.

So Vattimo writes about Derrida and his disciples, while in the case of Deleuze, he seems to anticipate Badiou's criticisms of the vitalist ontology hidden behind the glorification of simulacra:

> Vitalism is at work here, in the sense that the alternation of codification and de-territorialization, of canalizing rigidification and the

---

80   Maurice Merleau-Ponty, 'Sartre and Ultrabolshevism', in *Adventures of the Dialectic*, trans. Joseph Bien (Evanston: Northwestern University Press, 1973), pp. 95–201.

liberation of fluxes, is simply referred back to life and its rhythms, without a real discussion of the problem.[81]

There are thus good reasons to read *The Adventure of French Philosophy* as a polemical extension to *Adventures of the Dialectic* and *The Adventure of Difference* – except to add that Badiou, unlike Merleau-Ponty and Vattimo, refuses to take the path of either phenomenology or hermeneutics, no matter how 'weak' or how 'worldly'. Badiou resolutely opts for the rigour of formalization and the power of the post-dialectical dialectic.

Within each part of this volume, Badiou's texts appear in the order of their original publication or composition. Unless otherwise indicated, English translations are solely my responsibility; wherever previous translations were available, they have been revised and adapted for the present edition. As for references within each text, I have tried to track down and annotate the numerous quotations for which Badiou does not provide a source; any errors therein are exclusively my own.

Bruno Bosteels

---

81   Gianni Vattimo, *The Adventure of Difference: Philosophy After Nietzsche and Heidegger*, trans. Ciprian Blamires with Thomas Harrison (Baltimore: The Johns Hopkins University Press, 1993), pp. 144, 146.

Preface: The Adventure of French Philosophy

to per.

Let us begin these reflections on contemporary French philosophy with a paradox: that which is the most universal is also, at the same time, the most particular. Hegel calls this the 'concrete universal', the synthesis of that which is absolutely universal, which pertains to everything, with that which has a particular time and place. Philosophy is a good example. Absolutely universal, it addresses itself to all, without exception; but within philosophy there exist powerful cultural and national particularities. There are what we might call moments of philosophy, in space and in time. Philosophy is thus both a universal aim of reason and, simultaneously, one that manifests itself in completely specific moments. Let us take the example of two especially intense and well-known philosophical instances. First, that of classical Greek philosophy between Parmenides and Aristotle, from the fifth to the third centuries BC: a highly inventive, foundational moment, ultimately quite short-lived. Second, that of German idealism between Kant and Hegel, via Fichte and Schelling: another exceptional philosophical moment, from the late eighteenth to the early nineteenth centuries, intensely creative and condensed within an even shorter time span. I propose to defend a further national and historical thesis: there was – or there is, depending where I put myself – a French philosophical moment of the second half of the twentieth century which, everything else being equal, bears comparison to the examples of classical Greece and enlightenment Germany.

1

2

3

Euro. – Wittgenstein - UK
Heidegger, Buber, Levinas,
G. Marcel, Hotzel, W., Nietz,

Sartre's foundational work, *Being and Nothingness*, appeared in 1943 and the last writings of Deleuze, *What is Philosophy?*, date from the early 1990s. The moment of French philosophy develops between the two of them, and includes Bachelard, Merleau-Ponty, Lévi-Strauss, Althusser, Foucault, Derrida and Lacan as well as Sartre and Deleuze – and myself, maybe. Time will tell; though if there has been such a French philosophical moment, my position would be as perhaps its last representative. It is the totality of this body of work, situated between the groundbreaking contribution of Sartre and the last works of Deleuze, that is intended here by the term 'contemporary French philosophy'. I will argue that it constitutes a new moment of philosophical creativity, both particular and universal. The problem is to identify this endeavour. What took place in France, in philosophy, between 1940 and the end of the twentieth century? What happened around the ten or so names cited above? What was it that we called existentialism, structuralism, deconstruction? Was there a historical and intellectual unity to that moment? And if so, of what sort?

I shall approach these problems in four different ways. First, origins: where does this moment come from, what were its antecedents, what was its birth? Next, what were the principal philosophical operations that it undertook? Third, the fundamental question of these philosophers' link with literature, and the more general connection between philosophy and literature within this sequence. And finally, the constant discussion throughout this whole period between philosophy and psychoanalysis. Origins, operations, style and literature, psychoanalysis: four means by which to attempt to define contemporary French philosophy.

CONCEPT AND INTERIOR LIFE

To think the philosophical origins of this moment we need to return to the fundamental division that occurred within French philosophy at the beginning of the twentieth century, with the emergence of two contrasting currents. In 1911, Bergson gave two celebrated lectures at Oxford, which appeared in his collection *La Pensée et le mouvement* (The Creative Mind). In 1912 – simultaneously, in other words – Brunschvicg published *Les Étapes de la philosophie mathématique* (The Stages of Mathematical Philosophy). Coming on the eve of the Great War, these interventions attest to the existence of two completely distinct orientations. In Bergson we find what might be called a philosophy of vital interiority, a thesis on the identity of being and becoming; a philosophy of life and change. This orientation will persist throughout the twentieth century, up to and including Deleuze. In Brunschvicg's work, we find a philosophy of the mathematically based concept: the possibility of a philosophical formalism of thought and of the symbolic, which likewise continues throughout the century, most specifically in Lévi-Strauss, Althusser and Lacan.

From the start of the century, then, French philosophy presents a divided and dialectical character. On one side, a philosophy of life; on the other, a philosophy of the concept. This debate between life and concept will be absolutely central to the period that follows. At stake in any such discussion is the question of the human subject, for it is here that the two orientations coincide. At once a living organism and a creator of concepts, the subject is interrogated both with regard to its interior, animal, organic life, and in terms of its thought, its capacity for creativity and abstraction. The relationship between body and idea, or life and concept, formulated around the question of the subject, thus structures the whole development of twentieth-century French philosophy from the initial opposition between Bergson and Brunschvicg onwards. To deploy Kant's metaphor of philosophy as a battleground on which we are all the more or less exhausted combatants: during the second half of the twentieth century, the lines of battle were still essentially constituted around the question of the subject. Thus, Althusser defines history as a process without a subject, and the subject as an ideological category; Derrida, interpreting Heidegger, regards the subject as a category of metaphysics; Lacan creates a concept of the subject; Sartre or Merleau-Ponty, of course, allotted an absolutely central role to the subject. A first definition of the French philosophical moment would therefore be in terms of the conflict over the human subject, since the fundamental issue at stake in this conflict is that of the relationship between life and concept.

We could, of course, take the quest for origins further back and describe the division of French philosophy as a split over the Cartesian heritage. In one sense, the post-war philosophical moment can be read as an epic discussion about the ideas and significance of Descartes, as the philosophical inventor of the category of the subject. Descartes was a theoretician both of the physical body – of the animal-machine – and of pure reflection. He was thus concerned with both the physics of phenomena and the metaphysics of the subject. All the great contemporary philosophers have written on Descartes: Lacan actually raises the call for a return to Descartes, Sartre produces a notable text on the Cartesian treatment of liberty, Deleuze remains implacably hostile. In short, there are as many 'Descartes' as there are French philosophers of the post-war period. Again, this origin yields a first definition of the French philosophical moment as a conceptual battle around the question of the subject.

FOUR MOVES

Next, the identification of intellectual operations common to all these thinkers. I shall outline four procedures which, to my mind, clearly exemplify a way of doing philosophy that is specific to this moment; all, in some sense, are methodological ones. The first move is a German one – or rather, a French move upon German philosophers. All contemporary French philosophy is also, in reality, a discussion of the German heritage. Its formative moments include Kojève's seminars on Hegel, attended by Lacan and also influential upon Lévi-Strauss, and the discovery of phenomenology in the 1930s and 40s, through the works of Husserl and Heidegger.

Sartre, for instance, radically modified his philosophical perspectives after reading these authors in the original during his sojourn in Berlin. Derrida may be regarded as, first and foremost, a thoroughly original interpreter of German thought. Nietzsche was a fundamental reference for both Foucault and Deleuze.

French philosophers went seeking something in Germany, then, through the work of Hegel, Nietzsche, Husserl and Heidegger. What was it that they sought? In a phrase: a new relation between concept and existence. Behind the many names this search adopted – deconstruction, existentialism, hermeneutics – lies a common goal: that of transforming, or displacing, this relation. The existential transformation of thought, the relation of thought to its living subsoil, was of compelling interest for French thinkers grappling with this central issue of their own heritage. This, then, is the 'German move', the search for new ways of handling the relation of concept to existence by recourse to German philosophical traditions. In the process of its translation onto the battleground of French philosophy, moreover, German philosophy was transformed into something completely new. This first operation, then, is effectively a French appropriation of German philosophy.

The second operation, no less important, concerns science. French philosophers sought to wrest science from the exclusive domain of the philosophy of knowledge by demonstrating that, as a mode of productive or creative activity, and not merely an object of reflection or cognition, it went far beyond the realm of knowledge. They interrogated science for models of invention and transformation that would inscribe it as a practice of creative thought, comparable to artistic activity, rather than as the organization of revealed phenomena. This operation, of displacing science from the field of knowledge to that of creativity, and ultimately of bringing it ever closer to art, finds its supreme expression in Deleuze, who explores the comparison between scientific and artistic creation in the most subtle and intimate way. But it begins well before him, as one of the constitutive operations of French philosophy.

The third operation is a political one. The philosophers of this period all sought an in-depth engagement of philosophy with the question of politics. Sartre, the post-war Merleau-Ponty, Foucault, Althusser and Deleuze were political activists; just as they had gone to German philosophy for a fresh approach to concept and existence, so they looked to politics for a new relation between concept and action – in particular, collective action. This fundamental desire to engage philosophy with the political situation transforms the relation between concept and action.

The fourth operation has to do with the modernization of philosophy, in a sense quite distinct from the cant of successive government administrations. French philosophers evinced a profound attraction to modernity. They followed contemporary artistic, cultural and social developments very closely. There was a strong philosophical interest in non-figurative painting, new music and theatre, detective novels, jazz and cinema, and a desire to bring philosophy to bear upon the most intense expressions of the modern world. Keen attention was also paid to sexuality and new modes of living. In all this, philosophy was seeking a new relation between the concept and the production of forms – artistic, social, or forms of life. Modernization was thus the quest for a new way in which philosophy could approach the creation of forms.

In sum: the French philosophical moment encompassed a new appropriation of German thought, a vision of science as creativity, a radical political engagement and a search for new forms in art and life. Across these operations runs the common attempt to find a new position, or disposition, for the concept: to displace the relation between the concept and its external environment by developing new relations to existence, to thought, to action, and to the movement of forms. It is the novelty of this relation between the philosophical concept and the external environment that constitutes the broader innovation of twentieth-century French philosophy.

WRITING, LANGUAGE, FORMS

The question of forms, and of the intimate relations of philosophy with the creation of forms, was of crucial importance. Clearly, this posed the issue of the form of philosophy itself: one could not displace the concept without inventing new philosophical forms. It was thus necessary not just to create new concepts but to transform the language of philosophy. This prompted a singular alliance between philosophy and literature, which has been one of the most striking characteristics of contemporary French philosophy. There is, of course, a longer history to this. The works of those known to the eighteenth century as *philosophes* – Voltaire, Rousseau or Diderot – are classics of French literature; these writers are in a sense the ancestors of the post-war alliance. There are numerous French authors who cannot be allocated exclusively either to philosophy or to literature; Pascal, for example, is both one of the greatest figures in French literature and one of the most profound French thinkers. In the twentieth century Alain (aka Émile Auguste Chartier), to all intents and purposes a classical philosopher and no part of the moment that concerns us here, was closely involved in literature; the process of writing was very important to him, and he produced numerous commentaries on novels – his texts on Balzac are extremely interesting – and on contemporary French poetry, Valéry in particular. In other words, even the more conventional figures of twentieth-century French philosophy can illustrate this affinity between philosophy and literature.

The surrealists also played an important role. They too were eager to shake up relations regarding the production of forms, modernity, the arts; they wanted to invent new modes of life. If theirs was largely an aesthetic programme, it paved the way for the philosophical programme of the 1950s and 60s; both Lacan and Lévi-Strauss frequented surrealist circles, for example. This is a complex history, but if the surrealists were the first representatives of a twentieth-century convergence between aesthetic and philosophical projects in

France, by the 1950s and 60s it was philosophy that was inventing its own literary forms in an attempt to find a direct expressive link between philosophical style and presentation, and the new positioning for the concept that it proposed.

It is at this stage that we witness a spectacular change in philosophical writing. Forty years on we have, perhaps, grown accustomed to the writing of Deleuze, Foucault, Lacan; we have lost the sense of what an extraordinary rupture with earlier philosophical styles it represented. All these thinkers were bent upon finding a style of their own, inventing a new way of creating prose; they wanted to be *writers*. Reading Deleuze or Foucault, one finds something quite unprecedented at the level of the sentence, a link between thought and phrasal movement that is completely original. There is a new, affirmative rhythm and an astonishing inventiveness in the formulations. In Derrida there is a patient, complicated relationship of language to language, as language works upon itself and thought passes through that work into words. In Lacan one wrestles with a dazzlingly complex syntax which resembles nothing so much as the syntax of Mallarmé, and is therefore poetic – confessedly so.

There was, then, both a transformation of philosophical expression and an effort to shift the frontiers between philosophy and literature. We should recall – another innovation – that Sartre was also a novelist and playwright (as am I). The specificity of this moment in French philosophy is to play upon several different registers in language, displacing the borders between philosophy and literature, between philosophy and drama. One could even say that one of the goals of French philosophy has been to construct a new space from which to write, one where literature and philosophy would be indistinguishable; a domain which would be neither specialized philosophy, nor literature as such, but rather the home of a sort of writing in which it was no longer possible to disentangle philosophy from literature. A space, in other words, where there is no longer a formal differentiation between concept and life, for the invention of this writing ultimately consists in giving a new life to the concept: a literary life.

WITH AND AGAINST FREUD

At stake, finally, in this invention of a new writing, is the enunciation of the new subject; of the creation of this figure within philosophy, and the restructuring of the battlefield around it. For this can no longer be the rational, conscious subject that comes down to us from Descartes; it cannot be, to use a more technical expression, the reflexive subject. The contemporary human subject has to be something murkier, more mingled in life and the body, more extensive than the Cartesian model; more akin to a process of production, or creation, that concentrates much greater potential forces inside itself. Whether or not it takes the name of subject, this is what French philosophy has been trying to find, to enunciate, to think. If psychoanalysis has been an interlocutor, it is because the Freudian invention was also, in essence, a new proposition about the subject. For what Freud introduced with the idea of the unconscious was the notion of a human subject that is greater than consciousness – which contains consciousness, but is not restricted to it; such is the fundamental signification of the word 'unconscious'.

Contemporary French philosophy has therefore also been engaged in a long-running conversation with psychoanalysis. This exchange has been a drama of great complexity, highly revealing in and of itself. At issue, most fundamentally, has been the division of French philosophy between, on one side, what I would call an existential vitalism, originating with Bergson and running through Sartre, Foucault and Deleuze, and on the other a conceptual formalism, derived from Brunschvicg and continuing through Althusser and Lacan. Where the two paths cross is on the question of the subject, which might ultimately be defined, in terms of French philosophy, as the being that brings forth the concept. In a certain sense the Freudian unconscious occupies the same space; the unconscious, too, is something vital or existing yet which produces, which bears forth, the concept. How can an existence bear forth a concept, how can something be created out of a body? If this is the central question, we can see why philosophy is drawn into such intense exchanges with psychoanalysis. Naturally, there is always a certain friction where common aims are pursued by different means. There is an element of complicity – you are doing the same as I am – but also of rivalry: you are doing it differently. The relation between philosophy and psychoanalysis within French philosophy is just this, one of competition and complicity, of fascination and hostility, love and hatred. No wonder the drama between them has been so violent, so complex.

Three key texts may give us an idea of it. The first, perhaps the clearest example of this complicity and competition, comes from the beginning of Bachelard's work of 1938, *La Psychanalyse du feu* (The Psychoanalysis of Fire). Bachelard proposes a new psychoanalysis grounded in poetry and dream, a psychoanalysis of the elements – fire, water, air and earth. One could say that Bachelard is here trying to replace Freudian sexual inhibition with reverie, to demonstrate that this is the larger and more open category. The second text comes from the end of *Being and Nothingness* where Sartre, in his turn, proposes the creation of a new psychoanalysis, contrasting Freud's 'empirical' psychoanalysis with his own (by implication) properly theoretical existential model. Sartre seeks to replace the Freudian complex – the structure of the unconscious – with what he terms the 'original choice'. For him what defines the subject is not a structure, neurotic or perverse, but a fundamental project of existence. Again, an exemplary instance of complicity and rivalry combined.

The third text comes from Chapter 4 of *Anti-Oedipus*, by Deleuze and Guattari. Here, psychoanalysis is to be replaced by a method that Deleuze calls schizoanalysis, in outright competition with Freudian analysis. For Bachelard, it was reverie rather than inhibition; for Sartre, the project rather than the complex. For Deleuze, as *Anti-Oedipus* makes clear, it is construction rather than expression; his chief objection to psychoanalysis is that it does no more than express the forces of the unconscious, when it ought to construct it. He calls explicitly for the replacement of 'Freudian expression' with the construction that is the work of schizoanalysis. It is striking, to say the least, to find three great philosophers – Bachelard, Sartre and Deleuze – each proposing to replace psychoanalysis with a model of their own.

PATH OF GREATNESS

Finally, a philosophical moment defines itself by its programme of thought. What might we define as the common ground of post-war French philosophy in terms, not of its works or system or even its concepts, but of its intellectual programme? The philosophers involved are, of course, very different figures, and would approach such a programme in different ways. Nevertheless, where you have a major question, jointly acknowledged, there you have a philosophical moment, worked out through a broad diversity of means, texts and thinkers. We may summarize the main points of the programme that inspired postwar French philosophy as follows:

1. To have done with the separation of concept and existence – no longer to oppose the two; to demonstrate that the concept is a living thing, a creation, a process, an event, and, as such, not divorced from existence;

2. To inscribe philosophy within modernity, which also means taking it out of the academy and putting it into circulation in daily life. Sexual modernity, artistic modernity, social modernity: philosophy has to engage with all of this;

3. To abandon the opposition between philosophy of knowledge and philosophy of action, the Kantian division
   between theoretical and practical reason, and to demonstrate that knowledge itself, even scientific knowledge, is
   actually a practice;

4. To situate philosophy directly within the political arena,
   without making the detour via political philosophy; to
   invent what I would call the 'philosophical militant', to
   make philosophy into a militant practice in its presence, in
   its way of being: not simply a reflection upon politics, but a
   real political intervention;

5. To reprise the question of the subject, abandoning the
   reflexive model, and thus to engage with psychoanalysis –
   to rival and, if possible, to better it;

6. To create a new style of philosophical exposition, and so
   to compete with literature; essentially, to reinvent in
   contemporary terms the eighteenth-century figure of the
   philosopher-writer.

Such is the French philosophical moment, its programme, its high
ambition. To identify it further, its one essential desire – for every
identity is the identity of a desire – was to turn philosophy into an
active form of writing that would be the medium for the new subject.
And by the same token, to banish the meditative or professorial
image of the philosopher; to make the philosopher something other
than a sage, and so other than a rival to the priest. Rather, the
philosopher aspired to become a writer-combatant, an artist of
the subject, a lover of invention, a philosophical militant – these are
the names for the desire that runs through this period: the desire
that philosophy should act in its own name. I am reminded of the
phrase Malraux attributed to de Gaulle in *Les Chênes qu'on abat*:

Seek no find.

'Greatness is a road towards something that one does not know.' Fundamentally, the French philosophical moment of the second half of the twentieth century was proposing that philosophy should prefer that road to the goals it knew, that it should choose philosophical action or intervention over wisdom and meditation. It is as philosophy without wisdom that it is condemned today.

But the French philosophical moment was more interested in greatness than in happiness. We wanted something quite unusual, and admittedly problematic: our desire was to be adventurers of the concept. We were not seeking a clear separation between life and concept, nor the subordination of existence to the idea or the norm. Instead, we wanted the concept itself to be a journey whose destination we did not necessarily know. The epoch of adventure is, unfortunately, generally followed by an epoch of order. This may be understandable – there was a piratical side to this philosophy, or a nomadic one, as Deleuze would say. Yet 'adventurers of the concept' might be a formula that could unite us all; and thus I would argue that what took place in late twentieth-century France was ultimately a moment of philosophical adventure.

PART I. ESSAYS AND TALKS

1

The Current Situation on the Philosophical Front

Philosophy as partisanship. Philosophy as concentration of antagonism, in terms of worldview. Philosophy thoroughly summoned by history. The servant not of the sciences but of weaponry. Not the reign of the eternal, much less of wisdom, but the trenchant figure of the actual, of the divided, of class. Not heaven and air, the place of contemplative transparency. Not at all the nocturnal waters of reconciliation. But the resilient earth of production, the weight of interestedness, the fire of the historical ordeal.

Here we are going to place a few names, three notable names on the whole apparent surface: Lacan, Deleuze and Althusser. Does this not say it all? No, because our philosophical time, since the revolt spread, no longer finds an emblem in a name. Every list of notables is foreclosed. We will explain why these names are at best masking and misleading the philosophical novelty that is at stake. What they tell us about the forces of the real is foreign to these names themselves.

There is only one great philosopher of our time: Mao Zedong. And this is not a name, nor even a body of work, but time itself, which essentially has the current form of war: revolution and counter-revolution. There is nothing else to say, philosophically speaking, than the anteriority of this division with regard to any philosophy. Which is why what matters is the line drawn at the front.

When our Chinese comrades talk about 'struggles of principle' that take place on the 'philosophical front', they have in mind the stages of revolutionary politics. Philosophical attacks and counter-attacks accompany the historical periodization. The philosophical preparation of two *camps* aims at drawing up a *balance sheet* of one stage and concentrating the forces for the new stage that is just opening up. Philosophy possesses no more permanence than does the revolution. It enters the scene at the great turning points of history.

For three or four years now, philosophy enters the scene by way of a practical question that occupies all philosophers, whether avowedly or not: what has been the significance of May 1968? We will show that everything that is said about Power and Desire, about the Master and the Rebel, about the Paranoiac and the Schizophrenic, about the One and the Multiple, takes a stance and resonates with regard to this question – what has happened in May 1968? What has happened *to us*? And, within this national variant, the universality of this particularity, still only one question: what happened in the USSR after the October Revolution? What happened during the Great Proletarian Cultural Revolution in China? What happened to Marxism? There lies the front line where everyone battles, rallies, mobilizes or wavers.

There are so many 'philosophers' today! You have the dealers in nihilism, the inflationists of petty and personal misery, the flute-players of capital and nomadic subversion, the Nietzschean undermen and the proclaimers of Sex. You have the anthill of laborious epistemologists. In the heavens, the procession of Angels, Virtues, Thrones, Dominations and Seraphim; on earth, the resignation to the Master and the Law. The exegetes of Discourses, and the eulogists of textuality. Those who, in *Le Nouvel Observateur*, solemnly declare that God is not as dead as He looks. Those who, in stupor at the exit from the latest Seminar, tie together the obscure threads of the Borromean knot. Those who with their own eyes have seen that the seventy-fourth burial of Marx, or of Lenin, was undeniably the good one. Those who hate: thought, Marxism and the proletariat (but do they even possess the force of hatred?). Those who love: their ego, their sex and their voice (but do they even possess the force of love?). And the apostles of bad faith: those who amass their clientele by baptizing 'Marxist' the antiquated bourgeois conclusions about Stalin or about the Lysenko affair. Those who offer the friendly advice to the PCF that its window dressers better keep the dictatorship of the proletariat in the jars on the shelves, just in case. Those who rely upon the forgotten sciences, the crushed revolts, the falsified texts, in order to represent the tenor voice in the operetta chorus in honour of 'Eurocommunism'.

But all these speculative fortune-tellers, charlatans or honest retirees meet in the place assigned to them by history: where do we stand today with regard to the revolution? And even those who, together with their soul, sell to the bourgeoisie the pompous formulae of vulgar defeatism, must be seen as standing on the front line, such as it seems to become fixed between two storms.

Marxists have always said that the decomposition of a revolutionary impulse causes the two faces of selfish reinvestment to flourish among the exalted petty-bourgeois who have fallen from on high: pornography and mysticism. Today we can see both: Desire and the Angel. However, history is never a simple story of forms, it deforms and splits even that which it repeats.

II. POINT OF DEPARTURE: A SILENT THUNDER

May 1968, and even 1969, 1970, 1971: the masses front stage, the omnipresent Maoist ideology, albeit with Linbiaoist inflections – this was the silence of the garrulous philosopher, of separated philosophy. There is nothing more surprising than to compare this strong and violent uprising, this real and simple philosophy, which is everywhere at work in the substance of the movement in revolt, that is, the retreat and vacuity of academic discourse, with the logorrhea of the confessional in which everyone today spills their misery and their apocalypse. What then has happened?

In the end, the years 1968–1971 lent themselves only to the most real philosophy, the one that forms a single body with the practical questions of the revolution. In the heat of the moment people worked on 'One divides into two' in order to analyze the revolts; they called upon the class origin of ideas to bring down the reign of the mandarins. 'Antagonism' and 'non-antagonism' were distinguished in order to push to the end the workers' struggle against the PCF and against the unions. 'Identity' and 'difference' referred back immediately to the place of the organized Maoists in the movement and to the inventive force of the popular masses.

The historical breadth of the phenomena simplified the task of formal thought, barred speculation, and by force led back to the practice of masses and classes. The idealist deviations, which did not fail to appear, especially among the 'Maos', remained powerfully subservient to the immediate density of their contents.

Mao's philosophical writings themselves were inexhaustible, since they were supported by the inexhaustible force and capacity for rupture of the real movement. All the rest disappeared into futility. Roused out of itself through the relaying of the student revolt by the working masses, the so-called revolutionary intelligentsia of the petty bourgeoisie continued to feel exalted, on top of history. With enthusiasm it gave up its ordinary sophistication, because it imagined itself at the heart of the storm, with nothing more to do than to fuse its ideological and moral virulence with the harsh battalions of the factory revolt, in order to reach *its* victory.

III. THE REVERSALS OF 1972

This great and violent era sees its cycle come to an end around 1972. The mass of petty-bourgeois intellectuals understood little by little that, appearances notwithstanding, it was not the paladin of history. The fury of its ideological tumult, its exalted passion for 'struggles', its devastating impatience, if they were not organically linked to *the people's revolutionary politics* – at the heart of which stands the proletariat as the only antagonistic class of the bourgeoisie, and its avant-garde as the leading nucleus of the people in their entirety – became inverted into their opposite under the recovered weight of the fundamental clash, that of classes and their programmatic interests. The discovery of the masses was an anti-revisionist impact force of the first order; and the discovery of Maoism, a cultural revolution without precedent. But Maoism is not solely the apologia of revolt, it is the Marxism of our time, it is the thought and practice of proletarian revolution in the space opened up, on a worldwide scale, by the Great Proletarian Cultural Revolution. Maoism, too, puts the petty-bourgeois intellectuals *in their place*, just as starting in January 1967 the Chinese revolutionary proletariat, taking control of the storm, gave both its strength and its limitation to the spirit of revolt among the young red guards.

If one did not hold onto this historical and theoretical truth and translate it into the facts – as is the path of Marxism-Leninism-Maoism – what did one see? The ideologico-moral tumult turned into hollow terrorism, or flipped over into shapeless decadence; the passion for 'struggles' washed out into cautious conformism behind the bourgeois unions; the impatience slipped into defeatism.

These reversals were accelerated by the fact that the bourgeois counter-offensive, via the Union of the Left and the Programme Commun,[1] in the end left our ideologues completely disarmed. The

---

1   *Translator's Note*: Badiou is referring to the electoral alliance of the 1970s between the French Communist Party, the Socialist Party, and Left Radicals

adversaries, who up to this point had been on the defensive in the face of the revolts and the ideological rapid fire, finally started talking *politics* (that is, programmes and power), which is something of which the petty-bourgeois would-be revolutionaries are congenitally unable, being only the bearers of a principled, and thus abstract, vision of politics. For them, the strong antagonistic patience of the programme of the revolution is nothing more than popular materialism. They dream of a formal antagonism, of a world broken in two, with no sword other than ideology. They love revolt, proclaimed in its universality, but they are secondary in terms of politics, which is the real transformation of the world in its historical particularity.

The programmatic return to the proletariat and to the people, inevitable to keep steady in the face of the two bourgeoisies – which after the storm, and then in the form of the economic crisis, reconstituted their political space, their plans and their combats – was for the 'leftists' an unbearable test. They had believed in the blinding *coincidence* of their newfound morality and the historical aspirations of the people. Now they discovered that once more, in order to be the fortune-tellers of the revolution, they had to submit themselves to the internal process by which the proletariat appropriates its new historical dimension, formulates its programme, and strengthens the nuclei of its future party. To suppress oneself as a bourgeois intellectual was not some *parousia* but a labour.

The majority, it must be said, threw in the towel and returned to their sheep. Which is when they discovered the avenging virtues of philosophy.

---

under the leadership of François Mitterrand, who would eventually come to be elected president as a result of this alliance. The contents of the Common Programme, originally signed on 27 June 1972, can be found in *Le Programme commun de gouvernement de la gauche: Propositions socialistes pour l'actualisation* (Paris: Flammarion, 1992).

IV. REVANCHISTS OF THE IDEA

Chased away from the front stage, our 'Maos' from the night before, and most notably their petty chiefs now gone astray, swore to take their revenge in philosophy for the trick that history had played on them. Since no one still wanted them to take the leading role, they were going to show that the play was bad and its principal actor (the proletariat) would henceforth be responsible for a vile fiasco.

Since it was established that, not being a true political class, a state-bound class, the petty-bourgeois intelligentsia had no chance of ever exerting power, well then, they were going to show that Power is Evil. In this way they would remain the heroes of the whole affair, ideally changing the defeat of their vain ambition into the noble disapproval of its stakes.

Since they had been carried away by the ideological exaltation over the *revolt* of the masses, but now it seemed that without class structure, or without the antagonistic proletarian framework, the revolt does not carry the revolutionary *politics* for very long, they were going to say: the Masses are good, but the Proletariat is bad. The revolt is good, but politics is bad. The spokesperson is good, but the militant is scary.

Since Marxism was the means for the proletariat to exert its theoretical hegemony in the camp of the revolution, they would not hesitate to reveal a great secret: Marxism is bad.

The 'philosophers' of the moment, with their brilliant paraphernalia, have no other function than to organize the following three theses:

a) the masses (revolts) are good;

b) the proletariat (Marxism) is bad;

c) power (the State, in whatever form) is Evil.

All these discourses filter their dismal balance sheet of May '68 and its aftermath through the *political* matrix of mass/class/State, for which they propose singular universalizations. The political essence of these 'philosophies' is captured in the following principle, a principle of bitter resentment against the entire history of the twentieth century: 'In order for the revolt of the masses against the State to be good, it is necessary to reject the class direction of the proletariat, to stamp out Marxism, to hate the very idea of the class party.'

Everywhere to substitute the couple masses/State for the class struggle (that is, everywhere to substitute ideology for politics): that is all there is to it. And this is because the petty-bourgeois intelligentsia can parade around in the ineffective revolt, but it is in agony in the prolonged proletarian class struggle.

It does not like the dictatorship of the proletariat, it does not seek the dictatorship of the proletariat, as long as imperialism nourishes it to satisfaction. Nothing else exists in politics? Then, at its lowest, it will say: long live the Nothing! In the vicinity of the retreat after 1972 roams the nihilist sarcasm, the profound apoliticism, the pre-fascist aestheticism of these petty old men of history.

So that is the soil where our 'philosophies' grow. We will see through all these 'balance sheets' of May 1968, of October 1917, even if instead of the Masses, we obtain: the body, or desire, or the multiple. Instead of Class and Marxism: Discourse, or the Signifier, or the Code. Instead of the State: Power, or the Law, or the One.

Indeed, it is from the point of view of the reconstitution of their vacillating identity and from the restoration of their social practices that our intellectuals transmit their memory and their vengeful verdict. *Everyone*, including the Maoists, is after all called upon today, after the Cultural Revolution and May '68, to take a stance, to discern the new with regard to the meaning of politics in its complex articulation, its constitutive trilogy: mass movement, class perspective, and State. Such is clearly the question of any possible philosophy today, wherein we can read the primacy of politics (of antagonism) *in its actuality*. The difference is that the Maoists practice this question under the sign of the revolutionary politics of the people, the core of which is the antagonism bourgeoisie/proletariat. And our philosophers do so in the denial of antagonism, through their newly shared disengagement and their vindicated ignorance of the popular political realities. At a time when what counts is the question of the programme of the revolution, the petty-bourgeois intelligentsia finds itself largely out of place, cut off from politics, bound to a clear class choice from which its entire being desperately turns it away. And yet, politics is what makes it talk, it is the balance sheet of the storm that has it all worked up. So there it is forced to manipulate the poor, miserable content of its immediate social life (I read a little, I talk, I teach, I publish, I make love), to stage it in the place and stead of that which makes up the true backbone of their own history. The impoverishment, the abstract sophistication of the contents, the exaltation of the most individualistic and rarefied 'lived' experience: all this is what refracts, in the recuperation of social uses, the muffled thunder of the shaking up of history, whose features the petty-bourgeois intelligentsia no longer recognizes, even if it continues to carry along the question they pose.

We could propose a figure for the thread of this progressive misrecognition, in which the following contradiction can be read:

a) What forces the petty-bourgeois intelligentsia to think is the massive nature of the historical interpellation since 1968, the core of which is politics, that is, the system mass/class/State in the actuality of antagonisms.

b) Thrown back upon the periphery of the antagonism and dominated by the idealist restoration, the petty-bourgeois intelligentsia progressively misrecognizes that which constrains it and disguises it in generalizations whose referent is nothing else, in the final instance, than its immediate social practice (hence the Body, Writing, Enjoyment, etc.).

This gives us, for example, with variable sedimentations and measures of transparency:

	Historical form	Theoretical form			Misrecognition					
	Movement	Mass			Revolt	Body	Desire	Desire	Art, Play	Multiple
Class politics			+	Change of sign	+	+	+	+	+	+
	Organization	Class			Marxism	Discourse	Signifier	Code	Politics	Dialectic
			+		?	?	?	?	?	?
	Dictatorship	State			Gulag	Power	Law	Despot	Reason	One
					−	−	−	−	−	−

(Right margin bracket: *Metaphysical nihilism*)

This is the trilogy (the real movement, the organization, the dictatorship) with its metamorphoses, but taking a resentful stance on May '68, on the revolutions of the twentieth century, and bracing itself for the categorical refusal of the only confirmed, practicable revolutionary road, which can be read here and now: that of the dictatorship of the proletariat and of Maoism.

As for us, placed up close to their source, practicing the politics that they deny, which is the only *real* referent of philosophy, including theirs, we will always be able to translate statements such as the following into their historical actuality: '*Discourse* is that which disposes the *body* as the effect of a *power*.' Let us read: for us, historically responsible (or irresponsible) for vacillating formations, we refuse that the *proletariat* (Marxism) directs the *processes* (the movement) in their revolutionary relation to the *State* (the dictatorship of the proletariat). And, if we are told: 'The desiring *multiplicity* is inverted by the *coding* into *the axiomatic unity of capital*', we will read in it the same denial. Or again: 'The *plebs* is subordinated by *Marxism* to the *Gulag*', this is once again: mass, class, State, in the stubborn denial of their political articulation.

To break up the ineluctable proletarian link: leadership, organization, Marxism, dictatorship. To leave out in the open the atemporal masses: revolt, spontaneity, utopianism, democracy. Under the pretence of attacking its despotism, to deploy the gigantic omnipresence of the State under the metaphysical banner of the concept of 'power', alibi of all renunciations, of all cowardice: we are being told nothing else. Nothing, *nihil*. At the end of this nothing, inevitably, we find fascist violence. This is what the hatred of the proletariat, combined with the abstract cult of the 'masses' and the aesthetic despair, is preparing public opinion for.

V. THE OWLS OF THE REVISIONIST NIGHT

Then come the counterfeiters, the company of prebendaries of false Marxism. Annulled by Maoism, nihilism puts them back in the saddle. This is because Althusser and company are more radically nihilist in that, for them, quite plainly *nothing happened* in May '68. It is not a question of a negative balance sheet, but of denying the need for a balance sheet to begin with. Revolts? Masses? The people's revolutionary politics? Where? You have been dreaming! 'Scientific' Marxism, that monument sheltered from the storm, offers you, without counterpart, the academic serenity of the conservatories. It allows you, with no attributes other than those of some handsomely remunerated doctors in philosophy, to *pronounce yourself* about everything and to make heard, albeit in the register of the official oppositions, the great voice of the Party and of the Proletariat. It allows you to scold the petty anti-Marxist nihilists and to envisage History from the lofty heights of the great nihilism, that of the false Marxism, that of the card-carrying professors.

For the moment, politics is the occupation of Marchais and Séguy, Mitterrand and Maire.[2] Let them go where they want, provided that they beware of what they say. Our safekeeping

---

2   *Translator's Note*: Georges Marchais, as the General Secretary of the French Communist Party, co-signed the Common Programme for the Union of the Left with François Mitterrand as his Socialist counterpart. Georges Séguy and Edmond Maire are leading figures in the major French unions, the CGT (Confédération Générale du Travail) and the CFDT (Confédération Française Démocratique du Travail).

mission is that of concepts: the Programme Commun must be able to coexist with the regular allegiance to ossified Leninism.

Scholastic owls of the night of the PCF, the Althusserians are more dangerous than they seem. To pretend that there is any sense whatsoever, today, in continuing the battle for the Marxist and 'proletarian' purity of the PCF is to justify, even without wanting to, the worst: the politics of the bourgeois State in the name of the proletariat, the forced indoctrination of class politics, the anti-popular terrorism in the name of Marxism. Yes, when to the Masses of nihilism, to the pure multiple of desire, the revisionist philosophers object by invoking their fake conceptual proletariat, their oppositional allegiance to the One of the PCF, because then what they deny is at once the real proletariat, its work on itself, its revolted insurrection in the element of Maoist politics, they open the way to a 'red' despotism, under the pretence of white fascism. We say: the Althusserian company of concepts, of science above classes, does not organize in any way the 'left' of the PCF. Indeed, there is no worse bourgeoisie than the new bourgeoisie, the one who only speaks of the proletariat and of the dictatorship of the proletariat.

VI. THE SCEPTIC

Standing apart, tall dinosaur with his old rational step, idealist dialectician, true successor of the one and only Mallarmé, of the only productive Hegelian of our dominant national tradition of thought, drowned in the coquetry of his opacities, prey to the frenetic rhythm of sofas and doctors where plenty of repented *enragés* meant to use psychoanalysis to silence the commotion of politics: Lacan, bourgeois sceptic, also spreads the dangerous conviction – that there is nothing new under the sun.

What saves him, however, is the fact that he never pretends to draw any politics whatsoever from this, except to say that, after all, it is only ever a question of being subjected to the least bad master possible.

Those who extract or bet on a form of politics for him – that is to say, those who fuse with or split off from Lacanianism in the wake of their assessment of '68 – find no other ground to stand on, no other determination to bring to bear, except their apparent enemies, the nihilists and the naturalists of desiring multiplicity. Same refrain of the pure but unlikely Revolt, of the sinister proletariat and the unavoidable Master. Same trilogy. Same despair to scrutinize the points of desire where the enjoyment of Power becomes anchored. Same blindness.

About Lacan himself, one will say that his most extreme misfortune is to validate, by way of his atemporal scepticism, the counter-revolutionary *continuum* in which the Union of the Left prospers: the species of Lacano-Althusserians, alas, has not yet died out.

VII. THE PRINCIPLE OF DOUBLE FLUCTUATION

So goes the philosophy of those scalded by May '68, the weapon of war against the truth of May '68, against its popular and worker's truth, the truth of its force and of the prolonged Maoist work of its force: fluctuating and fascinated now by nihilistic fascism and now by 'scientific' social-fascism.

In the 'crisis' of philosophy, for those who confess it, we will see a single fallacious problem, fabricated in the movement of historical and political *foundering* after 1972: how to give life, in the wedging of fascism and social-fascism, of Deleuzian banditry and Althusserian science, to the tri-logical principle that all the exhausted old combatants seek to sell to the highest bourgeois bidder? For the *masses* to be purged of the *State*, we must hate the *proletariat*. For *sex* to be without *Law*, we must make a hole in the *text*. For the *multiple desire* to be without *One*, we must recuse *reason*. For the *body* to be detached from *Power*, we must fissure *discourse*. And so on.

Here we are no longer talking about the fortune-tellers and the professors, the charlatans and the spokespersons but about those – the vast majority – who *inherit* this falsified balance sheet, its immense weariness, and carry on their backs the infamous problem that is handed down to them: the problem of renegacy. Those who read Deleuze, and Lacan, and Foucault, and Althusser, and all the epigones, and think: where do we stand? What are people telling us here?

To this question we must again and always answer: history, class struggle, politics.

It is a stupid illusion to imagine that the philosophical conjuncture could be independent not only of the general set of phenomena of the class struggle but also of politics, of what gives structure at a given moment to the political scene in a dominant fashion. Today, what apparently predominates this scene is the rivalry of two bourgeois projects: that of the classical monopoly bourgeoisie, whose political expression, itself complex, is the coalition of 'advanced liberalism' of Giscard and Gaullism; and that of the new state bureaucratic bourgeoisie, which finds its parliamentary form in the Union of the Left and its syndicalist support system. With regard to this rivalry, the popular working movement is in search of its political autonomy. The class struggle thus unfolds on two fronts.

To clarify the sense of disarray and complexity in the face of philosophical proliferations, it is thus indispensable to understand that the petty-bourgeois intelligentsia is today historically situated in a force field with three poles, finding itself subservient to what we will call a *principle of double fluctuation*:

a) First of all, as intermediary social force, the petty-bourgeois intelligentsia oscillates in function of the moment's relations of force between the proletariat and the bourgeoisie – that is, from the point of view of the conception of the world, between Maoism (the Marxism of our time) and anti-Maoism (whether anti-Marxist or pseudo-Marxist).

b) The petty bourgeoisie is furthermore subject to the attraction and the attempts at hegemony of two bourgeois projects. It oscillates between classical reaction and modern revisionism – that is, from the point of view of philosophical expression, between anti-Marxism and pseudo-Marxism.

We cannot therefore offer a linear figure of the system of ideological and philosophical trends that structure at such or such a moment the petty bourgeoisie. It is important to represent it in the space of the class struggle on two fronts, as a kind of triangle that becomes deformed according to two axes of fluctuation whose engine is, on the one hand, the *antagonism* of bourgeoisie/proletariat, and on the other hand, the *rivalry* of the old bourgeoisie and the new bourgeoisie. It is with regard to this 'triangle of forces', anchored in the historico-political class struggle, that we can map the philosophical reference points of the double fluctuation, and thus draw up the *political cartography of philosophy in France*.

VIII. A MAP

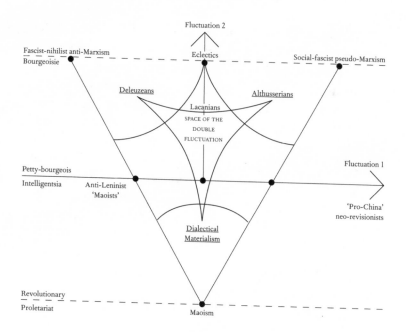

Some legends:

1) About the place of Deleuzians and Althusserians, as well as of dialectical materialism, we have nothing to add, except that the *philosophical space* they occupy stands in variable proximities to the pure expression of political interests whose service they guarantee. To grab the 'horns' of this fluctuating triangle in space means that there exist, of course, as collective phenomena, fluctuating Deleuzians who are by no means incorrigible fascists; there also surely exist fluctuating Althusserians who are capable of feeling repulsed by the real practical form of social-fascism; and also philosophical partisans of dialectical materialism who are still inconsistent and hesitant with regard to Maoist politics.

2) By 'anti-Leninist Maoists' we understand those who, under the pretence of preserving Marxism from revisionism, accuse the Leninist theory of the party and the class essence of Marxism-Leninism-Maoism for the degeneration into social-fascism. In so doing, whether they are council communists or theoreticians of the 'abolition of wage-labour', sectarians of the plebs or of popular memory, or apologists of the peasantry as the only true revolutionary class, they objectively tend towards proximity with the Deleuzian 'massists' and their anti-militant fury. Their utopias of the countryside – workerist or anti-repressive, depending on the case – are disarming in that they are opposed to the historical task of the moment: the constitution of the proletariat into the political class (which is something altogether different from its existence solely as a social class).

3) By 'pro-China neo-revisionists' we understand the ossified Marxist-Leninists, of the *Humanité Rouge* kind.[3] Their philosophical vacuity is, in reality, extreme.

4) The '*eclectics*' are those who discern full well the *common essence* of the 'desiring' faction and of Althusser: the disavowal of the autonomy of the proletariat and the hatred of Maoist militants. The eclectics validate both the sexo-fascism and the theoreticism. Typical example: Macciocchi or *Tel Quel*.[4]

IX. WHAT FOR?

Yes, what good is this cartography for? The fact is that there is fluctuation, that today the hegemonies are broken. The muted and organic rise of workers and the people to the antagonistic struggle on two fronts is reflected, by the petty-bourgeois intelligentsia, in the philosophical need – that is, the need *to be done with* the bilateral bourgeois subjections, even if this is not yet clear.

What we see today is that around and upon the initiative of the Maoists – or else more sporadically, even blindly and inconsistently – a double rejection of bourgeois impostors is taking shape in the field of philosophy:

---

3   *Translator's Note*: *L'Humanité Rouge* represents one of three tendencies that in 1970 split off from the (Maoist) Parti Communiste Marxiste-Léniniste de France (PCMLF). Badiou's own Maoist organization, the UCFML, always treated this tendency as a 'rightist' deviation. See UCFML, *La Révolution prolétarienne en France et comment construire le parti de l'époque de la pensée Mao-Tsé-toung* (Paris: François Maspero, 1970), and *Première année d'existence d'une organisation maoïste, printemps 1970/printemps 1971* (Paris: François Maspero, 1972).

4   *Translator's Note*: The UCFML, Badiou's Maoist group, also frequently attacked the 'sexpol' varieties of dialectical materialism, which they identified with the work of *Tel Quel* and figures such as Philippe Sollers and Maria Antonietta Macciocchi. See the texts in their collective volume, *Marxisme-léninisme et psychanalyse* (Paris: François Maspero, 1972).

- the anarcho-desirers are attacked by a growing fraction of the petty-bourgeois intelligentsia and of the youth who draw up the balance sheet of the disarray, the historical impasse in which these apologists of anything whatsoever have totally led them astray between 1972 and 1975;

- the Althusserians are put into question by the ever more evident incoherence between their apparent formal fidelity to certain principles of Leninism and the flagrant opportunism of their political operations vis-à-vis the PCF.

Our fundamental aim is, in the final instance, that this double critique, combined with the search for a rationality of a new type and with a living thinking of the history of our time, may go forward and break the encirclement attempted by the two bourgeoisies so as to formulate, with Maoism as its axis, its own expression, which is itself the reflection of the historical activity of the proletariat to constitute itself into the political class.

We are strongly convinced that this is an ever-growing aspiration, even if innumerable charlatans try their best to close the gap.

The following studies seek to be at the service of the mobilization for this task, in order to enable the dominant camaraderie of philosophy and of the mass movement, as class confrontations.

The aim is clear, which is why we put forth some provisory markers here and make a general call: may all genuinely revolutionary philosophers arm themselves for the true balance sheet and the antagonistic struggle on two fronts. May they contact us and join us. In this way they will contribute, in the work of preparation for a revolutionary public opinion, to breaking the worst threat to which our people have been exposed: that of a forced recruitment into one or the other of two bourgeois camps. In this way, too, they will play an integral part in the autonomy of the people's revolutionary politics.

2

Hegel in France '78

Hegel's vitality in France, aside from the fact that it is a recent phenomenon, follows a singular trajectory, which to this day has only obscured both its relation to Marxism and a renewed detachment of the rational kernel of the dialectic.

In our eyes, it is to Alexandre Kojève's seminar in the 1930s that we ought to date back a certain non-academic inscription of the Hegelian reference in the ideological concerns of the time. From this moment onward, a figure of Hegel is sketched out from which it will take us more than thirty years to extricate ourselves – and even then, the game is far from being over.

Kojève's Hegel is exclusively the one of the *Phenomenology of Spirit*, seized in the idealism of the scissions of self-consciousness, captured in the ascending metaphor that leads from immediate sense-certainty to absolute knowledge with, at its heart, the dialectic of lord and bondsman. The formalism of the confrontation with the Other has the poetic virtue of standing under the sign of risk and death: this Hegel will find an audience with the revolutionary romanticism of Malraux and, even more so, among the surrealists. Bataille and Breton will state all their debts to Kojève.

With the solid support of Jean Hippolyte's translations and essays, this unilateral figure reaches its massive promotion after the War, in the person of Sartre. The pessimist doctrine of the for-the-other (hell is the others) finds nourishment here. On the side of psychoanalysis, Lacan himself, further supported by his surrealist friendships, finds in his first texts a way to develop his doctrine of the imaginary: narcissism and aggressiveness are strictly symmetrical to lord and bondsman.

In short: surrealists and existentialists find in Hegel the wherewithal to forge a tense romanticist idealism, which places the affective subject back at the heart of the experience of the world, and which can be measured in its pathos against the backdrop of the terrible historical uproar provoked everywhere by the effects of the Bolshevik revolution. With regard to the forms of consciousness that October 1917, the crisis, fascism, and the two World Wars remodelled as in a storm, the young Hegel – the man who drew up the balance sheet of 1789 and the Napoleonic wars – served as siege-engine against the dusty positivism of the national academy, against the sinister humdrum of French post-Kantians, against the secular humanism of the 'thinkers' of the radical party.

Hegel in France was first and foremost the struggle of tragic idealism against scientistic idealism. In this sense, his irruption bears witness to the time in a masked way and, in the most profound depths of subjective ideals, substitutes the twin figure of the cursed writer and the professional revolutionary of the Third International – violent and secretive men from all over the world – for the slightly sub-prefectoral good-heartedness of the decorated member of the Institute.

On this terrain, the encounter with Marxism was unavoidable at the same time as it was impossible. Subjectively, the Hegelians of the moment placed their bet on the revolution and hated the bourgeois order. Breton and Sartre both had to come to this necessary crossing: becoming fellow travellers of the communists. But, being the bearers of romantic individualism no less so than Malraux, they could not withstand to the end all the mental consequences of this fellow-travelling. In the exemplary case of Sartre – which moreover came at the time of great ambivalence regarding the proletarian nature of the party – this contradictory situation gave way to a gigantic enterprise for which, on the other hand, he had had a number of recurrent predecessors, most notably in Germany: to force Marxism into subjective idealism. Hegel returned this time – by a reversal of the Marxist reversal – as an apparatus to put dialectical materialism back on its head. Such is the whole history of this Hegelianized Marxism, whose central category is that of alienation and whose fate revolves around a key text of the young Marx: the *Manuscripts of 1844*. Here too, Kojève's lesson was not lost on anyone, since it underscored, as the outcome of the dialectic of lord and bondsman, the generation of the category of Work – that focal point with which to solder together (if only apparently) the Marxist political economy and the avatars of self-consciousness.

In the *Critique of Dialectical Reason* – but after the young Lukács, after Korsch – Sartre hailed Marxism as the unsurpassable horizon of our culture and, in a single movement, undertook to dismantle this Marxism by forcing it to realign itself with the original idea that is most foreign to it: the transparency of the cogito. And such was, in fact – outside of the narrow circle of party intellectuals, who stuck to a scientism in the style of Jules Guesde[5] – the only available Marx on the French market, and at the same time the only Hegel.

Both this Marx and this Hegel are equally false, the first for being reduced to the second, and the second for being separated from that part of himself that precisely cleared the path for the first: *The Science of Logic*.

The counter-current took shape as soon as the historical horizon changed at its base. Once the cycle of the effects of the Second World War was over, once the revolutionary public of Soviet Russia implacably came undone, the PCF was clearly committed to bourgeois and chauvinistic revisionism (the experience of the war of Algeria was decisive in this matter), and proletarian rigor was on

---

5 *Translator's Note*: Jules Guesde (1845–1922) was an important French socialist intellectual, instrumental in the formation of the Parti Ouvrier and the Section Française de l'Internationale Ouvrière.

the rise in China, with every single person being summoned to take a stance on the wars of national liberation, the intellectuals had to invent another playground and organize different ideals for themselves. The 'fellow traveller' died of starvation. With him the guarantees of the philosophies of consciousness ceased to have purchase, since their role had been to preserve, with regard to a fascinating revolution, the double rapport of commitment and the for-oneself.

Solitary for a moment, the intellectuals were forced to identify themselves as such and to redefine their relation to Marxism on the basis of this re-identification. The first task produced that absolute valorization of knowledge and the intellect known as structuralism. The second, by a violent turnabout, made of Marx, instead of a metaphysician of the Other and of Work, a scholar of social structures. In both cases, there was a noisy break with Hegel.

As is well known, it is Althusser who concentrated the attack on the idealized Marxism of the previous period, who discredited the young Marx of the *Manuscripts of 1844*, and who made of Hegel the absolute foil, up to the point of stating the thesis of a radical discontinuity between Hegel and Marx as the vantage point from which everything becomes clear.

This cleanup project had positive effects in its time (1963–1966), supported from afar by the assaults of the Chinese against modern revisionism, in the doctrinal form these assaults took at the time. Althusser restored a kind of brutal trenchancy to Marxism, isolating it from the subjectivist tradition and putting it back in the saddle as positive knowledge. At the same time, Marx and Hegel, even though in opposite terms, found themselves no less foreclosed than in the previous moment. The latter insofar as his unilateral figure, taken as target, by the same token finds itself vindicated: the materialist Hegel of the *Greater Logic* is equally mute for Althusser and for Sartre. And the former insofar as, once adapted to the concepts of structuralism, he gained in scientificity what he lost in terms of class historicity. The Hegelianized Marx of the 1950s was a speculative, but virtually revolutionary figure. The anti-Hegelian Marx of the 1960s was a savant, but one devoted to the seminar rooms. Or, to give the alternative a concentrated philosophical form: Marx-Hegel was the idealist dialectic; the anti-Hegelian Marx was metaphysical materialism.

What the Cultural Revolution and May 1968 made clear on a massive scale was the need for something entirely different from an oscillation of national intellectual traditions (between the Descartes of the cogito: Sartre; and the Descartes of the machines: Althusser), in order to reinvest Marxism in the real revolutionary movement. Put to the test by the storm, Althusser's positivist Marx was found to be even more threatening, due to its connections with the 'scientific and technical revolution' of the PCF, than was Sartre's idealist Marx. This became visible in the choices they made in times of urgency: Althusser on the side of Waldeck Rochet,[6] when push came to shove; and Sartre with the 'Maos', in spite of everything.

In France today it is no doubt necessary to establish what Lenin in 1922 (and in reference to Trotsky's mistakes about trade unionism...) wished to call for: a kind of 'Society of Materialist Friends of Hegelian Dialectics', to which he assigned nothing less than the task of generating a 'propaganda of Hegelian dialectics'.[7]

The fact of urgency becomes clear when we look at how the joyous 'new philosophers', with André Glucksmann at the helm, attempt to *come full circle*.[8]

During the first half of the twentieth century, Hegel had served as the idealist mediation to acclimate a certain Marx to the needs of our intelligentsia. Then came the revenge of the all-powerful

---

6 *Translator's Note*: As late as 1974, Althusser dedicated his *Elements of Self-Criticism* to Waldeck Rochet, who between 1964 and 1972 had been General Secretary of the French Communist Party.

7 V.I. Lenin, 'On the Significance of Militant Materialism', *Collected Works* (Moscow: Progress, 1972), vol. 33, pp. 227–36.

8 *Translator's Note*: See André Glucksmann, *The Master Thinkers*, trans. Brian Pearce (New York: Harper and Row, 1980).

scientistic tradition: it was the apolitical Marx of the doctors in philosophy who held the podium, while Hegel disappeared behind the bitter curtains.

The Maoist aim is to break with this alternation, with this avoidance. Now, what do we see? The new philosophers come and bandy about Hegelianism as a spectre, as the rational monster of the State. Because of the avowed hatred of the dialectic, this brings them closer to Althusser, were it not for the fact that the latter sought to draw from this shadow-play some more light to shed on Marx, whereas the former aim to shove Marx and Hegel, once more made identical, into the same sombre bag of master thinkers who are at the origin of all Evil.

Thus, against the grain of the process started in the 1930s, this time it is in order to de-acclimate ourselves from Marxism, and in order to have us confess its horror, that once more that sphinx of our central philosophical tradition of thought is manipulated: the maintaining and the splitting of the dialectic between Hegel and Marx.

In truth, everything must be taken up again from scratch so as at last to see that, philosophically, Marx is neither the Other of Hegel nor his Same. Marx is the *divider* of Hegel. He assigns simultaneously the latter's irreversible validity (the rational kernel of the dialectic) and his integral falsity (the idealist system).

Hegel remains the stake of an interminable conflict, because the belaboured understanding of his division alone is what prohibits, in thinking the relationship Marx/Hegel, both the idealist-romantic deviation and the scientistic-academic deviation, as well as, finally, the pure and simple hatred of Marxism.

To restore Hegel in his division is not a vain enterprise, for it is always under the banner of his exclusion, or of his totality, that the bourgeois philosophies of assault proceed – those that propose for themselves not to ignore Marxism, but to invest and neutralize it.

Still, all this requires that we give back a voice to the Hegel who has been gagged – the essential Hegel, the one so feverishly annotated by Lenin, the one whose knowledge was required, as Marx declared, for understanding *Capital*: the Hegel of the *Science of Logic*.

We try, we begin.

3

Commitment, Detachment, Fidelity

When I recall the philosophical lightning strike that fell upon me in the *lycée*, it seems to me to be entirely contained in a single formula from Jean-Paul Sartre, which provided the inexhaustible matrix for my loquacious adolescence: 'Consciousness is a being such that in its being, its being is in question in so far as this being implies a being other than itself.'[1] The remark has already been made before, not without malice: so many mentions of being in order to say the nothingness of the for-itself! But the power of this formula lies elsewhere. It operates the synthesis of dialectical interiority, captured in the principle of being that is in question, and of intentional exteriority, of the constitutive projection onto the Other. It fixates a double maxim, which I must say continues to organize my thinking:

- On the one hand, the ego or interiority are deprived of all interest and thus despicable, if they do not carry an effect of meaning for which the only measure can be the whole world, the totality of whatever is disposed when thought seizes it in its disposition. This can be said as follows: psychology is the enemy of thought.

---

1   Jean-Paul Sartre, *Being and Nothingness*, trans. Hazel E. Barnes (New York: Washington Square Press, 1966), p. 24.

was human-
ego-choice & universal

On the other hand, the whole world, such as it is disposed,
is of no interest if it is not taken up and treated in the subjective prescription of a project that is equally extensive. The
world must literally be put into question. This can be said
as follows: pragmatic empiricism, adaptation, 'we must
cultivate our own garden', are also enemies of thought.

That interiority is the whole world as disposition and that exteriority is the whole world as imperative: this is the idea of which
philosophy, such as Sartre in my eyes incarnated it, convinced me
forever. If the ego is the measure of all things, philosophy is not
worth an hour of our effort. It has meaning only through everything in thought that exceeds our inevitable petty stories. Philosophy
is by no means destined to make us satisfied. Since always, and
forever, it agrees only with eternity, which we know is the eternity
of the True only in the future anterior of a temporal fierceness.

OK

Key against relativism

Thanks to Sartre and to him alone, this central conviction originally *seized* me. Today, when the narrowest sense of prudence
seems to have been restored as far as the ends of humanity are
concerned, and when a grave suspicion weighs down on the slightest proposition of universality, I nevertheless cannot but stick by
this conviction: Humanity, insofar as the word retains a meaning
that is not abject, is that being which is sustained in its being only by
projects or procedures whose identity with respect to the world *as it
is* must necessarily appear as inhuman.

Today I call truth, or generic procedure, this essential inhuman-
ity in which the human is summoned by that which makes that in
certain situations something else happens than their being.

This is not to say that the human being, as Nietzsche thought, is
what must be overcome. What must be overcome – this is a decisive
intuition on Sartre's part – is being, such as it is qua being. And the
human being is this chance that is unrelated to humanity, this
inhuman chance, which stands out qua subject in the generic and
infinite becoming of a truth.

But if the conviction remains that the subject is that which detaches itself from being so that there may be some truth, the articulation of this conviction had to give up, piece by piece, the Sartrean formula. I can thus say that the trajectory of my thinking may be perceived as the paradoxical combination of an energetic fidelity to the Sartrean message and the formal pulling to pieces of the dialectical schema that undergirds this message.

With regard to the philosophical supremacy of Sartre's schema, I should add that, from the beginning, as in a disjointed aesthetic, there were completely heterogeneous preferences and usages of thought.

There was mathematics, of which the least we can say is that they left Sartre rather cold, in spite of the subtitle of the *Critique of Dialectical Reason* – *Theory of Practical Ensembles* – which I have never been able to read without thinking that it recognizes Cantor's founding role for modernity.[2] Now mathematics in my eyes necessarily had some relation (but I did not know which one) with the question of being, or with the being in question – a relation that the Sartrean doctrine of consciousness did not elucidate.

Symmetrical to mathematics there were also the poets, and singularly, Mallarmé. Was there a supplementary crossing of paths with Sartre's concerns, since the figure of Mallarmé, literally, haunted him?[3] No doubt, except that in my eyes Sartre underestimated the *affirmative* capacity of the poet's thinking, in favour of a historico-subjective exegesis of his machinations of nothingness. It was not the alleged failure of the Book that attracted my passion, nor the fact (which is Sartre's thesis) that this Book would have

2 Jean-Paul Sartre, *Critique of Dialectical Reason*, vol. 1: *Theory of Practical Ensembles*, trans. Alan Sheridan-Smith (London: Verso, 2004). [*Translator's Note*: In French, *ensemble* is also the technical term for the mathematical 'set', with 'set theory' being rendered as *théorie des ensembles*.]

3 *Translator's Note*: See Jean-Paul Sartre, *Mallarmé: Or the Poet of Nothingness*, trans. Ernest Sturm (University Park: Pennsylvania State University Press, 1991).

been nothing but a pathetic mystification. I was even less interested in the temptations of suicidal despair. I saw in Mallarmé's poems and prose the most radical effort ever conducted to *think thinking*, an effort manifested in the accomplished appearance of the Constellation, the Swan, or the rose in the darkness.

Finally, there was Plato, to whom I constantly return with a quiet remorse, because of the degree to which the 'objective' ideality and much-flaunted primacy of essence over existence seemed absolutely to contradict the Sartrean doctrinal body. It was as if philosophy, aside from its most effective modern maxims – and here Sartre was so irreplaceable to me that for a long time I was accused of producing nothing but pastiches of him – possessed an intrinsic virtuosity that was totally detached from all interiorization, from all pathos of consciousness.

Thus, in an anarchic coexistence of sorts – perhaps analogous to the one that in Sartre allowed for the coexistence of the piano and Chopin, silently and without concept, with *all the rest* – I literally inhabited the Sartrean philosophy of consciousness of freedom, all the while reserving the domain of the poem as affirmation and of the matheme as Idea.

In what I call today the four generic procedures (politics, science, art, and love), there was at bottom only politics – the politics of commitment against the colonial wars, which at the time stemmed from simple principles of opinion, and which seemed to me capable of being subsumed under the Sartrean concept of freedom. Thus in these combats there was in my eyes a kind of *direct* link between Sartre's philosophy and the practice of the committed intellectual.

No doubt this is why, in the final instance, what was needed was the rupture inaugurated by May 1968 and the years that followed – that is, the entrance into militant politics 'on the ground', as an autonomous process that includes the immanent determination of its concepts – for me to abandon the dialectical schema of interiorization, though not without certain detours and regrets. I can certainly say without paradox that it is the fact of having practised and continuing to practise thought in its detour through the factory, of participating in the elaboration of a renewed vision of emancipatory politics, of holding onto the idea that in politics, no matter how bloody the turmoil and the apparent triumph of Capital, the signifier 'worker' has not yet said its last word – all this is what progressively distanced me from the prestige of the dialectic.

However, this distancing was never accompanied by any depreciation of Sartre as an active thinker. In that tormented decade, he was the thoughtful and curious companion of a generation that was not his (nor, truth be told, was it exactly mine). Especially today, against the grain of the hackneyed theme of 'Sartre's mistakes', we must salute the rigor that he displayed in always standing in the thick of things. The fact that progressively there has been a distancing, both in the order of political prescription and in that of the apparatus of thought, should by no means be seen as an objection to this essential historical community.

What would I say today, considering the almost magical formula that held my thinking spellbound thirty years ago? Let us restate it: 'Consciousness is a being such that in its being, its being is in question in so far as this being implies a being other than itself.'

The word 'consciousness', first of all. I will no longer maintain its philosophical pertinence. It seems to me that 'consciousness', designating a concept with a philosophical history that is definitely glorious, can no longer be used except as a *political* category – as in, 'political consciousness' – or perhaps as a category of psychoanalysis. No doubt nothing indicates better the distance that I affirm today between politics – as a *sui generis* form of thought-practice – and philosophy than the destiny of the word 'consciousness', which at bottom is a very technical concept of modern politics since at least Lenin. I can no longer believe – and I am tempted to say: alas! – in the happy transitivity between philosophy and politics, for which Sartre provided me with the paradigm and in which the philosophical concept of consciousness (or of praxis) played a pivotal role.

By contrast, I do not think that we can give up on the intraphilo-sophical unfolding of the concept of the subject, once it is disjointed or decentred from its conscious or transcendental supposition under the decisive effect of Freud and Lacan's inventions. The subject, then, is not the reflective or pre-reflective movement of the self-positing of the I; it is exclusively the differential point that supports, or endures, the becoming-generic of a truth. I call 'subject' a point of truth, or a point traversed by a truth, seized in its chance. It is the 'old man' of Mallarmé, the one who is defined by having to sustain a 'supreme conjunction with probability'.[4]

I now think that Sartre's subject-consciousness was a last and brilliant avatar of the *romantic* subject, of the young man given over to a world whose inertia little by little bogs down, except for a few flashes, both the infinite liberty of desire and the universality of the project. I would gladly say that the still incomplete redeployment of the concept of the subject finds an index, as we see after Mallarmé in the work of Beckett, in the replacement of the young man by the old man, in which we can see stated that no subject is ever truly young, for there is a subject only from the point at which he turns out to be as old as at least one truth.

With regard to the era of Sartrean commitments, this is also one of the aspects of the mutation in political thought, or rather in poli-tics as thought: the revolutionary theme went hand in hand with that of a youthful world, of a rejection of the 'old world'. But the youth is too young for the truth that it inaugurates in the event. Whence its common barbarism. And, symmetrically, what is most horrible in the world of Capital that is ours is its perpetual and monotonous, artificial youth. All forms of radical politics will restore, in accordance with the infinite measure of the generic, the time to grow old that is needed for there to be truths, 'the time taken

---

4   *Translator's Note*: See Stéphane Mallarmé, 'A Dice Throw', *Collected Poems and Other Verse*, trans. E.H. and A.M. Blackmore (Oxford: Oxford University Press, 2006), p. 168 (translation modified).

to have been true', says Beckett in *Watt*, 'the time taken to be proved true'.[5]

But let us continue on with Sartre's formula: 'Consciousness is a being . . .'

For a long time, I did not care about being, because like Sartre I rejoiced only in the meaning-giving functions of Nothingness. Being had the painful thickness, the massiveness, the superfluousness, the practical inertia, of the roots of the chestnut tree. What got me out of this – awoke me from my Sartrean slumber? – is an interminable meditation on set theory, and especially on its two existential extremes, which are the axiom of the empty set and the axiom of infinity. The decision to hold the historical corpus of mathematics for that which has said what there is to say about being qua being, and thus for ontology in the strict sense, sums up the renunciation of the blocked metaphors of massive and ultimately unthinkable being ('without raison d'être', says Sartre, and 'without any relation whatsoever to any other being'). In contrast, by confiding being to the safeguard of pure multiplicity, such that the matheme takes hold of it, we prepare it for the most subtle and ramified form of thinking possible, all the while subtracting it from all experience. Being such that mathematics thinks its being is neither contingent (as Sartre declares) nor necessary (as the classics say). It infinitely exposes itself to thought, and subtracts itself from it at the same time. This is why mathematics is both and at the same time immense and interminable, proceeding by way of axiomatic decisions (*as if* it were contingent) and by way of constraining demonstrations (*as if* it were necessary).

By demonstrating that the double original support of the thinking of being is the void, as suture onto the inconsistency of all consistency, and then the infinite, whereby the otherwise genial and romantic idea of the limit becomes secularized and de-sacralized in

---

5 *Translator's Note*: See Samuel Beckett, *Watt* (New York: Grove Press, 1953), p. 110.

favour of the lacunary number, we truly accomplish, without existential drama, the proposition – so exemplarily Sartrean in the tension that it induces in thought – of the death of God.

Next: 'A being such that in its being, its being is in question.'

The subject, such as I today conceive of it – a subject plotted or woven out of the cloth of some truth – has no interior, even a transparent one, nor any interior-exterior, in which a questioning (of) self can be generated. It is even, properly speaking, the unquestionable, for it is that from which an answer proceeds, the evental answer as to the being of a situation.

The vocabulary of the question and the questioning no doubt marks the highly original manner in which Sartre related to German thinking, and especially to Heidegger. And I should say that, precisely in its Sartrean version, displaced from the care of being towards the anthropology of liberty, this vocabulary of being as the nullifying question of the self exerted a tenacious power of seduction on my thinking. With time passing, this seduction has become inoperative. The question of the question is, it seems to me, the enjoyment of thought. But the answer alone is its action. The answer is often disappointing, so that one regrets the inexhaustible charm of the question. For the answer substitutes joy for enjoyment. Thinking thinks only in the un-enjoyment [dé-jouir] of self, which is also the way in which it un-joins or evades [dé-joue] the question. This is after all something that Sartre also said, having always thought, as he confessed, 'against himself'.

If God is dead (and Sartre convinced me of this more than Nietzsche, who was too concerned with disentangling himself from the Nazarene), this does not mean that everything is possible – and even less that nothing is. It means that there is precisely nothing better, nothing greater, nothing truer, than the answers of which we are capable. The ethic of the answer completes that of the inhuman ends by which the human becomes worthy of Humanity. It means that there are truths and, consequently, nothing is sacred, except precisely the fact that there are truths.

'In so far as this being implies a being other than itself', said Sartre, reading Husserl in his own way.

My reticence with regard to the theme of intentionality is grounded in the fact that it requires the maintenance of the category of the object, as the correlate of conscious intention, and more generally of the dialectic subject/object, of which the Sartrean motif of the in-itself and the for-itself is a genial *projection*. I defend a doctrine of the subject *without object*, of the subject qua vanishing point of a procedure that originates in an unmotivated evental supplement. In my eyes there is no being-other of the subject, except the situation of which a truth is the truth. I have no doubt paid my debt to Sartre by taking back the theme of the 'situation', of which he spun variations with a confusing virtuosity. But for me, as well as for Sartre – from a completely different angle – this apparent Other of the subject is the Same, for truth in an immanent way realizes the generic being, the whatever, the indiscernible of the situation itself.

The true is not said of the object; it is said only of itself. And the subject is not said of the object either, nor of the intention aimed at it; it is said only of the truth, such as it exists in a point that vanishes from itself.

Is all this, however, really as decisive as I make it out to be? Beyond the technical elaborations of thought, I am attached to Sartre by a determining 'existential' motif, which is that philosophy is not of matter of life or of happiness. But neither is it a matter of death or unhappiness. We will live or die in any case, on top of it all, and as for being happy or unhappy, it is what we are constantly required not to care about – neither for the others nor for ourselves.

The point is to throw the dice, at least once, if possible. Mallarmé's old man does not come to this resolution easily, it is true. He 'hesitates a corpse cut off by its arm from the secret it withholds rather than plan the game like a hoary maniac in the name of the waves'.[6]

---

6 *Translator's Note*: See Mallarmé, 'A Dice Throw', p. 166.

What ordinarily is called life, but also culture, leisure, elections, work, happiness, balance, flourishing, performance, economy, is exactly that: the hesitation to play the part in the name of the waves. And thus – precisely for this reason the signifier 'life' is involved – to live *forever* as 'a corpse cut off by its arm from the secret it withholds'. Life, the life proposed to us, about which Sartre said that it barely lifted itself above that of ants, is resolved in the disjunction between a corpse and a secret. Every human being holds a possible pass for at least one truth. Such is its secret, which our common lot under the law of Capital turns into the other extreme of a cadaver.

For if 'every thought emits a dice throw', we must admit that where there are no dice throws, there also is no thought. More so than Pascal, it was Sartre who for me decided the concept of this unconditional demand of the wager. At least he was able to do without God.

The secret for Sartre could be said in the form 'every man is worth as much as any other',[7] whereas I will say: All humans are capable of thought, all humans are aleatorically summoned to exist as subjects. And if all humans are capable of thought, the guideline is clear: throw the dice, play the part in the name of the waves, and then be faithful to this throw, which is not so difficult, since once thrown, the dice come back to you as Constellation. This Constellation is said 'cold with neglect and disuse',[8] but why should philosophy have to promise that the truth keep us warm and fuzzy, that it be convivial and affective? If Sartre's thinking keeps its trenchancy it is because it dispenses with such a promise, without

---

7 *Translator's Note*: Reference to the famous last lines of Sartre's autobiographical *Les Mots*: '*Tout un homme, fait de tous les hommes et qui les vaut tous et que vaut n'importe qui*' ('A whole man, composed of all men and as good as all of them and no better than any'). See Jean-Paul Sartre, *The Words: The Autobiography of Jean-Paul Sartre*, trans. Bernard Frechtman (New York: Vintage, 1981), p. 194.

8 *Translator's Note*: See Mallarmé, 'A Dice Throw', p. 181.

for this reason lapsing into nihilism. The truth is not convivial or affective, because its power goes no farther than to be or not to be.

The guideline is for a truth, or some truths, with regard to any situation whatsoever, to be suspended from their being. We will also say: let us be, without too much hesitation, '*maniaques chenus*', hoary maniacs of the generic. Then – strange thing – we will discover the truth of that other saying of some old man, the one who crawls in the mud and the darkness with his bag, in Beckett's *How It Is*: 'In any case we have our being in justice I have never heard anything to the contrary.'[9]

We can indeed name 'justice' that there are some truths, the 'there is' of truths thought in its pure 'there is'. Justice is then another name for the inhuman ends of humanity.

I do not believe that on this point, though by way of a series of mediations which in the end are very far from what I report here, Sartre has ever given up.

Humanity is what does justice to humanity, because if there is some event that summons it to do so, it has in it enough of a secret to chuck its corpse and crawl with its bag in the darkness of truth.

Of this darkness, which he knew to be dark – and that will remain no matter what one says – Sartre was, already almost half a century ago, one of our rare *illuminating* guides.

---

9   *Translator's Note*: See Samuel Beckett, *How It Is* (New York: Grove Press, 1964), p. 124.

4

Is There a Theory of the Subject in the Work of Georges Canguilhem?

skip

So I ask the question: Is there a doctrine of the subject in the work of Georges Canguilhem? Of course, it might seem unnecessarily complicated to put to a work of history and epistemology a kind of question that this work explicitly avoids. I allow that this complication may be a philosopher's failing, and in my defence I call upon witnesses who are so disparate that it may well be impossible to conclude whether they are witnesses of moral or immoral character.

The most suspect of these witnesses is none other than Heidegger, who, in his *Introduction to Metaphysics*, claims that 'it is in the very nature of philosophy never to make things easier but only more difficult'.[1] The less suspect witness is Georges Canguilhem himself, who concludes his essay on 'The Question of Normality in the History of Biological Thought' in this way: 'For I maintain that the proper function of philosophy is precisely to complicate matters, not only for the historian of science but for man in general.'[2] So, let us complicate things and, if I may put it in this way, complicate them *unreservedly*.

---

1   Martin Heidegger, *Introduction to Metaphysics*, trans. Ralph Manheim (New Haven: Yale University Press, 1974), p. 11.
2   Georges Canguilhem, *Ideology and Rationality in the Life Sciences*, trans. Arthur Goldhammer (Cambridge, Mass.: MIT Press, 1988), p. 144.

It is clear that there is no explicit doctrine of the subject in Georges Canguilhem's work. Such is the simple fact of the matter. What complicates things is that the subject, often employed by Canguilhem in the capitalized form of the Subject, nonetheless functions as an operator brought in at strategic points of the intellectual enterprise to which we are giving homage.

No doubt all of these strategic points are situated on a line of cleavage and have a seismographic value. They indicate the fault lines or discontinuities between the tectonic plates of Canguilhem's thought and what it controls in its actualization. I believe three such discontinuities can be identified:

- A quasi-ontological discontinuity which within the natural presentation separates the living from the non-living.

- An operational discontinuity which distinguishes technique from science.

- A primarily ethical discontinuity which, in medicine, links together the dimension of knowledge and what might be called the dimension of closeness.

If, for Canguilhem, the living is always in some way a pre-subjective disposition on the basis of which any possible subject arises, it is because the living can be understood only in connection with the three essential notions of centre (or centring), norm and meaning. A first approximation, a sort of formal schema or virtuality of the subject, is to be found here in this knot of centre, norm and meaning. The knot will be formulated in the following way, for example: every living being is a centre because it constitutes a normed milieu in which behaviours and dispositions have meaning with regard to a need.

Conceived of in this way, such centring refuses the notion that the reality of scientific theory would lay in a single, univocal description. The plurality of living beings immediately attests to the plurality of worlds, if by world one understands the place of meaning, such that around a centre it is related to norms. Hence there is what must be called a conflict of absolutes which is precisely picked out in the famous text of 'Le Vivant et son milieu' (The Living and its Milieu).

First of all, Canguilhem absolutizes reality in the unified form that, at least ideally, physical science attributes to it:

> In all rigor, the qualification *real* can be applied only to the absolute universe, the universal milieu of elements and movements disclosed by science. Its recognition as real is necessarily accompanied by the disqualification, as illusions or vital errors, of all subjectively centered natural milieus, including that of man.[3]

In passing, we can see that centring is explicitly associated here with a subjective connotation. However, this is only in order to discredit this connotation by confronting it with the point of view of the absolute character of the scientifically determined universe.

However, this absolute character is immediately contrasted with another. For, Canguilhem says, 'the natural milieu of men is not situated in the universal milieu like a content in its container. A centre is not resolved into its environment.' And, moving from centring to the effect of meaning, he affirms 'the inadequacy of any biology which, in surrendering completely to the spirit of the physico-chemical sciences, would eliminate from its domain any consideration of meaning'. Finally, tying the knot, Canguilhem passes from meaning to the norm so as to conclude: 'From the biological and psychological point of view, meaning is an

---

3   Georges Canguilhem, 'Le Vivant et son milieu', in *La Connaissance de la vie*, 2nd edition (Paris: Vrin, 1980), p. 153; 'The Living and Its Milieu', in *Knowledge of Life*, trans. Stefanos Geroulanos and Daniela Ginsburg (New York: Fordham University Press, 2008), p. 119.

assessment of value in relation to a need. And, for the one who experiences and lives it, a need is an irreducible, and thereby absolute, reference system.' The word 'absolute' is not there by chance. Canguilhem insists: 'There is a centre of reference that could be called absolute. The living being is, precisely, a centre of reference.'

So it can be seen that the absolute character of the objective universal milieu is coupled with the absolute character of subjective need, the latter giving its energy to the triplet of centring, norm and meaning. This conflict of absolutes implies that what is truly real, what determines differences within reality, varies from one whole to the other depending on the place from which one is speaking. With regard to the absolute universe, or universal milieu, living milieus have no meaning that would enable them to be classified or compared. As Canguilhem says, if one adopts the point of view of the in-itself then one has to say that 'the milieu of man's sensory and technical values does not in itself have more reality than the milieus proper to the woodlouse or the gray mouse'.[4]

On the other hand, everything changes if one is placed within the pre-subjective configuration of centring, norm and meaning – that is, if one is a woodlouse, a grey squirrel or a human being. With regard to the absolute character of need, the absolute reality of the universal milieu is an indifferent anti-nature. The Moderns know this; they have given up the harmony of these two absolutes.

Canguilhem praises Fontenelle precisely for having been the author who was able to give an amusing twist to what was 'an absurd and depressing idea in the eyes of the Ancients, that of a Humanity without destiny in a limitless Universe'.[5] I would add: it is precisely for this reason that, in an exemplary fashion, the concept

---

4   Canguilhem, *Knowledge of Life*, p. 119.
5   Georges Canguilhem, 'Fontenelle, philosophe et historien des sciences', in *Études d'histoire et de philosophie des sciences concernant les vivants et la vie* (Paris: Vrin, 1968), p. 58.

of the subject is a modern concept; it picks out the conflict of absolutes.

But there is a further, supplementary twist to the complication. It would be too simple to oppose the absolute character of the universal milieu to the pre-subjective absolute character of the centring by the living being. For its part, the human subject in any case is entailed in both terms of the conflict. As the subject of science, through mathematics, experiment and technique, it constitutes the absolute real universe from which every centre is absent. As a living subject, it objects to this universe through the changeable singularity of its own centred, normed and meaningful milieu.

Henceforth, the notion of a 'subject' somehow designates not just *one* of the terms of the clash of absolutes, but rather the enigma of this discordance itself.

It is precisely the status of the knowing subject in the life sciences that brings this enigma into sharp relief. Is the knowing subject an instance of the scientific subject, attached to the decentred universe, or of the living subject who produces norms that are always centred by an absolute need? Almost all of Canguilhem's texts are motivated by this question. And certainly, he comes to maintain that the subject of the life sciences is precisely the point at which this conflict of absolutes is brought to bear.

On the one hand, Canguilhem repeats that the living being is the original condition of any science of life. The formula expressed in the 'Introduction' to *Knowledge of Life* is well known: 'The thought of the living must take from the living the idea of the living.' This is taken further with Canguilhem's observation that to do mathematics it suffices to be an angel, but that to do biology 'we sometimes need to feel like beasts ourselves'.[6] It is because we share in the pre-subjective singularity of centring that the living offers itself to knowledge. It is this that, in contrast to the object of physics, makes the living resistant to any transcendental constitution.

6   Canguilhem, *Knowledge of Life*, p. xx.

More generally, as Canguilhem says in 'Le Concept et la vie' (Concept and Life), as soon as the living is taken into account there is 'a resistance of the thing, not to knowledge, but to a theory of knowledge which proceeds from knowledge to the thing'.[7] Now to proceed on the basis of the thing is to place oneself on the ground of its absolute character and so on the basis of centring and meaning.

Canguilhem never gives way on this point, and in 'The Question of Normality in the History of Biological Thought', he still claims 'questions about the vital meaning of these norms, though not directly matters of chemistry and physics, are questions of biology'.[8] In this precise and limited sense, biology necessarily has a subjective dimension.

However, on the other hand, insofar as it is subjected to the scientific ideal, biology shares in a break with the centring and singularity of the milieu. It connects up with the 'neutrality' governing the concepts of the universal milieu. It is therefore also a-subjective. Certainly science is a normed activity, or, as Canguilhem says in 'The History of Science', an 'axiological' activity which, he adds, is called 'the search for truth'.[9] But does this 'search for truth' arise from the absolute character of the living being's need? Is the norm governing the search for truth nothing more than an extension of the vital norms that centre the subject of need? This could only be established within the framework of a doctrine of the subject, so that we seem to be caught on a wheel.

Ultimately, it would seem that science – and indeed, more generally, the human action it informs – cannot be understood within the strict natural framework proposed by the knot of centring, norm and meaning. With reference to a text by Adam Smith on polytheist

---

7   Canguilhem, 'Le Concept et la Vie', in *Études d'histoire et de philosophie des sciences*.

8   Canguilhem, *Ideology and Rationality in the Life Sciences*, p. 144.

9   Georges Canguilhem, *A Vital Rationalist: Selected Writings from Georges Canguilhem*, ed. François Delaporte, trans. Arthur Goldhammer (New York: Zone Books, 1994), p. 30.

religions, Canguilhem pays tribute to 'the unostentatious profundity of the observation that man is only led to forge the supernatural to the extent that, within nature, his actions constitute a counter-nature'.[10] Does this mean that the subject, or at least the human subject, is the being that, in the supernatural illusion, goes beyond the counter-nature of its action? In any event, we must no doubt remember here that the subject of biological knowledge is concerned with the discordance between its scientific procedures and its object, between nature and counter-nature and, finally, between absolutes. In this the subject of biological knowledge is reducible neither to the living being nor to the scientist.

This means also, and here I evoke the second great discontinuity where the word 'subject' is called upon in some way, that this subject is neither technical nor scientific. Canguilhem, in a line of descent from Bergson, likes to present technique as a continuation of the effect of vital norms, whereas science goes beyond the limits of centring. It is in this sense that, in 'Machine and Organism', he writes: 'The solution we have tried to defend has the advantage of showing man in continuity with life through technique prior to insisting on the rupture for which he assumes responsibility through science.'[11] Thus, at the point we have now reached, I would suggest that the subject is the empty name for the articulation of a natural continuity and a counter-natural discontinuity, itself cast within the complex of technique and science, and in which a conflict of absolutes is realized.

The consideration of medicine comes to saturate or complicate once again this provisional statement. If there is one theme that is particularly constant in Canguilhem's work, it is the irreducibility of medicine to what within it presents itself with the efficacy of science. In 1951, he declared forcefully that 'the medico-surgical act is not just a scientific act, for the sick man who entrusts himself to his doctor's conscience – even more than to his science – is not only a physiological problem to be resolved: he is above all in a distress from which he seeks to be rescued'.[12] In 1978 there is an overwhelming recourse to subjective connotations:

> The sick person is a Subject capable of expression who recognizes himself as a Subject in all that he can only designate in terms of possession: his pain and his representation thereof, his anxiety, his hopes and his dreams. While on the part of rationality these possessions will be identified as so many illusions, nevertheless the authentic nature of the power of illusion must be acknowledged. It is objective to acknowledge that the power of illusion is not the capacity of an object . . . The subjectivity of the sick person's lived experience cannot be nullified in the objectivity of medical knowledge . . . This protest of existence deserves to be listened to, even if it opposes to the rationality of a well-founded judgement the limit of a sort of ceiling that cannot be pierced.[13]

In the first text, the distress invoked amounts to the fact of subjective centring being ineluctably given within the field in which the doctor works. In the second text, the subject is a being with the capacity for illusion through which he or she eludes any process of pure objectification. The capacity for illusion and error is the decisive test of the subject here. It brings to mind the phrase used by Canguilhem when commenting on the doctrine of fetishism in Comte: 'In the beginning was Fiction.'[14] What begins in the world of fiction is the resistance of the human subject to the destruction of

---

12   Canguilhem, 'Experimentation in Animal Biology', in *Knowledge of Life*, p. 20.
13   Georges Canguilhem, 'Une pédagogie de la guérison est-elle possible?' *Nouvelle revue de psychanalyse* 17 (1978): 408–9.
14   Georges Canguilhem, 'Histoire des religions et histoire des sciences dans la théorie du fétichisme chez Auguste Comte', in *Études d'histoire et de philosophie des sciences*, p. 85.

the absolute character of his centring. On its own account, and not just through its knowledge, medicine must be able to enter into a dialogue with the fiction in which the subject expresses this resistance.

Finally, the theme of the subject weaves a triple negative determination:

- Centring, which is an absolute of the living being, blocks the objective laying out of an absolute universe.

- Meaning, which passes through the supposition of norms, blocks the realization of a biology completely reduced to the physico-chemical.

- Fiction, finally, blocks an approach to the living being's distress through pure knowledge.

This negative egology could be transcribed on the model of Bichat's famous definition of life, frequently cited by Canguilhem. We will then say: 'The subject is the ensemble of functions which resist objectification.'[15] But immediately we must add that there is nothing ineffable in this. In Canguilhem's eyes, there clearly exists a discipline of thought that seizes on the *dispositif* of these functions of resistance. This discipline is philosophy.

The question then becomes: from what preferential philosophical angle does Canguilhem approach this theme of the subject that is only indicated in outline by epistemology and history?

With respect to the subject of knowledge, or the subject of science, the best starting point seems to me to be found in a very

---

15   *Translator's Note*: Xavier Bichat's original formula, frequently cited by Canguilhem, states: 'Life is the ensemble of functions that resist death.' See, for instance, Canguilhem, *Knowledge of Life*, p. 104.

terse and complex text in which Canguilhem broaches the reserva-
tions, or the questions, that certain developments in Bachelard
provoke in him. Here are some essential fragments of this text:

> Bachelard continues to employ a psychological and intrapsycho-
> logical vocabulary to set out an axiological type of rationalism. The
> divided Subject whose structure he presents is only divided because
> it is an axiological Subject. 'Every value divides the evaluating
> subject.' Now, if the concepts of normative psychic life and norma-
> tive psychology are admissible, do we not have good reason to be
> surprised before the subject of a 'psychologism of normaliza-
> tion'? . . . In any case, we will not deny Bachelard's total lucidity
> concerning the difficulty of constituting the vocabulary of a ration-
> alist epistemology from top to bottom without reference to an
> ontological theory of reason or without reference to a transcenden-
> tal theory of categories.[16]

Here Canguilhem firmly maintains, albeit against Bachelard, that
the doctrine of the subject which upholds the objectivity of science
cannot be a psychological doctrine.

Canguilhem has continued to maintain this anti-psychologist
axiom with basically the same vigour as Husserl before him,
although for completely different reasons. It seems to him that
Bachelard, when he addresses the crucial question of norms, does
not sufficiently extricate himself from an improved psychologism.

It is clear, even so, that a transcendental type of solution will not do
for Canguilhem either. It is all the less fitting for him in that modern
biology seems to him to confirm one of his oldest intuitions: in the
knowledge of life, the *a priori*s do not exist on the side of the subject
but on that of the object or the thing. That the living prescribes the
thought of the living is explicitly opposed to the assumption of a

---

16   Canguilhem, 'Dialectique et philosophie du non chez Gaston Bachelard', in
Études d'histoire et de philosophie des sciences, pp. 205-6.

transcendental subject when Canguilhem writes in 'The Concept of Life': 'It is not because I am a subject, in the transcendental sense of the word, but because I am living that I must look for the reference of life within life itself.'[17] And, commenting on the discovery of the genetic code, a veritable *logos* inscribed within the chemical combinatorial, he concludes: 'To define life as a meaning inscribed in matter is to acknowledge the existence of an objective *a priori* that is inherently material and not merely formal.'[18] Hence it can be seen that meaning itself, the major category of subjective centring, works against the hypothesis of a transcendental subject.

Canguilhem finally seems also to reject a subject drawn from what he calls an ontology of reason, be this a subject detached from the site of the Ideas, as in Plato, or one coextensive with a thinking thing, as in Descartes. There is nothing surprising in this, since such subjects, instead of dealing with the conflict of absolutes, tend to force the union of the centred subject and the absolute character of the universe, which bars their way to an adequate conception of the living being.

If it is neither psychological, nor transcendental, nor substantial – then what can this subject, the entire visible effect of which is subtractive or a resistance to objectification, be positively? It seems to me that Canguilhem, with the philosophical discretion that was for him like an ethic of speech, suggests two tracks.

In the text on Galileo, Canguilhem takes up the scientist's trial and concludes by absolving him. Why? Because, according to Canguilhem, in the absence of realizable proofs of his hypotheses, Galileo was right to invoke the infinite future of their validation. We have in this a crucial dimension of the subject of knowledge – its historicity. As soon as the singular position of such a subject has been got under way, it naturally considers itself to be infinite both in its rule and its effects.

---

17   Canguilhem, 'Le Concept et la Vie', p. 352.
18   Canguilhem, *A Vital Rationalist*, p. 317 (translation modified).

I cite: 'In his human existence, Galileo took upon himself an infinite task of measurement and the co-ordination of experiments which requires the time of humanity as infinite subject of knowledge.'[19]

If the subject of science can simultaneously take up the two conflicting absolutes of his living centring and the neutral ideal of the universal milieu, it is because in each singular case he can be represented as captive to an infinite task. This task works, precisely, in the gap between the two absolutes. The singularity of the living being is thereby taken up and relayed through the infinite history of the consequence of his thoughts and his acts. 'Humanity' is thus the generic name of any singular living subject, insofar as this subject is situated within the history of truths.

The other track concerns the nature of the task itself, as pursued on the assumption of an infinite subject of knowledge. Here we find what I think is, next to that of the centre, perhaps the most important of Canguilhem's concepts, that of displacement or moving around. The most developed text concerning this concept is the following, taken from 'The Concept and Life':

[Man] makes mistakes when he chooses the wrong spot for receiving the kind of information he is after. But he also gathers information by moving around [*se déplacer*], and by moving [*en déplaçant*] objects around, with the aid of various kinds of technology. Most scientific techniques, it can be argued, are in fact nothing more than methods for moving things around and changing the relations among objects. Knowledge, then, is an anxious quest for the greatest possible quantity and variety of information. If the *a priori* is in things, if the concept is in life, then to be a subject of knowledge is simply to be dissatisfied with the meaning one finds ready at hand. Subjectivity is therefore nothing other than dissatisfaction. Perhaps that is what life

19   Canguilhem, 'Galilée: La signification de l'œuvre et la leçon de l'homme', in *Etudes d'histoire et de philosophie des sciences*, p. 49.

is. Interpreted in a certain way, contemporary biology is, some-how, a philosophy of life.[20]

We can see that movement or displacement – which, just before this passage, Canguilhem calls human errancy – is what is presumed of free subjectivity at the source of all knowledge, including error. This freedom looms up as dissatisfaction with a meaning. It is the living energy that invests truth as a trajectory. For a truth is obtained in a constant displacement of situations, a movement that, in my own terms, I have called the regime of investigations. And it is along the trajectory of the investigations – or, for Canguilhem, in the freedom of displacements – that successive truths work.

I do not use the word 'freedom' lightly. In the article on the normal and the pathological, Canguilhem states: 'The norm in matters of the human psyche is the reclamation and use of freedom as a power of revision and institution of norms – a reclamation that normally implies the risk of madness.'[21] Now, the obligatory method of this capacity to revise norms is by displacement, so the use of freedom is ultimately governed by the rules which authorize or limit the direction taken by the possible and by experiments.

It is certainly not without interest that, for Canguilhem, the allegation of 'madness' can under no circumstances be an acceptable reason for strictly pinning down everything which moves or wishes to move about. Truth is at stake.

Fundamentally, displacement remains an activity of the living being, since it always develops from within the normative centring, or carries with it the requirement of a displaced centre, which is also a shift of meaning. But the infinity of displacements also approxi-mates to the absolute decentred reality, precisely because, besides the living subject and through the living subject, it assumes a subject

20   Canguilhem, 'Le Concept et la Vie', p. 364; *A Vital Rationalist*, p. 319.
21   Canguilhem, 'The Normal and the Pathological', in *Knowledge of Life*, p. 133.

free to move about – that is to say, a historicized subject in the true sense of the term. And, in turn, such a subject does not renounce fiction.

On the contrary, for, as Canguilhem writes in 'On the History of the Life Sciences Since Darwin':

> The imaginary (*fictive*) construction of a possible development is not intended to deprive the past of its reality. On the contrary, it highlights its true historical nature and clarifies the responsibility of individuals, whether scientists or politicians; it purifies history by demonstrating that the historical record was in no sense dictated by Fate.[22]

Finally, then, the subject is three things: under the name of humanity, it subjects singularity to the infinite becoming of truths; under the name of knowledge, it creates a breach in the neutral plenitude of the universe through the native dissatisfaction of the living being; and, under the name of fiction, it subtracts itself from the temptation of the inevitable fate. This cognitive and fictitious humanity is first and above all freedom of displacement, the freedom to come and go. My conclusion is that there is a subject for Canguilhem only insofar as we can say that in the universe there exists a living being that, dissatisfied with meaning and fitted for moving around the configurations of its objectivity, always appears, in the order of life and in the ambiguity of the adjective, as a somewhat *displaced* living being.

---

22 Canguilhem, *Ideology and Rationality in the Life Sciences*, pp. 112–13 (translation modified).

5

The Caesura of Nihilism

We know that, among the disciplines contributing to the training of analysts, Jacques Lacan attributed a pre-eminent place to anti-philosophy.[1] He thus opened up a new career for this old word, which in the eighteenth century designated the position of all the enemies of the Enlightenment. In fact, his position is a reversal of the conservative sense of the word. For, if it was expedient that analysts be antiphilosophers, this was precisely in the name of the Enlightenment, philosophy being assigned by Lacan to an essential 'not-wanting-to-know', namely (to speak like the Master), to the voluntary ignorance of anything concerning the effects of enjoyment [*jouissance*] at the heart of thought.

If philosophy does not want to know anything about enjoyment, it is because of the connection between enjoyment and the unnameable Thing, as unsymbolizable as it is despotic, which analytic orthodoxy assigns at its origin to the body of the mother. Philosophy is constituted literally by foreclosing the consideration of this thing, without which it would not be entitled to state that the all, or even the All, can be raised to the status of the concept.

---

1 *Translator's Note*: In 1975, at the University of Vincennes, Jacques Lacan suggested that analysts in his school train themselves not only in linguistics, logic, and topology, but also in what he proposed to call antiphilosophy. See Jacques Lacan, 'Peut-être à Vincennes', *Autres écrits* (Paris: Seuil, 2001), p. 314.

enjoy · Vague — *S-m: child? molesting?*

If, from Plato to Husserl, philosophy does not stop declaring that it will finally return 'to the things themselves', it is indeed – says the Lacanian analyst –because it exists only by virtue of the fact that it has turned away from the Thing.

This exclusion of enjoyment in the examination of thought results in the constantly reformed connection between philosophy and asceticism. This connection is one of the paths chosen by Nietzsche for his personal entry into antiphilosophy. If for him the philosopher is 'the criminal of criminals',[2] it is because the effect of philosophy's refusal of the native power of enjoyment is merely to arm resentment.

We can here note that Nietzsche and psychoanalysis are in agreement insofar as both hold that the essence of philosophy is ascetic, at least if we define 'ascetic' as a doctrine for which the price of thinking is the avoidance of any knowledge concerning enjoyment. Philosophy would be edified within something like an un-joying or de-joicing [*dé-jouir*], whereas life can only be reinforced by a re-joicing [*ré-jouir*]. Refusing to see that enjoyment – the only way to attain access to the Thing – is at the heart of thought, philosophy would be one of the variants of the religious imposture.

But what relation is there between these considerations and contemporary nihilism? A relation of major clarification. For, the present moment incontestably stands under the emblem of enjoyment. At a time when, we are told, the old 'ideologies' are fortunately dead – ideologies which, like the Carthaginian Moloch, were devouring human lives by millions in an entirely vain ascetic sacrifice – the quasi-familial imperative 'enjoy as you wish, enjoy as you can', holds from now on and forever: it is modest, modern and realist.

2   *Translator's Note*: Nietzsche calls the philosopher 'the criminal of criminals' in 'Law against Christianity', in *The Anti-Christ, Ecce Homo, Twilight of the Idols and Other Writings*, ed. Aaron Ridley and Judith Norman (Cambridge: Cambridge University Press, 2005), p. 25.

There are two versions of this imperative. One libertarian, the other liberal.

The libertarian version, which differs from the other in being presented as emancipating, or even 'radical', is concentrated in a May '68 slogan: 'Enjoy without shackles' [*jouir sans entraves*]. In fact, is this possible? Can we attain enjoyment that would exonerate us from any ties? This commandment is much more restrictive than the classical anarchist opposition to laws and rules. We are beyond what the Maoists of the epoch called 'the anti-authoritarian revolt'. Let us say that the slogan 'enjoy without shackles' concentrates in it what we could call a *drugged conception of existence*. I refer you, for the poetics of this conception, to most of Philippe Garrel's films, in particular *Le vent de la nuit* (which speaks with force of May '68, of the impossibility of transmitting it) and *Sauvage innocence* (which tracks down the exact point of nihilism: the point at which enjoying and dying are indiscernible). We clearly see in this film that a drug is something quite different from an adjuvant, a dependency or a pleasure. Drugs are a metaphysics: a metaphysics of the de-linking. It is what renders inactive – temporarily – any link, and artificially produces a truly unshackled enjoyment. One is 'high as a kite', outside any connection.

However, the real world being nothing but a system of links, we can say that, in the drugged conception of existence, as long as it remains within the ideal of the suspension of the link, the enjoying is purely and simply the negation of the world. It really is then a question of nihilism. In its libertarian version, nihilism is the enjoying in itself. It is a question of turning oneself through enjoyment into the debris of the connections of the world, and so of being dead to the world, like a saint – but all the more miserable, since what one sacrifices the world to is only the absence of any God.

In its liberal version, the imperative is to purchase some enjoyment. This is what keeps the world turning today. The problem is that this imperative is empty, because enjoyment is, by definition, and by its connection to the unnameable Thing, what remains forever without an equivalent. It is radically impossible to purchase enjoyment; at the most we can pay for the wrapper, as is shown by the principal model of this sort of commodified imposture, prostitution, and particularly the prostitution which, in our world, takes the prize over all others, the prostitution of transvestites. Understand by 'wrapper', always isomorphic with the stockings and high-heeled shoes of transvestites, the endlessly replaceable surroundings of a failed attempt at enjoyment.

This essential lack around which the transaction is made obviously induces a second kind of nihilism. (And we are reminded here of Bernard-Marie Koltès's admirable play, *Dans la solitude des champs de coton*, in which we see that instead of the Thing, we have an endless transaction concerning its attire. For in wanting to sell wrappers, for which there is no other veritable use except to throw them out, we transform the world into litter, into a pile of trash. The wrapper – and we can obviously include in this the totality of advertising devices – is, by its essence, rubbish.)

We might just mention that ecology consists, essentially, in wishing that the detritus of the missed-purchased enjoyment be biodegradable. Enjoyment, then – which, even aborted – would be 'healthy' and 'natural' by the fact of its wrapper being non-polluting. Perhaps ecology is only a reformism of the nothing, a rectified nihilism. Or a soft nihilism.

If the drugged conception of existence comes down to turning oneself into the waste of the world, its generalized mercantile conception comes down to turning the world into waste. In both cases, under the sign of enjoyment.

The synthesis of the libertarian conception and the liberal conception, a synthesis realized in the explicitly 'liberal-libertarian' person, Dany Cohn-Bendit,[3] comes down then to turning oneself

---

3 *Translator's Note*: Daniel Cohn-Bendit, member of the March 22 Movement that was key in the events leading up to May '68 in France, would later become a politician and member of the European Parliament for the Green Party.

into the waste of a wasteland. There is little to be thought here. But this is certainly the ineluctable consequence for anyone who poses that enjoyment, sometimes re-named 'happiness', or even 'humanism', is the unique defendable human project (if not, of course, we will suffer the return of 'totalitarianism', absolute Evil).

We might then say that philosophy was right to leave enjoyment aside. Never, undoubtedly, more than today did the ancient Greek figure associating philosophy and asceticism have better arguments to put forward. We find, moreover, an ascetic proposal from all the contemporary philosophers of any importance, including the most resolute partisans of Nietzschean vitalism – Deleuze, for example.

And yet the most interesting course is probably not that of the restoration of wisdom. Rather, enjoyment must be conceived otherwise within philosophy. We must redefine and rehabilitate enjoyment, rather than re-establishing ancient asceticism.

This is precisely the challenge that Jean-Luc Nancy took up by proposing an assertive thinking of enjoyment. I am referring to his 1986 article 'L'amour en éclats' (Shattered Love), an article which for the most part treats the question: What do we mean by enjoying?

This article is built on three essential propositions:

- A double negation: 'Sexual enjoyment is no more impossible, as Lacan maintained, than it is possible, as sexologists maintain.'[4] This means that the two dominant conceptions of sexual enjoyment, both the liberal and the libertarian, must be dismissed. Sexual enjoyment neither requires death, nor can it be purchased. (By the way: I do not believe that Lacan had ever wished to say that sexual enjoyment was impossible. But we will leave that aside.)

---

4 Jean-Luc Nancy, 'Shattered Love', trans. Lisa Garbus and Simona Sawhney, in *A Finite Thinking* (Stanford: Stanford University Press, 2003), pp. 245–74.

- A definition: sexual enjoyment is traversing being as Other. It involves the touching of being itself, but being itself as Other. This definition authorizes a play on the words 'joy' (the joy of the-other-in-being) and 'enjoy' (traversed for joy).

- An ontology of the offering: 'Sexual enjoyment is an extremity of presence, *self* exposed, *of self* enjoying outside of self, in a presence that no present can absorb, and which is not (re)presented, but which offers itself incessantly.'

The attempt is clear: asserting that sexual enjoyment is neither narcissistic nor selfless; neither pure relation to the self nor pure devotion to the other. Sexual enjoyment is in a relation to self outside of self. It is the exposition of self outside of self. It is not theatre, a representation, but a presentation, an offering. (Offering, exposition, these are two fundamental words for Jean-Luc Nancy: exposing oneself is something like a response to an offering.) Sexual enjoyment then becomes an experience of being itself, an experience of the traversing of sense. And nihilism is vanquished.

The misfortune – and this, after all, is *my* misfortune – is that I am not at all convinced by Nancy's very elegant attempt, which seems to me to be oriented towards an angelic myth. I believe his definition to be entirely false, and the consequences he draws from it obviously false. I mark my opposition in five steps, in a deliberately brutal manner.

Sexual enjoyment is not an extremity; it is a fragment, a cut. Any enjoyment picks up its motif from a dislocated continuum. This is moreover why coming out of any sexual enjoyment is always a bit disconcerting: the return to continuity allows nothing to subsist, within it, of this obscure piece of flesh in which the fertile obscenity of the real had come to glow.

Sexual enjoyment is not an exposition. That is where too much angelism is harmful. Sexual enjoyment is first an imposition. We can say it is the exposition of an imposition. The aleatory question, when there is a risk of the advent of sexual enjoyment, is always knowing at what moment the imposition is possible. We cannot reasonably avoid the question of a time of violence inherent in any sexual enjoyment – even, and above all, if we recognize that this time is the result of a certain toil, of the sweat of bodies at work.

The 'outside of self' can only be conceived in what Nancy attempts to leave out (at least in this article): sexuation, the differences in the positions of the sexes. There is no indeterminate 'outside of self', and any determination is also a dissymmetry. We can add that for Lacan the self is taken up in the paradoxical logic of the Other to such an extent that there is no relation 'outside of self'. There exists an intransitivity between the self and the outside of self. We understand then why Nancy, in a brilliant and tender essay, vainly attempted to restore the existence, denied by Lacan, of a sexual 'rapport'.[5]

Sexual enjoyment, says Nancy, is a 'presence that no present can absorb'. I would willingly hold exactly the contrary: Sexual enjoyment is a present that no presence can absorb, a pure present. It has no intrinsic temporality. Enjoyment-in-the-present presents no presence. It is only in the post-enjoyment that there is a return, to the other as well as to oneself, within the modality of presence. The necessary place must then be accorded to tenderness, which is the absolutely unrecognizable reverse of sexual enjoyment, its absolute Other. Sexual enjoyment is a demoniac present. In fact, Nancy's formulation defies the authority of fantasy in enjoyment. A representation adheres to the enjoyment itself, and is dissolved in its unpresented present.

---

5 *Translator's Note*: Jean-Luc Nancy's essay *L' 'il y a' du rapport sexuel* (Paris: Galilée, 2001) from its very title presents itself as a refutation of Lacan's famous dictum *'il n'y a pas de rapport sexuel'* ('there is no such thing as a sexual relationship'), all the while connecting enjoyment to the question of being, especially through the Heideggerian reference to the *'es gibt'* ('there is') usually translated in French as *'il y a'*.

Something in sexual enjoyment, Nancy says, 'is offered incessantly'. But is the 'incessantly' not the devouring of the 'offer', or of the offering? This enjoyment is implacably of the order of repetition. What can be done with an instance of sexual enjoyment, if not desire its repetition, the return 'to the same place' of the real which sustained the delight and the horror of it? The sweetness of the 'offering' weakens the dimension of the useless consumption of the enjoyment, which consigns it to the repetitive scansion of its pure present.

What can we conclude? Nancy's effort to assert enjoyment opens the way: it is out of the question to come back to asceticism without mediation. However, we must elaborate the question of sexual enjoyment starting with something other than itself, to avoid falling into the Edenic conception that Nancy proposes. In this sense, we are partly obliged to accept the verdict of psychoanalysis: Philosophy cannot find its starting point in the consideration of enjoyment. It is true that it must turn away from it. It is also true that philosophy must nourish the hope of coming back to it, and without this hope, thought falls under the nihilist jurisdiction of the contemporary world. But by wanting to short-circuit asceticism too quickly, philosophy only opposes to this jurisdiction the uncertain figure of the Angel.

The starting point of a veritable anti-nihilism is found in four maxims:

Contest the democratic emblem. This is the decisive task, the first liberation. Let us be very clear about this: It is not a question of abandoning the word 'democracy', but just the contemporary fetish the word represents. We hold that the only legitimate use is found with the adjective. 'The' democracy is a state fetish, 'the' democracies only designate the imperial comfort. But there can be democratic situations, or a fragmentary democratic politics. Part of the problem is to separate the adjective from the noun.

- Break with the naked power which underlies this emblem, the power of the imperial attack and of the 'one-and-only politics', that of capitalo-parliamentarianism.

- Exalt exceptions, without ever being intimidated by the denunciation of elitism or 'totalitarianism'.

- Find the faults of the 'democratic' transcendental, and work for its logical and real ruin.

How does the democratic emblem function today? It proposes a possible peace. The planetary extension of the democratic regime would represent a definitively pacified, and so a 'happy' world. This means that only the non-democratic exceptions are blocking the advent of this pacified world. In short, there are still the wicked – the non-democrats, 'terrorists', 'Islamists'. If we are to have democratic peace, we must wage wars against them.

The democratic emblem is that of a world which has already found its principle. But ill-will is preventing the world from organizing as a whole with respect to this principle, recognized by all as the best, and whose name is 'democracy'.

What is supposed in all this is that there is a world whose principle and whose immanent perfectibility we know. This perfecting requires going through a war, which is bothersome, but inevitable.

My thesis, which also takes its starting point in the consideration of endless wars and innumerable acts of violence, certainly does not propose a democratic 'perpetual peace' which is thwarted by a few evil, autocratic leaders. I hold that we are at a very special moment, a moment at which *there is not any world*. This is obviously a thesis which recognizes the radicality of contemporary nihilism. But in its connection to the existence of the world, we must introduce a new distinction. For 'nihilism' then can mean two things:

1) There is a world, but this world is meaningless. We can speak then of existential nihilism.

2) There is not any world. Which means that this nihilism is ontological and not existential: There is an inconsistent multiplicity, there is incohesion of what there is.

In his 1990 collection of essays, *Une pensée finie* (A Finite Thinking), Jean-Luc Nancy includes a long note on the world, a theme to which he has since consecrated an entire book. For him, a world is the extension of existence to something other than humanity (stones, stars, animals . . .). 'World' is a response to the question: Why is there all there is and nothing but what there is?[6]

I am once again fraternally in disagreement with Jean-Luc Nancy. There is not 'all there is' because 'all' is an inconsistent determination with respect to the infinite multiplicity of worlds. And as very often something else than what there is happens, neither is there 'nothing but what there is'. Nancy again gives too much place to Leibniz's questions ('Why is there something rather than nothing?' and 'Why is there this rather than that?'). This is because, for Nancy, and for many others, 'world' is a category of existence. More precisely, says Nancy, the world is the place of the event of existence. It is then a generic category of the sense of being.

For me, 'world' cannot be a category of the sense of being. For there would then be no sense in saying, as I maintain, that there is not any world, except to hold that this 'there is not' is an 'ontological' defection of sense, a nihilist episode in the history of the sense of being. But this historic construction is entirely foreign to me.

I will say that there is a world when there is a certain logic of being-there, and so of contingency. It follows, to begin with, that

---

6   *Translator's Note*: Badiou is referring to Nancy, 'Changing of the World', *A Finite Thinking*, pp. 300–10; and Jean-Luc Nancy, *The Sense of the World*, trans. Jeffrey S. Librett (Minneapolis: University of Minnesota Press, 2008).

there is a plurality of worlds due to a plurality of possible logics. And then the possibility that there is not any world is inferred from the fact that logic can be suspended in an interval between two distinct logics, which affects the being-there with a great vacuity as to its disposition, or as to the names which are suitable to it.

In reality, for philosophy, 'world' has two meanings. Either it means the source of sense, or else it is a simple logical figure for appearance.

These two meanings were born at the same time, because Plato holds both of them undivided in his great founding work on the world, *Timaeus*. *Timaeus* is a plausible narrative on the construction of the cosmos. In this narration, Plato plays with subtlety on the two meanings of the word 'world'. Let us look at the very end of the text, one of the rare conclusions to his dialogues in which Plato seems quite content with what he has done:

> And so now we may say that our account of the nature of the universe has reached an end. The world has received and teems with living beings, mortal and immortal, and has become a visible living being containing the visible – the sensible god, image of the intelligible Living Thing, its greatness, goodness, beauty and perfection are unexcelled. Our one universe, indeed the only one of its kind, has come to be.[7]

A very beautiful and very mysterious text, which has two meanings:

a) The world thus narrated is in the perfection of sense, it is a sensible god whose appearance is perfect, since it is that of an icon of the intelligible god.

---

7   *Translator's Note*: See Plato, *Timaeus*, trans. Donald J. Zeyl, in *Complete Works*, ed. John M. Cooper (Indianapolis: Hackett, 1997), p. 1291 (translation modified).

b) The world is also a visible living being which situates and envelops all the visible living beings. It is then a logic of visibility, a topology of the visible, a logic of the strata of appearance.

We can simply say that I take 'world' in Plato's second sense, while Nancy has chosen the first. For me, 'world' means for the moment nothing else than the logic of the situation which envelops all visible living beings.

I hold that, today, the world deprives the vast majority of human beings of their visibility. It is a protocol of exclusion of the visible, and not the transcendental distribution of a situation in the visible.

The fundamental question of the world is in reality that of names. Who receives a name? It is not to begin with the question of wealth and its distribution. It is the question of knowing who is counted under its name, and who is not.

The old world, which subsisted until the beginning of the 1980s, was in no way perfect, and it was even regularly sinister – but it was a world. There was a world because any worker from a city, any peasant from the (well-named) 'third world' had, as a possibility – opened up by the world itself – his or her own political name. One belonged to the struggles of national liberation, to the working class, to the socialist camp, and so forth. The world distributed its names and inscribed them in a situation. Under the name they adopted, each one had a future, even if it was improbable or illusory. We can say that the world was the place of the names of a History that could be shared by all, even in its moments of paroxysm.

Today, we are in an intervallic period in which the great majority of people do not have a name. The only name available is 'excluded', which is the name of those who have no name. The great majority of humanity counts today for nothing. 'Excluded' is the name of the absence of a name, and 'market' is the symmetrical counterpart of this 'excluded': it is the worldly name of what is not a world.

The question of contemporary nihilism, including its ties to the philosophical re-assertion of enjoyment, can then be formulated: Where lie the names with which logic will make the world to come?

Philosophy has no other legitimate aim except to help find the new names that will bring into existence the unknown world that is only waiting for us because we are waiting for it.

In a play written in his youth, *Emperor and Galilean*, Henrik Ibsen presents the story of Julian the Apostate, so named because he wanted to restore paganism after Constantine, after the conversion of the Empire to Christianity. And according to Ibsen, Julian the Apostate, hesitating between the aesthetics coming from the Greeks and the revelation of the Christians, declares magnificently: 'The old beauty is no longer beautiful, and the new truth is not yet true.'[8] What is the present time, for us, who carry the burden of a return to Marxism? A time in which former politics are no longer active, and in which the new forms of politics experiment, with some difficulty, their truth. We are the experimenters of the interval. We are between two worlds, one of which is falling little by little into oblivion, while the other is only fragmentary. What we have to do is pass through. We are passers. We create by fragments a politics without fetishes – not even, above all, the democratic fetish. In *The Balcony*, Jean Genet's prophetic play, one of the characters, a rebel, an insurgent, declares:

> How can we approach Liberty, the People, Virtue, and how can we love them if we magnify them! If we render them untouchable? They must be left in their living reality. Let there be poems and images prepared, which do not satisfy but irritate.[9]

---

8   *Translator's Note*: See Henrik Ibsen, *Emperor and Galilean: A World Historical Drama*, trans. Brian Johnston (Lyme, NH: Smith and Kraus, 1999), p. 36.
9   *Translator's Note*: See Jean Genet, *Le Balcon*, ed. David H. Walker (London: Methuen, 1982), p. 210.

Let us prepare then – if we know how to, but we always do know a bit – those poems and those images which fulfil none of the desires we are a slave to, but which name the future bearers of liberty.

6

The Reserved Offering

① virtues books?

Jean-Luc Nancy's singular position among us – by 'us' I mean the brutal and acrimonious corporation of philosophers – can be summarized as follows: nobody can reasonably say or think anything bad about him. In a word: in this milieu where hostile indifference towards one's colleagues is the rule, Jean-Luc Nancy constitutes a double exception. First, because of his equanimity and strong sense of serenity towards all; and, second, because he is loved by all.

For a moment I wondered whether the only possibility of being original – the sombre path of justice, as well as the most ungrateful and most difficult task – was perhaps to try and speak badly of this uncontested man, to address him in the forms of what he calls 'evildoing'. Jean-Luc Nancy indeed names evildoing as opposed to the accidental Evil of the classics, the essential Evil of which our century is everywhere supposed to have invented the experience. It is, to quote him, 'existence [that is] unleashed against itself', or the claim 'that existence can grasp its own being as essence and hence as the destruction of existence'. The senseless, which is not only the ruin of a given sense but, worse, which 'closes off the aspect of existence that opens onto the need for sense'.[1] Did I have the strength of

---

1   Jean-Luc Nancy, *A Finite Thinking*, ed. Simon Sparks (Stanford: Stanford University Press, 2003), p. 17.

being, not just severe or critical towards Jean-Luc Nancy – which comes naturally enough, and which he himself is at regular intervals – but 'evildoing'? The strength of will, properly to will, not to debate with him or to refute his spiritual disposition, but to bring him down? To cast a shadow over his aura, to mar his beautiful soul, to excoriate everything that his uprightness signals in terms of intellectual civility?

Well, in this direction I did not manage anything at all. I completely failed. One should not even dream of evildoing with respect to Jean-Luc Nancy. I do not even think myself capable of using the sharp words that he uses to stigmatize the customary ways of thinking of our time. I read, for example, the following:

> If there *is* anything like thinking, it's only because there's sense, and if there's anything like sense it's only in the sense that sense is always given and gives itself as something to be thought. But as well as thinking there's also intelligence or, worse, intellectuality: each of these are more than capable of devoting themselves to the job in hand as if, in the first instance and exclusively, it were *not* a matter of sense. This cowardice, or this laziness, is pretty common.[2]

To say 'cowardice' and 'laziness' is not nothing. They certainly are not tender words. And while I doubtless know that Jean-Luc Nancy is absolutely not thinking about me, I on the other hand can think of myself and several others. For with a few others, I explicitly hold that thinking is not a question of sense; with a few others, I write the praise of the senseless character of truth. Conferring an essential, ontological, value upon the literal blindness of mathematics, I tell myself that the one who devotes himself to the exercises of intellectuality is me.

And if I continue, things get even worse. Thus:

---

2   Ibid., p. 3.

Yet it seems that this fin de siècle has more or less its own form of cowardice and intellectual irresponsibility, carrying on precisely as if it did not remind us, if only by virtue of its symbolic value (but also because of other circumstances, other politics, technologies, aesthetics), with a certain brusqueness, of the question of sense, its chance or its concern. Won't the century that has just come to an end have been a century of innumerable destructions of sense, innumerable deviations, derelictions, weaknesses – in short, the century of its ultimate *end*?[3]

Again we find 'cowardice' and 'irresponsibility'. Now, I do not agree with Jean-Luc Nancy. I even find that his vision (at least in appearance and in this text) of the century that just ended and of the present moment is consensual, in a sense that is infraphilosophical. I do not think that the twentieth century will have been the century of the destructions or derelictions of sense but, on the contrary, that of its imposition, to the detriment of the ab-sense of disparate truths. Nor do I feel summoned, in this fin de siècle, by the chance or the care of sense but rather by the rigour – which I would gladly call aristocratic – of formalization and, yes, the obscure exercise. Finally, I do not believe that the injunction concerns the end, the finite, and finitude. My conviction is that it is the infinite that is lacking. And, on the threshold of this new millennium, I would gladly propose to lay off all usage of the words 'end', 'finite' and 'finitude'. Since Jean-Luc Nancy speaks of cowardice, of laziness, and of irresponsibility, and since I can, on my part, recognize myself in the places that he thereby designates – even though I know that he has never dreamed of putting me there – let me then for a moment be violent as well. Let us say, let us proclaim: what we must urgently break with and put an end to is finitude. In the motif of finitude are concentrated the denial of emancipation, the deadly reign of the pure present, the absence of people to themselves, and the

---

3   Ibid., p. 4 (translation modified).

eradication of truths. All this to the benefit, to be sure, of sense – at least as the invasion of sensing, of extreme sensation, which is identical to anaesthesia.

But, immediately, I realize that it cannot be a question of Jean-Luc Nancy in my polemical statements. Indeed, it is impossible to claim in any sense whatever that he would participate in the renegacy and the submission to the democratic stupidity of our time. About 'democracy', in the sense in which the uninterrupted discourse of journalism sees it as the unsurpassable horizon of our liberties, Nancy repeatedly says that it is not up to the task of the question of sense today and even that it mobilizes the means of a certain deafness to, or an avoidance of, this question. And then, above all, Jean-Luc Nancy more so than many others, more so than myself, is in a refined sense the last communist. It is he and nobody else who writes, not in 1960 or 1970 but in 1991 that '*Communism*, without doubt, is the archaic name of a thinking which is still entirely to come'.[4] Oh how I fraternally salute this statement! I nonetheless try one last time to be an evildoer. 'A thinking which is still entirely to come'! How irritating this post-Heideggerian style of the perpetual announcement, this interminable to-come, this kind of laicized propheticism which does not cease declaring that we are not yet in a position to think what there is to think, this pathos of the having-to-respond for being, this God who is lacking, this waiting in front of the abyss, this posing of the gaze that looks deep into the fog and says that the indistinct can be seen coming! How I feel like saying: 'Listen, if this thinking is still entirely to come, come back to see us when one piece of it at least will have arrived!'

But I cannot bring myself to being persuaded by this blasphemy. What gains the upper hand is the happiness of reading, a bit further

---

4   *Translator's Note*: See Jean-Luc Nancy and Jean-Christophe Bailly, '*La comparution* / The Compearance: From the Existence of "Communism" to the Community of "Existence"', trans. Tracy B. Strong, *Political Theory* 20:3 (1992): 377–8.

down: 'Communism wants to say that *being* is *in* common. It wants to say that we are, insofar as we "are", in common. *That we are commonly.*' And even more so, knowing the weight the word has for Nancy: 'Communism is an ontological proposition', assuming that 'the ontology under question is not the ontology of "Being", or of that "which is": it is the ontology of *being* insofar as it is nothing of that which is'.[5]

Here we are so close that I can no longer distinguish us. The advent of that which, of being, is nothing of that which is, not even of that which is being, together with Nancy himself and with some others we call an 'event'. And for me the event gives birth to the generic character of truths, which after all means exactly their being-in-common, the 'commonly' of their creation. So then, every event is 'communist', that is what Jean-Luc Nancy affirms and for me this is so true that I come to lose track of the sheer lexicon of evildoing.

What is to be done, at this point, with the antinomy about finitude? It is an understatement to say that this is a crucial notion for Nancy. With a provocative borrowing from the discourse of Lacan, with whom Nancy has rubbed shoulders somewhat, I would gladly claim that 'finitude' is the master-signifier of his philosophical discourse.[6]

'Philosophical discourse'? What did I just say? Here we have the occasion for a double disputation.

First of all, for Nancy, discourse is exactly the means by which irresponsibility insinuates itself into thinking. And even worse, Nancy declares that 'from the very moment that there is discourse', cowardice and laziness are 'unavoidable in every effort or

---

5 *Translator's Note*: Ibid., p. 378 (translation modified).
6 *Translator's Note*: For Nancy's take on Lacan, see Philippe Lacoue-Labarthe and Jean-Luc Nancy, *The Title of the Letter: A Reading of Lacan*, trans. François Raffoul and David Pettigrew (Albany, NY: State University of New York Press, 1992).

inclination to think'.[7] Sure, with his customary equanimity, he adds that 'there's always discourse', given that – a repudiation of the directly mystical perspective – there is never a silent *ekstasis* of sense. However, this does not render discourse any more innocent. As for philosophy, we must – this much we know since Heidegger – declare its end. This end even names the programme of thinking. Nancy speaks without let-up about 'the task that follows philosophy, our task'.[8] Having written an entire manifesto against the motif of the end of philosophy, I find myself ousted from this 'we' at work in our time. Moreover, Jean-Luc Nancy writes that what reacts badly to the word 'end', to the expression 'the end of philosophy', is simply 'intellectual cowardice'.[9] Ouch! Shall I remobilize the extremely meagre resources of evildoing? Let us say that there is already enough evildoing in merely keeping the thesis: 'Finitude' is the master-signifier of Jean-Luc Nancy's philosophical discourse.

Indeed, in this discourse, finitude is the master of thinking in a double sense.

First, because it recapitulates all the terms charged with the task of naming, of ill-naming – in the sense in which Beckett thinks the 'ill-seen ill-said' – what thinking is.

Nancy's very peculiar style is one that is entirely affirmative, built as it is almost monotonously around equivalences signalled by the verb 'to be'. The matrix of Nancy's statements is very simple. It is an equation of the type: this is that. The great sophistication of his writing, which is remarkable as well, stems from having to make the simplicity of such equations appear in the persuasive context of a soft insistence, an almost irresistible invocation. And this

---

7   Nancy, *A Finite Thinking*, pp. 3–4.

8   Ibid., p. 6.

9   Ibid., p. 4.

pressure, this invocation, simultaneously organizes the necessity of the identity, 'this is nothing but that', as well as its always-still enigmatic character, always-still to be re-thought. Consider, for example, the way it will be said that the limit, and hence finitude, is sense itself – the whole of sense:

> In fact . . . whatever the content or the sense of what I am calling 'finitude' (and this collection of essays is concerned with nothing else, even though it's a long way from being a treatise on the subject), we can at least be sure that any attempt to think such an 'object' is going to have to marry its form or condition, while also being a finite thinking: a thinking that, without renouncing truth or universality, without renouncing *sense*, is only ever able to think to the extent that it also touches on its own limit and its own singularity. How are we to think everything – sense as a whole, even though it's not as if we could *not* do so, sense being indivisible – in *a* thinking, within the limit of one trifling study? And how are we to think the fact that this limit *is* the limit of the *whole* of sense?[10]

In passing you will have noted that, concerning the collection of essays *A Finite Thinking*, Nancy clearly states that it deals with nothing else than with finitude. Here we have the confession of the signifying sovereignty of 'finitude', of the One that it imposes on the text.

The paragraph just quoted contains the complex protocol for establishing the equation: finitude = sense. This happens by way of the notion that the thinking of finitude is itself necessarily finite, and thus touches upon its own limit.

But this equation will actually absorb its mediation. If sense is finitude because thinking is finite, then, in truth, thinking too is finitude. This will be said a number of times, for example: '*Finitude is the responsibility of sense*.'[11] Now, obviously, the responsibility of

10   Ibid., pp. 4–5.
11   Ibid., p. 13.

*freedom from its humans forces. Pain, death?,
limits*

sense – we have already seen this, against the irresponsibility of intellectuality – is thinking itself.

How do we pass from the equation 'finitude is sense' to the equation 'finitude is thinking'? Simply by way of an intermediary equation, which holds that 'finitude is existence'. Because existence is nothing else than sense itself. For example: 'Sense is existence that is always being born and always dying.' Or again: 'Existence is the sense of being.'[12] Thus, if finitude is sense, and if sense is existence, then finitude is existence.

What remains is the passage from 'finitude is existence' to 'finitude is thinking', evidently by way of the equation 'existence is thinking', which, in truth, is contained in the equation 'existence is the sense of being'. But a subtler course – Nancy is fond of deriving his equivalences by the detour of an apparent non-equivalence – is going to propose yet another intermediary equation. It is admitted, since Heidegger, that the essence of truth is freedom, which is something that Nancy, in the complex book *The Experience of Freedom*, elaborates in a direction that subsumes 'truth' under 'thinking'.[13] Thus, thinking is existence, but existence as freedom – or, in a truly beautiful formula from Nancy, 'the restoration of existence *to* existence [*remettre l'existence à l'existence*]'.[14] If one establishes that finitude is freedom thusly conceived, one will arrive at the desired equation: finitude is thinking; and this is indeed what takes place. Nancy writes: 'Hence, the *sense* of "freedom" is nothing other than the very finitude of sense.'[15]

You see that, ultimately, 'finitude' is the nominal polarity of a trajectory that includes sense, the sense of being, the responsibility of sense, existence, freedom, and thinking. 'Finitude' is the master-signifier in that it absorbs the totality of these positive terms.

---

12 Ibid., pp. 10, 12.
13 *Translator's Note*: See Jean-Luc Nancy, *The Experience of Freedom*, trans. Bridget McDonald (Stanford: Stanford University Press, 1993).
14 Nancy, *A Finite Thinking*, p. 18.
15 Ibid., p. 14.

Philosophy, or the philosophical discourse, consists in unfolding these terms in such a way as to render visible their absorption into a single one of them. Thus, formally, we are indeed dealing with a defence of finitude.

But in that case, 'finitude' is a master-signifier in another sense as well, namely, as injunction or duty – though obviously not in the sense of the exteriority of a commandment, but in the sense already attached to Nancy's meditation on the categorical imperative, in his beautiful book on Kant. Most notably, with regard to that which a word indicates as belonging to the responsibility of thinking, or what it indicates as that by which freedom is obliged to itself, without delay, 'as its own end in the double sense of the word'.[16]

And this word, once more, is indeed 'finitude'. As Nancy writes: 'Duty indicates the finitude of being.'[17] The contemporary call for an ethics is the call 'to conserve and to augment the access of existence to its own inappropriable and groundless sense',[18] which means the call to keep thinking within the realm of the responsibility of finitude.

What am I then to think, if for me the duty is to summon thinking to the dissident exercises of its own *infinity*? Is it a question of a quarrel over master-signifiers, as in politics, at the time of Maoism, the quarrel between the political sovereignty of the party and the political sovereignty of the masses? One could easily claim that, in the sound and fury of the time, the masses had the duty to render infinite the party's mediocre finitude.

I know that Jean-Luc Nancy thinks that what I call the 'infinite', as he has often told me, is in any case situated at exactly the same point as the thought that he calls 'finitude'.

Now, you see, this is Nancy's reserved offering. On the one

---

16   *Translator's Note*: For Nancy's reading of Kant, see Jean-Luc Nancy, *L'impératif catégorique* (Paris: Flammarion, 1983).
17   Nancy, *A Finite Thinking*, p. 18.
18   Ibid., p. 18.

hand, thinking, in the inevitable mode of discourse, offers us a master-signifier that is appropriate for the injunction of our time. And yet, on the other hand, this proposition, this offering, must be there, exposed, without imposing its presence on us. Besides, this is proper to any genuine offering according to Jean-Luc Nancy:

> The offering retains of the 'present' implied by presentation only the gesture of presenting. The offering offers, carries, and places before (etymologically, of-fering is not very different from ob-ject), but it does not install in presence. What is offered remains at a limit, suspended on the border of a reception, an acceptance – which cannot in its turn have any form other than that of an offering.[19]

The result of this non-imposition of presence is that the word carried by the offering – for example, the word 'finitude' – could as well signify another word that appears to be its total opposite – for example, the 'infinite'. Since it has already absorbed being, sense, existence, and freedom, what would this word 'finitude' *not* be capable of semantically? Indeed, a final equation is the following: 'There is no sense of the words "end" and "finite" that would allow us to think that whose *index*, held out at the very limit of our history, bears the name "finitude" – or, equally well, the name *the absolute of existence*.'[20] I am talking of the equation 'finitude = absolute'. Consequently, it is true that 'finite' does not allow us to think 'finitude'. So, then, why not 'infinite'? The infinite as the absolute of finite existence? We are extremely close to Hegel, in truth an essential companion of Nancy's thinking, to whom he has devoted several admirable essays.[21] Hegel too is after all the great master of

---

19   Ibid., p. 237.
20   Ibid., p. 29 (translation modified).
21   *Translator's Note*: For the works on Hegel, see Jean-Luc Nancy, *The Speculative Remark (One of Hegel's Bons Mots)*, trans. Céline Surprenant (Stanford: Stanford University Press, 2002); and *Hegel: The Restlessness of the Negative*, trans. Jason Smith and Steven Miller (Minneapolis: University of Minnesota Press, 2002).

the re-absorption of terms into an essential re-capitulation under one ultimate name. He too attempts to think the absolute of existence. And of course Nancy writes: 'Finitude does not end, being precisely not the infinite' [*La finitude ne finit pas, n'étant pas l'infini*]. But precisely, is this 'not ending' not the infinite – another infinite than this infinite which ended the end? In that case we would not be caught in a quarrel about finitude, but in what I and others take to be the true challenge of modern thought, since Cantor: the discernment of the plurality of infinites, and of its consequence for the fundamental orientations of thinking.[22]

Well then, I throw in the towel, not even dreaming any more of either evildoing or disputing. And I turn towards the other Jean-Luc Nancy, the one for whom the enigma of sense is that of our five senses, the enigma of sense as sensible, the aesthetic finitude of a thinking of the heteronomy of the sensible.

Along this path, however, I promptly and very intimately come upon the writing of Jacques Derrida, in that immense book that he has dedicated to Nancy, turning it into the powerful tabernacle of his admiring friendship. A book that not only re-exposes the doctrine of sensible-sense, but that finally is something like a rewriting of Aristotle's *Treatise on the Soul* for our time.[23] Why bother then with a bad sketch, or a poor copy, of what is already there?

And so I resign myself purely and simply to invite everyone to take delight in what Jean-Luc Nancy writes about the body, in *Corpus*; about painting, in 'The Look of the Portrait'; about poetry, in 'To Possess Truth in One Soul and One Body'.[24] In these texts,

---

22 *Translator's Note*: For the role of Cantor in discerning the fundamental orientations of thought, see Meditation 27, 'Ontological Destiny of Orientation in Thought', in Alain Badiou, *Being and Event*, trans. Oliver Feltham (London: Continuum, 2005), pp. 281–5.

23 *Translator's Note*: See Jacques Derrida, *On Touching Jean-Luc Nancy*, trans. Christine Irizarry (Stanford: Stanford University Press, 2005).

24 *Translator's Note*: See Jean-Luc Nancy, *Corpus*, trans. Richard A. Rand (New York: Fordham University Press, 2008); 'The Look of the Portrait', in

obviously, one will once again find the offering held in reserve, that is, the certitude that any sensible exposure duly responds to an offering of the sense of being, since it is its finitude; but also, precisely because it is its finitude, it reserves it for a self that is beside oneself, to a traversing of the other in the same, to an infinite and essential gap, in which thinking creates a new mode of restoring existence to existence. Exposure, retreat, finitude: at bottom that is the unfolding of finitude in all its range. Now let us see how this is said:

> A body is an image offered to other bodies, a whole corpus of images stretched form body to body, local colors and shadows, fragments, grains, areolas, lunules, nails, hairs, tendons, skulls, ribs, pelvises, bellies, meatuses, foams, tears, teeth, droolings, slits, blocks, tongues, sweat, liquors, veins, pains, and joys, and me, and you.[25]

Offered to the other, that is the offering. The fragments are the exposure. And you and me, the reserve.

But in this same register, I feel a very particular tenderness for the little book from 1997 titled *La Naissance des seins* (The Birth of Breasts). Formally, the offering is here the capture of what a woman offers of herself, or offers to herself, in the existence of her breasts. She is reserved by a kind of amorous and enchanting discretion. The book's texture speaks of both. It contains an exposition, in the ordinary sense: reproductions, pictures, and, above all, against a grey background, an extraordinary set of texts, of quotations, indicative of the creative proliferation, the perpetual counter-offering, induced by that which, in the body of women, is innately presented. But Nancy's whole effort consists in establishing that what responds to the offering in thinking is not on the order of the object. The

---

Multiple Arts: The Muses II, ed. Simon Sparks (Stanford: Stanford University Press, 2006), pp. 220–48; 'To Possess Truth in One Soul and One Body', in *The Birth to Presence*, trans. Brian Holmes et al. (Stanford: Stanford University Press, 1993), pp. 284–306.
25   Nancy, *Corpus*, p. 121.

birth of breasts, thought as the sensible coming of a shared delight, is absolutely other than the cut-out of an object, absolutely other than the object-cause of desire that conjures up a fantasy. It is of the non-objective breast that Jean-Luc Nancy wants to tell the marvel.

Now, this effort leads to the erasure of the word 'offering' itself. It is no doubt at the point of this erasure that one seizes the potential of the feminine in thinking. For to think what is exposed by a woman leads to the rescinding of the key-word 'offering', and thus, in the 'reserved offering', to giving precedence to the reserve over the offering.

Everything begins, as I said, with the critique of the object and of the origin. 'The fantasy or the object – the fantasy of the object – is the disfiguration of the breast, a hallucination without tact. How can one talk about it with tact, without swallowing it up?'[26] This tact is another name for the reserve.

Three quotations will lead to this question of the reserved erasure of the offering as proof of tact – as proof of the pre-eminence, within finitude, of the reserve. We should read them:

On the poop of the Onassis yacht, the Old Lion gave Garbo 'a salacious look'. Would she oblige by showing him her breasts? The spoils of women belong to the victors. He will see what nobody has ever contemplated.

Huddles up while crossing her arms on her young breasts,
And holds them tight, one in each hand.

Sight, smell, taste, touch and hearing . . .
In the face of God will be saintly pleasures.
In Abraham's breast our desires will flourish
Desires, perfect loves, intense desires without absence,
For the fruits and flowers will only be one birth there.[27]

---

26   Jean-Luc Nancy, *La Naissance des seins* (Valence: Erba, 1997), p. 45.
27   Ibid., pp. 46–7. [*Translator's Note*: The three fragments are quotes,

So then, one can speak of the body of love, of the body as exposure (of) love, of which the breast is simply the announcement, 'announcement of complete nudity'. This is where, putting the offering under erasure, Nancy commits the Platonic parricide with regard to himself:

> It is suspended between the gift and the refusal. It is neither the waiting nor the potential of the one or the other. It is not caught in this fierce gigantomachy of great categories or of sublime postures. It is something other. The gift and the refusal are on the order of the exchange and the latter may consist of the exchange of goods and services or of pain and suffering. There is offer and demand, and the offer itself is a demand: the demand for there to be some demand. But here, it is something other. Neither offer nor demand – and, thus, to finish, not even an offering. This word is still too religious, too sacrificial, and too grandiloquent. Too intentional.
>
> Now, it is a question of what is without intention: wholly in extension. It is a question of what is extended without intention, offered without demand, proposed without invitation.[28]

The reserved offering is not an offering, because the breast of a beloved woman is 'offered without demand, proposed without invitation'.

This is precisely the place where Nancy wants to keep the discourse proper to him. He offers it to us, through and through affirmative, but without demanding anything. He proposes it to us, without inviting us to follow him. Shall I say that he desires for his books to be, for the desire of thinking, like the birth of breasts for the amorous desire? And can one really occupy this place, without

respectively, from Françoise Ducout, *Greta Garbo la Somnambule* (Paris : Stock, 1979); Catherine Weinzaepflen, *Totem* (Paris : Flammarion, 1985), p. 97 ; and Agrippa d'Aubigné, *Les Tragiques*, in *Œuvres* (Paris : Gallimard, 1969), p. 243.]
28   Ibid., p. 48.

something vaguely maternal? Without diminishing the necessary violence and blindness too much? Without reducing the share of dry exercise and fierce dissidence too much, in favour of an assured benevolence? Yet here I am once again on the brink of 'evildoing', which in the case of Jean-Luc Nancy is impossible to achieve. Let us greet the friend, the loyal man, the last communist, the thinker, the intellectual artist of sensible disparity. Let us say with him, since we all love him: 'There is this brilliant, shattering constitution of being. "Love" does not define it, but it names it, and obliges us to think it.'[29]

---

29 Nancy, *A Finite Thinking*, p. 273.

7

Foucault: Continuity and Discontinuity

I. FOUCAULT: A DISCURSIVE ANTHROPOLOGY

To what register of thought do Foucault's writings belong? The character himself, tender and sardonic – tender when needed, streetwalker at night, voracious library rat – would have liked this question. Was he not meant always to seduce and to disappoint at the same time? What better way than by never being there where you are assigned a place, by not fitting into any classification? Especially when one is a formidable thinker of all modes of classing, when one is oneself an enraged classifier.

Since it is a question of continuity and discontinuity, let us ask ourselves with which classical disciplines Foucault's writings present some continuity and with which ones they break.

This question poses itself above all with regard to philosophy and history. Sylvain Lazarus argues that Foucault is a philosopher who engaged in historiographical investigation. His conclusion is that, as always happens whenever a philosophy leaves the discipline of the concept for a particular investigation, Foucault is an empiricist. But what begs for a justification is the statement according to which Foucault is a philosopher, as well as the one that defines his singular practice as that of a 'historiographical investigation'.[1]

---

1   *Translator's Note*: See Sylvain Lazarus, 'Pensée de la singularité et Michel

Philosopher? In my view it is difficult to identify Foucault as such, at least in the first part of his oeuvre, before *The Will to Knowledge*. In its most general acceptation, philosophy is the thought of thought qua real. The result is that its privileged 'outside' is constituted by that which is excepted from opinions, such as the sciences, the arts, the politics of emancipation . . . and that its singular production, as Deleuze recapitulates, is the production of concepts. Now, for Foucault, the concept stems from what he calls the 'overall discourse', so that he cannot rely on it as a fixed horizon, since his purpose is to think singularities. As for the 'historical' materials of his constructions, as a rule they exclude everything that makes sense for philosophy. Neither mathematics, nor artistic breakthroughs, nor the slow course of revolutionary ideas enter the textual stratification from which emerge the 'epistemes' or the discursive singularities that characterize an epoch. We can thus observe in Foucault's works a rather singular eighteenth century indeed, in which one will find money and botanics, but neither differential calculus nor democratic contract theory; in which one finds the juridical and repressive arsenal, the treatises on onanism, or the chimerical physiology of the school of Montpellier, but neither pre-Romantic German poetry, nor Italian opera, nor the epistolary novel, nor celestial mechanics. In truth – an eighteenth century without Rousseau or Lagrange, without Euler or Marivaux, without Lavoisier or Goethe, without Haydn or Schiller's plays. In short – without all that which for philosophy, anxious to envelop itself in the few universal propositions of which humanity has been capable, makes it that the eighteenth century *exists*.

This is because Foucault – and we will see the extreme importance of this point, its strategic position – who knew better than anyone what a given century was really *worth*, adopts the ascetic method of never concerning himself with what he himself calls 'the buried knowledge of erudition'. He always tries to work against the

Foucault', *Anthropologie du nom* (Paris: Seuil, 1996), pp. 105–108.

grain of historical judgements and the selections that history operates on the formless mass of intellectual productions. This authorizes
some captivating finds and montages, but peddling under the name
of 'knowledges' in the dead figures of opinion and its immanent
structure, we do not gain any foothold from where to carry the
concept to a sufficient level of intensity.

Let me remark in passing that Deleuze, no matter how curious he
may be at times for lateral objects and despised writers, in order to
carry his philosophical creation, always stuck to the uncontested
and canonical figures, both insofar as philosophers are concerned –
from the Stoics to Nietzsche and Whitehead, via Leibniz and
Spinoza – as well as for novelists – from Melville to Beckett, via
Henry James. This is one index among many of the fact of which I
have been convinced for a long time, that the pairing Deleuze/
Foucault, even if its empirical virtue – their friendship and admira-
tion – is incontestable, nonetheless is philosophically empty.
Everyone knows that Foucault went so far as to say 'maybe, one
day, this century will be known as Deleuzian'.[2] But we can and
should understand this: it will be known as such *philosophically*
speaking, exactly to the extent that I, Foucault, *am not a philosopher*
in that sense, and finally in no sense at all.

Here it is not a matter of indifference to mention the history of
Foucault's election to the Collège de France. In this institution one
begins most often by giving a name to a chair, in order subsequently
to make the election of someone to this chair self-evident. In sum,
one mechanically makes the person correspond to his anticipation
by a name. Yet another history of words and things . . . And so the
Collège agreed in 1969 to create a chair with the name 'History of
Systems of Thought', and elected Foucault to this chair in the spring
of 1970. What is interesting is that he succeeded Jean Hyppolite,

2   Michel Foucault, 'Theatrum Philosophicum', in *Language, Counter-Memory,
Practice: Selected Essays and Interviews*, ed. Donald F. Bouchard, trans. Donald F.
Bouchard and Sherry Simon (Ithaca: Cornell University Press, 1977), p. 165.

whose chair was named 'History of Philosophical Thought'. If one compares these chairs' names, one observes that the word that disappears completely between Hyppolite and Foucault is 'philosophy'. This is surely an important remark: 'thought' and 'history' are kept, and 'system' is added. From this we could draw two conclusions. First, that it is a matter of pursuing a history of thought, or of thoughts. Second, that Foucault proposes, under the name 'systems of thought', much vaster frameworks than philosophies or philosophical systems. In doing so he assumes a properly non-philosophical, or even antiphilosophical, position, which consists in the promise that one is going to think philosophy starting from something other than philosophy itself.

Should we then arrive at the thesis of Foucault as a historian, and even more simply, as a historian of ideas? There certainly has been a Foucauldian legacy in history. A number of young historians found in his work the tools to renovate the objects and methods of their discipline, particularly with regard to everything that has to do with the borders between social practices and legitimating discourses of these practices. However, to this recruitment of Foucault – our great faun of erudition, our great twisted baldhead – by the terrible union of historians, I would raise three objections that are as brief as they are peremptory:

- History seeks out regularities, whereas Foucault constructs singularities.

- History is a thinking of time, whereas for Foucault the discursive combinations, which rather compose a kind of mental spaces, are more important than time. Or to be more precise: these spaces prescribe the forms of time.

- The formal object that is central to history is the pair society/State, whereas Foucault wants to subvert this duality with the use of transversal categories that socialize the State all the way to the top and that 'statify' society all the way down to the microscopic level. The principal two categories used to this effect are, as is well known, those of 'knowledges' and 'powers'.

I would thus propose to say that Foucault is neither a philosopher nor a historian nor a bastardized combination of the two. Foucault proposes a *linguistic of discursive anthropology*. In this anthropology, the unit is neither the name (as in what Lazarus calls an anthropology of the name), nor the sentence or statement. The unit is that which a discourse prescribes as a correlation between words and things, or between sentences and practices.

The (latent) philosophy of this anthropology – as furthermore is the case of the anthropological stratum, which also exists, in Nietzsche's complex work – is nominalism, more so than empiricism. Indeed, we can hardly speak of empiricism when, clearly, there exists no concept of experience. Foucault to be sure investigates certain practices, but without presupposing that any describable domain of experience ever comes to unify, gather, or even just centre them. What is true, by contrast, is that there exists no real invariant referent to measure the pertinence of such or such discursive assemblage. You enter by way of words into a relation of words to things, of statements to practices, which is always operative even – or especially – on bodies. But this operative dimension does not bear witness to any underlying element of the real beneath the operation itself, such that the discourse, or the relation words/ things, would be its code.

Nothing is intelligible except the words by which one enters discourse as the interface between statements and practices and the operations or treatments of bodies prescribed by discourse.

Based on these axioms, all you need is virtuosity in the decipherment of the archives and the correlated construction of great discursive operations.

In *Theory of the Subject*, in 1982, I had written about Foucault that he was a 'Cuvier of the archives who with some bookish bones examined with genius gives you the entire brontosaurus of a century'.[3] I later found out that he took this badly. I nevertheless stand by the sentence, only to punctuate with force that word 'genius', which a great many epigones of Foucault – unfortunately for them and for us, being philosophers or historians rather than anthropologists – have shown us should certainly not be forgotten in the definition.

II. GENEALOGY *VERSUS* ARCHAEOLOGY

Yet little by little it turns out that this 'classical' Foucault, the great builder of closed epistemic configurations delivered over to their purely textual coherence, is haunted by something else, which stems from the May 1968 that he partially missed (he was in Tunisia) and from a proximity to the different forms of leftism (especially, militant Maoism) that he assumed, all the while maintaining his ironic independence and subjecting himself, even in the most intense commitments (for he could also be violent) to a kind of duty of reserve. This 'something' is the question of real struggles, the question of the present, of its division and its potential or impotence. What good does the archivist's work of constructing epistemes or the archaeology of knowledge do, when one accepts the urgency of collective action? The answer reactivates a fundamental term from the Nietzschean lexicon, which Foucault had already put to great use: the term 'genealogy'. Proving once more – as Foucault moreover proclaimed on numerous occasions – that together with Heidegger, Nietzsche is the great philosophical reference of his discursive anthropology. Even before the care of self enters the stage, the positive discipline of archaeology is displaced, perhaps even annulled, by this care for genealogy that results from a real

---

3 Alain Badiou, *Theory of the Subject*, trans. Bruno Bosteels (London: Continuum, 2009), p. 188.

experience this time, namely, from the revolts and political combats of the 1970s.

For Foucault, the situation can then be summarized as follows: Sure, there are thinkable singularities, which are the epistemes. At the cost of a harsh labour on the traces of the archive, which is a constructive labour and not an exegesis, one can become the archaeologist of these singularities and *lay bare* their assemblages. But it is possible, and within the conjuncture necessary, to orient this work towards the concerns of the present. The archaeologist can *open up* the archaeological labour towards a finer determination of what holds *potential* in today's struggles. Put otherwise, the archaeological finesse can be articulated upon a genealogy of its tactical efficacy.

In reality, this articulation amounts rather to a tension, which will only increase and will lead Foucault in a direction from which it seems that his positive endeavour should have cleared him, namely, in the vicinity of philosophy and, what is more, of philosophy in its generic sense: philosophy as wisdom, as leading 'the good life'.

This tension operates from the beginning, between the archaeological objectivity, conceived of as the archival montage of singularities, and the genealogical commitment, seen as the clarification of tactical struggles. It also evokes the tension that Nietzsche both organizes and (with great difficulty) suffers, as is highly perceptible in the late works (after 1880): the tension between the *typology* of figures of power, active or reactive, and the *affirmative resolution* that is opposed to the latest avatars, decadent or nihilist, of the figure of the priest. A tension, we might say, between the archaeology whose emblem is the Crucified and the genealogy of the great 'Yes' whose name is Dionysus.

Nietzsche will find a way out of this tension only by personally assuming the totality of figures – by becoming, in his poetic body, and under the name 'Nietzsche', the impossible coexistence of Dionysus and the Crucified. Which is what one rightly calls his madness.

But Foucault? It is precisely to a first attempt at a resolution of this tension that his famous course from 1976 is dedicated: *Society Must Be Defended*.

III. FROM 'KNOWLEDGE OF THE STRUGGLES' TO A THEORY OF POWER?

A central thesis in the 1976 course – in actual fact its axiom, or its hope, rather than something it establishes or demonstrates – is that of a strange harmony between the archaeology of knowledge and the genealogy of tactics of struggle. This thesis seems to ignore the discontinuity of epistemes. Foucault indeed has some good news to announce: 'people's knowledge', such as it is active in the struggles of the present (at least in the popular struggles), is homogeneous with the discoveries of erudition. In both cases, in effect, we are dealing with censured forms of knowledge, with discursive figures repressed by the dominant classifications. This is why the 'critique of discourse', underneath its academic and erudite appearance, has a real political force: 'Well, I think it is the coupling together of the buried scholarly knowledge and knowledges that were disqualified by the hierarchy of erudition and sciences that actually gave the discursive critique of the last fifteen years its essential strength.'[4]

Let us note that the homogeneity is negatively founded: in both cases, we are dealing with a 'memory of combats' that has been 'confined to the margins'; we are dealing with a 'knowledge of struggles' that is quietly opposed to what must be abolished as much as possible, which is 'the tyranny of overall discourses'.[5]

Should we understand this as saying that a negative essence of knowledges associated with popular struggles is continuous, or

---

4 Michel Foucault, *Society Must Be Defended: Lectures at the Collège de France, 1975-1976*, ed. Mauro Bertani and Alessandro Fontana, trans. David Macey (New York: Picador, 2003), p. 8.
5 Foucault, *Society Must Be Defended*, p. 8.

transversal, whereas only the tyrannical economy of dominant knowledges constitute discontinuous epistemes? In that case, we would once again be less at a distance from Hegel and Marx than we think.

In any case, it is this negative continuity that grounds the new definition of genealogy: 'If you like, we can give the name "genealogy" to this coupling together of scholarly erudition and local memories, which allows us to constitute a historical knowledge of struggles and to make use of that knowledge in contemporary tactics.'[6]

However, in 1976, the question is more precise. It is a matter of knowing if we can go further than the partial genealogies that respond exactly to the programme of 'coupling'. Sure, one can show that a historical knowledge of the prisons, of psychiatry, of sexual codes, and so on, was genealogically articulated upon contemporary tactics. There is homogeneity between Foucault the savant of *Discipline and Punish* and Foucault the militant of the Prison Information Group (GIP). But we remain, as far as the mechanisms of subjugation and combat are concerned, within the labyrinth of singular genealogies. Is it possible, Foucault asks, to advance a more global interrogation, to situate 'what is at stake in all these genealogies' and, finally, to conceive of a logic of power arrangements? The risk is obviously that we would fall back into 'theory' and thus into conceptual tyranny. But Foucault nevertheless seeks out a middle path, for which the essential programme is as follows:

I am not suggesting that we give all these scattered genealogies a continuous, solid theoretical basis – the last thing I want to do is give them, superimpose on them, a sort of theoretical crown that would unify them – but that we should try, in future lectures, probably beginning this year, to specify or identify what is at stake when

---

6   Ibid., p. 8.

knowledges begin to challenge, struggle against, and rise up against
the institution and the power- and knowledge-effects of scientific
discourse.[7]

We clearly sense that a new tension is latent here, the one that
operates between the multiplicity of partial genealogies and the
potential unity of the stakes involved. The middle path refuses, as is
often the case, both the empiricist acceptance of the pure contingency of dispersed singularities and the theoretical engagement in
an external conceptual unity. It is a *critical* path, of which we still
have to find the intellectual operators.

We will first of all remark that Foucault vindicates a certain type
of historical unity, at least in the form of the unity of a question –
the question of power, such as the twentieth century has put it on
the agenda:

> What is at stake in all these genealogies is this: What is this power
> whose irruption, force, impact, and absurdity have become palpa-
> bly obvious over the last forty years, as a result of both the collapse
> of Nazism and the retreat of Stalinism. What is power?[8]

Observe how Foucault confirms, in his typical slightly distant
manner, the analysis proposed between 1975 and 1978 by a whole
series of renegades of leftism (and particularly of Maoism), according to which the fundamental question of our time is that of the
crime of the State. Once one thinks of it as the 'ethical' analyzer of
all politics, this State crime brings to light, under the name 'totalitarianism', the profound identity of communism and Nazism.

Foucault – thank god – does not dwell on this commonplace of
opinion, against which Deleuze also instantly rose up in protest. Let
us say that the unified reference to a historical 'line' serves Foucault

7   Ibid., p. 12.
8   Ibid., pp. 12–13.

to give its full breadth to the genealogical investigation into the topic of power.

Indeed, in the lectures that follow in 1976, no matter how restricted or 'bloated' the textual sources may appear to be (especially the legitimation, via Boulainvilliers, of a kind of counter-revolution of the nobility), genealogy is given an impressive horizon. In the end, the task is to think the emergence and coming into being of those fundamental categories that the nineteenth century handled as political categories: races (referring to the 'collapse' of Nazism) and classes (referring to the 'retreat' of Stalinism).

What is striking here is that we are no longer dealing with singularities. Foucault certainly engages here in a *theoretical* gesture, even if he defends himself against it. This gesture consists in using the genealogical trajectory in order to *disjoin the question of power from the economic analysis, so as to turn it towards something else*. This 'something else' is what Foucault will call 'a historico-political field', or 'the foundation of the history of politics', or again 'the functioning of politics to calculate historical relations of force'.

In other words, nothing less than a putting into question of 'classical' Marxism. Foucault's thesis indeed can be recapitulated in two points:

1. We must maintain the idea of an articulation of politics and history.

2. This articulation passes neither through the juridical theory of sovereignty nor through the economic theory of the distribution of wealth.

Foucault proposes to construct a categorial autonomy of the historico-political field, both with regard to the philosophies of sovereignty and with regard to economic positivisms. It is clear that a doctrine of 'fields' substitutes that of sequences (or of epistemic singularities). A bit as if he replaced the archaeological construction of knowledge arrangements with a sketch of history in the long run, constructed on the basis of the concerns of the present. The return to the Greeks, in Foucault's subsequent work, seems to confirm this point.

In any event, the thesis to be defended is certainly that the theory of power, insofar as it is of interest to the tactics of struggles, belongs neither to philosophy, nor to the doctrine of right, nor to economy. We will note that this genre of interrogation re-launches Althusser's doctrine about thinking the articulation of the 'instances' of the Whole, their relative dependence, and, among them, the relations of domination 'in the final instance' or of overdetermination.

IV. POLITICS AND WAR

Can we then envision that Foucault's lecture course from 1976 opens the path towards a thinking of the autonomy of politics? Such would be the true meaning of the developments on biopower, justifying the contemporary considerations on 'biopolitics'.

Along this path, we promptly stumble upon two obstacles. The first is that 'politics' remains identified with power, or with powers in the plural. The second is that the underlying category, charged with unifying the different genealogies, is finally the category of war.

What Foucault asks of the nobility's reaction at the end of the seventeenth century and of its mouthpiece Boulainvilliers is the authorization to anticipate the inversion of the famous formula of Clausewitz: 'War is the continuation of politics by other means.' One should rather say: 'Politics is the continuation of war.' And since 'politics' here means 'State politics', or 'power politics', we will finally understand that war is the true essence of that which unifies the arrangements of power.

But what is the status of this thesis? What does it mean, if we think in the direction of the autonomy of politics, that we must enter the intelligibility of power by way of the intelligibility of war? In any case, the thesis implies that, like war, *power is a relation and not a property*. Let us read Foucault:

> Power is not something that can be possessed, and it is not a form of might; power is never anything more than a relationship that can, and must, be studied only by looking at the interplay between the terms of that relationship.[9]

Clearly, this is a formal thesis, or one that bears on 'power as form'. Power is thinkable only on the basis of the play among several terms. Now, this play among terms is strategic and historical. We thus see with great clarity that the debate regarding a possible autonomy of politics (with regard to the economy or the doctrine of right) finds its true stake in the coupling together of politics and history in the guise of a relation between history and the State. And on this point, Foucault takes great care to propose the hypothesis of a continuity:

> That a continuity has been established between historical narrative and the management of the State is, I believe, of vital importance. It is the use of the State's model of managerial rationality as a grid for the speculative understanding of history that establishes the historico-political continuum. And that continuum now makes it possible to use the same vocabulary and the same grid of intelligibility to speak of history and to analyze the management of the State.[10]

The consideration of this *continuum* (characteristic of the 'modern' episteme?) imposes first of all the equation 'politics = State = power', and second, the equation 'history = war'. Finally, the major paradigm of the continuity between politics and history is to be found in the formal (strategic) dimension of war. It is under this

---

9   Ibid., p. 168.
10   Ibid., pp. 170–71.

condition that – in a decisive formula – 'there is now a link between the political fight and historical knowledge'.[11]

Of such a conception of politics it is no exaggeration to say that it is, from beginning to end, *historicist*.

V. RACES AND CLASSES, MEDIATIONS OF THE NON-RELATION BETWEEN SOVEREIGNTY AND CONTROL?

Within the framework of this historicism, Foucault endeavours to construct a genealogy of the political uses of the concept of 'race' (and even of 'class') and to propose the outline for an analysis of Nazism.

Racism for Foucault is an operator, one that serves the conjunction between two apparently contradictory givens. On the one hand, 'biopower' as defined starting in the nineteenth century supposes that the State takes care of populations (hygiene, medicine, demography, territoriality . . .); on the other, the old doctrine of sovereignty relies on the right over life and death, the right to kill. Racism articulates both terms, by defining the living beings that, for reasons that touch upon social hygiene and the well-being of 'genuine' populations, can, or must, be eliminated:

> I think that, broadly speaking, racism justifies the death-function in the economy of biopower by appealing to the principle that the death of others makes one biologically stronger insofar as one is a member of a race or a population, insofar as one is an element in a unitary living plurality.[12]

Let us say that 'race' is an operator for coupling together heterogeneous historical series. The first series, the archaic one: under the paradigm of war, the sovereign conception of power, which

---

11   Ibid., p. 171.
12   Ibid., p. 258.

concentrates the right to kill. The second series, the modern one: under the paradigm of the life of populations, biopower, the maxim of which is 'make live and let die'. State racism serves as the junction of this disjunction, that which archaicizes the modern, or modernizes the archaic. Indeed, what it declares is that in order to 'make live' certain populations it is indispensable to exterminate others:

> We have, then, in Nazi society something that is really quite extraordinary: this is a society which has generalized the sovereign right to kill. The two mechanisms – the classic, archaic mechanism that gave the State the right of life and death over its citizens, and the new mechanism organized around discipline and regulation, or in other words, the new mechanism of biopower – coincide exactly.[13]

So here we are confronted with a novelty as concerns the synthesis, or the enjambment, of the relation discontinuity/continuity: with operators such as race, we have the means to conjoin heterogeneous dispositions that refer to distinct historical epistemes.

This goes to show that we can involve ourselves in long-term genealogies, *because we have what it takes to think the mediation between those closed historical segments that are epistemic sequences.*

Foucault's new orientation, which will progressively bring him back to the concept and to philosophy, consists in making the genealogical continuities traverse the archaeological discontinuities. For example, in the modern world, the sequence is identified by biopower, but the continuity is assured by the new forms of war, which is always intricately linked to the old *dispositif* of sovereignty. The question that we inherit is clearly that of the disjunctive synthesis (as Deleuze would have said) on a historical scale: 'How can one both make a biopower function and exercise the rights of war, the

---

13   Ibid., p. 260.

rights of murder and the function of death, without becoming racist? That was the problem, and that, I think, is still the problem.'[14]

We can easily agree that *if* one accepts the opposition between sovereignty and biopower (or the power of control), such indeed is the problem. But are we forced to confirm this opposition?

VI. QUESTIONS

The general construction finally seems to me to be precarious, as witnessed by the fact that between continuity and discontinuity there is a need to intercalate operators (such as 'racism') that are lifted from the empirical evidence of the historical record. Besides, regarding this point I would agree with Lazarus: on the path that seeks to move beyond the archaeological closure, Foucault does not go much further than whatever empiricism authorizes. For lack of a concept of politics that is truly disjoined from a theory of power, genealogy alone cannot safeguard the sought-after communication between scholarly knowledges and the actual tactics of struggles.

Let me dryly enumerate the difficulties:

Nominalism in the end always confronts whatever it presupposes, without saying so, in terms of effects of the real. Thus the abyss that opens between the counter-revolutionary fable of Boulainvilliers and the real of war and its avatars, especially the opposition – present, but masked in Foucault – between state war and revolutionary war, or war of the people. Considered as a generic or transversal category, war becomes too much or too little. It ends up being an emphatic and indistinct name (to speak like Jean-Claude Milner) for 'strategy', or even, for 'calculation'.

Power, says Foucault, must be thought as relation. True. But if one refuses the dialectical schema (the relation is contradiction), how to think the distinction between terms and relations to begin

---

14 Ibid., p. 263.

with? What is the *logic* of Foucault? Nominalism necessarily renders the distinction evasive, and the logic improbable.

Is politics identifiable as such? Foucault wedges politics between the theory of powers and the tactic of struggles, between the strategy of wars and the marginal subtraction of forms of control. What we have here is only a slightly more sophisticated version of the always disappointing opposition between the State and the 'movements'. In my view – and this is no doubt his principal, negative commonality with Deleuze – it is impossible to find in Foucault an affirmative doctrine of politics.

All things considered, what stands in for political analysis, on the side of the operations of power, is very close to the Althusserian thought of overdetermination. A point of confusion, an occasion, a paradox of power, is never anything but the disjunctive synthesis of two contrasting apparatuses. Consider this presentation of the death of Franco after an interminable coma:

> And so the man who had exercised the absolute power of life and death over hundreds of thousands of people fell under the influence of a power that managed life so well, that took so little heed of death, and he didn't even realize that he was dead and was being kept alive after his death. I think that this minor but joyous event symbolizes the clash between two systems of power: that of sovereignty over death, and that of the regularization of life.[15]

But the immanent legibility of politics, as irreducible thought-practice, is never guaranteed by the analysis of powers, not even by that of their paradoxical overdetermination. Beyond the simple tactical clarification, the genealogical saturation of archaeology fails to delimit not only the invariants but also the successive forms of the politics of emancipation.

This is no doubt why the late Foucault turned towards forms of

---

15   Ibid., pp. 248–9.

life and wisdom. Except that he momentarily hallucinated, during the Iranian revolution – and I have a certain tenderness for this moment, when paradox exposed him to such great animosity – the mythic figure of what would conjoin the fury of insurrections and the sweetness of spiritualities.

8

Jacques Rancière's Lessons: Knowledge and Power After the Storm

I will announce right off that I am only going to speak well of Jacques Rancière. In the past, I have spoken critically of him so often that my stock of negative comments has run out.[1] Yes, yes – we are brothers. Everyone sees that, and in the end, I do too.

To speak only well of Jacques Rancière is not an easy task, given the positions that the two of us occupy. Perhaps my constant praise might in fact be the worst fate that I could have in store for him. Would doing so be precisely the most underhanded way to attack him? If, for example, I were to announce that we are in agreement on a number of important points, how would he take that? Would he rather just as soon change his mind on all those points and leave me behind?

The ethical principle that I am advancing up front is to stay away from all manner of comparisons with myself. I will say nothing about myself, neither in agreement nor in disagreement – nothing of the sort. Rather, we should maintain a pure Rancière, praised in his totality. In order thus to approach his work from a point of departure that is as far removed from my own as possible, I have

---

1 *Translator's Note*: Badiou's criticisms of Rancière can be found in two essays, 'Rancière and the Community of Equals' and 'Rancière and Apolitics', included in his *Metapolitics*, trans. Jason Barker (London: Verso, 2005).

chosen a point of entry that seems to belong to someone else: the relation between knowledge and power. This dialectic of knowledge and power is today thoroughly academicized in the established systematic reference – one-sidedly, no doubt – to Foucault. Indeed, its vulgar form ('All knowledge is power, down with the authority of knowledge!') has been a sort of commonplace since the end of the 1960s and the beginning of the 1970s. Certainly, if someone can rightly claim to have developed this conceptual frame more and better than Foucault, it has been none other than Rancière. This was the intention from the beginning, as is clear from the title of his first book, *Althusser's Lesson*, which meditates on the relationship between the 'theoreticism' of Althusser, his defence of science, and the reactionary political authority of the French Communist Party; between the knowledge of the intellectual and the power of the party of which he is the fellow traveller with or without deviation.

To understand the provenance of this meditation, we should return to the context of the 1960s and particularly to the crucial sequence between 1964 and 1968, reaching its culmination in 1966. For the question we are concerned with, this context was absolutely paradoxical: it prepared and organized a tipping of the balance, from 1968 onwards, from a scientific position that fetishized concepts to a 'practicist' position that fetishized action and the immediate ideas of its agents. We should not forget that these were Rancière's formative years.

Let us see what happened around 1966-1967. The reign of structuralism in those years was also incontestably the reign of science. Its motif was profound, because this was no ordinary scientism. Rather, this neo-scientism centred on the theme of formalization, having learned its lesson from the achievements of structuralist linguistics, particularly with respect to phonology. In the dominant methodologies of the human sciences – those of Marxism and psychoanalysis – it is able to read veiled theories of form: in the former, the modes of production constituted the forms of History;

in the latter, the psychic apparatuses constituted the forms of the Subject.

Althusser and Lacan, each in his own way, led the way in these movements and took on the ideal of science, that is, the ideal of formalization: Althusser by radically distinguishing between science and the history of ideology; Lacan by making this formalization, in a canonical text, the ideal of psychoanalysis itself. We thus find ourselves in a context where the question of knowledge in its most rigorous and solid sense is paradigmatic, in the formalized sciences like logic, mathematics and the phonological core of linguistics.

However, in the mid to late 1960s, there appeared a completely opposite disposition. Such was the initial paradox that one needs to keep in mind for a well-grounded understanding of Rancière's trajectory. This paradox is perhaps the originary example that was also to be subjectively decisive for what he will later name (as his primary categories) the relation of a non-relation, or the non-relation conceived as a relation.

We should recall that during the period of intense activity of the Cultural Revolution in China, between 1965 and 1968, the main question was that of the forms of intellectual authority. The student revolt rallied against what the Red Guards named the 'monkish academics', demanding their dismissal without hesitating in their cruel persecution. We had, on a large scale, an anti-authoritarian revolt aiming at the reversal of hierarchies founded on the access to knowledge. The revolts in the factories established their political form precisely in Shanghai in January '67, when anti-hierarchical revolts challenged the engineers and bosses whose status was founded on the authority of techno-scientific knowledge. The idea was that the direct experimentation of workers should be at least as important as the authority of their leaders. Here we had a sequence which was to be the key reference for a number of young philosophers – Rancière, myself and others – who at the same time were engaging in the apology of the scientific concept and its liberatory authority. The question of knowing whether we were rightly or wrongly fascinated with the Cultural Revolution is a marginal debate. The fact is that an immense political phenomenon seemed polarized on the question of the denial or radical contestation of the set of authorities based on the centralization of knowledge. That being the case, for the revolutionary scientists that we were aspiring to be, this constituted the most violent of our internal paradoxes.

Now let us return to France. Beginning in 1967, there were a series of factory revolts leading to the month of May 1968. These revolts were qualitatively new because, being organized by nuclei of young workers who frequently were not unionized, they also proposed to overturn the internal hierarchy of the factory, with actions that constituted a particular form. These actions began first as a reticence towards or even a frank opposition to the overall unionized framing of the movements, and, then, developed into a fairly systematic humiliation of all existing authorities. In the months after May '68, this was followed by the spread of a rather confrontational practice: the sequestering of factory bosses. I just want to mention a kind of stylistic résumé of all this in a film by Jean-Luc Godard, *Tout va bien*, which we might consider as an artistic document of the way in which consciousness was formed by the experience of this upheaval in the relation between knowledge and power.

Finally, prepared as well by the many prior dissident movements, notably on the question of sexual and social inequalities, the student revolts of May '68 and the following years were explicitly directed against the top-down organization of the transmission of knowledge. These revolts questioned academic authority, the choices concerning one's education and the courses of study, the testing of knowledge and the possibility of self-led education by students who would organize themselves in the absence of any figure of the professor-scholar.

All of these events organized the paradox: the tension between a kind of dominant philosophical ideology under the paradigm of the absoluteness of scientific knowledge, and a series of politico-ideological phenomena which, on the contrary, strengthened the conviction that the connection between knowledge and authority is a politically oppressive construction that should be dismantled, if necessary by force.

Although we each lived with the paradox in our different ways, Rancière, I and many others were met with the same considerable question: How do we untie or undo the existing configurations of the relation between knowledge and authority, between knowledge and power? This question emerged naturally in the context that I spoke of, from the moment we rallied to the side of the movement, which at the time was our inaugural gesture as young professors. But I think that the question develops into a more complex form around the following problem: If it is necessary to depose the authority of knowledge, instituted as a reactionary function in the oppressive figures by which knowledge is monopolized, how then will experience be transmitted? The question of transmission becomes a particularly acute question. If it is not the concept but rather practical and actual experiences that form the real sources of emancipation, how does this experience transmit itself? In the first place, of course, we are speaking of the revolutionary experience itself. What are the new protocols of this transmission? What emerges once we have undone, untied and terminated the canonical joint authority of power and knowledge that has served institutionally as the space of this transmission? What is a transmission that is not an imposition?

We can also ask: What is the new figure of the master that results if one excludes all validation by the institutional authority? Are there masters outside of the institution? Or are there no more masters at all? The importance of the question of the master is certainly clear for Rancière, but it is also absolutely crucial in the work of Lacan. It not only emerges contextually in the abstract or genealogical question of the relations between knowledge and power, but also and above all in the immediate consequences of the engagement in the mass global movement of youth and workers between at least 1965 and 1975.

Since the start of the Cultural Revolution, this crucial question of transmission outside the institution had been formulated by Mao when he inquired about the successors of the cause of the proletariat. Given that he supported the students and the workers in their revolts, it became clear that this question of transmission could neither pass through the channels of the established authority nor through the channels of the Communist Party in power. The party, as the depository of authority and the supposed concentration of experience, became with each passing day the principal target of these activities. The result was the movement's establishment of Mao as the figure of the absolute master. On the question of whether there are masters outside the institution, the response was: the master untied from the institution is the master of the movement itself. He is a paradoxical master, since he is the master of the movement that aims to depose the masters. But what then was Mao if not a proper name? What the Red Guards proposed was the subsumption of revolt, infinite and dispersed, under the transcendence of a proper name. The authority of the singular name replaced those of disparate institutions and bureaucracies. To transmit meant: to study collectively what is equal to the name. Such was the role of Mao's little red book: to give form to what is guarded by the name in the fire of experience. It is almost impossible today to imagine the enthusiasm around this donation of form, the exaltation that prevailed around the theme of study, which was tied to those previously unseen political trajectories and those unprecedented actions.

In this we find a characteristic example of the problems and particular solutions of the time. Lacan himself personally took on the question of mastery. Not only did he produce a matheme of the discourse of the master but he meditated on the relation between mastery, transmission, and institution as well. He had, in particular, advanced the remarkable idea of a sort of equivalence for the new schools of psychoanalysis, as spaces of transmission, between foundation and dissolution. If one follows the genesis of a veritable institution for the case of Lacan, one will first notice that it proceeds nonetheless under the radical guarantee of the proper name of a master who takes exception to the instituted forms of mastery (there again, 'Lacan' just like 'Mao' expresses a condition of transmission). And then one notices that if an institution, in an effort to avoid the *'effet de colle'*, attempts to assure the transparency of transmission, it must approach the edge of its own dissolution with each passing day.[2]

This whole context, this historical and subjective paradox, constitutes our origin – for us, for the 'generation', as one might say, who were struck by lightning in May '68. This origin illuminates Rancière's trajectory of thought, and it does so in the long run for the simple reason that, in contrast to so many others, Rancière never reneged on it. This is the same reason why it illuminates my trajectory as well. It is so much the case that, in renouncing the opening comments of my own essay, I believe it obligatory to engage in some comparisons between Rancière and myself.

I obviously return to my initial difficulty: how do I compare myself to Rancière without immediately implying that he is wrong and I am right? The Rancière/Badiou comparisons are, little by little, on their way to becoming somewhat canonical in some limited but international, and – without appearing too shameless – significant contexts. We do not – neither I nor Rancière – draw any

---

2   *Translator's Note*: *L'effet de colle* literally means the 'sticking effect', and has resonances with *l'effet d'école* or the 'effect of school', and with *faire école*, which means 'to acquire a following'. The term itself was used by Lacan in the development of independent study groups at the École Freudienne de Paris, called 'cartels'. The main point was that cartels are only truly productive if they do not continue beyond a certain period of existence. Members in different groups should split up, form other groups with other people. In this way there is no one individual who constantly occupies the 'leadership position' or who acquires the status of 'most diligent worker'. This form is discussed in Lacan's founding text of the school, 'L'Acte de foundation de L'Ecole Freudienne de Paris' (21 June 1964), as well as in the later, more theoretical discussion in 'D'écolage' (11 March 1980). These texts can be found on the website of the École de la Cause Freudienne at causefreudienne.net/orientation-lacanienne/cartels/.

particular pride from this. Full of good sense, Jacques told me one day, 'You know, we are advancing only by virtue of seniority'. That's true, but we might congratulate ourselves on the passage of a faithful seniority and not that of the social advantages found by some colleagues in their trumpeted renunciations ('We were mistaken, oh dear – we believed in communism, we were totalitarians – yes, yes, yes, long live democracy').

Some words are in order about the methodology concerning this recent practice of the comparison between Rancière and myself. As a general rule, it has three functions. The comparisons serve above all to open a critical apparatus, in demonstrating our differences with respect to certain figures like Mallarmé or Plato, or Straub or Godard. Sometimes comparison serves as a synthetic method for constituting a supposedly unnoticed problem that circulates 'between' the two of us. And finally, it serves to positively shed light on the work of one of the two of us. This third function is the one that I shall undertake, trying at each instant – more or less clumsily – to place myself in the negative role. I will maintain the axiom to 'speak only well of Rancière', albeit at the cost of speaking negatively of myself.

On the problem at the heart of the context that I have mentioned – that is, on the question concerning not only of the relation between power and knowledge, but also the singularity of transmission in the undoing of an instituted relation between knowledge and power – I would say that Rancière holds a democratic hypothesis with respect to the possible configuration of a new type of transmission. I call a hypothesis 'democratic' insofar as it relates to an eruption, a movement of the masses, a lightning-like rallying together. I also refer here to a 'social' separation between those at the bottom and those on the top. The two descriptions establish a correlation between a new regime of transmission and mastery, on one hand, and an always incomplete unraveling of old instituted practices, on the other. In the background, one also finds the correlation of the themes of equality and inequality in their current modes of articulation, that is, in the non-relation which is, in turn, a relation.

My first remark is that this hypothesis constrains Rancière to mediations of a historical character. In effect, a democratic hypothesis thusly conceived applies itself to observations concerning the dysfunction of certain instituted regimes of distribution. In this dysfunction what insinuates itself as if in a breach is the possibility of a different distribution of power, of knowledge, of active bodies, and finally of the visible order itself. This different distribution reorganizes a new modality of transmission, a fragile and transitory modality, which no longer passes through the channels of instituted knowledge at all but rather, changing the insignia of power-knowledge, inscribes itself into the part of that which, in the former distribution, was the no-part. This transmission is truly democratic because it articulates itself directly on the differential of the instituted regime of distribution. It is articulated at the point where the '*polis*', the virtual city of the collectivity of equals, separates itself suddenly, while at the same time remaining in contact with the 'police'. In this, the 'police' indicates not only the regime of the established distributions with their unequally distributed parts but also the no-part, the necessary figure of all subsequent redistributions.

I insist on the fact that Rancière's epochal account unites the consequences of a renewed democratic hypothesis, simply because my own hypothesis is not his. To speak honestly now, and this is where I begin to take on a negative role. I believe that my hypothesis is, simply put, aristocratic. The emergence of a new transmission, for me, presupposes a post-evental constitution of the effects of a heterogeneous body. However, this heterogeneous body is not immediately democratic in nature because its heterogeneity affects the multiplicity – the *demos* – at the heart of which it is constituted, in an immanent but separating manner. What makes possible the existence, or at least the propagation, of the egalitarian hypothesis is not itself an immediately equal regime.

It is a bit like mathematics: what is more egalitarian than the pure connections in an equation? Thoughts are strictly identical in the face of this formal game where rules are entirely explicit, where everything is inscribed and nothing is hidden. This is exactly why Plato accorded to mathematics the status of an obligatory stepping stone on the way to the dialectic, leading us through the most evident case of equality. Such is his democratic ideal: equality before the Idea. However, it is clear that the formation of the body of theorems and the organization of their proper transmission is ultimately always the work of a small group of inventive mathematicians. Hence, the mathematicians properly speaking form a particularly aristocratic milieu, even if their personal disinterestedness and the total dedication of their capacities to the universal are never in doubt. It is from this case or this paradigm of deep democracy that Plato drew his conclusions about the rarity of guardians. This rarity is maintained while at the same time asserting their position of radical equality – with the inclusion of women – and the commitment to absolute communist disinterestedness in the forgoing of private property. It is in this sense that I speak of an aristocracy of transmission, a 'communist' aristocracy, which is today faced with the problem of having to distance itself from everything reminiscent of the form of the political party.

To sidestep the problem, Rancière sticks closely to the collective process in its operation to undo the established forms of transmission rather than going further along in the investigation of the very means of the material organization of consequences.

Here, we find the most condensed form of our differences: we have two distinct oxymorons. For Rancière, it is the *ignorant master*, and for me it is the *proletarian aristocracy*. In certain regards these two oxymorons, taken as maxims of judgement, are very similar. Viewed from afar, they are the same thing, but focussing more closely now, we find them to be extremely different. Why? Here we have a philosophical question that we might say is precise or well formed. Why is this 'ignorant master' not substitutable by the 'proletarian aristocracy' as a balance sheet of the paradox of the 1960s and 70s?

The oxymoron of the ignorant master activates its place, which is the place of the non-place, in contingent collectives. There, it undertakes a transmission without any guarantee of what takes place or what it affirms under this title. The ignorant master is an activation disposed in a sort of potential universality, an activation of what exists and what is becoming. The historical phenomenon of this transmission is at the same time immediate and sequential.

That which I call a 'proletarian aristocracy' is an aristocracy that is contingent as well as prescriptive. It does not democratically testify to the powers of taking place [*l'avoir-lieu*], of the becoming placed [*devenir placé*] of the out-of-place [*hors-place*]. It prescribes what it considers important, and this it transmits without any guarantee as well. However, its transmission occurs by way of *incorporation into its own duration*, which is a completely different mode of transmission than that practised by the ignorant master. Here I am simply introducing this term of 'proletarian aristocracy' for the sake of clarifying the oxymoron of the 'ignorant master' and also to say that these two new and paired names serve conceptually to name a certain account of the paradoxical context which I spoke of a little earlier.

This duality leads to many shared usages but also to all sorts of differences. We can take Plato as an example. Rancière and I certainly understand – as did Foucault, who would have laughed at seeing all this attributed to him – that the disjunctive dialectic of knowledge and power is first of all, in philosophy, a Platonic affair. Plato argues, in innumerable pages, for the proposition that there should be a privileged relationship between the protocols of the acquisition of knowledge and the distribution of the positions of power – that is, the hierarchical constitution of the city (the guardians, the warriors, the artisans...). For Rancière and me, with respect to this proposition, Plato has been a constant and fundamental interlocutor. Plato is something like a fault line, a shared edge where I believe we walk. In this, we are nevertheless facing in different directions.

If you observe the construction of the *Republic*, which is thematically paradigmatic, you could say that the text can be treated either from the aspect of the global distribution of occupational positions – the aspect of its social vision, as we might say today – or alternatively by concentrating our attention on the education of the guardians. In the first case, we have the conclusion of Rancière, that the essence of Plato is a critique of democracy. Why? Because the principle that governs the distribution of places is that those who only perform one duty, who are constrained to only perform one duty, cannot really participate in the direction of political affairs. Rancière insists strongly on this point. In the end, that which founds the 'social' anti-democracy of Plato is not really the need of a scholarly idleness or the rigid division between manual and intellectual work. No, what is essential is once again the question of the One and the multiple. The hierarchical distribution of powers according to Plato is guided by the conviction that whoever is assigned a productive task cannot properly perform it unless they only perform that task. For the artisan (here the 'technique' comprises the poetic technique, art) the principle of the One is strict: one task, one person. What we have then is a *practical univocity*. On the contrary, the guardians of the city – in other words, the political leaders – are obliged to do several things all at once, even if they are excluded from manual production. For example, they have to do mathematics, gymnastics, martial arts, dialectical philosophy . . .

One can say that, in our general approach to Plato, Rancière insists on the reactive dimension of this practical univocity (everyone in his place) while I focus on the theoretical multiplicity (the place of the leaders, always, is displaced). If, with the abstraction of the social schema, we consider the guardians as a metonymy of a polyvalent humanity, we can find in Plato a communist paradigm. Here we find a coexistence, in the dialogues, of a severe hierarchy that places the productive artisan at the bottom but also affirms a generic communism that hypothesizes, despite being a terrifying but inevitable hypothesis in the eyes of Socrates, the participation of women in leadership. Plato's division is thus a projection of the division between the oxymoron of the ignorant master who organizes thought according to a practical univocity, a 'social' hierarchy, and according to its unbearably anti-democratic side, and on the other hand, the oxymoron of a proletarian or communist aristocracy, which on the contrary extrapolates the Platonic vision of guardians as the paradigm of a polyvalent multiplicity, of a generic humanity (without class), as the real support of an authentic equality.

Plato concludes this relation between knowledge and power with the suggestion that the key question of politics is education. It is thus interesting to ask oneself how Rancière treats education philosophically. To introduce a bit of tension, we might remark that, for Foucault, the anti-dialectic of knowledge and power does not lead towards a theory of education. Foucault seeks rather to uncover what we might call the unforeseeable diagonal of practices and, in particular, the pathological and local practices, plebeian and excessive, which border on the unnamable and which in this sense trace all kinds of diagonals across the schema for the articulation of knowledge and power.

It is time to affirm that Rancière occupies an absolutely original position due to the system of formalization that he has constructed, little by little, from the paradoxical experience of which we spoke in the beginning. Rancière's work merits particular mention in terms of the circulation, produced by his writing, between the properly philosophical origins of the question as well as materials gathered from the experiences of the worker's actions in the nineteenth century; between the theses of his contemporaries, in particular those of Foucault, as well as the study of the positions of sociologists and historians, among them some significant polemics with the *Annales* School. He also investigates literature as well as, more generally, aesthetics and, finally, cinema. In looking at this broad interweaving, we might see how it makes for a possible formalization of our situation in the 1960s and 70s. The heterogeneous material in Rancière's work prepares, in my view, a convincing formalization of the original paradoxical experience.

What are the stakes of the problem of education? Rancière does not affirm that education occupies a central place in the political process. In this sense, he does not confirm the Platonic position. Yet neither does he affirm the contrary, that education should not have any privilege as a superstructure. This is a good example, but perhaps also the source of what I might call Rancière's 'median' style. By 'median', I do not mean centrist, but rather, one that is never immediately conclusive. This median style stems from the fact that Rancière always looks for a point where the inherited solutions encounter problems that obscure them, while this obscurity, in turn, proves that the inherited solutions are not as clear as they pretended to be.

The events that I spoke about earlier were foundational for Rancière. He took from them, as did I, the conviction that the struggle is always *a struggle on two fronts*. This was the principal lesson of Maoism. In politics, the struggle was naturally against the strongholds of bourgeois power, against the capitalist and the imperialist power, but this principal struggle could not succeed if we did not also struggle equally against the Communist Party and institutional trade unionism. It was certainly necessary to fight American imperialism, but we could not hope to reach the other side without stigmatizing the complicity of Soviet social-imperialism. To be brief: a true leftist revolutionary fights the official 'left' as well as the right. Such was the very powerful and vast context of upheaval right up to the beginning of the 1980s, framed by this idea of a struggle on two fronts.

With respect to the theoretical points that remain important today, there was also a struggle on two fronts. There was the struggle against the idea that politics can be dependent on science and, thus, on institutional transmission, a model according to which politics should be taught to the 'ignorant workers' and 'common people' by the experts or the party of the working class. However, Rancière equally struggles against the idea that politics is a blind spontaneity, a vital energy foreign to the concept and totally encapsulated by the gesture of revolt. There is neither a knowing party overseeing movement from on top, nor is there an immanent vital movement such that the gesture of revolt absorbs or encapsulates the totality of political substance.

With respect to the first front, Rancière had to enact a break with Althusser – just as I did in those years – in his writing *Althusser's Lesson*. For Althusser, science remained the fixed point from which ideology could be divided. This might be why he remained faithful to the Party for such a long time, long after the sequence of years that I spoke of. It is important to realize that behind Althusser, who was the figure of the knowing master, we found what the Maoists of the time called 'ossified Leninism'. This was the conviction that apart from any movement, consciousness comes to the workers from the outside, rather than being immanent in workers' knowledge, and that this outside is the positive science of the history of societies – in other words, Marxism.

But we should not forget that there is a second front. Here Rancière must detach politics from all its vitalist identifications, and maintain its status as a declaration, its discursive consistency, and its status as a figure of exception. Against the active prolonging of forms of life such as they are, his thesis is rather that if politics is not transitive to science, on the first front, it is nonetheless productive of various forms of knowledge that are necessary to the workers engaged in conflicts. Here, on this front, he puts in place an entirely new dialectic of knowledge and ignorance.

In the end, the question of the political unbinding of knowledge and power, constrained by the necessity of achieving nonetheless something like a new type of transmission, results – in the conceptual field – in the proposition of a new dialectic of knowledge and ignorance, and more generally, of mastery and equality. These are the dialectics that in my eyes form the heart of Rancière's work – the part of his work that formalizes those original experiences mentioned earlier.

This dialectic can be laid out in two very subtle theses, it seems to me. Their interrelation is subtler still. Formalizing Rancière's formalization, here is how I would write these two theses:

1. Under the condition of a declared equality, ignorance is the point from which a new knowledge can be born.

2. Under the authority of an ignorant master, knowledge can be a space for equality.

To be clear, we retain an essential point, which has become synonymous with the accomplishment of Rancière's work as a whole: equality is declared and is never programmatic. This may be obvious for the convinced Rancièrians that we are, but we should also stop to punctuate this major contribution of his enterprise. It was he who first introduced into the contemporary conceptual field the idea that equality is declared rather than programmatic. This was a fundamental reversal, and I announced my absolute agreement with this thesis very early on.

Here we pause again for another short comparative sequence. Rancière and I are in agreement on the declared dimension of equality, but we do not share the same hermeneutics with respect to it. For me, that equality is declared rather than programmatic means that equality is, in reality, the invariant axiom of all real sequences of the politics of emancipation. This axiom is (re)declared each time that an event opens a new sequence of emancipatory politics. It is what I called in 1976, during the period contemporaneous with the initial context, the 'communist invariants'.[3] The communist invariant par

---

3   Alain Badiou and François Balmès, *De l'idéologie* (Paris: François Maspero, 1976).

excellence is the egalitarian axiom as the axiom of a given political sequence. A declared equality is the maxim of an aristocratic politics that is grappling with a specific or singular form of inequality. This contingent aristocratic politics is an active body that carries out the maxim in a singular sequence and that has no other task than its deployment to the extent it is possible in a given situation. This aristocracy is absolutely contingent and uniquely identifiable in the sense that it is articulated in the very effects of the embodiment of the maxim in a given sequence.

All this is quite different for Rancière, who distrusts principles and more still the idea of a prescriptive relationship between principles and sequences. I would say that for him, equality is simultaneously a condition and a productive process. Such is the profound sense of the two theses that I formalized just a moment ago. On the one hand, equality is the condition of a new figure of knowledge and transmission. On the other hand, under the sign of an ignorant master, this new figure in turn strengthens equality by creating a new place or space for it in society.

Equality is a condition insofar as its declaration institutes a new relation to knowledge, creating the possibility of knowledge there where the distribution of places did not foresee any such possibility. This is why the master of such a sort of knowledge must be declared ignorant. In its capacity qua condition, the egalitarian prescription institutes a new regime of knowledge and its transmission in the guise of an unexpected undoing of the established relation between knowledge and ignorance.

Equality is a production insofar as the new configuration of knowledge brings about a space of equality that did not previously exist. We had given our blessings on the beautiful formula according to which a part of no-part comes to exist. But I have always felt it just a little too structural to truly summarize Rancière's thought. Everything here is process, occurrence, a lightning bolt of meaning. And in this process what is key is that equality is a double occurrence, one of condition and one of production. It is the knotting of these two functions that makes equality *the event par excellence*.

This tempts me to once again enter into the forbidden terrain of comparison. Yes, one can say that the declaration of equality is, for Rancière, the event itself, the event insofar as it provides a space to an indelible trace. In my vision of political matters, the egalitarian declaration is *made possible* by the event and is not to be confounded with it. It is that which organizes the body but in the context of a given evental condition, which is thus not homogenous with the declaration itself.

To draw out this comparison with even more complexity, we might consider the fact that we took leave of the Party in different ways, something that our shared experience made necessary.

Rancière's departure from the Party was not accompanied by a maintenance of the motif of organization: he left that in suspense. If I decided to change the title of my piece, for the moment I would rename it, 'Rancière or the organization in suspense'. In his departure from the Party he is concerned with staying as close as possible to the point of inscription of politics. This does not mean that he was for the movement and against the Party. He left, but remained close to its inscription. And yet – as a supernumerary point – this inscription was ineffaceable; all this happened in the gap, in the non-related relation. Of this one was sure. This much existed. Perhaps it still exists at times. History testifies to it and we continue to stand by this insight.

Even more than Rancière, I was fraught with concerns and difficulty over my departure from the Party. I was concerned since my conviction was that we could not sacrifice the notion that political *continuity* is always something necessarily organized. What is it that constitutes a heterogeneous, aristocratic embodiment of equality which is not also an inherited form or an imitation of the wise post-Leninist Party, the party of experts? Philosophically, the difference between putting the organizational principle in suspense and giving it a central place in political preoccupations has considerable impact on the treatment of the relation between event, participation, body and consequences. We thus arrive at two philosophical definitions of politics that, while being close to one another, are also sufficiently distinct as to not always be in friendship.

As such, we might have presupposed that the two theses (on the double occurrence of equality) could have helped us complete our understanding of Rancière with a few definitions about politics. However, the difficulty of extracting a few *precise* definitions from Rancière's texts is not theoretical in origin. Nor do I believe that it is the anti-Platonic slant, a difficulty with the transcendence of Ideas, which results in the resistance to definition. On the contrary, his prose is very definitive. There are clearly many surprising formulae that resemble definitions to the point that sometimes I tell myself that his prose is all *too* definitional and not sufficiently axiomatic. That perhaps it is too Aristotelian . . . but, for me, that is an accusation so serious that I would immediately strike it from the record.

Rather it is necessary to think that the difficulty concerning precision is a formal difficulty connected to Rancière's philosophical style. This style is very singular. It is direct and compact and has certainly not finished charming us. However, for a Platonist such as I am, charm is always something ambivalent in philosophy. This was true even, or above all, for Plato! When Rancière charms us, what he looks to do is to cut a path across an equivocation.

Rancière's style has three characteristics. He is assertive. He connects affirmations, but he does so with a singular fluidity that makes it seem as though his assertions are derived only by virtue of his style. It would be very interesting to compare this in detail with the style of Deleuze, who exhibits an equally assertive style, although of a different sort. Second, Rancière's is a style without argumentative discontinuity. One does not find moments where he proposes an isolated demonstration to support a given thesis. It is, finally, a style that seeks a conceptual unfolding of examples with the goal of creating certain zones of undecidability between actuality and the concept. It is not a question of empiricism. Rather, if Jacques will forgive me, it is a Hegelian inflection: it is a question of showing the presence of a concept *there*, in the real of historic eruptions, in the effectiveness of its rhythmic behaviour. Certainly my own style is more axiomatic and formulaic, containing more separations in the various dimensions of arguments. In any case, Rancière's stylistic approach – the fluid affirmation without argumentative discontinuities, the smooth unfolding of examples – renders it difficult to extract precise definitions.

I would like to examine this style, taking a famous passage, one that clearly approaches a definition of politics and rearticulates almost all of the themes that we have brushed against in this essay. It is the beginning of the end of *Disagreement*:

> [P]olitics exists wherever the count of parts and parties of society is disturbed by the inscription of a part of those who have no part. It begins when the equality of anyone and everyone is inscribed in the liberty of the people. This liberty of the people is an empty property, an improper property through which those who are nothing purport that their group is identical to the whole of the community. Politics exists as long as singular forms of subjectification repeat the forms of the original inscription of the identity between the whole of the community and the nothing that separates it from itself – in other words, the sole count of its parts. Politics ceases wherever this gap no longer has any place, wherever the whole of the community is reduced to the sum of its parts with nothing left over.[4]

Now, that is the direct and compact style of which I spoke. The intelligibility of the movement is completely guided by the syntax. In saying that Rancière's style is essentially syntactic, with a singular semantic distribution between the concept and the example, it

---

4   Jacques Rancière, *Disagreement: Politics and Philosophy*, trans. Julie Rose (Minneapolis: University of Minneapolis Press, 1999), p. 123.

would thus be difficult, in this text, to extract the precise definitions of politics, equality, mastery, knowledge . . . But I will attempt to do so all the same.

Let us begin with a very singular definition. What can we call the 'end' of politics or even the 'end' of the very existence of political action in a particular conjuncture? It is a question of sequences wherein a politics of emancipation exists. Politics ends, Rancière tells us, when the whole (the collective) of the community is reduced to the sum of its parts with nothing left over. On this point, I indicate a very suggestive difference between Rancière and myself, a difference more esoteric than other differences, since it concerns an ontological question. This question of the sum of the parts presupposes an ontology of the multiple that Rancière does not really provide for us. If we are speaking truly rigorously, a set cannot simply be brought back to the sum of its parts. There is always something in the count of the parts that overflows the set itself. This is precisely the excess that I name the state – the state of the multiple, the state of the situation. When a collective is nothing but the management of the sum of its parts, we have what Rancière calls the police and what I call the state. But the similarities end here. For Rancière, the protocol for the cessation of politics is the moment where the collective state, or the policing of the parts, is restored. In my view, there is no possible cessation of politics in this sense, since the excess of the state is irreducible. There is always some element in the state whose capacity overflows the pure presentation of the collective. There is always some non-presented in the state. One cannot then imagine that politics ceases in the figure of the collective brought to the sum of its parts. I will not continue further on this point but to say that, for me, there is no possible structural description of the cessation of politics. This is the reason why I do not share Rancière's political diagnostic of the *existence* of politics: because we do not share the same protocols for diagnosing its cessation. For him, there is a definable structural form for the end of politics; it is the moment where the supernumerary is abolished for a restoration without remainder of the totality as the sum of its parts. The affirmation of such a protocol of cessation of politics allows him to designate its absence, its end. Since I do not share this protocol, politics, at least structurally, always remains an open question for me. This is probably the place where a difference in the diagnostics of our conjunctures receives a purely ontological expression. And no doubt we can find here the root of an empirical difference. Unlike me, Rancière has not engaged in organized politics for quite some time now.

Now, can we define equality? Equality is a declaration. Although situated in a given regime of inequality, it affirms that there occurs a time of the abolition of this regime. Equality is not the *programme* of this abolition, but rather the affirmation of its *occurrence*. I am profoundly in agreement with this essential gesture. We see then that this exercise of equality is always registered on the order of its consequences, and never on the order of the pursuit of an end. What is affirmed is causality or consequences, but not finality. This is essential. What we have, and what we need to organize, are the consequences of an egalitarian declaration, not the means by which we pursue equality as an end. On this point, too, I am absolutely in agreement. In Rancière's conception, what follows is that equality is never an idea. It is not susceptible to being an idea since it is a regime of collective existence in a given time in history. The fundamental declaration, in its varying and locally situated forms, is that 'we are equal'. Although historically supernumerary, it is actualized in the series of consequences that follow from it. Such is the vision of Rancière. For me, equality is fundamentally an Idea, but in a very particular sense. It is an Idea because it is an invariant in the political declarations such as they are constituted in the various sequences of a politics of emancipation. It is thus eternal in its *being*, even though its local constitution in a determined world is its only possible form of *existence*. In speaking of 'eternity' and the difference between 'being' and 'existing', I continue to play the role – you might agree – of the lingering dogmatic. It is without doubt on this point, at the heart of political action, that the separation continues to play between Platonism and non-Platonism or anti-Platonism: the status of the idea of equality. At the same time, Rancière and I agree that the exercise of equality is always registered on the order of consequences. However, is this practical agreement sufficient to counterbalance our ontological disagreement? Certainly not, or perhaps only in some local circumstances, but never across the board, as we will eventually find ourselves at odds simply because the eternity of the egalitarian axiom relies on a sort of continuity that Rancière simply cannot maintain.

On the basis of politics and equality, we can enter into a critique of the figure of the master, something like a third definition of Rancière's work. On another occasion, it might be very interesting to do a comparison of the figures of the master in contemporary French philosophy. The well-established critique of mastery has led to a new figure that Rancière has described with much refinement. Through the doublet, ignorant master and community of equals, this figure has the capacity of undoing the relation instituted since Plato between the master of knowledge and the leader of the city, between knowledge and power. In Lacan's terms, this means putting an end to the confusion between the discourse of the master and that of the university. I believe that, on this terrain, Rancière demonstrates the fecundity of resources drawn from the inventions and revolutions of the working class in the nineteenth century. We need to salute this extraordinary gesture of the activation of the archives, something that, in my opinion, is more efficient and less melancholic than Foucault's earlier achievements. The worker's archive, dusted off and reactivated by Rancière's magnificent texts, shows its speculative fecundity. Precisely on the question of an absolutely original figure of transmission, it constitutes a direct engagement with the original questions we spoke of at the start. In my own terms, I would say that Rancière has found a form for the eternal conceptualization of our original paradoxes. He has produced a new Idea of transmission outside of the institution.

All this, in the end, turns on the question of what knowledge is. That is to say, what is knowledge when it is thought under the condition of an egalitarian maxim, in a new relationship with ignorance, and in the opening of a new space for equality? It is obviously a form of knowledge that is displaced with respect to the institution. In my own jargon, this would mean that we obtain a form of knowledge that is *equal to the status of one truth at least*. For Rancière, I believe knowledge – true knowledge – is what a declaration of equality illuminates or accentuates in a regime of inequality. What presumed ignorance, named as such in a regime of inequality, produces under the authority of an egalitarian declaration is a new figure in discourse. In earlier times we would have said that it is a revolutionary or emancipatory knowledge – a *true* knowledge, in the sense that Nietzsche speaks of a 'gay science'. We might also say that such knowledge is the effect produced on consciousness by an encounter with an ignorant master. Besides, here, we are rather close to what Rancière would consider to be the 'good' Plato. Evidently, as with all anti-Platonists, he has his good Plato. It was Plato who encountered, or perhaps invented, the ignorant master. The first to have said, 'The only thing that I know is that I do not know anything' and, thus, to have presented himself as the ignorant master was certainly Socrates. What was produced in the conscience of the youth in this encounter with an ignorant master merits the name of a new knowledge or a true knowledge.

I have not approached anything but the tip of the iceberg, but with all this in mind, we might return to the question of education. I believe that the overturning of the question 'Who educates whom?' is Rancière's principal reformulation of the question of education. More to the point, the problem is that this question is poorly posed. It poses a false dilemma between the assumption of the figure of the master and that of anarchy where knowledge and non-knowledge are equivalent in the capacity of life. If everyone educates everyone else, then no one educates anyone. This is a canonical example of the struggle on two fronts. We neither accept the One of the knowing master nor the inconsistent multiple of spontaneous knowledge. The struggle continues against the university and the party, but also against the spontaneous vitalists; the partisans of the pure movement or what Negri refers to as the multitude. The new conception of the relation between knowledge and politics neither confirms the vision of enlightened parties, which is despotic, nor the anarchist vision, which is at the service of opinion; remaining more or less merely the manipulation of the regime of inequality. In both cases, following Rancière's vocabulary, the *polis* dissolves under the police.

The appropriate formula is the following: *the anonymous process of education is the construction of a set of consequences with respect to a situated egalitarian declaration*. Here we find a form of emancipatory education. The question 'Who educates whom?' disappears. All that we can say is '*We*, we educate ourselves in this process'. Here, the 'we' is understood as being singular at each point, where each point in the situation reaffirms that the only universal maxim is equality. Conceived in this manner, education is neither a condition of politics as it is the case for Plato, for ossified Leninism, or for Althusser; nor is it indifferent to politics, as it is in the spontaneous vitalisms of the immanent creation of the movement. We are led to a difficult expression that I hesitate to propose with Rancière, or in his name: *Education is a fragment of politics*, a fragment equal to other fragments.

There is no doubt of my formal agreement on any of this. The difficulty, the space of our contestation, is over the definition or the delimitation of the anonymous 'we', in the formula 'we educate ourselves in the process'. Rancière does not provide us with a prescription on this point; there is no true opening, because of the defence of democracy. Democracy, in a certain sense, takes as a fundamental precaution not to circumscribe any 'we' even at the level of the concept. It certainly speaks abundantly to the central motive of utopian communisms, the community of equals. Yet it clearly takes this to be a regulative myth, which is moreover a social result and not an instrument of the political process. We might say that for Rancière, there is no established figure of the militant. On the other hand, in the Platonic lineage that I named aristocratic, the 'we' is the body of equality, the body of the maxim in a given moment of its process. As a contingent aristocracy, of course, the 'we' does not have any other function than the treatment of the relation of the non-relation, the relation to that which is heterogeneous, in bearing out the consequences of the maxim of equality to the full extent of its possibility. It is thus defined by a group of militants, the militants that constitute a body situated in the consequences of truth.

Being a militant means to take on the trajectory, to redefine the limits, to draw improbable connections . . . Within the context with which we began our discussion, this meant the very improbable connection between intellectuals and workers. In the end, this whole affair is simply the history of that connection. We have been discussing, without giving the impression of really touching upon it, the philosophical or speculative history of the connection between intellectuals and workers, as a possible or impossible relation, as a relation or a non-relation, as a gap, and so on. With the Maoist elements of the time, this is what we called the link with the masses, but this link dialectically implied the power of delinking. It is the originary delinking that unleashed, in an incredible newness, the possibility of this linkage. This possibility, however, only constructs its own temporality within a political organization.

In more conceptual terms, we might summarize Rancière's thought as follows. For Rancière, that which has value is always the fleeting inscription of a supernumerary term. For me, that which has value is the discipline of putting a fixed measure on an excess. For Rancière, the supernumerary term can be described, in a given regime of inequality, as the part of no-part. For me, the result of the discipline of a truth can be described as generic multiplicity, subtracted from all predication. For Rancière, there is no other exception than the epochal or historic. For me, there is no other exception than the eternal.

This allows me to finish by giving consistency to my ethics of praise with a pointed critical remark. It concerns Richard Wagner and the question of the power of the delinked, or the generic, such that art can produce its embodied multiplicity. In one of his books, Rancière proposes an interpretation of the third act of Wagner's *Die Meistersinger von Nürnberg* (Mastersingers of Nuremberg).[5] The subject of *Die Meistersinger* concerns the necessity of a reconstitution of the relationship between the people and art. The 'mastersingers' were an artistic corporation of artisans who maintained and taught a particular tradition of singing. In Wagner's opera, the key character of this institution was an artisan of the lowest degree. He was a cobbler. We could think of his status as close to that of an 'untouchable' in the Indian sense. Yet, as it happens, here we find ourselves at a juncture where it becomes necessary to institute a non-relation as a relation between the people and art. What is clearly illuminated in this fable is something exemplary for Rancière and me – here, once again, with respect to our original imperatives. In the figure of a young aristocrat, Walther, we find the emergence of a new artist, a new art, a new song. Walther, whose name echoes the name Wagner, competes in a singing contest organized by the masters. The prize of this competition is the hand of a maiden in marriage, the beautiful Eva. The prize of a maiden as the reward for a new art is certainly agreeable to Wagner, and to other artists as well. This competition is directed by the horrible Beckmesser, whose name echoes the name Meyerbeer, and who represents the most entrenched advocates of tradition obviously opposed to the new song. The central character, the cobbler Hans Sachs, was to be the mediator in this reconstruction of the relation where the non-relational dimension of the new

---

5   *Translator's Note*: Rancière includes a long discussion of *Die Meistersinger von Nürnberg* in the second section of *The Philosopher and His Poor*, trans. John Drury, Corinne Oster and Andrew Parker, ed. with intro. Andrew Parker (Durham: Duke University Press: 2003), pp. 57–124.

song could be inscribed. He resorts to cunning and intrigue. The details are far too complicated to explain here. All we need to recount is that the young gentleman is allowed to compete, takes the prize, and through this we find a public construction of a new internal relation interweaving art, tradition, the people, and invention. The 'militant' goal of Hans Sachs is to articulate artistic invention to tradition, and to do so in such a way as to reconstitute a new fundamental relation between the people and its historicity in the medium of art.

Rancière and I propose somewhat different interpretations with respect to the section where the knight, surmounting all obstacles, comes to the competition, sings his new melody, and captivates the people. He then is told, 'Now, you should go and join up with the mastersingers'. But having experienced all the humiliations inflicted on him, the arrogant and solitary Walther, unrepentant romantic that he is, refuses the mastersingers. At this point, the cobbler intervenes with a major declaration. He explains to his young protégé that he needs to accept the guild, because it is only in establishing this non-relation as a relation that a new *organon* of the collective becomes possible. The people will not be constituted by art unless the non-relation between the traditional and the new, in one way or another, is exercised as a relation. In Sachs's long tirade he continues in laying out a vision of the destiny of Germany. Here, Hans Sachs supports a very particular thesis, which in my view is quite accurate: that the 'true' – that is, universal – destiny of Germany is none other than German art. Finally, the knight accepts. However, the people do not cry out 'Long live Walther!', but instead 'Long live Hans Sachs!' It is the cobbler that is crowned with laurels under the chorus of cheers. All told, the master of the whole process, as recognized by the people, is the miserable cobbler.

Rancière remarks that this is all quite melancholic since the epoch of the possibility of a true relation between a new art and cobblers has passed. When Wagner composed his opera, he staged a pure nostalgic fiction – the nostalgia of the young Wagner who climbed onto the barricades of Dresden in 1848 – to imagine the public crowning of a cobbler, a spiritual sovereign of the figure of art. Wagner knew quite well that we were already well along the way towards a complete disjunction between the arts of the avant-garde and the collective of the people.

It is on this point that I note my differences. This scene announces that, in the crossing of a non-relation, if art is not reconciled with the powerful assent of the people, then it will become insignificant and will be replaced everywhere by consumable 'culture', the stereotype that Beckmesser embodies. Hans Sachs lends a theatrical and musical figure to an anticipatory Idea, still in suspense today, one that even 'socialist realism', which attempted to recapture it, could not replace: the Idea of a great art which is neither reserved for the educated bourgeois nor degraded as booming sing-a-longs. The Idea is a great art of the masses, something that may sometimes be found today, from Chaplin to Kitano in cinema. This Idea, since the nineteenth century, has been in the torturous process of the becoming of its actual eternity. To crown Sachs the cobbler in this scene for having realized this idea in its course of becoming eternal is certainly justice rendered even in view of the difficult history of this process in the last century and a half. All this might perhaps have been more convincing if in place of a singer singing a new song, Walther had come onto the scene saying: I have a camera, I have invented cinema. In fact, he does not really bring forth an art that, while inheriting the legacy of popular traditions, would also be the creation of a strong artistic novelty. It is really nothing more than a singer singing a somewhat newer song. Indeed, it is one of the most beautiful of Wagner's arias . . . Yet in the end, the real of the scene is in that which it affirms rather than in what it does not. Neither Walther's aria nor Sachs's declaration is musically dominated by melancholy. This opera, from the spring-like architecture of its overture onwards, is *artistically* the opera of constructive gaiety. It is interesting to see the dimension of Sachs's abandonment (he knows that the new song is for Walther to sing and that he is nothing but a mediator, and thus, even if he is the symbolic father and an admirer of Eva, it is the young man who should marry her). This abandonment, like the lively softness of the theme of the midsummer's night – the sonic invention of the scent of lime tree – is absorbed in the general energy of a folk tale, under a sort of comic hullabaloo in the second act, and, in the third, a blend of patriotic and working-class imagery.

From this we can see how music creates on its own a generic figure of *artistic discipline as an analogy of political discipline*, which, for its part, remained in suspense after 1848 and would remain in suspense, after the crushing of the Paris Commune, until Lenin and the revolution of 1917.

This minimal difference is interesting because it concerns the question of history. Rancière incorporates our contemporary standpoint into his evaluation of Wagner's allegory. It is true that the hopes of the revolution of 1848 were all but undermined by 1850, but I take my reading in a reverse direction. I argue that the artistic allegory is prospective, anticipatory, and a temporal beacon of the becoming-eternal of the Idea. The circumstantial failures of history should not force us into melancholy, but should rather activate the deployment of the Idea in the tension of its future, albeit a future to be persevered for a long time. This is what Wagner, through the artistic fanfares, understands by the crowning of Hans Sachs the cobbler. This Wagnerian question, 'Who is the master of the arts?', has all the while been present in my efforts concerning the work of Rancière, particularly in what has been said about cinema.

Ideas, in their process of becoming within disparate worlds, should be judged not by what determines the circumstances of their apparent failure in this or that sequence of history, but by the becoming – point by point, through their traversal of unforeseen new worlds – of their universal imposition.

*Translated by T*z*uchien Tho, re̶v̶i̶s̶e̶d̶ b̶y̶ Bruno Bosteels*

PART II. BOOK REVIEWS

9

The (Re)commencement of Dialectical Materialism[1]

Althusser's work is attuned to our political conjuncture, for which it provides a grid of intelligibility by indicating its own urgency therein. What is frightening and essentially *deviant* in the propositions of Communist parties in the 'West' and, above all, in the Communist Party of the USSR, can be defined on the basis of the permanent efficacy of a certain theoretical silence: whereof one does not speak, except to give form to the non-saying in the chatter of condemnations – schematically: Stalinism and China – completely structures that of which one speaks. Indeed, the lacunae must be covered over and the whole chain of arguments must be deformed so that the signifiers of the cover-up may come to find their place. All this does not happen without some damage, the rigour of the Marxist

---

1 Review of Louis Althusser, *Pour Marx* (Paris: Maspero, 1965); Louis Althusser, Jacques Rancière, Pierre Macherey, Étienne Balibar and Roger Establet, *Lire le Capital*, 2 vols (Paris: Maspero, 1966); Louis Althusser, 'Materialisme historique et matérialisme dialectique', *Cahiers marxistes-léninistes* 11 (April 1966). These appear in the notes, respectively, as PM, LC, and MH-MD. English translations are Louis Althusser, *For Marx*, trans. Ben Brewster (London: Verso, 1990); and Louis Althusser et al., *Reading Capital*, trans. Ben Brewster (London: Verso, 1979). These appear in the notes as FM and RC, while contributions to *Lire le Capital* that are not translated in *Reading Capital* will be cited as LC, followed by volume and page number.

discourse being in a situation of close proximity to the collapsed
parties and leading its own clandestine life underneath the nominal
parades of revisionism. So as better to keep quiet, the official ideological offices are thus progressively constrained to abandon all
theory in order merely to *collect* in the portable chats of the moment,
or even in the dirty little streams of post-conciliatory ecumenism,
whatever is posted under the name of Marxism.

These damaged goods are all the result of a general effect that
Marx began to analyze with reference to the passage from classical
economy (Smith-Ricardo) to vulgar economy (Bastiat-Say, etc.):
the effect of the *re-inscription*, into the ideological space, of the
concepts of science, previously transformed into homonymous
notions. We know that this operation takes advantage of the philosophical heritage in order to proceed with its specific deformation in
three different ways:

a) By staying *near the source* of science, it pretends to ground
   its concepts in an inaugural gesture and to resolve the articulated complexity of theoretical discourse into a foundational
   transparency.

b) *At the far end*, it uses the pseudo-concept of the result in
   order to absorb the concepts into the systematic extrapola-
   tion of a Whole in which the alleged 'results'[2] come to

---

2   The pseudo-concept of the result pretends to describe science as the
assemblages of 'truths' that are in principle disjointed from the process of their
production. It is precisely in the name of this disjunction that Hegel pronounces
his condemnation of mathematical knowledge: 'The movement of mathematical
proof does not belong to the object, but rather is an activity external to the matter
in hand.' See G.W.F. Hegel, *Phenomenology of Spirit*, trans. A.V. Miller (Oxford:
Oxford University Press, 1977), p. 24. The result is that, for Hegel, science
'reduces what is self-moving to mere material, so as to possess in it an indifferent,
external, lifeless content' (p. 27). The whole contemporary polemic against the
coldness, exteriority, closure of scientific knowledge; the whole effort that is put
into opposing the totalized inertia of scientific objects to the totalizing movement

figure as the mediocre doubles, of that ancient shadow theatre in which a god, recognized-misrecognized under the rags of the humanist or naturalist philosopheme, victoriously pulls the strings.

c) *Sideways*, or above, it invents a code with which to translate, export, double the scientific coherence in an empirical region that is thus simply *formalized* yet arbitrarily declared *known*.

Whence the three species of 'Marxism': fundamental, totalitarian, and analogical.

Fundamental Marxism, which is almost exclusively consecrated to the interminable exegesis of the *Manuscripts of 1844*,[3] turns out to be indifferent to the scientific construction of Marx, to the singular

---

of scientific thought, refers in the final instance to this figure of death to which Hegel confines the result of science without memory.

In a falsely Hegelian article, Robert Paris does not fail to give us the classical *colour* version of this argument: '. . . Mr. Althusser's attempt to free Marx from the Hegelian dialectic and to redefine the "level" of Marxism does little more than reduce us, and even make us regress, not only beneath Marxism but even to the *grey and sad universe* of a pre-dialectical, pre-Hegelian rationalism', in 'En deça du marxisme', *Les Temps modernes* 240 (May 1966): 2001 [Badiou's italics].

This means not having read Bachelard and perpetuating the insidiously religious ideology that discredits science, which is considered to be an unbearable petrification of souls. But science is something else altogether: organized production of its objects, as a specific transformation, in which 'nothing is given. Everything is constructed' (Gaston Bachelard, *La formation de l'esprit scientifique* [Paris: Vrin, 1938], p. 14), science announces that its domain is *nothing but* the process of production of which apparently it is the result, and thus that it coincides with the protocol of its appearance.

The Hegelian critique of the result therefore has no relation to its target (science). By contrast, it prepares the correlated valorization of suffering experience, of sublimated Christianity, which is the outcome of this 'critique'.

3   It is therefore not surprising that Althusser would devote long developments to the genealogical situation of the works of the young Marx. See for example PM, pp. 49–86; see also the text by Jacques Rancière, LC I, pp. 95–210.

determination of its objects of knowledge, and proposes a general anthropology centred on the multivocal notion of work. History, as the place of exile and scission, is captured as the deferred *parousia* of transparency, as the essential *delay* in the invention of the total Man. The covariant notions on the basis of which an exhaustive reading of experience is declared possible are those of praxis and alienation,[4] whose 'dialectical' combination unconsciously reiterates the old muddled lullaby of good and evil.

Totalitarian Marxism certainly exalts scientificity. But the concept of science to which it refers is the schematic application of the so-called 'dialectical laws', not the least burdensome of which is the famous transformation of quantity into quality. For totalitarian Marxism, Marx fits entirely within Engels' fragile system of extrapolations. To the young Marx of fundamental Marxism, it opposes the posthumous and vicarious Marx of 'natural' dialectics.[5]

Analogical Marxism at first sight seems to offer a more centred reading: it is concerned with the configurations and levels of social practice. It is glad to stick to *Capital* as the essential work and to the economic categories as founding paradigms. It is not difficult, however, to observe that it uses Marxist concepts in such a way as to *undo* their organization. It conceives indeed of the relation between the structures of the base and the 'superstructures', though not following the model of linear causality (totalitarian Marxism) nor that of expressive mediation (fundamental Marxism),[6] but as pure isomorphism: knowledge here is defined by the system of functions that allow one to *recognize* on one level the *same* formal organization as on another level, and thus to

---

4   See the critique of this false concept in the article by Étienne Balibar, 'Les idéologies pseudo-marxistes de l'aliénation', *Clarté* (January 1965): 59.

5   It is a miracle to see the speed with which Roger Garaudy has moved on from totalitarian to fundamental Marxism – from freedom according to Stalin to freedom according to Pope John XXIII.

6   Althusser distinguishes three concepts of causality: Cartesian, Leibnizian and Spinozist (RC, pp. 186–90).

approve of the invariance of certain figures that are not structures so much as 'planar' combinations among distinct elements. Analogical Marxism is a Marxism of identity. In its most vulgar form, moreover, it rejoins both totalitarian Marxism, with which it shares the mechanical rigidity, and fundamental Marxism, from which it restores the spiritual transparency, under the sign of the principled unity of its figures.[7] In its most refined form, it does no more than replace the problematic constitution of an object of knowledge with the undefined *transference* of pre-given questions, subject to the recurrence of more or less isomorphic levels of the social totality.[8] There where, in the order of discourse, the key question of structural causality – that is, of the *specific* efficacy of a structure on its elements – should have appeared, we are supposed to be content with a hierarchical system of resemblances and dissimilarities. The result is a retroactive adulteration of the real theoretical elements incorporated into the construction. For, in the process of occupying the place that the *description* of correspondences assigned to them, these elements are transformed into disjointed *results* and henceforth function, in turn, as simple descriptive indices.

The importance of Althusser's work consists first of all in reconstructing before our very eyes the *commonplace* of what henceforth, following Marx's example, we will call the variants of vulgar Marxism. Here again, it is the mapping of what these variants do not

---

7   Thus it is with the most recent works of Lucien Goldmann, which go so far as to *identify* purely and simply the homological structures 'discovered' by its author: 'Thus, the two structures, that of an important novelistic genre and that of exchange, turn out to be rigorously homologous, to the point where one might say that one and the same structure manifests itself on two different planes' (*Pour une sociologie du roman* [Paris: Gallimard, 1964], p. 26). Admirable simplicity!

8   The most accomplished example is no doubt Jean-Pierre Vernant's 'historical psychology'. It fortunately transgresses its theoretical presuppositions. One will grasp its ambiguity by reading, among others, the final chapter in *Mythe et pensée chez les Grecs* (Paris: Maspero, 1965).

say, that is, the system of their erasures, that constitutes the secret of their unity well beyond their apparent antagonism.

The effect proper to vulgar Marxism is the *effacing of a difference*, which operates throughout the complete spectrum of its instances.

The form of appearance of this suppressed difference, its *form of presentation* in empirical history, is the old question of the 'relations' between Marx and Hegel. The variants of vulgar Marxism have this in common, that they *produce the question of this relation* on the basis of variations on a *single* answer, whereby its *essential* importance, in any event, is affirmed. The concepts of 'reversal', opposition, realization, and so forth, successively come to fill the possible places originally designated by the essential nature of this relation. And, as is necessarily the case according to the ready-made dialectic of vulgar Marxisms, every apparent negation of the continuity Hegel-Marx produces the reflexive form of its affirmation.

Althusser's first texts are above all devoted to disinterring this buried difference. To restore the difference means to demonstrate that the problem of the 'relations' between Marx's theoretical enterprise and Hegelian or post-Hegelian ideology is properly speaking irresolvable, that is, un-formulatable.[9] Un-formulatable precisely because its formulation *is* the gesture that covers up the difference, which is neither a reversal, nor a conflict, nor a borrowing of method, and so on, but an epistemological *break* – that is, the rule-bound construction of a new scientific object whose problematic

---

9 'Mankind sets itself only such tasks as it is able to solve': this famous formulation has served as guarantee for the most variegated corruptions of Marxism, above all the empirical historicism put on trial by Althusser (RC, pp. 119–44) and the obscure speculations relative to 'the unity of theory and practice' (which is a problem devoid of meaning in post-Bachelardian epistemology, in which theory itself is originally thought as process of production, that is, as *theoretical practice*). The 'famous formula' simply means that a (scientific) problem cannot be *produced as problem* unless the space of its position – the problematic of its object – has itself been produced.

connotations have nothing to do with Hegelian ideology. Most literally, beginning in the 1850s, Marx stands *elsewhere*, there where the quasi-objects of Hegelian philosophy and their forms of linkage – the 'dialectic' – cannot be reversed or subjected to critique, for the simple reason that one no longer *encounters* them: they have become impossible to find, to the point that one would not even be able to proceed to their expulsion, since the space of science constitutes itself on the basis of their radical *lack*.[10] And no doubt the epistemological break produces, in retrospect, the specific *other* of science – that from which epistemology can teach us how science separates itself. In the *discovery* of science, we may try to map the 'edge' of the break, that is, the ideological place that indicates, in the form of an answer without a question, the necessary change of terrain.[11]

---

10   Thus, for example, the Aristotelian concept of 'Nature', whose lack – the impossibility of constructing it therein – determines post-Galilean physics. Properly speaking, *there is no* relation – not even a negative one, not even an inverted or a criticized one – between the new 'physics' and what bears this name in Aristotle's philosophy. For positive physics would not even be able to affirm the existence of the Aristotelian object. Of this object, it has *nothing to say*. This 'nothing' is what Bachelard names the epistemological break.

11   This mapping constitutes the *genealogy* of a science. The works of Alexandre Koyré or Georges Canguilhem are genealogical in this sense. What sets Althusser apart from the astonishing enterprise in which Michel Foucault is involved – an enterprise of which a true masterpiece, *The Birth of the Clinic: An Archaeology of Medical Perception*, trans. A.M. Sheridan Smith (New York: Vintage, 1994), manifests the exceptional importance – is the theoretical conviction that, if a *genealogy of science* and an *archaeology of non-science* are possible, by contrast there could not exist an *archaeology of science*. Science is precisely the practice without systematic substructure other than itself, without fundamental 'bedrock', and this precisely to the extent that any constituent bedrock is the theoretical unconscious of *ideology*.

On the basis of this discordance, we would try to explain:

a)   Foucault's inability to produce against the structural backdrop that he draws, in spite of its universality, the distinctive operators of science and non-science; and thus his *necessary* limitation to the archaeology of the pseudo-sciences.

Except that, in a number of remarkable pages,[12] Althusser has clearly determined the ideological *other* of Marx, and it is not Hegelian speculation: it is the classical economy of Smith and Ricardo.

This is not by chance: a youthful work constantly mentioned by fundamental Marxism is titled *Critique of Hegel's Philosophy of Right*; the scientific work, *Capital*, bears the subtitle *Critique of Political Economy*. By producing the concepts of an entirely new discipline (the science of history), Marx has not only abandoned the space of Hegelian ideology but he has also, so to speak, *changed his other*: the elsewhere where he stands is not the elsewhere of some Hegelian fatherland. Thus he appears, with respect to post-Hegelian ideologies, in the radical *fact* of his being-other.

The simple theoretical consideration of this fact – Marx has founded a new science – indicates for us that conceptual difference of which the dissimulation of the historical break produces, in a secondary effect, the suppression. This essential difference, which this time is *interior* to Marx's theoretical project, and of which the difference of Hegel/Marx is the historico-empirical evidence, is the difference of the Marxist science (historical materialism) and *the discipline within which it is possible in principle to pronounce the scientificity of this science*. Following an otherwise perhaps questionable tradition, Althusser calls this second discipline *dialectical materialism*, and the 'second generation' of his texts is centred on the distinction historical materialism/dialectical materialism. This distinction is of capital importance, even if only within the theoretical *strategy* that Althusser never loses sight of. The variants of vulgar Marxism can indeed be specified according to the different procedures for effacing this difference:

---

b) The pre-theoretical superficiality of his judgements about Marx (cf. *The Order of Things: An Archaeology of the Human Sciences*, trans. A.M. Sheridan Smith [New York: Vintage, 1973], pp. 260–2).

12 LC I, pp. 17–31; RC, pp. 18–28.

- Fundamental Marxism forces dialectical materialism into historical materialism. Indeed, it takes Marx's work to be a dialectical anthropology in which historicity becomes a founding category, rather than a constructed concept. By thus *undoing* the concept of history, it enlarges it to include the notional dimensions of a totalizing milieu in which the *reflection* of the structures, their 'interiorization', is a mediating function of the structures themselves.[13]

- Inversely, totalitarian Marxism forces historical materialism into dialectical materialism. Indeed, it treats contradiction as an abstract law applicable to any object whatsoever, and considers the structural contradictions of a determinate mode of production as particular cases subsumed under the universality of the law. Under these conditions, the procedures for the constitution of the specific object of historical materialism end up being suppressed, and Marx's 'results' incorporated into a global synthesis that could never transgress the rule that attributes to the imaginary any assumption of the Totality. Strange metempsychosis, from which Marx emerges saddled with the 'cosmic' robe of Father Teilhard de Chardin . . .

---

13   Here Sartre is a striking example, and from this point of view the *Critique of Dialectical Reason* is a monument of 'metaphysical Marxism'. However, the theoretical case of Sartre is more complex than it seems and Althusser is rather quick to rank him among the 'rationalist idealists'. Between the originary transparency of individual praxis and the formal inertia of structures, there is in Sartre a specific decentring at work, provoked by the radical and anti-dialectical exteriority of the in-itself: the Sartrean dialectic is a broken dialectic within which it is possible to reflect in part certain structural distortions, and even, at the cost of a slightly allegorical use of its concepts, to posit or at least to translate the fundamental problems of dialectical materialism. See *Critique of Dialectical Reason*, vol. 1, *Theory of Practical Ensembles*, trans. Alan Sheridan-Smith (London: Verso, 2004), p. 251.

- Analogical Marxism, finally, establishes between historical materialism and dialectical materialism a relation of correspondence juxtaposing two terms, with the Marxist philosophy at every moment being the structural *double* of a given state of the social formation, and particularly of the objective form of class relations.

Determination of one of the two terms by the other – or else pure redundancy: such are indeed the three general procedures for the purification of difference. But, as Jacques Derrida forcefully observes, a purified difference is only the defeat of an identity. Every authentic difference is *impure*.[14] The preservation of the concepts of historical materialism and of dialectical materialism – the theory of the primitive impurity of their difference, its complexity, and the distortion induced by the spacing of the terms – all this enables *at the same time* the systematic classification of the variants of vulgar Marxism. Which is already not nothing.

But what is more, the difference of historical materialism and dialectical materialism – we will henceforth note them HM and DM – signals the breadth of the Marxist theoretical revolution. To the foundation of the science of history, this revolution adds this unique fact in the becoming of knowledge, which is the foundation of an absolutely new *philosophy*, a philosophy 'which has enabled the passage of philosophy from the ideological state to the state of a

---

14 Jacques Derrida, 'The Theater of Cruelty and the Closure of Representation', in *Writing and Difference*, trans. Alan Bass (Chicago: University of Chicago Press, 1978), p. 333 n. 20. Can we think 'at the same time' the reading of Marx by Althusser, that of Freud by Lacan, and that of Nietzsche and Heidegger by Derrida? Headline, in our conjuncture, of the most profound question. If we take these three discourses in their integral actuality, I think the answer can only be negative. Better yet: to approach indefinitely that which keeps all three *at the greatest distance* from one another is the very condition of progress for each one of them. Unfortunately, in our instantaneous world in which concepts immediately become commercialized, eclecticism is the rule.

scientific discipline',[15] such that Marx's work presents itself as a double foundation in a single break – or rather: a double break in a single foundation.

Clearly to distinguish HM from DM, the science (of history) from the science of the scientificity of the sciences, thus means to *take the measure* of Marx and, consequently, to assign him his fair place, his double function – scientific and scientifico-philosophical – in the complex intellectual conjuncture in which, before us, the dominant post-war ideologies are coming apart: phenomenological idealism.

Thus restored to its strategic context, Althusser's work can be traversed in the order of *its own* reasons. It is not a matter here of retelling its story, nor of confronting it either with existing theories or with an undifferentiated concept of the real, but rather of folding it back upon itself, introducing some play into it, qua theory, according to the meta-theoretical concepts that it produces – to investigate if this work obeys the rules whose operation it isolates as the law of construction of its objects. And if there appear any lacunae, any *gaps* between that which the text produces as the norm for itself and the textual production of these norms, our goal is less to contest the project than to 'suture'[16] its lacunae, to introduce *into* the text the problems whose absence it indicates. Thus what we engage with in the discourse of Marxist theory, without ever separating ourselves from it, is a self-recovery of its blank spaces.

Rationalism is a philosophy that has no commencement; rationalism is of the order of the recommencement. When one defines it in one of its operations, it has already re-begun for a very long time.[17]

---

15 MH-MD, p. 113.

16 It is well known that the concept of 'suture' was introduced by Jacques Lacan and Jacques-Alain Miller in order to think the displaced-place of the subject in the psychoanalytical field. Cf. *Cahiers pour l'analyse* 1 (January 1966). The use I make of this concept in passing is only indicative.

17 Bachelard, *Le Rationalisme appliqué* (Paris: PUF, 1949), p. 123.

We might be tempted to proceed according to the inaugural difference that splits the Marxist revolution, so as to distribute the
problems into two registers: Althusser's contribution[18] to historical
materialism, on one hand; and, on the other, to dialectical materialism. Let us say immediately that this would be a way of dissimulating
what is essential, namely, the impurity-complexity of the difference
in question. Indeed:

a) The distinction of DM and HM is *internal to DM*, which
   renders vain all symmetry, all analytical distribution of our
   problems.

b) Can we truly pronounce here the theoretical discourse of
   HM?

Either we elliptically tell the story of this science, whereby we
lapse into the trap of saying precisely that which Althusser's work
has the function of forbidding us to say. In determining Marxism as
the foundation of a science, Althusser indeed reminds us that it is
impossible to jump over the detail of the proofs towards the illusory
results, since the objects of a science are one with the structure of
apodicticity in which they appear.

Or we try to separate out the specific form of rationality of HM,
and we operate 'the "reprise" of a basic scientific discovery in philosophical reflection, and the production by philosophy of *a new form
of rationality*'.[19] And undoubtedly we then talk *about* HM, we
undoubtedly produce the discourse of that which is the silent condition of its discourse. But the place where we operate precisely is not
HM: the place where we operate is the place from where we can

18 Let me stress once and for all that by limiting our study to the essential
concepts introduced by Althusser, I by no means pretend to hide that already this
(re)commencement of Marxism is a collective work. More collective than any
other, which is due to its exclusive *political* destination.
19 LC II, p. 166; RC, p. 185.

think, not the *scientific object* of HM (the 'modes of production' and the 'forms of transition'), but its *scientificity*; the place, therefore, and by definition, of DM.

Of HM we can exhibit here *only* what takes place in DM. Our exposé will thus be entirely interior to DM, including the difficult problems, which we will tackle in the end, concerning the theoretical status of DM itself.

c) And yet, in conformity with what we would have to call the paradox of the double break, *DM depends on HM*, in a theoretical dependency that is still obscure: not only because DM naturally cannot produce the concept of 'new forms of rationality' except by considering some existing sciences in which, in an enigmatic expression from Althusser, these forms exist 'in a practical state'; but more importantly because, as opposed to idealist epistemologies, DM is a *historical* theory of science. DM is 'the theory of science and of the history of science'.[20] For in truth, there is no other theory of science than the theoretical history of the sciences. Epistemology is the theory of the history of the theoretical; philosophy is 'the theory of the history of the production of knowledge'.[21] And this is why the revolutionary foundation of the science of history, insofar as it renders possible a scientific history of the production of scientific knowledge, *also* produces a philosophical revolution, designated by DM.[22]

We thus see up to what point the difference of DM and HM is not distributive. We have here a non-differentiating difference, which in principle is mixed: impure. The intricacy of DM and of all the sciences, but especially of HM, does not put an end to the autonomy

---

20   LC II, p. 110; RC, p. 145.
21   LC I, p. 70; RC, p. 56.
22   For all this see MH-MD, p. 115.

of the process of scientific knowledge. And yet, it constitutes this autonomy, this retreat, so to speak, 'flush' with science in such a way that the lack of science (the silence in which its discourse is kept at a distance) is the determining lack of *epistemology*, in which this science is constantly *mentioned by its lack*. This is because the knowledge of scientificity is at the same time knowledge of the specific impossibility of a *narrative* of science, knowledge of the non-presence of science elsewhere than in itself, in the real production of its objects. Internal to DM, our testing of Althusserian concepts nonetheless will be structured by the *withdrawn immanence* of HM, the figure of the lack that remains *its own*.

For reasons that will appear gradually further along, I will organize the analysis around two differences: that of science and ideology; and that of determining practice and dominant practice. Thus, I will speak successively of the *theory of discourse* and of the *theory of structural causality*.

I. Science and ideology

From the definition of DM (discipline in which the scientificity of HM is pronounced) we immediately derive that the determining concept of its field is that of science. DM would not be able to exhibit the identity of science in an un-decomposable 'seeing': thus, what comes first is the differential *couple* science-ideology. The object proper to dialectical materialism is the system of pertinent differences that both and at the same time disjoins and joins science and ideology.

In order to characterize this pair at first in grossly simplified terms, let us say that science is the practice that produces forms of knowledge, whose means of production are *concepts*; whereas ideology is a system of representations, whose function is practico-social and which designates itself in a set of notions. The effect proper to science – the 'knowledge effect' – is obtained by the regulated production of an object that is essentially different from the given object, and different even from the real object. Ideology, by contrast, articulates *the lived* – that is, not the real relationship of human beings to their conditions of existence but 'the *way* in which they [human beings] live the relation between them and their conditions of existence'.[23]

Ideology produces then an effect of *recognition* [reconnaissance], and not of knowledge [*connaissance*]. It is, to speak in Kierkegaard's terms, the relation insofar as it relates to me. In ideology, the presented conditions are represented, and not known. Ideology is a process of redoubling, intrinsically – even though mysteriously, at least in the current state of our forms of knowledge – tied to the specular structure of fantasy.[24] As for the function of this redoubling, it consists in implicating the imaginary and the real in a specific form of *necessity* that assures the actual fulfilment, by determinate human beings, of tasks prescribed 'in the void' by the different instances of the social whole.

If science is a process of *transformation*, ideology – insofar as the unconscious comes to constitute itself therein – is a process of *repetition*.

The fact that the *pair* comes first, and not each one of its terms, means – and this is crucial – that the opposition science/ideology is not distributive. It does not allow us immediately to classify the different practices and discourses, even less to 'valorize' them abstractly as science 'against' ideology. Truth be told, the temptation is all too evident. In the midst of the political confusion and faced with the theoretical laxity of the Communist Party, there is a great risk of making the pair of the opposition work as a *norm*, and

---

23   PM, p. 240; FM, p. 233.

24   It is precisely *on this point* that we would have to situate the articulation of Marxism and the status that psychoanalysis accords to the imaginary. But also the risk that this articulation may be provisorily *impossible to find*. Lacan's most recent speculations on the subject of science should not disguise for us that, for Marxism, the subject is a *properly ideological* notion.

of identifying it with the (ideological) couple truth/error. In this way a theoretical difference would be reduced to the game in which Good and Evil perpetuate the closed infinity of their reciprocal images. It is clear, though, that a practico-social *function* that orders a subject to 'keep to its place' cannot be the negative of the *production* of an object of knowledge. And this is precisely why ideology is an *irreducible* instance of social formations, which science will not be able to dissolve: 'it is not conceivable that communism, a new mode of production implying determinate forces of production and relations of production, could do without a social organization of production, and corresponding ideological forms'.[25] In reality, the opposition science/ideology, as the opening of the domain of a new discipline (DM), is itself developed therein not as a simple contradiction but as a process. In effect:

a) *Science is the science of ideology.* Except to repeat that science is the science of its object, which is a pure tautology, the question 'Of what is science the science?' admits no other answer than that science produces the knowledge of an object of which a determinate region of ideology *indicates the existence.* The notions of ideology can indeed be described as 'indicators'[26] on which certain functions of linkage come to operate. The linked system of indicators re-produces the unity of existence in a normative complex that *legitimates* the givenness of the phenomena (what Marx

25   PM, p. 239; FM, p. 232.
26   The best term perhaps would be 'denotator', or some equivalent of the English 'designator' (see Rudolf Carnap, *Meaning and Necessity* [Chicago: University of Chicago Press, 1956], p. 6). The formal theory of denotation and more generally the formal semantics developed in Anglo-Saxon logical empiricism provide us, in my eyes, with the framework for a structural analysis of *ideology*. Naturally, for Carnap, semantics is a theory of *science*: this is because logical empiricism is itself an ideology. The fact remains that it takes up the systematic classification of the general forms of *linked description*, of the discourse of reproduction – that is, of the most abstract forms of any ideological discourse.

calls appearance). As Althusser says, ideology produces the *feeling* of the theoretical. The imaginary thus announces itself in the relation to the 'world' by way of a *unifying pressure*,[27] and the function of the whole system is to furnish a legitimating thought of *all* that is given as real. In these conditions, it is clear that it is from within the same ideological space that the designation of 'real objects' is produced, of which science produces the object of knowledge, *just as it produces, furthermore, the indication of the existence of the object of knowledge itself* (but not the *knowledge effect* that it induces). In this sense, science appears *always* as 'transformation of an ideological generality into a scientific generality'.[28]

b) Reciprocally, ideology is always the ideology for a science. The ideological *mechanism* of totalizing and normative designation of existents is discovered (known) only for the region in which the existents of *a science* are designated, that is to say, the real objects of which a science accomplishes the cognitive appropriation. We can no doubt formally *designate* as ideological a great number of discourses. There is no shortage of them in political practice. But precisely insofar as it is a designation, this evaluation is *itself ideological*. The only discourses that are *known* as *ideological* are such in the *retrospection* of a science.

Marx only gave us the developed theory of *a single* ideology (and even he was supposed to dedicate to it all of volume four of *Capital*!): the *economic* ideology, itself divisible between classical

---

27 The concept of totality, taken in its absolute sense, is the archetypical example of a theoretical fantasy. Sartre's totalization is the fantasmatic critique of fantasy: an intra-ideological displacement-progress.

28 PM, p. 189; FM, p. 185.

economy (ideology 'on the verge of the break') and vulgar economy (ideology proper).[29] This is due to the fact that in *Capital* he
produced only *regional* scientific concepts – those of the economic
instance – in whose retrospection he could think only *this*
ideology.

We can thus measure the complexity of the relations between
science and ideology, that is, their organic mobility. It is not
exaggerated to say that DM is at its highest point in this problem:
How to think the articulation of science onto that which it is not,
all the while preserving the impure radicality of the difference?
How to think the non-relation of that which is doubly related?
From this point of view, we can define DM as *the formal theory of
breaks*.

Our problem thus takes place in a much vaster conceptual
context, which concerns *all* forms of articulation and rupture
between and among instances of a social formation.

---

29   Vulgar economics is characterized in a number of places. For example:
'vulgar economists . . . of those relations, ceaselessly ruminate on the materials
long since provided by scientific political economy, and seek there plausible
explanations of the crudest phenomena for the domestic purposes of the
bourgeoisie. Apart from this, the vulgar economists confine themselves to
systematizing in a pedantic way, and proclaiming for everlasting truths, the banal
and complacent notions held by the bourgeois agents of production about their
own world, which is to them the best possible one' (*Capital*, vol. 1, trans. Ben
Fowkes [London: Penguin, 1992], p. 174-5 n.34). Thus, ideology:

   a) repeats the immediate (appearance), that is, objective illusion;

   b) re-inscribes in this re-presented immediacy the scientific concepts themselves
       (elaborated materials);

   c) totalizes the re-presented (system) and thinks it as Truth: Ideology self-desig-
       nates as science;

   d) has the function of serving the needs of a class.

II. Structural Causality

Here I will try to be as rigorous as possible, albeit at the risk of taking into account only one part of Althusser's effort.

Like any construction of a concept, the knowledge of the 'mechanism of the production of this *society effect*' (the object proper to HM)[30] presupposes (invisibly) a *general* theory.

Science is indeed a demonstrative discourse that is related, as far as the order of succession of the concepts is concerned, to a systematic combination that hierarchizes them 'vertically'. The linguistic analogy would have us say that *the process of the exposition* in which the object of science apodictically manifests itself is the syntagm of a *theoretical paradigm*: the 'organizational structure of the concepts in the thought-totality or *system*'.[31] For example, Marx's demonstration regarding the law of the tendential fall of the profit rate appears logically as subordinated to a number of 'previous' conceptual constructions (theory of value, construction of the concept of surplus-value, theory of simple reproduction, etc.). But this diachronic subordination refers to a complex synchronic ensemble in which we find: (1) an interconnected system of concepts that obey certain laws of combination, (2) forms in the order of discourse that organize the evidentiary *unfolding* of the system.

The aim of the theory of the knowledge effect is to thematize the difference/unity, the 'dislocation' [*décalage*],[32] between the order of combination of the concepts in the system and their order of presentation-linkage in the scientific discursivity. The whole problem lies in the fact that the second order by no means represents

---

30   LC I, p. 84; RC, p. 66.

31   LC I, p. 87; RC, p. 68.
The essential distinction between object-of-knowledge and real-object, the theory of knowledge as production, the difference between system and process of exposition: all this is the fruit of a tight reflection upon a 'canonical' text from Marx: the 1857 Introduction to the *Critique of Political Economy*.

32   LC I, p. 87; RC p. 68.

the trajectory of the first, nor its redoubling, but its *existence*, determined by the very *absence* of the system, and the immanence of this absence: its non-presence within its own existence.

We might as well say that the system does not become explicit as an effect of the (scientific) discourse, whose functioning requires precisely the non-explicitation of the 'vertical' combination that it makes exist. Consequently, the theoretical presentation of the *system* of a science does not belong to this science.[33] In fact, the presentation of the system of HM, the theory of the special type of causality that it exhibits as the law of its object, does not and cannot belong to HM. Althusser's fundamental texts on the structure in dominance,[34] and on the object of *Capital*,[35] do not belong to HM either – but to DM. It is in DM that these concepts are unfolded according to certain diachronic forms of succession that are

---

33   Michel Serres sustains with brio the opposite thesis as far as mathematics is concerned. See M. Serres, 'La querelle des anciens et des modernes en épistémologie et en mathématiques', *Critique* 198 (November 1963): 997–1007. According to Serres, modern mathematics has taken itself as object and has progressively imported its own epistemology. More generally, a science arrived at the stage of maturity is 'a science that comprises the self-regulation of its own region, and thus, its autochthonous epistemology, its theory of itself, expressed in its language, according to the description, the foundation and the norm' (p. 1001). The precise discussion of this thesis has no place here. Let us simply indicate that the *foundation* to which Serres alludes is placed in a transcendental perspective. If on the other hand one takes care to define science as the *production* of a specific effect, and epistemology as the theoretical history of the modes of production of this effect, then it appears that such epistemological importation is impossible. In reality, what mathematics effectively has 'treated' is not the real law of its process, but an ideological re-presentation of mathematics, an epistemological illusion. And this treatment was indeed necessary for it, since like any science, mathematics is science *of ideology*. The singularity of mathematics lies in that its determinate 'exterior' is none other than the region of ideology in which *mathematics itself* is indicated. Such is the real content of the 'a prioric' character of this science: it never cuts itself off from its *own fact* such as it is indicated in re-presentation.

34   PM, pp. 163–224; FM, pp. 161–218.

35   LC II, pp. 127–85; RC, pp. 158–98.

themselves linked to *the most general (absent) system that can be indicated* – the system of DM, or Theory.

Let us therefore consider the systematic organization of the concepts of HM such as DM produces it.

This organization begins by providing itself with some primitive words, that is to say, *undefined* notions that will be transformed into concepts by their 'axiomatic' linkage into the system. These elementary notions are gathered in the definition of the most general concept of DM: the concept of *practice*.

> By *practice* in general I shall mean any process of *transformation* of a determinate given raw material into a determinate *product*, a transformation effected by a determinate human labour, using determinate means (of 'production'). In any practice thus conceived, the *determinant* moment (or element) is neither the raw material nor the product, but the practice in the narrow sense: the moment of the *labour of transformation* itself, which sets to work, in a specific structure, men, means and a technical method of utilizing the means.[36]

The primitive notions are in fact: (1) the labour force, (2) the means of labour, (3) the forms of application of force to the means. The two extremes – raw materials at the point of entry, product at the end – are only the *limits* of the process.

A *specific combination* of these three terms, considered in the structure that is proper to them – 'which, in all cases, is the structure of a production'[37] – defines *a* practice.

The first *ensemble* or *set* that is thus constructed, then, is the *list of practices*. Althusser provides several lists, most of them open-ended. The invariant segment of these lists contains: economic practice (whose limits are nature and the products of use); ideological practice; political practice; and theoretical practice.

---

36   PM, p. 167; FM, pp. 166–7.
37   LC I, p. 74; RC, p. 58.

To say that the concept of practice is the most general concept of DM (its first regulated combination of notions) amounts to saying that in the 'social whole' there exist *only* practices. Any other so-called simple object is not an object of knowledge but an ideological indicator. This also means that the generality of this concept *does not belong to HM*, but only to DM. *The* practice *does not exist*: 'there is no practice in general, but only *distinct practices*'.[38] Let us understand: history, such as HM thinks it, knows only determinate practices.

In these conditions, the only conceivable 'totality' in all evidence is 'the complex unity of practices existing in a determinate society'.[39] But what *type of unity* articulates the different practices among one another?

Let us first agree to call *instance* of a social formation a practice *such as* it is articulated onto all the others.[40] The determination of the differential autonomy of the instances with regard to one another, that is to say, the very construction of their concept (which explains why we can speak of a history of science, a history of religion, of 'the political', etc.), is *at the same time* the determination of their articulation and their hierarchy within a given society. Indeed, to think the relations of foundation and articulation among the different instances means to think 'their *degree of independence* and their type of "relative" *autonomy*'.[41] An instance is entirely defined by the specific relation it maintains with all others: what 'exists' is the articulated structure of instances. What remains to be *developed* is its knowledge.

In the assignations of places that are thus determined, for the state of a given society, there may exist a privileged instance:

---

38   LC I, p. 73; RC, p. 58.
39   PM, p. 167; FM, p. 167.
40   In the texts from *For Marx*, out of a lingering respect for tradition and so as better to find support in a famous text by Mao, Althusser still calls the articulated practice a *contradiction*. We resolutely abandon this confused designation.
41   LC I, p. 74; RC, p. 58.

the instance whose concept is required to think the actual *efficacy* of the others. Or, to be more exact, the instance *on the basis of which*, for a given 'stasis' of a social totality, we can rationally traverse the complete system of instances in the actual order of their degrees of efficacy. Let us agree to call *conjuncture* the system of instances such as it is thinkable according to the trajectory prescribed by the mobile hierarchy of efficacies. The conjuncture is first of all the determination of the *dominant* instance, whose mapping fixes the *point of departure* of the rational analysis of the whole.

The first great thesis of DM – here considered to be the epistemology of HM – posits that the set of instances *always* defines a conjunctural kind of existence, in other words, that 'the complex whole has the unity of a structure articulated in dominance'.[42]

Now, it is clear that the conjuncture changes. By this we mean to say that the conjuncture is the concept of the *forms of existence* of the structured-whole, and not of the variation of its forms. To place ourselves from the start in the midst of the maximal hypothesis, we could admit that, if a *conjunctural type* is defined by the instance that occupies 'the principal role'[43] – which is dominant – all types are thinkable: the conjuncture with a dominant that is political (crisis of the State), ideological (anti-religious combat, as in the eighteenth century), economic (general strike), scientific (decisive break, as in the creation of Galilean physics), and so on. Thus, it matters to determine the invariant of these variations, that is, the *mechanism for the production of the conjuncture effect*, which moreover coincides with the *effect of existence* of the whole.

Let us agree to call *determination* the production of this effect. It will be remarked that determination is exhaustively defined by its effect: the change in the conjuncture, which itself can be identified with the displacement of the dominant. This being said, what is the efficacy from which this displacement is the result?

---

42   PM, p. 208; FM, p. 204.
43   PM, p. 219; FM, p. 213.

A preliminary warning: the secret of determination in any case cannot be found in the *instances*, or practices, thought according to their complete relations to all other instances. At the level of the instances, there exists *only* the articulated structure in dominance. To believe that one *instance* of the whole determines the conjuncture inevitably means to confuse determination (law of displacement of the dominant) with domination (hierarchizing function of the efficacies in a given conjunctural type). Besides, such is the root of all ideological deviations of Marxism – especially the most notorious among them, economism. Economism indeed postulates that the economy is always dominant; that each conjuncture is 'economic'. Now, it is true that an economic instance always figures in the articulated whole. But it can have a dominant function therein, or not: it all depends on the conjuncture. As such, the economic instance has no privilege of principle.

If no *instance* can determine the whole, it is by contrast possible that a *practice*, thought in the structure that is proper to it, which is thus a structure that is so to speak *dislocated* [*décalée*] with regard to the one that articulates this practice as an instance of the whole, plays the determining role with regard to a whole in which it figures in a decentred manner. We can imagine that the displacement of the dominant and the correlated distortion of the conjuncture are the effect of the presence, subjacent to one of the instances, of a structure-of-practice in non-coincidence with the instance that *represents* it in the totality. We can imagine that *one* of the terms of the social combination (this time an *invariant* term) operates in its own complex form the articulated fulfilment of *two* functions: the function of instance, which relates it to the hierarchically structured whole; and the function of *determining practice*, which in real history is 'exercised precisely in the permutations of the principal role between the economy, politics, theory, etc.'[44] – in short, in the displacement of the dominant and the fixation of the conjuncture.

---

44   PM, p. 219; FM, p. 213.

Such a practice, like Spinoza's Nature, would be at the same time structuring and structured. It would be placed in the system of places that it determines. *Qua determining*, however, it would remain 'invisible', not being *presented* in the constellation of instances, but only *represented*.[45]

Such, brutally schematized, is the second great thesis of DM: There exists a *determining practice*, and this practice is *the 'economic' practice* (to be more precise: the practice whose limits are nature and the products of use).

We should take note of the fact that the *type of causality* of the determining practice is entirely original. Indeed, thought of as principle of determination, the economic practice *does not exist*: that which figures in the articulated whole in dominance (which is the only effective existent) is the economic instance which is nothing but the representative of the homonymous practice. Now, this representative is itself *caught* in the determination (according to whether the economic instance is dominant or subordinate,

---

45   The fundamental problem of *all* structuralism is that of the term with the double function, inasmuch as it determines the belonging of all other terms to the structure, while itself being excluded from it by the specific operation through which it figures in the structure only in the guise of its *representative* (its *lieutenant*, or place-holder, to use a concept from Lacan). It is the immense merit of Lévi-Strauss, in the still mixed form of the zero-signifier, to have recognized the true importance of this question. See Claude Lévi-Strauss, 'Introduction à l'œuvre de Mauss', in Marcel Mauss, *Sociologie et anthropologie* (Paris: PUF, 1950), pp. xlvii–lii. Pinpoint the place occupied by the term indicating the specific exclusion, the pertinent lack – that is to say, the *determination* or 'structurality' of the structure. Jacques-Alain Miller has given an exposé of this problem to which we must refer. See 'La Suture', *Cahiers pour l'analyse* 1 (January 1966): 37–49. We will nevertheless try to show elsewhere:

a) that the – extraordinarily clever – use of Frege's construction of number for the purpose of illustrating the problem of structural causality is epistemologically inadequate;

b) that we cannot think the logic of the signifier as such (of the signifier 'in general'), without reduplicating the structure *of metaphysics*.

according to the extent, prescribed by the correlation of instances, of its conjunctural efficacy, etc.). The causality of the economic practice is thus the causality of an absence on an already-structured whole in which it is represented by an instance.[46]

The problem of structural causality, which is the problem of 'the determination of the phenomena of a given region by the structure of that region',[47] and, more specifically, each instance being itself a combined form, the problem of the 'determination of a subordinate structure by a dominant structure',[48] thus finds itself posited in the form that MH assigns to it: *decentred unity* between the combination of instances – 'structure of unevenness (in dominance) of the ever-pre-given complex whole'[49] – and the determination-displacement of this whole – 'the complex process' – by a represented practice, but without existence other than that of its effect.

This problem, which according to Althusser 'sums up Marx's extraordinary scientific discovery . . . as an extraordinary theoretical question *contained* "in the practical state" in Marx's scientific discovery',[50] is far from having been solved. It is not even sure that we are capable of *posing* it (theoretically). It is possible that for the time being we can only *indicate* it. And this indication should no doubt take the unexpected form of a reading of Spinoza.[51] In any case – it is on the solution, or at least, on the posing of the problem of structural causality, that the ulterior progress of DM depends.

---

46   LC II, p. 156; RC, p. 179.
47   LC II, p. 166; RC, p. 186.
48   LC II, p. 167; RC, p. 186.
49   PM, p. 223; FM, p. 217.
50   LC II, p. 167; RC, p. 186.
51   See for example LC I, p. 49; RC, p. 40. The immanent causality of substance is indeed *nothing else* than its effect: the intra-modal mobility of *Natura naturata*, of which *Natura naturans* is the absent determination. However, God is effectively *represented* as mode (by its adequate idea). In the structural configuration called the human, this representative of *determination* can be *dominant* (freedom) or not (servitude): wisdom is a conjuncture.

We must finally come to the principal 'blanks' of the project, those whose deforming effects on the text itself are tangible at the levels that I have distinguished (inaugural difference between science and ideology; theory of structural causality). These blanks can be listed, not without a certain rigidity, in the form of two questions:

a) What is the theoretical status of DM itself?

b) Are the *structures* on which determination exerts itself defined on the basis of *sets*?[52] And, if not, can we really conceive of a combination without giving ourselves the concept of a 'space' of places, and without specifying, by their typical capacity to occupy-distribute certain places, the *elements* that are combined?

The question of the status of DM does not fail to evoke the second question, because it puts into play certain enigmas of representation. Indeed, the point is to know whether DM is *represented* in the operative distinctions that make it possible and that organize its proper discursivity. Is DM caught in the formal configuration of 'cognitive' practices that it has the function of sketching out?[53] Is DM a science? And if not, is it an ideology?

Althusser shows some hesitation with regard to this topic, even though he most often designates DM as *philosophy*. This designation barely allows us to make any progress. Indeed, the oppositional

---

52 *Translator's Note*: Badiou here as elsewhere in this chapter uses *ensembles*, which can be translated both as 'ensemble' (as in Marx's 'ensemble of human relations', mentioned in his 'Theses on Feuerbach') and as 'set' (in the mathematical sense associated with Cantorian set theory).

53 The complete field of these practices, such as Althusser here and there indicates it, would comprise, aside from theoretical practice and ideological practice, 'technical' knowledge and 'empirical' knowledge, probably reducible to certain transitional configurations between the known, the re-presented, and other effects, interior to other instances of social formations.

pair ideology/non-ideology also applies to philosophy; and the stroke here (/), which marks the break, bears witness precisely to DM at the source of which appears, now finally announced and denounced, the mirror-relation in which the old (ideological) problem of knowledge comes to a close:

> In other words, the whole of Western philosophy is dominated not by the 'problem of knowledge,' but by the ideological *solution*, i.e., the solution imposed in advance by practical, religious, ethical, and political 'interests' foreign to the reality of the knowledge, which this 'problem' *had to* receive.[54]

Would the best definition of DM that one could give perhaps be 'non-ideological philosophy'? But this nominal addition is meaningful only if one thinks the intrinsic relation of philosophy to the non-ideological (to science) as such.

Althusser does in fact think this relationship, in terms of the 'production by philosophy of new theoretical concepts which resolve the *theoretical problems* contained "in the practical state", if not explicitly posed, in the great scientific discoveries in question'.[55] To each scientific break there comes to correspond a philosophical 'reprise' that produces in reflective and thematic form the theoretical concepts that are involved at the practical – that is, operational level – within the different sciences. So it is with Plato for geometry, Descartes for the new physics, Leibniz for differential calculus, Kant for Newton, DM for HM, Marx (the philosopher) for Marx (the scientist).

But what Althusser does not tell us is the following:

a) What distinguishes this 'reprise' from the ideological *re-inscription*, pure and simple, of the new fact that is a

---

54   LC I, p. 66; RC, p. 53.
55   LC II, p. 166; RC, p. 185.

science; what distinguishes this reprise from a reflective disarticulation of the concepts of science leading to the reflection-misrecognition of the absolute *difference* of the scientific discourse within the fantasmatic *unity* of the ideological discourse, via the ideological operators of 'truth' and 'foundation'; what distinguishes the philosophy of a particularly delicate region of ideology, the region in which operates the ideologization of that which is in principle radically non-ideological, namely, science; if the empirically evident correlation between science and philosophy is not tied to the fact that philosophy is indeed specialized 'in' science, I mean: specialized in the unifying-grounding *dissimulation* of the only discourse whose specific process is irreducible to ideology, the scientific discourse.

b) What distinguishes DM, represented as philosophy, from the previous (philosophical) epistemologies, devoted explicitly to producing, differentiating, and then reducing, the concept of science. Althusser does not tell us how to avoid, or circumvent, the isomorphisms that can be mapped between DM and the general form of philosophical ideology such that DM itself conceives of it. Althusser knows all too well that the clearest formal characteristics of ideological philosophy are those attributed to eclecticism: *theoretical teleology* and *auto-intelligibility*.[56] Now, DM, as the 'supreme' theoretical discipline for 'drawing up the formal conditions' of *each and every* theoretical practice,[57] necessarily possesses these two properties: DM is inevitably auto-intelligible and circular, if it is true that it produces the theory of all theoretical practice and, consequently (as

---

56   PM, p. 53; FM, pp. 56–7.
57   PM, p. 170; FM, p. 170.

opposed to *all* other sciences), *the theory of its own practice*.[58]
General theory of epistemological breaks, DM (as opposed
to all other sciences) must be capable of thinking its own
break, to *reflect its difference*, when *a* science is nothing but
the developed *act* of this very difference.

DM thus restores for its own benefit the ideology of the self-
presence of difference, the ideology of the identity of transparency;
'*capable of accounting for itself*, by taking itself as its own object',[59]
it differs less from absolute knowledge than Althusser concedes,
since it contains in itself the wherewithal to think, in addition to
its own essence, the *scientificity* of all science – its essence that is
not visible but actualized – and it thus articulates the theoretical
modes of production as formal *figures* of its own process. DM is
strongly at risk of being, this time with reference to HM, *one* 'philosophical' reprise among others, the perpetuation of the task to
which the history of philosophy is devoted: the impossible *enclosure* of the scientific opening in the illusion of closure typical of
ideology. Simply put, DM risks being the *ideology of which HM is
in 'need'*.

But – second blank – even in this limited perspective, the

---

58 As Althusser observes with respect to Husserl: to proclaim the circle as
circle is not the same as finding a way out. I would add: to name 'dialectical' the
circularity of the circle should not cloud the case in which this circle is clearly the
circle of ideology. 'The circle implied by this operation is, like all circles of this
kind, simply the dialectical circle of the question asked of an object as to its
nature, on the basis of a theoretical problematic which in putting its object to the
test puts itself to the test of its object' (PM, p. 31; FM, p. 38). Agreed. But when
the object, as is the case in dialectical materialism, is *knowledge itself* – that is,
precisely the relation of any possible scientific object to its problematic? Then the
question asked of the object institutes a problem of which the structure is
absolutely original: the problem of the problematic. Do we not risk observing
that this particular object is, like certain 'objects' in naïve set theory, a *paradoxical*
object? Do we not expose ourselves to not being able to designate this except by
way of *undecidable* statements?

59 PM, p. 31; FM, p. 39.

difficulties are considerable, since the dominant concept of DM as epistemology of HM (the concept of structural causality) poses more problems than it solves.

I already showed that between the determining practice (the economic practice) and its 'presence' in the guise of an instance in the whole, there was a highly enigmatic distortion-unification, of which the Cartesian-Spinozan relation between God and the adequate idea of God furnishes no doubt the first 'model'. But here, as in the case of Spinoza, the problem remains as to the 'deduction' of the modes – that is, of the determination of 'that which' is structured by the structure, from that *on the basis of which* the structure is defined. In all likelihood one will say that it is defined by the system of instances. But, first of all, this poses the problem of the list, or the enumeration, of practices: neither determination (which manifests itself *within* the linked multiplicity of instances by the effects of displacement, and thus of limitation of efficacy), nor the dominant (from which we can think the conjuncture, or the *existing* type of unity of the instances) allow us to produce the *collectivizing* concept of the instances. The distinction of levels of a social formation (politics, aesthetics, economics, etc.) is presupposed in the very construction of the concept of determination, since determination is *nothing else* than the structure-in-dominance defined *on* the set of instances.

There must exist a *previous* formal discipline, which I would be tempted to call the *theory of historical sets*, which contains *at least* the protocols of 'donation' of the pure multiples onto which the structures are progressively constructed.

This discipline, which is closely tied in its complete development to the mathematics of set theory, no doubt exceeds the simple donation of a procedure of *belonging*, or of an inaugural system of empty differences. Indeed, we have seen that the conjuncture had to be thought as a definite system of 'places' in which the instances come to articulate themselves onto one another. From this point of view the dominant (as any structure, according to Althusser) is essentially a distributor of places and a definer of functions.[60] The same goes for determination, which is the assignation of the dominant place to a determinate instance. Thus, the complete construction of the concept of determination presupposes the following formal operators.[61]

a) Set P, set of places, or (empty) space of combined efficacies.

b) Set F of functions, or practices, *which distribute certain places to the functions themselves*. These functions are thus defined on a part of F and they take their values from P: they distribute-occupy certain places. We define 'practices' as assignations of places to other practices.

The image in P of a function f by another function f' is called *instance of f according to f'*, or the 'distance of efficacy' $f - f'$. We can in particular consider, if *it is defined* (if the part of F on which f is defined contains f), the instance of f according to f itself (that is, $f(f)$). This is the *representative* instance of f: the place that f assigns to itself.

Subset H of F (thus a set of practices) will be said to be *historically representable* if the following two conditions are met:

I) A *condition of determination*. For example: There is *in H* a function $det(\ )$ which is a bi-univocal application of H on P: $det(\ )$ distributes therefore the practices of H on all the places of P, and in particular it distributes itself – it is *represented* in P by the instance $det(det)$.

---

60   LC II, p. 157; RC, p. 180.
61   The indications that follow are rather arid and extremely summary. Giving myself authorization based on the fact that Althusser generally determines the 'global' efficacy of an instance by the effects of displacement, I have built a more complete theoretical example, which uses as basic functions certain *permutations of permutations*. This example is too technical to be reported here; I merely signal its existence.

II)   A *condition of domination*. The theory of the conditions
      of domination is already extremely regional, in the sense
      that the concept of structural causality that we obtained
      depends essentially on the type of dominance adopted.
      The one that I wish to propose here by way of example
      purposefully stresses the conceptual difference between
      determination and domination: a trivial demonstration,
      which I will leave to the reader, shows indeed that the
      representative existence of the *determining* instance
      cannot occupy therein the *dominant* place.

Let us remark first of all that the bi-univocity of *det*( ) allows us to
consider that in each place of P stands a practice (completeness of a
social formation).

Given a function h of H, everywhere defined in H, and a place p
of P, we will define h (p) as being h (h'), with det (h') $= p$. In other
words, h (p) $= h$ (det$^{-1}(p)$): the function takes as its argument the
function that occupies the place p.

We can thus consider that a function h operates *on the places*
insofar as it operates on the functions that have been assigned to
these places by the determinant: in a given situation a function h
(defined on H) is taken to be an endomorphism of places.

Now take *dom* ( ) as a function of H defined on H. We will define
the *place n-dom* by recurrence:

$1\text{-}dom = det$ (*dom*)   (instance of *dom* by the determinant)

. . . .

$n\text{-}dom = dom$ (($n\text{-}1$)-*dom*)   (defined as h (p) above)

We see that *dom* operates first on itself (since $2\text{-}dom = dom$
(*dom*)), then on the function that is sent by *det* to the place, here *dom*
sends itself, finally on the function that occupies (by *det* always) the
place that is thus obtained.

We will say that *dom* is in a position of *dominant instance* if, for any place *p* there exist a number *n* such that:

$$n\text{-}dom = p$$

In that case, a kind of recursion on the dominant instance, a recursion that would be constructed on the 'distance' of a practice *h* to the determinant (that is *det* (*h*)), permits one to *traverse* in a certain order – hierarchy of instances – the linked system of places.

A subset H of F as historically representable that possesses *a single* determining instance and *a single* dominant instance will be said to be *historically represented*.

Starting from these forms, by progressively 'incorporating' the fundamental concepts of HM, one could *probably* construct the concept of a conjuncture. Without laying claims on a mathematization for which the above scheme all too obviously falls short, I think it is necessary to situate the abstract interval that separates, within DM, the concept of practice from the concept of articulation-unity, and to indicate the allure of its problematic filling.

Let me add that this construction is incomplete and obscure. But above all, based on the available evidence, *Althusser thinks he can do without it*. His entire effort is geared towards actualizing right from the start, for a discipline without tradition, what mathematics is at pains to obtain through the emerging theory of categories: a *direct* determination of the concept of structure that bypasses the underlying presence of a set.[62] I believe for my part that epistemological

---

62   The theory of categories is perhaps the most significant epistemological event of these last years, due to the radical effort of abstraction to which it bears witness. Mathematical structures are not properly speaking constructed in it according to operational links between elements of a pure multiplicity (set); but they rather appear as 'summits' of a network of trajectories in which the structural correspondences (the morphisms) are primary. In the Universe (such is the concept used) that is thus drawn, Structure of structures, multiplicity is not one structure among others: one will speak of the Category of sets as well as of the Category of groups, etc.

prudence for the time being imposes a 'classical' formalization. Any premature hyper-structuralism inevitably leaves the construction of the fundamental concepts of HM (structure in dominance, structure of structure, determination) incomplete and, to some extent, *notional* (pre-theoretical). *Within DM,* the moment of the 'pure' theory of historically representable sets seems to me to have to take precedence over the theory of historical structures.

To conclude, I would like to underscore both the absolute necessity and the risk of this (re)commencement of DM.

It is first of all clear to me that there currently exists no other resource, at least if one wants to be able to *speak* about that of which the silent reality (silent *in theory*) interpellates us and makes us into the 'bearers' of determinate historical functions. There exists no other resource if one wants to think what constitutes *our* political conjuncture: de-Stalinization and 'pacific coexistence', tied to that *form of regressive transition* defined by the Soviet regime; American imperialism; the Chinese revolution, which is another *species of transition.*

Since I am talking mathematics, I must underscore the latent danger of a certain 'Aristotelianism' in Althusser, a movement that is more 'organic' than mathematical. In Althusser's texts one indeed finds:

a) the subordination of mathematics to a nonmathematical conceptualization: 'Mathematical formalization must be subordinate to conceptual formalization' (LC II, p. 163; RC, p. 183);

b) the identification of concept and definition: '. . . the question of the status of the definition, i.e. of the concept' (LC II, p. 67; RC, p. 115).

This brings us back a bit abruptly to the old ideology of mathematics as language. Let us recall that the concepts of a science are necessarily words that are not defined; that a definition is never anything but the introduction of an abbreviating symbol; that, consequently, the regularity of the efficacy of a concept depends on the transparency of the code in which it figures – that is, its virtual mathematization; and finally that mathematics is not, in physics, in fundamental biology, etc., subordinate and expressive, but primary and productive.

We owe it to the epistemological lucidity of Marxists working around Althusser if we are capable of reflecting upon this political conjuncture *in our theoretical conjuncture*, and inversely: absent which we would be reduced to regurgitating the *descriptions* of vulgar Marxism and abandoning the vitality of science, in all its aspects, to the formalist right and to the theologians of Literature.

It is to these Marxists around Althusser that we owe the *actuality* of the concepts of HM, which we might say they have literally discovered, since we possessed them since Marx: not forgotten but disguised, re-inscribed, *repressed*. And insofar as I have not said a word about the science of history properly speaking, having devoted myself out of necessity to DM (but let us read Marx: from now on, we *can*), I here want to mention the *services* rendered, in political practice, by the surprising results that Étienne Balibar obtains regarding precisely the forms of transition.[63]

No doubt the theory of the political instance still remains to be done. But we know that there are Marxists busying themselves with this; and it is already an accomplishment that the *place* for such a theory is clearly designated. In a time when the conjuncture forces us, beyond the common critique of phenomenological idealism, to preserve – through and in novel scientific configurations – the rationalist and revolutionary rigor of class organizations, to think that the political practice will be assigned its status gives shape to our exigency.

And yet, Althusser's interpellating work finds itself in a situation of rupture. In more ways than one, it is still governed by theoretical *resentment*, which sometimes renders it blind to whatever therein stems from the philosophical, or even ideological, tradition.

No doubt we all must, each on our own terms, separate ourselves by way of murder from the greatest theoretical tyranny under which we have learned to speak – the tyranny of Hegel. But it is not enough to *declare* oneself outside of Hegel in order effectively to

---

63   LC II, pp. 277–332; RC, pp. 273–308.

exit an accursed reign in which, as we know, nothing is easier than endlessly to sing the song of departure while staying *in the same spot.*

If we provisionally sum up the Hegelian project in two corre-lated concepts, totality and negativity, we will say that there exist two ways of ridding oneself of the master, following the topics that these two concepts bar.

The fact that we are refused access to the totality is what the first Kantian critique establishes with rigour, placing itself from the start – and without pretending either to reduce or to deduce it – in the pure *fact* of science.[64] In several regards, the transcendental dialec-tic is the secret government behind the Althusserian polemic. It is not surprising if so many descriptions, in *Reading Capital*, relate the object of knowledge to its conditions of production (for example, to its problematic) in a manner that strongly recalls the progressive and constitutive approach of Kant. When even to escape the empir-icist 'circle' that endlessly confronts the subject to the object, Althusser talks about the '*mechanism* of the cognitive appropriation of the real object by means of the object of knowledge',[65] he is not so far from schematism, which also sidesteps the problems of the guaranteeing, of the 'policing' of the true, in the direction of the positive question of the *structures of the concept's functioning.* The theory of the production of forms of knowledge is a kind of practi-cal schematism. The philosophy of the concept, sketched out by Althusser as it was by Cavaillès before him, strongly resembles the exhibition of the structured field of knowledge as multi-transcen-dental field without a subject.

---

64   Reread the preface to the second edition of the *Critique of Pure Reason*: here Kant multiplies the indices of a singularity without concept, of a quasi-miracle that presides over the 'groping' rise of science, 'revolution brought about by the happy thought of a single man', 'light flashed upon the mind', etc. Science is the pure fact 'beneath' which there is *nothing*. See Immanuel Kant, *Critique of Pure Reason*, trans. Norman Kemp Smith (New York: St Martin's Press, 1965), p. 19.
65   LC I, p. 71; RC, p. 56.

If now we turn to the concept of negativity, with everything it connotes (expressive causality, spiritual interiority of the idea, freedom of the for-itself, parousic teleology of the Concept, etc.), we clearly see that its radical critique has been conducted the farthest by Spinoza (critique of finality, theory of the object-idea, irreducibility of illusion, etc.). This time the debt is publicly recognized, and there is no need to insist on it.

The true question finally consists in knowing if there is compatibility between the Kantianism of the multiple that we perceive in Althusser's 'regional' epistemology, and the Spinozism of causality that rules over the presuppositions of his 'general' epistemology. In other words, the question is that of the *unity* of DM, and even of its *existence* pure and simple as a distinct theoretical discipline.

Indeed, let us make no mistake about this: Kant and Spinoza can here be mentioned in the exact extent to which one *suppresses* that which could superficially bring them into proximity: suppressed, book V of the *Ethics* in which a form of co-belonging of the human being to its ultimate ground is restored in the intellectual love of God; suppressed, the second *Critique* in which freedom opens up a path towards the trans-phenomenal. What remains to be thought is the difficult juncture of a regional, historical and regressive epistemology with a global theory of the effect of the structure. Althusser – or, in order to think Marx: Kant *within* Spinoza. Such is the difficult allegorical figure on the basis of which we might decide whether, in effect, dialectical materialism (re)commences.

10

The Flux and the Party:
In the Margins of Anti-Oedipus[1]

It is tempting to give a warm round of applause. Yes, yes! Read:

> It is a question of knowing how a revolutionary potential is real-
> ized, in its very relationship with the exploited masses or the
> 'weakest links' of a given system. Do these masses or these links act
> in their own place, within the order of causes and ends that promote
> a new socius, or are they on the contrary the place and the agent of
> a sudden and unexpected irruption?[2]

Could Deleuze and Guattari be dialecticians? The revolutionary
dialectic as theory of discontinuities and of scissions, as logic of catas-
trophes – that is it, after all: the order of causes assigns no place where
a rupture could take hold. No quantitative accumulation incorporates
a new quality, or counts the latter's limit among its number of terms,
even though quality is, necessarily, produced as the limit.

---

1   Review of Gilles Deleuze and Félix Guattari, *L'Anti-Œdipe: Capitalisme et
schizophrénie* (Paris: Minuit, 1972). English translation is Gilles Deleuze and Félix
Guattari, *Anti-Oedipus: Capitalism and Schizophrenia*, trans. Robert Hurley, Mark
Seem and Helen R. Lane (New York: Viking, 1977). Page numbers in the body
of the text refer to this translation.
2   Translation modified from p. 377.

True, the revolutionary crisis is an irruption of large masses into history. The revolution is 'a sharp turn in the lives of vast popular masses'.[3] Deleuze-Guattari echo this here, with the touch of pedantry and some vain Latinisms that stick to the soles of these nomads weighed down by all their baggage. ('Promoting a new socius' – you call that cute?)

All Marxist-Leninist-Maoists learn in school (cadre school, of course) that the Parisian workers, the Soviet people, the Hunan farmers and the young workers of Sud-Aviation in May '68 one day rose in revolt; and they know better than anyone that all those who pretend to having read, in their mental horoscope, the precise sequence of the good news, by this lie merely want to justify, after the fact, their personal discomfort in the heat of the moment.

Marxist-Leninists precisely base their particular energy and unvarying persistence on two facts:

- 'Where there is oppression, there is revolt.'[4] But it is the revolt that, on its own time, passes judgement on the fate of the oppression, not the other way around.

- 'One has reason to revolt against reactionaries.'[5] The popular and proletarian revolt is the reason of the

---

3   *Translator's Note*: See V.I. Lenin, 'Lessons of the Revolution' (July 1917), in *Collected Works*, 4th English edition (Moscow: Progress Publishers, 1964), vol. 25, p. 229 (translation modified).

4   *Translator's Note*: This phrase is commonly attributed to Mao Zedong and circulated widely as a summary of Maoism. It appears, among other places, in Mao's 1965 interview with Edgar Snow, 'South of the Mountains to North of the Seas', in Edgar Snow, *The Long Revolution* (New York: Random House, 1971), p. 204.

5   *Translator's Note*: Mao coined this phrase in his 1939 speech 'Stalin Is our Commander', made in Yenan to celebrate Stalin's sixtieth birthday. See *Renmin ribao* (20 September 1949), translated in Stuart R. Schram, *The Political Thought of Mao Tse-Tung* (New York: Praeger, 1969), pp. 427–8. The phrase was widely used during the Cultural Revolution in China. See, for example, *Chairman Mao Talks to the People: Talks and Letters: 1956–1971*, ed. Stuart Schram (New York: Pantheon, 1974), pp. 260–1. Badiou will go on to play on the suggestion of the 'reason' or 'rationality' of the revolt.

bourgeois oppression, it is what gives reason, it is our reason.

True class revolt, in essence, surprises. It is a war by surprise, the generic brutality of scission. How could the established rule of the old (including the revolutionary old) put up with a deduction of what tends to break it asunder? How many people have we not seen enraptured by the fact that 'no one could have foreseen May '68'! I even suspect that the ascent of anti-Oedipus and all the fabrications about the pure mysteries of Desire take off from this question. The question is, strictly speaking, stupid. Can one imagine a 'foreseen' May '68? Foreseen by whom? Who does not see that the unforeseeable is a constitutive, essential component of the historical power of May '68? To baptize this unforeseeable element 'irruption of desire' does not even have the soporific properties of opium.

This baptism, however, is not innocent. It machinates the stage entrance of the irrational. Unforeseeable, desiring, irrational: follow your drift [*dérive*], my son, and you will make the Revolution.

It has been a while now since Marxist-Leninists ceased to identify the rational with the analytically predictable. The dialectic, the primacy of practice, means first and foremost affirming the historical objectivity of ruptures. Masses, not concepts, make History. No one can ever really know precisely how, and in which workshop, a revolutionary (anti-union) strike began. Why Tuesday and not Thursday? The masses' gesture closes one period and opens another. What was dividing itself reverses its terms, the working-class viewpoint takes over. A local, dialectical rationality opens for itself a new space of practice. The revolt condenses one rational time and deploys the scission of another. The revolutionary process of organization is itself reworked, recast, transformed and split by the primacy of practice: 'The composition of the leading group . . . should not and cannot remain entirely unchanged throughout the initial, middle and final stages of a great struggle' (Mao).[6]

The material objective base of everything (the revolutionary class practice) is never quite exhausted by its outcome. Revolutionary history renounces Hegelian circularity and imposes periodization, the uninterrupted by stages: one sequence's rationality cannot absorb the practical rupture from which the sequence deploys itself as such. The rupture can be thought in its dialectical generality; but, historically, it is only practiced. The concept, the strategy and the tactic, the organization, all have the solidity of a sequence; but behind them lies the historically new, that which founds the sequence and which the concept within the sequence necessarily leaves outside itself as its remainder. Masses make history; practice comes first with respect to theory. Therefore there is a leftover of 'pure' practice, the historical rupture as such, which historical materialism and theory will not be fully able either to deduce or to organize any longer, because their deductions and their organizing principles presuppose it as fact.

This remainder, however, is neither the cause nor the hidden essence. It is not at all unknowable: it is an infinite historical source, at least throughout a historical period governed by the same principal contradiction (bourgeoisie/proletariat). The 'remainder' is that which, in the periodizing scansion (Commune, October, Cultural Revolution . . .), deploys such force of rupture that the long work of ruptures to come is needed to clarify the historical contribution of the masses, which is what sustains and what carries forward both theory and organization, in an infinite approximation that is itself always split (battle of the two roads). Who does not see that the Shanghai workers' practice, in 1967, of the directive of the 'workers' commune' returns to the practical, historical inexhaustibility of the

---

6   *Translator's Note*: See Mao Zedong, 'Some Questions Concerning Methods of Leadership' (1 June 1943), in *Selected Works of Mao Tse-Tung* (Beijing: Foreign Languages Press, 1965), vol. 3, p. 118.

Paris Commune? And at the same time, the positive elaboration of this directive, in the new form of the three-in-one revolutionary committee, carries this return forward.

From Paris 1871 to Shanghai 1967, revolt is the furnace, the great production of class. From a just idea dismembered to a continental rupture, everything is there. The furnace of the class break, of the revolt, has no place to call home.

The good fortune of the Marxist-Leninist revolutionary has never been the prediction and determination of the revolt, but rather the irreparable suddenness of the storm. Whatever weapons the Marxist-Leninists have assembled for the people – in terms of organization, doctrine, prevision, patience, and compactness of the proletariat – they will be judged according to their capacity to have them all taken away without warning by those who, suddenly rising up, are indeed destined to possess them, but as a rule for later.

The revolt surprises Marxist-Leninists and their organization too. It must surprise, by a new kind of surprise. For the Marxist-Leninists must stand precisely where the surprise will slam right into them. The revolutionaries, who professionally prepare themselves for the mass uprising, for the irruption of the revolt, can obviously never be ready enough. Only for them does the historical 'not ready' have a rigorous meaning, since what is ahead is only for them, the professionals of class struggle, what they ceaselessly prepare for. But they are not ready: were they ready, how could they have left in reserve the revolutionary potential of the proletariat, which is the sole asset of this preparation? The Marxist-Leninists, who analyze, predict, lead, and who alone know the revolutionary potential at each moment, are the ones to pose the question of the timing of the revolt.

What is at stake, for the Marxist-Leninist organization, is not changing the 'it was for later' of its prevision, as an approximating reserve of tactical composure, into the repressive 'it is too early' of the Right. Here, its identity is played out all at once.

Marx before the Commune: the Parisian proletarian uprising is bound to fail, but I stand unconditionally by its side; its real movement instructs and reworks through and through the theory of my (correct) prevision: the historical failure, the proletarian uprising, works and displaces my prevision. It criticizes my prevision, even though it is correct, because it is correct.

Mao and the peasant revolt of 1925–1927: the peasant revolt – very good. Fundamental. Our tactical application of the primacy of the proletariat, as urban insurrection, must explode into pieces. The peasants in revolt teach us that it is not the demand of the countryside, but the proletarian uprising that is premature. The masses' violent rupture carries this rationality to come: the encirclement of cities by the countryside.

The Marxist-Leninist leaders are the ones who sunder and split themselves, between the objective form of the rational revolutionary preparation and the unconditional and unconditionally immediate reason of the masses' revolutionary revolt – that which Lenin called the actual moment. May my enlightened preparation break apart and be verified by the fire of irrefutable historical un-preparedness: such is the essence of Marxist-Leninist leadership, the leadership of the party!

There is no other leadership but of the new. The old is managed, it is administered – it is not led. The revolutionary leadership scrutinizes the conflicted state of things, the class struggle, the clues accumulated during the proletariat's revolution in process. From there the leadership systematizes a guiding prevision that is both strategic and tactical. Let us take an example: since 1970, the revolt of the OS[7] puts to work a dispersed programme of class against capitalist hierarchy. Condensing this programme as soon as possible, formulating combatant directives that have their origin in class power, we put ourselves forward. Granted. But such an advance is but the point where a new assault wave is received and accumulates.

---

7   *Translator's Note*: *Ouvriers spécialisés*, unskilled and mostly immigrant workers, were key in the Maoist mobilizations in post-May France.

Who clings to it too tightly, forever stays behind: with the Renault of '73, when it is about the Renault of '75.[8]

The same goes for analytical prevision: there is a capitalist crisis today, there will be an anti-capitalist revolt. This is Marxism. So, let us get ready: propaganda, worker schools, popular committees for anti-capitalist direct action. But where and on what will the masses make their violent judgement bear? This must be studied quite closely, enumerating the practical hypotheses that are half-living in the work of the masses. Then and only then the unexpected breach – armed with this previous work on itself, taking along the skeletal frame of a barely sketched-out organization, carrying its leading virtuality, draining and reworking the Marxist-Leninists' strategy – will tear down the oppressive web as far as it can.

A correct line is the open road to the most powerful striking force of the proletarian irruption. The party is an instrument of knowledge and of war in an ever-widening space of manoeuvre and irruption. A correct line, a vanguard organization, an iron discipline, an organic relation to the popular masses, a constant exercise of Marxist-Leninist analysis, reclaimed and unravelled and reworked to the most minute detail, carried forward to the shadow of the trace of the new; the bark of class struggle pressed down to its imperceptible acid; everything interpellated by directives: all of this – the party – is needed for the revolutionary revolt to strike completely, past the meshes of the situation, into the historical unicity of the new. The active leadership of the party must be

---

8   *Translator's Note*: Strikes of the OS at Renault-Billancourt, in March–April 1973; strikes, at Renault, of truck drivers in the spring and of line workers in December of 1975. See Laure Pitti, 'Grèves ouvrières versus luttes de l'immigration: une controverse entre historiens', in Sylvain Lazarus, ed., *Anthropologie ouvrière et enquêtes d'usine, Ethnologie française* 31.3 (2001): 465–76. The general context of the change is the incoming economic crisis on the one hand, the Union of the electoral, revisionist Left after 1972 on the other. The victorious 1973 strike brought forward the rupture between the demands and the strategies of the workers and the unions.

tireless, perfect, exhaustive; as the unexpected revolt and the unicity of the revolutionary hour will demand of it that it be split again, beyond anything it could and in fact did foresee, and inevitably constrained by the new of the class that casts it forward. At which point proletarian thought filters through and gathers, anew – itself establishes its kingdom, before destroying it again: 'There is no construction without destruction' (Mao).[9] To which we add: without construction, there is no destruction – before destroying in turn whatever cannot be deducted or managed any more.

Marxism-Leninism and the idea of the class party go further than the anti-dialectical moralism of the theoreticians of desire. Moralism – yes, and of the dullest kind. Look at the two-column chart with which these jingly subversives would like us to conclude:

The two poles are defined, *the one* by the enslavement of production and the desiring-machines to the gregarious aggregates that they constitute on a large scale under a given form of power or selective sovereignty; *the other* by the inverse subordination and the over-throw of power; *the one* by these molar structured aggregates that crush singularities, select them, and regularize those that they retain in codes or axiomatics; *the other* by the molecular multiplicities of singularities that on the contrary treat the large aggregates as so many useful materials for their own elaborations; *the one* by the lines of integration and territorialization that arrest the flows, constrict them, turn them back, break them again according to the limits interior to the system, in such a way as to produce the images that come to fill the field of immanence peculiar to this system or this aggregate; *the other* by lines of escape that follow the decoded and deterritorialized flows, inventing their own non-figurative breaks or schizzes that produce new flows, always breaching the

9   *Translator's Note*: See Mao Zedong, 'On New Democracy' (January 1940), *Selected Works of Mao Tse-Tung* (Beijing: Foreign Languages Press, 1965), vol. 2, p. 369.

coded wall or the territorialized limit that separates them from desiring-production; and, to summarize all the preceding determinations, the one is defined by subjugated groups, the other by subject-groups.[10]

And one should perhaps call this 'beyond Good and Evil'? All this cultural racket, all this subversive arm-pumping – only to slip us, at the end, that Freedom is Good and Necessity Evil?

Freedom. And by the way, what Freedom? 'Subject-group', Freedom as Subject. Deleuze and Guattari do not hide this much: return to Kant, here is what they came up with to exorcise the Hegelian ghost.

For quite a while, I wondered about this 'desire' of theirs, wedged as I was between the sexual connotations and all the machinic, industrial brass they covered it over with to look materialist. Well, it is the Freedom of Kantian critique – no more, no less. It is the unconditional: a subjective impulse that invisibly escapes the whole sensible order of ends, the whole rational fabric of causes. It is pure, unbound, generic energy: energy as such. That which is law unto itself, or absence of law. The old freedom of autonomy, hastily repainted in the colours of what the youth in revolt legitimately demands: some spit on the bourgeois family.

The rule of the Good, with Deleuze, is the categorical imperative stood on its feet, by means of the amusing substitution of the particular for the universal: always act so that the maxim of your actions be rigorously particular. Deleuze would like to be to Kant what Marx is to Hegel. Deleuze flips Kant upside down: the categorical imperative – but a desiring one; the unconditional – but materialist; the autonomy of the subject – but like a running flow. Sadly, if you turn over Kant, you will find Hume, which is the same thing – and Deleuze's first academic crush. Critical idealism has no obverse and no reverse, that is even its very definition. This is the Möbius strip

---

10   Translation modified from pp. 366–7.

of philosophy. On the swing of Desire, the head bobs down and up again, until it no longer knows one side from the other, object from subject. All in all, whether this or that is Good or Evil is just a reversible matter of mood, without much consequence: always act so that the maxim of your action strictly speaking does not matter to anybody.

Marxism-Leninism thinks of otherwise forceful 'schizzes' or 'splits', ones that secure themselves otherwise to the material of history. The unity of opposites, that is to say, the impossibility of grasping the One except as the movement of its own scission; the step-by-step struggle against all figures of reconciliation (two fuse into one: the essence of revisionism in philosophy); the refusal of all static dualisms, such as the moralism of desire, this structuralism full of shame. Yes, this is quite different from the catechism of the System and the Flux, the Despot and the Nomad, the Paranoiac and the Schizo – all that, under the colourless banner of freedom, invisibly leaks in its sterile other side.

It is so different that a major historical object, like a class party, completely evades the 'schizo' grip precisely insofar as it concentrates dialectical divisions to the extreme. The 'schizos' imagine they are done with the concept of representation. The party 'represents' the working class, it is the theatre, the image, the territorial subjection. And so it has to end with the Great Despot.

Bourgeois party, indeed, revised party: one facet, separately undecipherable, of the party as one in two. This theatre is a necessary threat from the inside, as the party is itself split. Short of that, it is a cadaver. 'If there were no contradictions in the Party and no ideological struggles to resolve them, the Party's life would come to an end' (Mao).[11]

More than any other historical object, the party is one in two: the unity of the political project of the proletariat, of its state-project,

---

11   *Translator's Note*: See Mao Zedong, 'On Contradiction' (1937), in *Selected Works of Mao Tse-Tung* (Beijing: Foreign Languages Press, 1965), vol. 1, p. 317.

the project of its dictatorship. And in this sense, yes: apparatus, hierarchy, discipline, renunciation. And so much the better. But at once, also, the historical flip side: the essential aspiration of the masses, whose iron hand is the party, to the non-State, to communism. Which is what gives the party, as leadership, all of its strategic content.

The party leads the withering away of what it must lead (the State, the separation of politics). The party's only proletarian reality is the turbulent history of its own self-dissolution. 'Concern yourself with the affairs of the State!', says Mao to the vast masses.[12] And this is precisely the party, a communist party, speaking. The State is the serious matter, the central matter. The petty-bourgeois leftist wallows in the mass movement and parades there with delight. But when matters turn to power, to the State – when matters turn to dictatorship, since all state-power is dictatorial – see how he gets all furious, clamouring loudly of the Right to Desire. He is even relieved: the shameful electoral rallying of all the 'leftists' to the Mitterand-Marchais clique proves that, showing their appetite for bourgeois parliamentary politics, this dictatorship that squashes the people, but in the end lets all the intellectuals babble on as they wish. In the end, the 'leftist' political daydream is a mass movement that proceeds straight on until it is joyfully proclaimed that the State has quietly faded away. And since confusion invariably belongs to the thought of the vacillating classes, it will come as no surprise that this tells both the true and the false.

The false, for the most part: the State is the only political question. The revolution is a radically new relation of the masses to the State. The State is construction. A rupture without construction is the concrete definition of failure, and most often in the form of a massacre: the Paris Commune, the Canton Commune, the anarchists of Catalonia . . .

---

12   *Translator's Note*: See Mao's statement at 'meeting the masses' in Beijing on 10 August 1966, *Peking Review* 34 (19 August 1966), p. 9 (translation modified).

The true, nonetheless: it is true that the mass movement engages in a necessary dialectic with the State. Between the two there is no continuity, but rather unity of opposites. If the State is a proletarian State, the contradiction can be of the non-antagonistic type. If it is a State of exploiters, the contradiction is antagonistic at heart. But in either case there exists a contradiction, and a severe one, in that the masses cannot concern themselves with the affairs of the State other than by pushing the State, brutally or organically, towards its own dissolution; by pushing the great dichotomies of the State – city and country, agriculture and industry, manual and intellectual labour, the military and the civilians, nation x and nation y – to their pure and simple disappearance. The masses take hold of the State with the communist design set on its withering away. Any other way, and we can be sure that it is the State that takes hold of the masses: the bourgeois State, the party infected by the bourgeoisie.

Actually: each great revolt of the working and popular masses sets them invariably against the State. Each revolt takes position against one power and in the name of another, of one thought as a step towards the dissolution of the State. Each extensive revolt, across its specific contents (the school, the country, the factory hierarchy), is an anti-state proposition.

This is what puts the party through an ordeal, while the masses' anti-state proposition has no other chance, no other way out than to succeed in the interpellation with which it summons the party or whatever takes the party's place. It is here that the party (which, as apparatus, as real historical object, nourishes its own permanent prevision towards power, towards the State), summoned to fall into temporary blindness by another political thought, the one that brings out the anti-State summons of the masses, must overcome its own fear. Here it will always be eager to say: 'It is too early.' And there is barely time for another sequence of political thought to tip the balance of what has already been opened up.

Look at 'The Crisis Has Matured', this truly inspired work of

Lenin.[13] The passage from 'it is too early' to 'it is almost too late' solders these pages into one bloc, where Lenin puts his resignation from the Central Committee on the scales. Brutally bound together, we have:

1) The unforeseeable constraint exerted by the popular uprising, accelerating practically in a matter of days.

2) The rational prevision of the party, itself in turn split into:

   — the wait-and-see approach of the Central Committee majority (it is too early);

   — the Leninist anticipation (only immediate insurrection brings the prevision of the party on a par with the violent practice of the masses; the masses in revolt broke with the State: they summon us to lead, to practice our own kind of rupture – the order of insurrection – or else become nothing. If we reject the insurrection, from one day to the next we, the great Bolshevik party, become leftover riffraff).

Lenin says: there is a peasant uprising. 'It is incredible, but it is a fact.'[14] This objective element of the 'incredible' does not surprise us – Bolsheviks, who analyze the class struggle. Kerensky's government protects the capitalists and landowners, it oppresses the peasant masses that hoped to be liberated. But the only revolutionary question is this: Will our broad theoretical prevision (our lack

---

13   V.I. Lenin, 'The Crisis Has Matured' (October 1917), in *Collected Works*, 4th English edition (Moscow: Progress Publishers, 1964), vol. 26, pp. 74–85.
14   Lenin, 'The Crisis Has Matured', p. 77: 'In a peasant country, and under a revolutionary, republican government which enjoys the support of the Socialist-Revolutionary and Menshevik parties that only yesterday dominated petty-bourgeois democracy, a peasant revolt is developing. Incredible as this is, it is a fact.'

of astonishment) let itself be transformed, revolutionized, by the truly incredible reality of the peasant uprising? How will the party carry forward its correct prevision under the unforeseeable historical constraint of the irruption of popular forces? How will it formulate, in the leadership of the vast masses, that which hits it in the face – this divided, sundered, immediate realization of what was given in the organized calm of Marxist knowledge? To this question, Lenin replies: immediate insurrection – whose signal, whose time, whose urgency, are in truth fully fixed by the movement of the masses, by concrete history. Meanwhile, so as not to infringe upon their necessary system, of causes, ends and deadlines, the majority in the Central Committee persist in their perpetual 'it is too early', sheltering their Marxist prevision from the storm. And Lenin, intuitively at the very heart of the popular rising, beside himself with rage, literally slashes through the party, bombards it with all that history demands:

> There is a tendency, or an opinion, in our Central Committee and among the leaders of our Party which favours *waiting* for the Congress of Soviets, and is *opposed* to taking power immediately, is *opposed* to an immediate insurrection. That tendency, or opinion, must be *overcome*.
>
> Otherwise, the Bolsheviks will cover themselves with eternal *shame* and *destroy themselves* as a party.
>
> For to miss such a moment and to 'wait' for the Congress of Soviets would be *utter idiocy*, or *sheer treachery*.[15]

Herein lies the source of all the party's strength, against 'sheer treachery' and self-destruction: it is the party to whom history addresses its summons, the party that must remain steadfast as the movement escalates, the party whom the revolt questions as regards leadership. You who have foreseen all and were thus at the heels of

---

15   Lenin, 'The Crisis Has Matured', p. 82 (original italics).

the irruption, what good is it to us now that you are close by? Will you remain close, or will you let yourself be left behind by that for which you said you were accountable?

Lenin here stands for the question cast, from within, by the revolutionary practice of the masses (the unforeseen, the rupture), to the party's vocation to lead (the prevision, the project). This is the party as one in two, the working class itself as one in two: its apparatus on one side, its anti-state focus on the State on the other. From one to the other, the vertigo, in the movement of history, comes from the scission between a settled tactical rationality and a rupture that demands more than political rationality, since it demands plunging into the spaces opened up by the masses. Insurrection, Lenin will say, is an art. Not a science, but an art.

The party always directs the proletarian transition. The party is the dialectic. Its proper effect is the creative scission of the masses and the State as a directed process, as dictatorship of the proletariat.

The party is a being of the thresholds. It holds out amidst the tearing apart of the foreseeable theoretical element and the unforeseeable practical element, of the project and the revolt, of the State and the non-State. 'Fusion of Marxism-Leninism and the working-class movement', the classics would say. 'Fusion' is a metaphor; it too must be divided. The party is the process of dialectical division of Marxism-Leninism and the proletarian movement. It is their torn encounter, always to be remade. Between Marxism-Leninism and the proletarian movement, there is no coincidence (neither spontaneism, nor theoreticism), nor is there simultaneity: theory is in advance, but the movement of the revolutionary revolt is in advance of this advance. Marx did say 'dictatorship of the proletariat' before the Paris Commune. But the Commune, which enacts this directive, is no less a decisive advance on the question of this dictatorship.

Yes, between Marxism-Leninism and the workers' movement there is unity, but it is a unity of opposites. The Marxist-Leninist party is the existence of this opposition. The party is that blind spot from which the proletariat grasps its own class practice, sorts it out, purifies it, concentrates it and prepares another stage of its war. This stage, though, is realized by the masses, not by the party, so that what the party apprehends is always both in front of it (the project) and behind it (the revolt), but never exactly on the same plane. The party is the ever-displaceable organization of the proletarian present, as the split unity of the prevision and the assessment.

That is what Mao means to say: 'The masses are the real heroes, while we ourselves are often childish and ignorant.'[16] The mastery of Marxism-Leninism is the essence of communist leadership. It is the solidity of science. But it is also childish and ignorant, if it believes that history can be done by delegation, by representation – if it believes that it can sidestep the heroic wisdom of the masses, the wisdom given in their irruption, in their practice, without appeal.

And Stalin: he emphasizes that the party certainly does lead, but at the same time it is part of the working class, its detachment.[17] Detachment is quite something else than representation, it is even its opposite: the proletarian party is the opposite of an image. The party is what cuts, what detaches. It is a body of the class at its cut: a threshold.

There is an essential historical instability of the party. This is why it is constantly threatened from within by bourgeois forces of restoration, which take hold on the separateness of the party. The

---

16 *Translator's Note*: See Mao Zedong, 'Preface and Postscript to Rural Surveys' (1941), in *Selected Works of Mao Tse-Tung* (Beijing: Foreign Languages Press, 1965), vol. 3, p. 12.

17 *Translator's Note*: See Joseph Stalin, 'On the Problems of Leninism' (1926), in *Problems of Leninism* (Moscow: Foreign Languages Press, 1940), p. 132 (et pass.). Stalin quotes Lenin's 'Greetings to Hungarian Workers' (1919); see Lenin's *Collected Works*, 4th English edition (Moscow: Progress Publishers, 1965), vol. 29, p. 388.

party, which concentrates the leading force of the proletariat, is also its latent weakness, its worst threat. Repress the revolt in the name of the prevision; smother the new in the name of legitimacy; crush the living present, give in to the shadows, abandon the mobile threshold; raise up the State against the vigorous communism of the masses: the bourgeoisie does not cease to work on the party's essential instability.

What makes of Stalin and Mao great proletarian leaders, aside from their enormous differences, is, among other things, the conviction that the proletarian project is ever to be re-conquered, is ever unstable and corroding from within; the conviction that all inertia tends towards restoration; that there is no place for mechanical adjustment. Lenin, Stalin, Mao submit to an ever more profound critique the reactionary mechanism, the pacifism, the treachery of 'wait-and-see' in the form of reformism and revisionism. The party, according to which the proletariat adjusts itself to its own class practice in terms of the project, must be adjusted in turn in terms of state-construction, since the party is where the greatest burdens accumulate as well. Against this threat, nothing but a counter-threat will do. From this point on, Stalin and Mao part ways completely, but this divergence lies within the history of the proletariat, within the dialectical movement of Marxism-Leninism.

Stalin saw only one possible counter-threat: ubiquitous terror. Be tirelessly wary, above all of the party (practically exterminated in the 1930s), then of the masses as well, at the slightest suspicion of softness or resistance during the magnificent industrial upheaval.

Mao set out from the same idea: the transition submits this dialectical object that is the party to a severe test. And it is a long transition: 'A very long period of time is needed to decide "who will win" in the struggle between socialism and capitalism.'[18] But the answer

---

18   *Translator's Note*: The quotation here is from Mao Zedong's 'Speech at the CPC National Conference on Propaganda Work' (12 March 1957), in *Selected Works of Mao Tse-Tung* (Beijing: Foreign Languages Press, 1977), vol. 5, p. 423

turns Stalin's upside down. The answer is this: have tireless confidence, above all in the masses (confidence in the masses is the central element of the counter-threat), then in the party too, and especially in the torn correlation of the two: the proletarian cultural revolution, which is at the same time an assault of the masses; their anti-State focus on the State, against the reactionary stabilizers of the party; and the reconstitution, regeneration, revolutionizing of the party itself as instability, as threshold, as dialectical inductor of communism.[19]

To these astounding dialectics of history, to these unstable objects, these proletarian uprisings of unheard-of violence and richness, what do the little professors oppose, from their ambush full of desire?

What do they oppose, here as well, to the toil of prevision and of revolt deeply immersed in the workers' divisions, which constitutes the unparalleled affirmative power of Maoist militants? What can they capitalize on against these thoughts, which are real in themselves, ever recast and traversed through and through by proletarian interpellations? Is there anything equal to the project of letting the idea of the party be torn from one's hands by the masses – the party which, in France, is not yet established, not yet decided upon, but still to be proposed and remade? What kind of 'desire' will ever equal the one deployed throughout the profound entanglements and counter-currents of our history, the one that Marxist-Leninists formulate: to hand back to the working class the question of its communist party of the new type?[20]

(translation modified). See also Mao's 'On the Correct Handling of Contradictions Among the People' (27 February 1957), p. 409.

19   *Translator's Note*: 'We must have faith in the masses and we must have faith in the Party. These are two cardinal principles. If we doubt these principles, we shall accomplish nothing.' See Mao Zedong, 'On the Co-operative Transformation of Agriculture' (31 July 1955), in *Selected Works of Mao Tse-Tung* (Beijing: Foreign Languages Press, 1977), vol. 5, p. 188.

20   *Translator's Note*: The project of the 'party of a new type' is a constant concern

What is the final word of these hateful adversaries of all organized revolutionary politics? Read: to complete 'this process that is always and already complete as it proceeds' (p. 383). In effect, to seep out like pus.

In the end, such maxims are innocent. Look at them – these old Kantians who pretend they are playing at scattering the trinkets of culture. Look at them – the time is nigh, and they are already covered in dust.

Translated, with annotations, by Laura Balladur and
Simon Krysl, revised by Bruno Bosteels

---

in Badiou's Maoist, militant thought, beginning with his political work from within the Parti Socialiste Unifié (PSU). See Alain Badiou, Henri Jancovici, Denis Menetrey and Emmanuel Terray, *Contribution au problème de la construction d'un parti marxiste-léniniste de type nouveau* (Paris: François Maspero, 1970). The concept itself was developed by Lenin at the 1912 Prague party conference that refused the party model of Western Social Democracy and split the Bolshevik party from the Mensheviks. It has received its canonic formulation in *History of the CPSU(b): Short Course* (1939), pp.138–42, 172; English at www.marx2mao.org.

11

The Fascism of the Potato[1]

Today we can draw up the most general – ontological – balance sheet of the 1960s and 1970s. At the heart of the matter, there is the idea that the *mass* uprising of May '68 – as unprecedented popular revolt – in the eyes of its intellectual protagonists would not have had a tangible *class* background and that, for this reason, it would be conceivable as an insurrection of the multiple. Students, workers, employees seemed to have risen up in parallel fashion, in a kind of horizontal storm, or a cumulative dispersion, in which on top of everything the petty-bourgeois intelligentsia could vindicate the role of tactical vanguard.

The immediate attack against the pseudo-centres of the unions, and even more so against their bourgeois political guarantor (the PCF) in its objective form, was an essential component of the storm. The entire external unity of the bourgeois type was violently rejected. But this revolt against the pseudo-centres was far from giving way on the spot to the new Maoist thought, which is that of a centre of a new type (of the party of a new type), new not only in its being, but also in its process.

---

1 Review of Gilles Deleuze and Félix Guattari, *Rhizome* (Paris: Minuit, 1976). English translation is Gilles Deleuze and Félix Guattari, 'Introduction: Rhizome', *A Thousand Plateaus*, trans. Brian Massumi (Minneapolis: University of Minnesota Press, 1987). Page numbers in the body of the text refer to this translation.

Contrary to numerous revolutionary workers for whom this was the dominant question, the petty-bourgeois intelligentsia resisted en masse letting itself be traversed by the Maoist question, because the latter concentrated anew the proletarian class point of view, the absence of which at bottom pleased these intellectuals. In order to protect that which had catapulted it onto front stage (the dialectic of an extended mass revolt and a defeated proletarian leadership; of a vigorous ideology and an inexistent politics), the petty-bourgeois intelligentsia forged in haste the concepts with which the organic weaknesses of the situation could be changed into so many apparent strengths. It unleashed into the clouds of pure thought the storm of the Multiple against the pretensions of the One. Down with the centres, whatever they are! Long live dispersion as such! Ontology returned to the Megarian school: only the multiple is affirmative, whereas the One is its oppressive spectre, puffed up with resentment.

Let us admit that the transitory force of this frenzied polycentrism was nourished by the realities of the tempest. To attack *on all fronts* the 'unities' of bourgeois type (labor unions, national unity, the union of the 'Left') gave the movement its vitality. Better the multiple storms of revolt than the unifying tutelage of a bourgeois politics. That is certainly true.

But at the same time, under the anti-organizational pretexts, it is not too difficult to see the rejection of the point of view of class. Its theme was the need to add up the revolts (immigrants, women, ecologists, soldiers, prisoners, students, homosexuals, etc.), to enumerate the punctual social forces to infinity, but obstinately to combat anything resembling the political unification of the people's camp, seized in its antagonistic inflection, in its living class being. Organization and its alleged 'castrating hierarchy' make for broad targets: the One of the multiple in revolt is a question of content, of the politics of the people. Some hid behind the blunders of the form, here and there, in order to deny the content.

Badly camouflaged behind the hatred of militancy was the hatred of the class struggle.

On this shaky ground, one soon would see the One takes its revenge in the depressing guise of the return of the bourgeois politicians from the Union of the Left. At the far end of the Multiple, there is the revisionist Despot; at the far end of Deleuze's literary pleasures, the ministerial smile of Marchais, or the fascist despot, the Medusa-like face of those verbose generals of which our history seems to know the secret. In effect, if the people do not have their own politics, they will enact the politics of their enemies: political history abhors the void.

The ideological leaders of the petty bourgeoisie always commercialize this void, which they praise in the figures of nihilism and the aesthetics of despair, concerned as they are above all with not having to choose and with benefiting from the – considerable – advantages conceded by bourgeois politics, particularly 'democratic' parliamentarianism, all the while bedecking themselves in the spoils of the revolt. What these people abominate and seek to drown out – depending on the case, in the absoluteness of the One or in the pulverization of the Multiple – is the division into two, that is, the dialectic.

In this regard it is interesting to note that, in *Rhizome*, the cunning monkeys of multiplicities, the heads of the anti-Marxist troupe, Deleuze and Guattari, openly strike out at the central dialectical principle: One divides into two. Let us look at the passage:

One becomes two: whenever we encounter this formula, even stated strategically by Mao or understood in the most 'dialectical' way possible, what we have before us is the most classical and well reflected, oldest, and weariest kind of thought . . . the book as a spiritual reality, the Tree or Root as an image, endlessly develops the law of the One that becomes two, then of the two that become four . . . Binary logic is the spiritual reality of the root-tree . . . This is as much as to say that this system of thought has never reached an understanding of multiplicity: in order to arrive at two following a spiritual method it must assume a strong principal unity. (p. 5)[2]

We will not take Deleuze and Guattari to be illiterate. We will thus take them to be crooks. Before giving their readers the shattering directive: 'Be the Pink Panther and your loves will be like the wasp and the orchid, the cat and the baboon' (p. 25), they should warn them that before all these metamorphoses they take their readers to be morons. Only a moron can confuse the Marxist dialectical principle 'One divides into two' with the genealogy for family trees concealed in 'One becomes two'. For what the dialectic says is the exact opposite of the 'strong principal unity' imputed to it; it is *the divided essence of the movement as One*, that is, a principle of *the double precariousness of the One*:

a) The One has no existence as entity, there is unity only from movement, all is process.

b) The process itself has its internal being in scission.

For a Marxist, to think the One is to think the unity of opposites, that is, the movement as scission. Dialectical thinking is the only thinking of revolt in that, precisely, it shakes to its roots the omnipotence of the One. For dialectical thinking, the essence of the One is the labour of antagonism that constitutes it, which is the Two.

Deleuze-Guattari's 'dialectical' arboriculture, all absorbed as

---

2   The rhizome is 'the subterranean stem of living plants that pushes bulbs to the outside and emits adventitious roots to its inferior side'. For Deleuze and Guattari, this botanical being that proliferates at the crossover between the floral and roots is the model of a multiplicity without unitary principle of generation. The rhizome is opposed to the pivoting root, or to the Cartesian tree layering its branches based on the solidity of the trunk. It is the potato against the dandelion or against the fir tree.

they are to oppose the 'multiple' philosophy of the potato to the vertical despotism of the tree, is only a painful falsification. Lenin already remarked that the essence of the dialectic is never the strong and presupposed unity, but unity of *opposites*, which at once relativizes the concept of the One beyond return: 'The unity (coincidence, identity, equal action) of opposites is conditional, temporary, transitory, relative. The struggle of mutually exclusive opposites is absolute, just as development and motion are absolute.'[3]

The problem of the dialectic is certainly not that of an excessive force of the One but rather that of its weakness. Nonetheless to think unity, albeit as tearing apart and as labour of division, this is what philosophy needs to apply itself to, against the leftist Manichaeism, which loses the thread of the unity of opposites and sees salvation only in the redoubling of the One, which flips into its opposite, for in the dialectic two times One does not equal Two but once again One – the only Two worthy of the name being the essence in becoming of the One.

'One divides into two' always means: 'One is equal to the self-dividing-into-two', and never: 'One becomes two'. This is true for the amoeba – as living unity that reproduces itself – as much as for capitalist society – as unity of a struggle to the death between two antagonistic politics.

What good comes from these small mistakes for Deleuze and Guattari?

The thing is that they have recognized in the dialectic their true adversary.

Deleuze's transitory historical strength has come to him from being the bard of the multiple in revolt against the bourgeois One (which, in turn, is only the One of the two that constitutes it as rivalry: two superpowers, two bourgeoisies, classical and

---

3 *Translator's Note*: See V.I. Lenin, 'On the Question of Dialectics' (1915), in *Collected Works: Philosophical Notebooks* (Moscow: Foreign Languages Press, 1961), vol. 38, p. 360.

state-bureaucratic). As long as the bourgeois One is the antagonistic target of Deleuze, at the time of the uprising against the pseudo-centres, there will be a clientele for the scattered revolts. What is to be done against the One of the proletariat, which qua scission is precisely that mobile and precarious One in which the revolt, through the element of antagonism that traverses it, finds not only its place but also its affirmative dimension? Deleuze and Guattari have discovered only this poor trick: forcefully to reduce the dialectic to the One of reactionary metaphysics. Thus they imagine that they can keep the monopoly of the ontology of the revolts.

Unfortunately, the ruse will not do, given that the ontology in question, by circumventing the dialectic, is built against any thought of antagonism. And so we can see how today it validates with total equanimity any figure of speech or action whatever. This is only logical: you cannot think and exalt the pure multiple (the rhizome) without throwing yourself into the flattest of conservatisms, the surest ratification of everything that exists. You will obtain not only the Pink Panther, the baboon and the orchid, but also the white bear – which owes its elongated figure, as we all know, to its exclusive fish-eating regime – the mangy jackal of the last oasis, the moth, and the whole panoply of pungent herbs that you find on the picket fences of the never-ending construction sites.

The great principles of the ontology of the multiple are by themselves the illustration of this conservatism, of this aesthete's acquiescence to the proliferating splendour of all rubbish.

Let us note that of all the possible multiplicities, Deleuze and Guattari hate only a single one: the Two, that detestable figure of choice (and of class choice), and the support of what they condemn the most in the world: morality, which implies options, but also politics (since there are only two of them, proletarian and bourgeois). 'That is why one can never posit a dualism or a dichotomy, even in the rudimentary form of the good and the bad' (p. 9).

All scission having been eluded, all choice circumvented, the rhizome follows its course towards the unbridled apology of the anything whatsoever. This is the first principle: 'Any point of a rhizome can be connected to anything other, and must be' (p. 18).

This 'must be' is famous. Let us understand:

- In a first sense, there exist only individuals, to whom it matters that they can touch each other without having any law, or any demand of class, *separate* them from the enjoyment of unlimited contacts – theory of 'social' relationships as immediacy of the body.

- In a second sense, the federalist political ideology, as the only outcome of a politics of the multiple, of an anti-dialectical politics: May all 'struggles' be in contact, and from this connected egalitarian magma, may they 'converge', as they say. But what will come out of this rhizomatic parliamentary potato? With a cold face, our innocent friends answer: the festival! History speaks another language. One knows since at least the Commune that these 'convergences' of dismembered struggles are the prequel to the failure, the massacre, and the restoration of the One in its most repugnant military forms. Sectarians of the rhizome, remember Chile!

- In a third sense, everything communicates with everything else, there is no irreducible antagonism. There is not the bourgeoisie on one side, the proletariat and the revolutionary people on the other. That is the reason why everything is a formless tubercle, pseudopods of the multiple.

As such, the One takes its revenge in the realm of the universal interconnection.

In truth, it is the Maoist dialectic that thinks the antagonistic weakness of the one, because it apprehends that there is something non-connectable – that in the unity of their conflictive movement, each term of the contradiction never ceases to *sever* that which connects it to the other term. Such is for example the process of the class party: to concentrate, through the practice of antagonism, the means radically to *separate* the people's revolutionary politics from *all* forms of bourgeois politics. Deleuze and Guattari only catapult in the realm of ontology the status that is their own: to run with the hare and hunt with the hounds.

This is what allows the 'pure' concept of multiplicity to take off. Let us study how:

> Principle of multiplicity: it is only when the multiple is effectively treated as a substantive, 'multiplicity', that it ceases to have any relation to the One as subject or object, natural or spiritual reality, image and world. Multiplicities are rhizomatic, and expose arborescent pseudomultiplicities for what they are. There is no unity to serve as a pivot in the object, or to divide in the subject. There is not even the unity to abort in the object or 'return' in the subject. A multiplicity has neither subject nor object, only determinations, magnitudes, and dimensions that cannot increase in number without the multiplicity changing in nature. (p. 8)

The only passage in these confused assertions that makes any sense lives as a parasite on the dialectic. In these 'dimensions that cannot increase in number without the multiplicity changing in nature', one will recognize a bizarre version of the law of conversion of quantity into quality. The rest is on the order of the incantation: the Multiple indeed is a thinkable category only in its contradictory relation to the One. All thinking of the pure multiple carries like its shadow a thinking of the pure One. Besides, one sees this spectre haunt Deleuze and Guattari's discourse all the way to the use of the large capital, as that against which it feigns to build itself up but which it comforts with the unilateral and exalted deviation of its opposite.

This is particularly clear in the recapitulating definition in which

Deleuze and Guattari, sensing that they are ensnared in the Greek traps of the One and the Multiple, imagine that they have changed terrains:

> The rhizome is reducible neither to the One nor the multiple. It is not the One that becomes Two or even directly three, four, five, etc. It is not a multiple derived from the One, or to which One is added ($n + 1$). It is composed not of units but of dimensions, or rather directions in motion. It has neither beginning nor end, but always a middle (*milieu*) from which it grows and which it overspills. It constitutes linear multiplicities with n dimensions having neither subject nor object, which can be laid out on a plane of consistency, and from which the One is always subtracted ($n - 1$). (p. 21)

Complete failure! The subtraction of the One merely metaphorizes the need for both the One and the Multiple, both 'n' and '1', in Deleuze and Guattari's construction of 'multiplicities'. The transparency of the political outcome is a schoolbook exercise, being a matter of the subtractive model '$n - 1$'.

The point is to call for the mass revolts, *minus* the antagonistic factor of unity – that is, minus their traversing by the point of view of class.

The point is to call for the ideas of the revolt, *minus* the Marxist systematization.

The point is to call for the forces of the revolution, *minus* the proletarian party.

But these multiplicities, which are pure only thanks to this 'minus', validate the latter *outside* of themselves as that which endures intact in the One that is so irreducibly hostile to them.

We have seen this in May '68: If you have the mass revolt, but not the proletarian antagonism, you obtain the victory of the bourgeois antagonism (of bourgeois politics). If you have ideas that are just, but not Marxism, you obtain the return to power of the bourgeois reformists of the Parti Socialiste. If you have the objective forces, but neither the programme nor the party, you obtain the revenge of Pompidou's parliamentarianism,[4] you obtain the return to the scene of the PCF and the unions.

The Deleuzian multiplicities are a zero-sum combination of weakness and impotence, of the multiple in revolt and the bourgeois One.

To think the multiple outside the two, outside scission, amounts to practicing in exteriority the dictatorship of the One.

To say that the grandeur and virtue of things lies in their being the 'minus' of (that is, in their external coexistence with) that which is antagonistic to them: that is ultimately all there is to it. There where the point is to accomplish a rupture, by forging the internal unity of that which, within the multiple, divides itself antagonistically from its adversary, Deleuze and Guattari propose a subtraction, a flat indifference. The multiplicities, subtracting themselves from each other as One, peacefully coexist. To play in one's own corner: such is the maxim of rhizomatic multiplicities.

And be sure to note that Deleuze and Guattari have made, in passing, a virtual discovery. What else do they tell us if not that the division of the people is not inherent to the people but is organized by the bourgeois State; that the character of separated unity of this State is the point where all the great differences, all the stratifications, all the hierarchies, are operative so that it is indeed because it is non-popular, subtracted from the people, that the State as One maintains the people as multiple, as partially raised up against itself? The Maoists immediately see in this aspect of things the *class* dimension of the State, at work in what is the real historical body and defines the permanent stakes: the organization of *all the people* in bourgeois dictatorship. The conclusion leaves no doubt: there can be no regained unity of the people except in the antagonistic affirmation of the other point of view of class, the proletarian one, and

---

4 *Translator's Note*: Georges Pompidou famously was France's Prime Minister under President Charles de Gaulle during and right after the events of May 1968, before succeeding de Gaulle as President in 1969.

in the destruction by the masses of the bourgeois unity, which has the State as its centre.

For Deleuze and Guattari, the situation is completely different. From the fact that the bourgeois One causes the division of the people, they infer the excellence of the division conceived of as indifference to the One, as non-antagonism. The State is the One of our multiple weakness? Let us be even more divided, let us subtractively affirm our division, and we ourselves will be plentiful. Which *we*? In truth, the *we* prescribed by the One. We should say: *In actual fact* Rhizome *draws the conclusion of the excellence of the bourgeois One*.

Can one dream up such disarmament, such complacency towards the worst? Whoever renounces antagonism and thinks in the element of indifferent affirmative multiplicity has the *need* sooner or later to kneel down, under the cover of the cult of the Self, before the real political powers, before the separate unity of the State. This is why Deleuze and Guattari are pre-fascist ideologues. Negation of morality, cult of natural affirmation, repudiation of antagonism, aestheticism of the multiple, which outside of itself, as its subtractive political condition and its indelible fascination, leaves in abeyance the One of the tyrant: one prepares for the kowtow, one is already bowing down.

To cleanse themselves of the accusation of fascism, it will not be enough for Deleuze and Guattari to argue – in a familiar pirouette – that they are even more so than people think.[5]

---

5 'We have been treated as fascists; we will never be so enough, so much are we aware, we at least, that fascism is not only that of others. Groups and individuals contain microfascisms just waiting to crystallize.'

[*Translator's Note*: Here, as in the rest of his review, Badiou quotes from the separate publication of *Rhizome* as a small separate volume in French (Paris: Minuit, 1976), p. 28. In the English translation of 'Introduction: Rhizome', as part of *A Thousand Plateaus*, the corresponding fragment no longer entails such a clear pre-emptive move against possible objections: 'You may make a rupture, draw a line of flight, yet there is still a danger that you will reencounter organizations that restratify everything, formations that restore power to a signifier, attributions that reconstitute a subject – anything you like, from Oedipal resurgences to fascist concretions. Groups and individuals contain microfascisms just waiting to crystallize' (pp. 9–10).]

12

An Angel Has Passed[1]

Lardreau and Jambet have this to tell us: the Cultural Revolution in China, or May 1968 in France, all this was not by any means a process, a politics, or anything whatsoever pertaining to our world. In order to ground such an insurrection of spirits, we need to have recourse to an ontology of the Two, to Manichaeism. The Rebel stood up, and it was not even *against* the Master, but elsewhere altogether, in a world the essence of which is the eternal contemplative insubordination, in which no master proffers his organizing discourse any more. Faithful in this regard to the spirit of 1793 that the ex-Gauche Prolétarienne reclaimed,[2] Lardreau and Jambet postulate that the revolution is nothing if it is not the instance of

---

1 Review of Guy Lardreau and Christian Jambet, *L'Ange: Ontologie de la révolution*, vol. 1 (Paris: Grasset, 1976).
2 *Translator's Note*: Guy Lardreau and Christian Jambet were part of the Maoist formation of the Gauche Prolétarienne, which was founded in September 1968 and brought together ex-members of the March 22 Movement and the Union des Jeunesses Communistes Marxistes-Léninistes (UJCML). After its official interdiction in May 1970, the GP continued its activity around the journal *La Cause du Peuple*. With their joint book *L'Ange*, Lardreau and Jambet became associated with the New Philosophers, many of whom likewise reneged on their Maoist past. Badiou discusses this trend in 'What is a Thermidorean?', in his *Metapolitics*, trans. Jason Barker (London: Verso, 2005), pp. 124–40; and in an interview with Eric Hazan, 'Roads to Renegacy', *New Left Review* 53 (2008): 125–53.

Absolute Liberty, the vanishing of any and all effects of domination. Their concept of the revolution is the bourgeois democratic revolution pushed to the end. It is the Great Democracy, that of the abolition of tyranny all the way into the concept. Any endeavour that, in closest proximity to the rebellion, restores in actual fact a new mastery – even, or above all, when it claims to be part of the revolution – is the specific form taken by the world of the master put to the test by that of the rebel. We thus must distinguish:

- the Cultural Revolution, the angelical assumption of the Rebel, advent of the other world, absolute liberty detached from the flesh and from death;

- the ideological revolution, the renewal of the master, the re-inscription in this world beyond the storm; novelty, to be sure, but novelty *of the cultural counter-revolution.*

This distinction becomes clear in a systematic comparison of the cultural revolution in China with the cultural revolution in Christianity. Just as Saint Paul, genius of the ideological revolution, founded the Church and its mastery in closest proximity to a massive spiritual revolution of Manichaean essence, which broke in two the history of the ancient world (a rupture of which subsequently the trace can be deciphered in all popular heresies), so Maoism has finally regenerated the party and Marxism in closest proximity to an uprising (that of the Red Guards) that posited, at the heart of bourgeois history, the pure demand for another world, for another history.

The ideological revolution, Christian or Marxist, is that through which the power of absolute alterity of the Rebel changes the world of the Master, so as to restore homogeneous submission. To invert rebellion into absolute submission: such is the trap set up for the rebel by the new masters and their new discourse. One sees this in what the monks have been able to capture and enslave from the hatred of the world delivered by the spiritual insurrection of the poor at the dusk of the ancient world. They have made this into an order, a prison, an implacable law. The absolute liberty of primitive vagrancy, the fury of egalitarianism and contempt for the world have become (after the ancient master has given way to the new Christian master, instructed by rebellion) the absolute obedience to the Superior, hierarchy, the divine order of a radically unified world.

One likewise sees this, according to Lardreau and Jambet, in what the party has been able to do with the Red Guards in China, under the law of a new concept of the dictatorship of the proletariat: laborious obedience, sacrificial soaking, indoctrination, endless cult of the Boss and the Text, barbarism of lifeless thought.

In both cases, one category supports the point of inversion: that of Work. The monks dig in the garden, the Red Guards clear the virgin soil. Those who were part of *the other world* chained themselves to the most menial of chores on earth. The ideological revolution is that by which they manage to do so on their own free will, caught in the *semblance* of the revolt that is revolutionary ideology.

And so it is that Lardreau and Jambet teach us how, having departed after '68 for the unlimited revolt, the advent of an other Thinking, the hatred of the revisionist semblance, they found themselves again made stupid, reciting in a drone three sentences from Mao, and bowed over to the ground under the absurd orders of the coterie of adventurers who 'led' the Gauche Prolétarienne. A sad story, indeed, from which few have come back and for which, we can imagine, they require vast detours in order to clarify the reasons.

Yet this book is discouraging from the start, being both fascist and idealist:

- absolutely idealist: 'The real is nothing but discourse. Or again: the world is a fantasy' (p. 18).

- fascist: 'At present I can write this directive, which no
  longer serves me any purpose but which we had to scream
  for five years now: *the hatred of Thought is 100 percent
  reactionary if it is not accompanied by the hatred of the
  Proletariat*' (p. 136).

The hatred of thought *and* the hatred of the proletariat: now there is
an exemplary ideological figure of fascism. One will not find shelter
behind the cult of the masses to ward it off.[3] Fascism, too, is a
violent doctrine of the masses.

We will thus cross this out: fascism is not up for discussion.

But could we not say the opposite? This is an anti-fascist text
insofar as it radically negates all political biology, evacuates all
naturalism, flushes out any pre-fascist abjection disguised behind
the undifferentiated apologies of enjoyment. Yes, we support the
effort behind this diatribe against Lyotard 'the liar' (p. 213),[4] this
furious demand for some morals, this indictment against Sade for
being the most detestable semblance of the rebel, the worst complacency, the worst of all masters (p. 184). We are satisfied when these
sectarians of the Angel say about Lyotard (and we would also say
about Deleuze) that 'this is not theory but a programme: that of the
spirit's fascization' (p. 219).

And it is a materialist text at least in that its question comes to it
from history, from a *well-centred* history, without mistakes in what

---

3   Masses that are themselves unconscious, registered in the in-itself: 'The
masses have no need for the Angel, since they are it' (p. 79). What appears here
is the treatment of the question of the intellectuals as separate, as the exception of
the for-itself: '[The Angel] here is only the demand, for the intellectuals, that they
should not make themselves any illusions about Ethics' (ibid.). In actual fact, the
Angels have no use for the masses or for their real movement. Only the salvation
of the intellectuals is at stake.

4   *Translator's Note*: In the final section of *L'Ange*, titled 'Le menteur' (The
Liar), Lardreau and Jambet deliver a vicious attack on Jean-François Lyotard's
'libidinal' works *Des dispositifs pulsionnels* (Paris: UGE, 1973), *Dérives à partir de
Marx et Freud* (Paris: UGE, 1973), and *Économie libidinale* (Paris: Minuit, 1974).

matters: unlike so many of their old comrades who infamously lent their hand, Lardreau and Jambet refuse to falsify the force and the novelty of the Cultural Revolution, May '68, the team of 'Maoists from *La Cause du peuple*', and do not deal in their oblivion. They remain the watchmen of that irreducible fidelity to the revolt, of that *other thing* of which they caught a glimpse and which they put into practice. The real trace of the movement of the world for them was not simply a misstep in the sand before the rising tide of bourgeois rewards.

More profoundly still, it is on the basis of this unprecedented experience and its trenchancy that they legislate philosophy, and not the other way around. By this we mean to say that Lardreau and Jambet stand steady on the question of the revolt, and must conceive of a system in which it would be radically averred, albeit against the pessimistic system inherited from Freud and Lacan.

In effect, for Lardreau and Jambet, philosophy means Lacan. But from the fact that Lacan forecloses the revolt, they courageously draw the lesson that another world must be found – that of the rebel – from which Lacan, as a way of thinking, would in turn be foreclosed.

And yet, this wager of fidelity, of which we measure the grandeur compared to the vast majority's self-abasement under the iron rule of the new bourgeoisie, progresses uncomfortably and, after all is said and done, changes over into a quasi-desperate prophecy, a millenarian Expectation. The suffocated shout: 'The Angel must come' (p. 36). What apparently was the bedrock of an indelible popular upheaval, in the facts as much as in its effects, evaporates into an aleatory question, into an empty allegory of Return. The Rebel is not at work in this world at all; he is, or he was, the Visitation:

> I have tried to show how the two great themes through which the cultural revolution spoke became rarefied and subverted. In the end, the Rebellion reverted back precisely to Obedience; such is

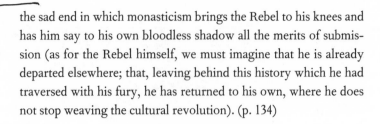

the sad end in which monasticism brings the Rebel to his knees and
has him say to his own bloodless shadow all the merits of submission (as for the Rebel himself, we must imagine that he is already
departed elsewhere; that, leaving behind this history which he had
traversed with his fury, he has returned to his own, where he does
not stop weaving the cultural revolution). (p. 134)

Traversing and obscure retreat: the cultural revolution is not
woven into the visible, or into what exists. Finally, one begins to
doubt the possibility of its reign, and Lardreau and Jambet, who
had started from the most exalting certainty – something of the
Revolution has taken place – fall into the banal and appalling
question of the whole petty-bourgeois intelligentsia that comes
undone after 1972: Have we not dreamed? Was it not perhaps
rather nothing, in fact? Ethical nihilism takes over from the
audacity of the wager for the Rebel. Suddenly, a modest calculation is all it takes for our precipitate angels to maintain their
rickety faith:

> And I would also say this: that even if we are wrong, we would still
> be right. Yes, if there were no one like us, as fooled as we are
> supposed to have been, and at the risk of playing the role of the
> halfwit, the world would still be worse than it is. It is in this sense
> that we say, like Rousseau and in the same sense in which he said it,
> that no man would dare say that he is better than us. (p. 153)

How can that which uplifted them so forcefully revamp its historical substance into that moral 'optimism' that on all sides is
surrounded by the powers of doubt?

This exemplary path, which pounces on a just idea (the history of
the world, starting in the 1960s, has given its course a new orientation) to the point of making it vanish, is one that we must follow
because it is the path towards a proper balance sheet. And this
assessment interests us, revolutionary Maoists for whom the

Cultural Revolution and May '68 are not memory sites but the substance of the present.

It is between two negatives that Lardreau and Jambet seek to take hold of the new, of the revolt.

First, the philosophy on the basis of which they operate: Lacan, theoretician of the discourse of the Master who negates any world that would not be this discourse. Let us schematically recall its main reference points: man is sex and language. His desire is nothing if not articulated, under the law of the signifier. But the signifier's leverage is the lack qua cause. Castration, which renders equivalent Desire and Law and ties them together in a space with neither outside nor inside, is what seals a destiny: that desire, because it is the desire of the Other, follows the rule of the Same. Caught in the defiles of the signifier in which its object presents itself only as absence, desire yields under the master-signifier, the signifier of lack, the signifier of the null signified. There is the (sexuated) body only under the Law, disposed by the discourse of the Master. Rebellion is, in its desire of the Other, desire of absolute submission. Lacan in 1969 interpellates the boisterous leftists at Vincennes: 'What you aspire to as revolutionaries is a master. You will get one.'[5]

Lardreau and Jambet want to think of rebellion according to this Freudian reasoning that, without hypocrisy, restates, as the Greeks had already done, its radical impossibility.

Let us consider the antinomy: Lacan necessarily institutes the revolution in the past tense, as a 'transcendental question'.[6] If indeed

---

5 *Translator's Note*: See Jacques Lacan, 'Analyticon' (intervention at Vincennes, 3 December 1969), in *The Seminar of Jacques Lacan*, ed. Jacques-Alain Miller, book XVII, *The Other Side of Psychoanalysis*, trans. Russell Griff (New York: W.W. Norton, 2007), p. 207.

6 A transcendental question of which the correlate, as in Kant, is faith – the obscurantist gnosis with its languor, its inoperative and honeyed style, which in Jambet's *L'Apologie de Platon* (Paris: Grasset, 1976) makes for a painful contrast with what the Angel is still capable of mustering in terms of force, thanks to its

what has taken place (Cultural Revolution, May '68, Gauche Prolétarienne) is measured by the fact that Lacan declares it impossible, then there is no other option but to formulate the question as follows: How is the revolution possible?

This is the point from which everything becomes derailed, because there is no reality to such a question. Not even for Lardreau and Jambet, unless they already stand on the threshold of oblivion. The revolution *is*. It is even historically, in a sense, the only thing that *is*, since its adversaries have no internal political being except by opposition to it: counter-revolution. To approach the ensemble of what is by asking the Kantian question of its possibility is to feign to extract oneself from this ensemble, it means to install oneself already in the fictive figure of the beyond.

The turning trick with the Angel consists in the following: to interrogate the Cultural Revolution from the point of its (Lacanian) impossibility, and thus as that which, by raising the question of its existence, leads one to establish this existence in inexistence: another world, a beyond, the kingdom of Angels.

Whereas the Maoists say, inversely: *the* world is the one averred in the revolution. Do not search for another one, not even that of the counter-revolution, of which we can decipher the internal law from the sole point of view of our reality. The Cultural Revolution and May '68 are not encircled, quasi-unintelligible exceptions. They are reality itself, and that from which all reality proceeds.

In the order of the history of the world, the revolt is first, and the master second. The intelligence of the world (and of discourses) is not the Law, it is antagonism.

No Lacanian balance sheet of May 1968 is possible. There is only an impossible balance sheet. It is of this impossibility that Lardreau and Jambet embroider the legend, in all its historical affectations (the origins of Christianity). Such is the first negative behind their statement.

---

connection with the jolts of history.

And the second: from May 1968 and the Gauche Prolétarienne, Lardreau and Jambet retain exclusively, as pure alterity, the negative aspect. End of knowledge, hatred of inherited culture, gruelling activism, annulment of the self. Consider this exalted portrayal:

> We all dreamed, at bottom, of arriving at an equally vulgar reading of *Capital* as of the Bible, that of the 'anthropomorphists'.
>
> We had the desire of a sovereign amnesia. Their fury to destroy the temples, to profane the pagan tombs in order to sell off the marble to the lime traffickers – all this was the same amnesia. We would have burned down the National Library in order to suffer as needed . . .
>
> We wanted humility; the saint, with his status of abjection, of refuse, of waste, with which the intellectual most naturally felt in agreement, that is what we were aiming for . . .
>
> And it was only normal that, wanting to break with all philosophy of survival, with that '*conatus*' that classical meditation puts in the place we know, we would meet up again with Christian detachment: contempt for all things, oblivion of parents and horror of the world itself; normal, too, that the most aberrant forms of the destruction of the body and the exhaustion of its desires would reappear. We say the resurgence of a craze for fasting, a dementia for wakefulness. And, filled with marvel, we understood that we were no longer in fear of death. (p. 132)

Lardreau and Jambet only have a subjective and empty memory of the storm. A bit earlier, they evoke the 'intellectual's contrition' and declare having been able to verify, in the 'pain of the soul', 'the tears of love that accompany those of penitence'. Of the rise of the workers, Lardreau and Jambet, in their incredible narcissism, have filtered only this absurd directive: we (the intellectuals) were all, let us be nothing.

And paradoxically, this is the reason why they have changed so little, no matter what they say. It is through and through their old being that speaks, that of the bourgeois intellectual who still cannot get over the fact that he has had to give up his ordinary delights, except that by making *his* renouncement into an exalted form – into a singular idealist philosophy – he in fact abstains from renouncing *all the way to the end*. Lardreau and Jambet have renounced so little that here they are back at it. If Lacan remains standing for them, it is because the revolted *askesis*, the madness of the extenuated body and the unravelled mind, which are the privileged and negative contents of their experience, assured the permanence of the ordinary intellectual in them.

The proletarian revolutionary is not about renouncing, it is affirmative scission.

Lardreau and Jambet have shared with their Deleuzian adversaries this aristocratic conviction that revolutionary militancy is first the absolute break, the spitting on oneself, the interior purge. Their sole force lies in vindicating this negative figure, instead of drawing from it a pretext, like all the others, to vilify what they were for four years and demanding the return of yesteryear's enjoyments.[7] The bottom line, however, remains, with its distinguished weakness: the frantic will of the bourgeois intellectual to survive, albeit in the tragic-imaginary representation of its dispossession.

Lardreau and Jambet will thus proceed between two negatives that respond and consolidate one another, even as they pretend to exclude each other: Lacanianism, which in the name of the world as discourse negates the revolution; and Manichaean *askesis*, which according to the revolt negates the world.

The encounter between Lacanianism and May '68 thus ends up in this variant of the transcendental question from which its object vanishes: how is the negation of the world possible?

7　That is, the serene benefit of imperialism's bread crumbs, the salary of anti-proletarian and anti-Marxist watchdogs, and the stipend for useless buffoonery.

The gigantic detour via the origins of Christianity, which occupies the bulk of the book,[8] thus becomes easy to clarify. 'My kingdom is not of this world' indeed serves as a maxim for the Rebel, insofar as this world is that of the Master.

What Lardreau and Jambet, as decided Linbiaoists, call 'cultural revolution' is the absolute and imaginary irruption of the outside-world, the definitive eradication of egoism. It means 'breaking the history of the world in two' (p. 226). It is the ideologism of the remaking of oneself, fascist in its sectarian ambition of absolute purity, of absolute simplicity, of starting anew *from scratch*.

Indeed, from scratch ultimately means from the people itself, the working people, in whom purity and simplicity must urgently and violently be inculcated. From the Angel to the militarized torturer, there is only a short step. We have seen this with Lin Biao and with the Japanese Red Army, just as we have caught a glimpse of this in the Gauche Prolétarienne.

Sure, Lardreau and Jambet know that 'negation of the world' means nothing. It is necessary to posit (to wager) an *other* world. The Angel tirelessly reiterates the simple proposition: there are two worlds (two discourses). Henceforth, everything thus splits according to an exemplary Manichaean ontology, yet starting from the 'common notions' of any petty-bourgeois balance sheet of May '68: Body and Discourse.

The body must be divided into non-sexuated body and sexuated

8 And which makes up its detailed interest. To apprehend the force of the masses and of rupture that for almost two millennia gave power to *this* religion is a historical project far superior to many others. To those who say, with their menacing eyes and believing they are taking us apart, that the Maoists are the Christians of our time, let us answer the following: If you mean that Marxist thought for us has popular power for centuries to come, agreed! We even hope to do better. There where Lardreau and Jambet go astray is when they think in terms of repetition and believe that our immobile question is that of Christianity: 'As long as the hitherto eternal model of cultural revolutions, as long as Christianity will not have been understood, what is this knowledge with its enchanting novelty to us?' (p. 232). It is for this eternity that we have no use.

body (or, according to the Church Fathers, into glorious body and flesh). The second comes from the Master, the first does not.

The discourse is the discourse of the Master that disposes the sexuated body. But the glorious body, the Angel, is standing according to the discourse of the Rebel:

> To say that sex is from the Master is a tautology, just as it is to say that the discourse of the master is from the Master. But if sex is not the body, then the discourse of the Master is not the discourse. And, since we are speaking about the West, reason is not thought . . .
>
> If we did not hold onto this disjunction between thought and reason, between body and sex, we would state the impossibility of the rebellion . . .
>
> There must be not two objects of desire, which is where the Church Fathers went astray, but two desires.
>
> Or rather a desire, that is, a sexual desire, and a desire that has nothing to do with sex, not even the desire of God: rebellion. (pp. 35–6)

At this point, the discouragement of critique seizes us anew. After all, this dualism with its two slopes is a piece of nonsense. It is as false to say that sexuated desire comes from the Master as that non-sexuated desire would have nothing to do with it at all. Let alone that the division of the worlds would pass through all this.

What to say, except that nothing, especially not the revolt, authorizes the pure Two of metaphysics? The revolt in an exemplary way is that which splits – so not the Two, but rather the One dividing into Two, and thus revealing what the One has always been – the becoming of its own scission. There is unity only of opposites. At this point, two contradictory ontologies (metaphysical and dialectical) confront each other without mediation. Lardreau and Jambet in fact maintain the non-split metaphysical consistency of the One, and thus cannot reduce it except by positing *on the outside* the heterogeneity of this One. Their maxim, against 'one divides into two', is 'two times one'.

One understands that Lardreau and Jambet are opposed to:

1) the anarchism of the multiple such as, on the basis of Nature, it prepares fascism (*any* desire *whatsoever* will do in the machinic multiplicities). Here is where their aphorism serves them: 'The Two is that which protects the multiple from the universality of the Master' (p. 68);

2) the usurpation of the One as semblance and perversion such as it is incarnated in the revisionist project of the State, in social-fascism (*no* desire will do, all mass experience is null and void, only the State, as the sole capitalist, produces politics).

But the bias they adopt is fictive. For it is the 'numerical' problematic itself that induces a falsified ontology. We will not escape the alternating constraints of the Multiple and the One by the angelical postulation of the Two. What shakes up the arithmetical framing of ontology is the unconditional primacy of becoming as scission. But this is what Lardreau and Jambet cannot want, *due to their politics*. What irreducibly supports dialectical thinking indeed is the fact that at the heart of the mass movement the class *antagonism* becomes actualized.

Lardreau and Jambet complain that the masses in the end for them (and, they pretend, for the Red Guards as well) have not been anything more than an abstraction:

- 'In fact, the masses are totally absent from our stories. All the time *named*, they are only a pure signifier, exactly identical to the name of the President' (p. 150);

- 'The Masses had never been anything else for us than a pure signifier, the master-signifier' (p. 136).

Let us leave the Red Guards for the time being. But, for the Gauche Prolétarienne, this is indeed what happened: You have taken the masses in their symbolic indivision, in the signs offered to you by democratic violence, the naked revolt, the story of oppression. Now, it is the masses worked by antagonism, in which a class point of view conflictually affirms itself, that make the politics of revolution. This is what you have rejected with the GP. This is what corners you into such a disastrous assessment. When you lacked the signs, you lost your head and the world. What took to the stage was no longer a symbol but the real: antagonism.

Antagonism is in fact the organizing element, *because it is absent*, of the balance sheet drawn up by the Angels. You present yourselves as heroes of two heterogeneous worlds, but the truth is that at the first approach of some effectively heterogeneous element – when your brutal exaggeration of symbolic violence was no longer worth anything – you have dissolved. And still today, you pay the philosophical price of what was the errancy of the GP: a fictive politics, insofar as the thought that governed it pretended to stick to the masses and to circumvent all class antagonism. For the masses without classes have no existence, and become indeed the pure sign of the Idea of the revolution.

The disavowal of antagonism is such that Lardreau and Jambet are forced to posit the two worlds, that of the Master and that of the Rebel, in an eternal coexistence:

   II. The multiple can be brought back to Two. The Duel is there from the Origin. The One perhaps can/cannot be conquered.
   III. Each Plerome always offers itself for an Aion, even if the contemplation may resolve it into history. (pp. 23–4)

History, in which the coexisting eternity of the two worlds resolves itself, is only a contemplative disposition. What offers itself as revolt is, in its very being, the opposite: *peaceful coexistence*.

What is properly excluded is that one world may come into being only in the destruction of another.

And this eternal juxtaposition of the Master and the Rebel sheds light on what is so striking about this book with its violent allure and 'people-like' intention (do they not write, on p. 142, that their goal is to 'give intellectuals reasons for putting themselves on the side of the people'? But what is given with one hand is taken back with the other, the good old hand of scepticism, which makes simple things into obscure enigmas: 'Of course, we would still need to know what is meant by the people!' Four years with La Cause du Peuple have left them apparently perplexed): *what predominates therein is the bourgeois conception of the proletariat.*

When the petty-bourgeois intelligentsia attributes the totality of the revolution to the sole movement of the masses in revolt, it completely dissolves its appearance, so much is it the case that the sporadic and circumstantial evidence of the massive storms enters into a contradiction with the very idea of a radical transformation (one that goes to the root) of society and the State. The only thing that gives the mass irruption its political body and changes the revolt into a world is the class nature of antagonism; it is the existence, *in this world*, and as the only law of its existence, of two modes of politics (of two conceptions of the world) that are rigorously contradictory, so that one of them can be practised only according to the actual destruction of the other. Outside of this, the revolt is only the vain repetition of infinite protest, whereby its historical being is unravelled and undone. But this is false: we hold and prove that history is the history of victories, and that there is no example of a class antagonistic to the existing order that, once built into a political class, does not vanquish in the end and remodel the world in its image.

Lardreau and Jambet want another path, because their concept of victory is entirely caught in the metaphysics of the *definitive* as their always silent and worn-out Master. Let us translate: they are afraid and despise the dictatorship of the proletariat. Their ontological

leap consists in ideally changing the sporadic nature of the movement into the eternity of coexistence.

This mental operation aims to annihilate (in the realm of ideas)
the proletariat. Stripped of its political essence, which is its totally
antagonistic dimension, reduced to being nothing more than a
component of the masses, the proletariat is dissolved into the
working class. The proletariat is no longer anything more than its
social being – that is, work. It then becomes easy to pretend, as
Lyotard and Deleuze have always done, that class is never anything
but a piece in the discourse of the (capitalist) Master, since it is
Capital itself, via the labour in which it is born and reproduces itself.

About this baffling idea we should energetically say that, since
Marx, it is very precisely *against* it that the Marxist theory of the
revolution has constructed itself. To make it into the main stum-
bling block in a 'critique' is one of those tenacious stupidities for
which petty-bourgeois anti-Marxism always has had a knack. On
the whole, when the openly and frankly reactionary bourgeoisie
sees in all violence and antagonism the hand of the Marxist conspir-
acy, and thus in the end the hand of the proletarians and the
commies, it shows that it knows more about Marxism than our
doctors of philosophy who pontificate about the enlarged reproduction of Capital and the 'alienation' of the workers.

We regret that Lardreau and Jambet flounder in these worldly
mistakes. Look:

> With Mao we used to say: 'Let the young children come to me who
> are like the sun at eight or nine o'clock in the morning.' With this
> old man, who was sufficiently in the grip of amnesia to speak only
> in logia, this supremely irresponsible old man who before the
> hordes, those torrents of Red Guards assembled on the square
> where the sun rises, launches the maddest and most profound idea
> of the Cultural Revolution, and whose Marxism rang out better
> than anything we have been able to say since then, than anything we
> will ever say: the proletariat is you! (p. 133)

This is a profound idea, indeed, but one that is exemplarily *Marxist*: to recognize the point of view of class *there where it exists*, that is, *in the fraction of the revolutionary people that materializes the antagonism*, has always been the very principle of Marxist action. Spearheading the revolt against the new revisionist bourgeoisie, against the bourgeoisie within the party, the Red Guards in 1966 are the proletariat, in the precise extent to which the proletariat is never anything else than what practises to the end the political antagonism with the bourgeoisie. And in January 1967, it is the working class of Shanghai that will be the proletariat, taking the lead in that the working class, when it takes the stage *qua proletariat*, delivers the overall unity of antagonism and irreversibly breaks the encirclement, which is something that nobody knows how to do in its place.

Whoever comes and tells us that the proletariat is the worker exploited by capitalism proves the nullity of his Marxism, at the most basic level: the grasping of the notion of the class struggle pure and simple.

In order for the proletariat to exist and construct itself, it must divide itself, purge itself from the *social* class of exploitation and unionism and take control of the whole political world, the revolutionary politics of the whole people. And it is true that Maoism and the Cultural Revolution have brought this Marxist certainty to its extreme.

The mediocre critique of Work, reflected as critique of the proletariat and of Marxism, is only the adoption of the categories of the adversary: the purely 'social' and objectivist vision of the phenomenon of the worker. Here we see the second component of the balance sheet of the GP, the terms of which Lardreau and Jambet are incapable of understanding. Because it was caught in the apolitical ideology of the masses, the GP transported everywhere the reduction of the worker to its social being – its 'mass' being, exactly. The factory, productive labour, the 'fascism' of the workshop: this was as far as people looked. *Because it was 'massist', the GP was also workerist.* And this is what made it fail in the face of the unions and the PCF, whose workerism is the cement that holds together the mass base at the centre of the working class.

Lardreau and Jambet are aware that they have been driven back into submission and into political stupidity by the disingenuous cult of labour, of work as it presents itself in the capitalist factory:

> One of the essential stakes of the ideological revolution, in the definition it proposes of the two lives, certainly consisted in authorizing a new doctrine, the fixation of work, by affirming its *dignity* . . . This considerable intellectual revision, of which we have tried to specify the articulations, is finally ordered around the notion that Work had to be posited as ideal . . . In this [original Christian cultural revolution] I thought I saw the same hatred that had driven us [in the Gauche Prolétarienne] in terms of what this break between Work and Thought had constructed as a rarefied life, the same hatred of those who possess the knowledge of this world. I did not yet realize that they and we had both been busying ourselves with an account that equally overestimated productive labour for the benefit of the Master. (pp. 128–31)

> It seems to me that in the end it was the same trick with the hatred of Thought that threw us into the arms of the Master, we who believed to have broken with him once and for all: we Marxists, too, had been subordinated to the love of work. (p. 136)

Marxism, the theory and practice of the political antagonism bourgeoisie/proletariat, has nothing to do with 'the love of work'! Let us leave that to the Giscardian propaganda about the rehabilitation of manual labour! The Gauche Prolétarienne, alas, was not far removed from it! Abstract hatred of thought, abstract love of working-class labour: the GP oscillated between the ideological revolt and the unionizing workerism before it disappeared, leaving at loggerheads the two antagonistic politics – bourgeois and proletarian, revisionist and Maoist.[9]

It speaks to Lardreau and Jambet's honour that they abhorred the workerist stupidity, which is the greatest contempt and the greatest obstacle that separates the working class from antagonism, from the revolutionary programme, from the political class. For what is political, what is fully antagonistic, is only that which concerns the people as a whole.

But, unable in a lasting way to peg themselves to the real movement, obsessed with the idea of Salvation, there they went – sliding from the hatred of workerism to the hatred of workers to the hatred of politics, of Marxism, and of the proletariat.

Unable to remove the proletariat from its pure social and objective being, they also do not manage to break with the object of their critique – the workerist definition of the worker, the unionist definition of Marxism, the apolitical, non-antagonistic and counter-revolutionary definition of the class struggle. And there they are – counter-revolutionaries in turn, spitting on class in the name of the masses, on the revolution in the name of the revolt, and on action in the name of contemplation.

Lardreau and Jambet are completely off when it comes to Maoism and the very essence of the Cultural Revolution; off when it comes

---

9   To what extent workerism shapes the memory of all those who were caught in the debacle of the GP, all the while comforting their catastrophic assessment with a completely revisionist and bourgeois social materialism, can also be seen in someone like Jacques-Alain Miller, another restored Lacanian. In his 'Discourse in Rome' (*Ornicar*), the only hint at his past as a 'Maoist' evokes the useful humility that overcame him when he found, among the workers, the superiority of people who can do things with their hands. This is certainly not a bad feeling. But one understands that a few years sufficed to exhaust the *political* charm of this lesson and to legitimize that beyond it one returns without too much fuss to the logic of the signifier. This is a fact of our time: when the lessons learned from history are exclusively lessons in 'materialism', one can attend to one's business and even find the Programme Commun reasonable. The only lesson from which there is no turning back is the lesson of antagonism.

to what might have saved them, perhaps, from the mystical duality of eternal worlds as well as from their Lacanian pessimism, namely: antagonism as such, the locus for which is the people's revolutionary politics that endlessly divides itself from bourgeois politics and, in the storms of revolt, sharpens the edge that organizes the new proletarian world.

Let us say that through the absurdly metaphysical demand for purity, through the hatred of the proletariat and of Marxism, and through the cult of the apolitical masses, what seems fascist about Lardreau and Jambet is not what they criticize in the GP but what they have kept from it, which is ultimately what tied their group to the bourgeoisie and to revisionism: a restricted and negative view of the proletariat, limited to the workshop and concentrated in the syndicalism of committees of struggle.

To separate masses from class is to annul both together with politics. The 'masses' become a pure name, class is absorbed into the union. And so Lardreau and Jambet come back to the point of departure: bourgeois intellectuals, nothing more – or if you like, nothing less.

This angelical account, no matter how senseless it may seem, in the end is only conservative. Nothing from what marked the adventure and collapse of the 'Maoists of *La Cause du Peuple*' is at bottom put into question. Taken at face value, purely at the level of its immediate consciousness, this experience is merely arranged and exported into the sumptuous décor of Manichaeism. The Angel brings no news that we did not know already, and, with its Gnostic paraphernalia, sinuous and savvy, is only the visitation of the shadow of a shadow.

13

Custos, Quid Noctis?[1]

I. A BOOK OF PHILOSOPHY

Philosophers have recently been eclipsed by their very overabundance, by the singular avatar of their 'newness'. However, if one reads them, which is perhaps an exercise for which they are not destined, the philosophers in question participate in newness only in the sense of the wise maxim from Don Leopold Augustus in Claudel's *The Satin Slipper*, who after having demanded novelty, which he loves, for he must have 'the new at any cost', clarifies: 'But what new?' He goes on: 'New is but the lawful issue of our past. New and not strange. New that is the development of our natural situation. New and new again, but let it be exactly like the old!'[2]

Jean-François Lyotard announces that, with *The Differend*, he has written his book of philosophy. Are we dealing with a novelty in every aspect identical to the old? It seems that Lyotard takes 'philosophy' in a sense that is heterogeneous to the one promoted in the magazines. That we are dealing with his book of philosophy, in

1 Review of Jean-François Lyotard, *Le Différend* (Paris: Minuit, 1983). English translation is Jean-François Lyotard, *The Differend: Phrases in Dispute*, trans. Georges Van Den Abbeele (Minneapolis: University of Minnesota Press, 1988). Page numbers in the body of the text refer to this translation.

2 *Translator's Note*: See Paul Claudel, *The Satin Slipper; or, The Worst is not the Surest*, trans. Rev. Fr. John O'Connor (New York: Sheed & Ward, 1945), p. 146.

the singular, furthermore amounts to the highly risky confession that what he previously put out in books was not philosophy but rather no doubt some pre-philosophical intervention, or philosophemes in the raw.

Already the style puts the Lyotard of the differend in a differend with the previous Lyotard. Here you have an upstanding and demonstrative prose, which stubbornly follows its own guiding thread; a will to investigate with care all possible objections; an overall argument as dense as it is lucid. As opposed to Gide's Prometheus, Lyotard has to throw no powder in our eyes, no smoke bombs, and no pornographic pictures, in order to convey his message and appease the readers of newspapers.

Lyotard's essential reference points go back to the Flood – before the blessed Ark of that pen-pushing Noah, before the zoo of essay-mixers. Look at his antiquities: Protagoras, Gorgias, Plato, Antisthenes, Aristotle, four notices on Kant and Hegel . . . All these respectable people are in each case given the treatment they deserve, following procedures of punctuation and transcription that showcase an astonishing novelty and a rectitude that, adapted to the most modern of tasks, knocks over our academic convictions.

Lyotard himself declares that his three sources are the Kant of the third *Critique*, the second Wittgenstein (the one from the *Investigations*), and the last Heidegger. From the first, he borrows the critical doctrine of multiple domains of judgement, the impossibility of the whole, the syntax of the imperative, and the function of feeling in justice; from the second, the analytic of language; and from the third, the withdrawn figure of Being. *The Differend* contains indeed nothing less than a taxonomy of genres of discourse and their incommensurability, an ethics, a politics, and an ontology. This goes to show to what extent, as Lyotard announces, we are dealing with a book of philosophy.

Let us nonetheless ask this announcement to appear before the conceptual tribunal of the book itself. In it, indeed, we can find written that 'The stakes of philosophical discourse are in a rule (or rules) which remains to be sought, and to which the discourse cannot be made to conform before the rule has been found' (p. 97). Does *The Differend* belong in this sense to the philosophical genre? Is it an autonymous book, insofar as it contains its very own definition?

The first disquieting fact is that the prescription of having to search for a rule constitutes a rule and, thus, that we dispose of a possible measure of conformity of the discourse to its own genre, contrary to what has been concluded. Let us begin by congratulating Lyotard for taking this type of 'sophistic' argumentation extremely seriously. Lyotard in effect rejects the (modern? postmodern?) temptation of considering the instruction of a proof a useless thing. He repudiates the style of the essay. This is confirmed by the new and convincing usage of the 'paradoxes' of Protagoras or Antisthenes. Just as Plato, according to Pascal, prepares Christianity, so scepticism, according to Lyotard, prepares the critique. After this, we will refute the refutation by saying the following: the fact that the philosophical discourse is in search of its rule does not constitute a rule for this discourse, because 'search' means that the type of linkage between phrases is neither prescribed in advance nor governed by a result.

The uncertainty as to the rule is averred in the properly de-regulated multiplicity of the procedures of linkage. In Lyotard's book you will find, alternatively, the argumentation that touches upon the logical genre, the exegesis of a name ('Auschwitz'), the textual insertion (authors), the putting into play of an addressee ('you say this . . ., then . . .'), the definition of concepts and their species, the formulation of an impasse, as well as many other techniques. In this sense the book is made up entirely of passages, following a trajectory from which no totality whatsoever results: 'What are we doing here other than navigating between islands in order paradoxically to declare that their regimens or genres are incommensurable?' (p. 135).

This book is philosophical insofar as it is archipelagic. The rule of navigation that the navigation itself allows to be mapped out is

none other than that of the differend, that is, the rule of a multiplicity that no genre can subsume under its rules. Philosophy here states
that its rule is to respect that which no rule can render commensura-
ble. This respect is therefore addressed to the pure 'there is' [*il y a*].
Evil can be philosophically defined: 'By evil, I understand, and one
can only understand, the incessant interdiction of possible phrases,
a defiance of the occurrence, the contempt for Being' (p. 140). The
book's last word thus will be: the 'there is' [*il y a*] is invincible. One
can, one must bear witness against the interdiction, in favour of the
occurrence.

Yet this last word still requires that we navigate our way up to it.

II. A LINGUISTIC ATOMISM

It has been a while since one of Samuel Beckett's heroes proclaimed
that 'what happens are words'.[3] Such is Lyotard's point of departure: the designation of 'what happens' as 'phrase'. With this
gesture, Lyotard places himself within what he calls the 'linguistic
turn' of Western philosophies. But, to be clear, this historical time-
liness is only an opportunity. It does not serve as a legitimation.
The philosophical rule sought after by Lyotard is not conformity
with the spirit of the time. In order to establish that there is no possibility of going back further than the phrases, a linked argumentative
chain is required. Lyotard rediscovers, subjects to critique, and
diverts the Cartesian procedure of evidence. What resists absolutely the radical doubt is not, as Descartes believes, the 'I think'
but the 'There was this phrase: I doubt'. Any resistance to letting
oneself be convinced that there was this phrase is itself, whenever it
produces itself, nothing but a phrase. Whereas Descartes thinks he
establishes the subject of the enunciation as the ultimate existential
guarantee of the enunciated, Lyotard limits himself to the following: the enunciation happens. What exists is therefore not the 'I

---

3   *Translator's Note*: See Samuel Beckett, *L'Innommable* (Paris: Minuit, 1953), p. 98.

think' that underlies the 'I speak', it is on the contrary the I (of 'I speak') that is an inference (an instance, that of the addressor) of the existent-phrase, or, to be more precise: of the event-phrase.

The central unity of the I thus finds itself emptied out. Insofar as what exists is of the order of the event-phrase (and not of its underlying unitary guarantee), there is no reason to subtract oneself from the evidence that there are phrases, and not one phrase. Thus, what is inaugural is a linguistic atomism in which nothing is anterior to the multiplicity of occurrences of phrases: neither the subject, as we have seen, nor the world, since the world is nothing but a system of proper names. 'Phrase' thus designates the One of the multiple, the atom of sense qua event.

Here begins an austere analytic, of which I give only the broad lines.

That the phrase is the absolute One also signifies the multiple, both in the order of simultaneity and in that of succession.

At the level of the simultaneous, the One of the phrase is distributed over four instances:

A phrase presents what it is about, the case, *ta pragmata*, which is its referent; what is signified about the case, the sense, *der Sinn*; that to which or addressed to which this is signified about the case, the addressee; that 'through' which or in the name of which this is signified about the case, the addressor. (p. 14)

The programme of investigation thus requires that one occupy oneself with presentation itself (chapter on the referent, on what is presented, then on presentation); with sense (critique of the speculative-dialectical doctrine of sense in the chapter on the result); and with the couple addressor/addressee (chapter on the obligation).

At the level of the successive, the fundamental axiom holds that if a phrase takes place, it is necessary to make a linkage. Even silence is a phrase, which links up with the preceding one. And, of course, there is neither a first phrase (except in the stories of origin) nor a final one (except in the anxiety before the abyss). This point is as simple as it is crucial: 'For there to be no phrase is impossible, for there to be *And a phrase* is necessary. It is necessary to make linkage. This is not an obligation, a *Sollen* [an ought to], but a necessity, a *müssen* [a must]' (p. 66).

No less crucial with regard to this necessity, however, is that the mode of linkage, for its part, is contingent: 'To link is necessary, but how to link is not' (p. 66). This time the investigation demands that one occupy oneself with the linkage of phrases. Now this task is in turn double: 'The rules of formation and linkage that determine the regimen of a phrase have to be distinguished, as we have been doing, from the modes of linking that stem from genres of discourse' (p. 136).

The study of regimens of phrases in some way is syntactical. The internal disposition of the four instances of the One of a phrase varies according to whether this phrase is cognitive, prescriptive, exclamatory, etc. The study of genres of discourse by contrast is strategic, because a genre of discourse unifies phrases in view of a success. Or again: the regimen of a phrase governs a mode of presentation of a discursive universe, and these modes are heterogeneous. A genre is defined by its stakes: 'A genre of discourse imprints a unique finality onto a multiplicity of heterogeneous phrases by linkings that aim to procure the success proper to that genre' (p. 129). These stakes are in turn heterogeneous. There is thus a double qualitative multiplicity – that of regimens, which is intrinsic because it concerns the syntax of presentation; and that of genres, which, unifying intrinsic heterogeneities according to a finality, organizes a veritable war around the question, 'how to link?'. For the contingency of the 'how to link?' combined with the necessity to link manifests the multiple of phrases as a conflict surrounding any occurrence of a phrase.

Now, the fact that there is the war of genres founds the omnipresence of politics. Lyotard in effect gives an intra-systematic concept of politics:

> Politics is the threat of the differend. It is not a genre, it is the multi-
> plicity of genres, the diversity of ends, and par excellence the question
> of linkage. It plunges into the emptiness where 'it happens that . . .'
> [Politics] is tantamount to Being [*à même l'Être*]. (p. 138)

Lyotard, as we see, does not concern himself with justifying politics
through sociology, or through the economy. It is not the extant-being
(the figures of the communitarian bond) that sustains politics, since
politics plunges into the gap where it is convenient and inconvenient
to link. The being of politics lies in naming the being-which-is-not, the
risk and suspense around which the polemic of genres revolves.

Turning his back on the modern anthropologization of politics
no less than on its postmodern economicization, Lyotard abruptly
proposes a concept of politics of which the discursive, trans-generic
inscription is, and can only be, ontological.

III. AN ONTOLOGY

Lyotard's ontology is not autonymous, it does not belong to the
genre of which the rule of linkage is that the second phrase must
present the presentation contained in the first (p. 78). In passing one
will recognize Hegel, the beginning of the *Science of Logic* – the
Nothing that presents the presentation of Being, and Becoming that
presents the presentative disintegration.

Lyotard is certainly not Hegelian, or at least: Lyotard does not
conform to the Hegel who figures in Lyotard under the rubric of the
result, of the speculative genre. What is said of being will not
present the presentation, but rather name the unpresentable. So
there is not a discourse on being but a displaced aphoristics, included
in the archipelagic trajectories.

Let us pinpoint the aphorisms of being:

- 'The necessity of there being *And a phrase* is not logical (the question "*How?*") but ontological (the question "*What?*")' (p. 66).

- 'There is *There is*' (p. 74).

- 'The occurrence, the phrase, as a *what* that happens, does not at all stem form the question of time, but from that of Being/non-Being' (p. 74).

- '*Is* doesn't signify anything, it would designate the occurrence "before" the signification (the content) of the occurrence . . . Rather *is* would be: *Is it happening?* (the *it* indicating an empty place to be occupied by a referent)' (p. 79).

And now the aphorisms of non-being:

- 'Joined to the preceding one by *and*, a phrase arises out of nothingness to link up with it. Paratax thus connotes the abyss of Not-Being which opens between phrases, it stresses the surprise that something begins when what is said is said' (p. 66).

- 'What is not presented is not. The presentation entailed by a phrase is not presented, it is not. Or: Being is not. One could say that when an entailed presentation is presented, it is not an entailed but a situated presentation. Or: Being grasped as an existent is non-Being' (p. 77).

- 'This is why negation is needed to present the entailed presentation. It is only presentable as an existent, that is, as non-Being. This is what the word *Lethe* means' (p. 78).

- 'Genres of discourse are modes of forgetting the nothingness or of forgetting the occurrence, they fill the void between phrases. This "nothingness" is, nevertheless, what opens up the possibility of finalities proper to the genres' (p. 138).

Put otherwise: from the fact that there are only phrases, it results that non-being encircles being. I say 'encircle', because there is a triple intervention of non-being.

First, insofar as any phrase presents a universe (according to the four instances of its One), it does not present this presentation, which is presentable only in a 'second' phrase and which thus, rigorously speaking, in the time of the occurrence itself, is not (for what is only is what the occurrence entails in the presentation).

Second, being itself is not, for no phrase is its occurrence. Being has no presentable, phraseable identity, or again: 'Being is not Being, but *There is*'s' (p. 138).

Third, the nothingness 'borders' upon each occurrence of phrase, an abyss in which the question *How to link?* plays itself out and which is covered up, filled, but never annulled, by the genre of discourse in which the contingency of the mode of linkage presents itself afterward as necessity.

The *There is* of a phrase, being unphraseable by this phrase, is not. Philosophy's polemical safeguarding tries to preserve the occurrence, the *Is it happening?* and thus, against the unitary pretence of a genre, to preserve the encircling of the *There is* by the triplicity of non-being. The philosopher keeps up the vigilant agitation surrounding the vulnerability of non-being in which the occurrence comes up. The philosopher is the armed guardian of non-being.

Who are the enemies of the philosopher? In philosophy (but this is the non-philosophy inherent in philosophy), the speculative (Hegelian) genre, which in the figure of the result pretends to disintegrate the non-being of being, to render explicit the *There is*, to present the presentation, to flaunt and thus to disavow the occurrence. In politics, the enemy is the predominance of the narrative genre, which tells of the origin and the destination, acts 'as if the occurrence, with its potentiality of differends, could come to completion, or as if there were a last word' (p. 151).

The apogee of this narrative politics is Nazism (the Aryan myth).

This politics wants the death of the occurrence itself, which is why it wants the death of the Jew – the Jewish idiom being par excellence the one that stands precisely under the sign, '*Is it happening?*'

As a subtle warrior, Lyotard makes the speculative genre and the narrative politics wage war against each other, showing that his two principal enemies are mutually annihilating. Indeed, of what possible result is Auschwitz the sign? What can the Odyssey of the absolute Spirit possibly find to 'sublate' in Auschwitz? The silence in which Nazism phrases itself stems from the fact that it has been beaten, like a dog – but it has not been refuted, nor will it be, and thus it will not be sublated and will not ever contribute to any result. With regard to the Nazi massacres, the linkage is a feeling, not a phrase, nor a concept. All speculative phrases are found wanting. Only the feeling denotes that a phrase has taken place and thus that a wrong, perhaps an absolute wrong, has been committed. The feeling in which an unphrased phrase announces itself is the watchman of justice, not in the place of a simple damage but in the essential place of a wrong.

What is a wrong? We will distinguish it from a damage, which can be pleaded, in a common idiom, determining a litigation for which there exists a power entitled to decide among the phrases. Wrong refers to the differend, just as damage refers to litigation: there is no recognized power of arbitration, but complete heterogeneity of genres, with the will of one of them to be hegemonic. A wrong cannot be phrased in the genre of discourse in which it should make itself recognizable. The Jew cannot be heard by the SS. The worker has no place in which to find recognition for the fact that his labour power is not a commodity.

The hegemonic will of a genre of discourse necessarily pretends to know what is the being of any occurrence. This will posits that the being-nothing is. Now, precisely (encircling of being by nonbeing), 'you never know *what* the *Ereignis* is. A phrase, in which idiom? In which regimen? The wrong is still in anticipating it, that is, in prohibiting it' (p. 85).

IV. CAPITALISM, MARXISM, DELIBERATIVE POLITICS

Is Marxism not the discourse that pretends that its genre – its success – consists in giving voice to the wrong? Is it not the heterogeneous speech of the victims of Capital? What does Lyotard think of Marxism today?

In a first approach, Marxism may seem nothing but a nefarious combination of speculative 'philosophy' (as Lyotard says: 'prisoner of the logic of the result') and a narrative politics ('purity' of the proletariat, myth of the final reconciliation). Alas, history over-abundantly illustrates that a certain Marxism is devoted to interdicting the occurrence, feeding the love of structures and the hatred of the event.

But things are more complex. Lyotard does not bog himself down in the muck of vulgar anti-Marxists. He thinks that 'Marxism has not come to an end, but how does it continue?' (p. 171). How does Lyotard inscribe this non-end, in which discursivity must give in to feeling?

There is first the analytic of capital, subsumed under what Lyotard calls 'the hegemony of the economic genre', of which he offers a concise and convincing description. He is right to say, against any metaphysics of the producer or of work, that the essence of the economic genre consists in the annulment of time in the anticipatory figure of exchange: 'The economic phrase of cession does not expect the phrase of acquittal (counter-cession), it presupposes it' (p. 173). The economic genre (capital) organizes the indifference to the 'there is', to the heterogeneous punctuality, since all that occurs has its reason in an accountable null sum to come. The economic genre 'dismisses the occurrence, the event, the marvel, the anticipation of a community of feelings' (p. 178).

It is above all under the hegemony of the economic genre that nothing has taken place but the place.

Should we at least recognize that this interdiction of marvels – which has the merit of rejecting all narratives of origins – involves a wager on a 'pluralistic' politics that protects our liberties? Such is, today, the common thesis, as is well known. It is even, at the level of facts, the quasi-universal thesis: the law of the market and the tyranny of exchange value are certainly not admirable, but parliamentary politics, which cannot be dissociated from them, is the least of all evils.

Lyotard does not make explicit references to pluralism, to parliaments, or to civil liberties. Democracy is not the axis of his value system. His path consists in gathering the determinations of modern politics under the unique concept of the 'deliberative form of politics', whose origin is Greek and whose peculiarity lies in the fact that it leaves empty the political centre and, thus, de-substantializes the phrase of power. On this account we can indeed say that 'deliberation is a concatenation of genres, and that suffices to let the occurrence and differends sprout up within it' (p. 150).

And yet, here comes a fundamental proof: not only is the deliberative form of politics not homogeneous with capitalism, but it is an obstacle to it. Let us quote the passage in its entirety for those who would be tempted to imagine that Lyotard is about to rally himself – for the cause of democracy, as always – to the politico-economic order of the West:

> Thus, the economic genre of capital in no way requires the deliberative political concatenation, which admits the heterogeneity of genres of discourse. To the contrary, it requires the suppression of that heterogeneity. It only tolerates it to the degree that the social bond is not (yet) entirely assimilated to the economic phrase alone (cession and counter-cession). If this is one day the case, political institutions will be superfluous, as national narratives and traditions already are. But then, without the deliberative concatenation where the multiplicity of genres and their respective ends can in principle be expressed, how could the Idea of a humanity, which is not the master of 'its' ends (a metaphysical illusion), but which is sensitive to the heterogeneous ends implied in the various known and

unknown genres of discourse, and capable of pursuing them as
much as possible, maintain itself? And without this Idea, how would
a universal history of humanity be possible? (p. 178)

So it is still and always against capital, in the name of the differend
– of which Marxism connotes the feeling – that the point is to save
the Idea of a humanity engaged along the paths of the multiple.

Deliberative politics remains for Lyotard a polemical ideal. It is
not supported but fatally threatened by the 'liberty' inherent in the
economic genre. Philosophy has not stopped being militant. And
there are grounds for hope, since the differend sprouts up relent-
lessly, since 'The *Is it happening?* is invincible to every will to gain
time' (p. 181).

V. SEVEN PUNCTUATIONS

1. The metaphors that present the theme of the differend in
   Lyotard's book are juridical in nature: litigation, damage,
   wrong, victim, tribunal . . . What is the (Kantian) presupposition wrapped within this apparatus? Once it is critical,
   is philosophy constrained to phrase itself in close proximity
   to law and right?

   I posit that there are two species of philosophical
   procedure, two ways of being faithful to the directive of
   having to search for one's rule without knowing it: the
   one whose paradigm is juridical, and the one whose paradigm is mathematical. Of course, I leave aside the
   speculative genre.

   Is Lyotard caught in the great return of right? Of human
   rights? Even if he correctly establishes that for the expression 'rights of man', which is inappropriate on account of
   both terms, it would be convenient to substitute 'authority
   of the infinite' (p. 31).

One could not have said it better. But, outside of the mathematical paradigm, 'infinite' is an erratic signifier. As for right, it is literally dominated by its hatred of infinitude.

2. I would also say: the burden of the juridical metaphor extends itself to Lyotard's definition of knowledge (of phrases from the cognitive genre). Everything for him depends on the question of the referent, as is the case for the judge, especially the English judge, who seeks to establish in a regulated manner which fact the statements of all parties involved can be assigned to. It is with the aid of the referential ('real') criteria that Lyotard distinguishes the cognitive genre from the purely logical genre:

> The cognitive genre is that of knowing whether the combination of signs with which it is dealing (the expression, which is one of the cases to which the truth conditions apply) makes it possible or not that real referents correspond to that expression. (p. 51)

I say that mathematical phrases just by themselves – but, in my mind, all phrases of which the effective stakes concern the truth – belie this definition of the cognitive genre. What makes the 'there is' of mathematical thinking is not governed by any procedure for establishing a real referent. And yet, we are not for this reason remitted to the pure 'possible truth' of the logical form. Lyotard's epistemology remains critical (juridical). It does not possess the radicality of his ontology. It is not oriented according to the good paradigm.

3. A wrong is committed in this book towards the mathematical paradigm, by reducing it to the logical genre. Here the filiation stems from Frege, Russell and Wittgenstein. As far

as I am concerned, I posit that the mathematical genre surely is not reducible to logic, in the sense that it is said about the latter that 'If a proposition is necessary, it has no sense' (p. 51). One recognizes what can only be called the irresponsible remarks that are recurrent in Wittgenstein. It is manifest that mathematical propositions make sense, and it is no less clear that they are necessary. The attempt to see in them only regulated and arbitrary word games has fizzled out and, besides, it never has been anything more than an inconsistent provocation.

I would like to phrase the feeling inspired in me by the wrong done to mathematics by the postulated hegemony of the logical genre. I will only say the following – which is close to Albert Lautman's theses – namely, that mathematics in its history is the science of being qua being, that is, being inasmuch as it is not, the science of unpresentable presentation. One day I will prove it.[4]

4. From this can be inferred that the book does not completely ground the fact that the phrase would be the One of the occurrence – or that it would be its appropriate name. The critique of the speculative genre, exclusively centred on the theme of the result, misses the essence of the dialectical message, which is the non-arithmetical primacy of the Two over the One, the logic of scission as form of the occurrence itself. We could establish this for the mathematical paradigm, inasmuch as its necessity lies in naming and giving consistency to pure being as existential scission of the nothing and the name (for example: 'the empty (nothing) set (name) exists').

---

4   *Translator's Note*: This 'proof' is, of course, the fundamental wager behind Badiou's *Being and Event* which, at the time of this review of Lyotard's *The Differend*, was already in the making but would not be published until five years later, in 1988.

Or again: in true knowledge, there is no case, there is a double. This is something that the juridical arrangement, which demands the case, forbids to perceive.

5. The notion that the occurrence may be Two allows us to respond differently from Lyotard (who answers negatively) to the question that he poses: 'Are some phrases and genres strong, and others weak?' (p. 158). From the point of view of politics, or of philosophy – which are not exactly genres – the occurrence that can be captured as Two, can be qualified according to its force in proportion to whether it breaks down the rule of the hegemonic genre that endeavours to count it as One. For politics, as well as for philosophy – precisely because their vocation is the safeguarding of the occurrence, the vigilance over the opening of the '*Is it happening?*' – there is no equality of occurrences. This is a serious differend with *The Differend*. I posit that what an event destroys in the genre in which it is phrased (hence the need for it to be two: inscribed and ex-scribed) measures the power of the scission, the singularity of the occurrence. 'What it destroys' means: the dysfunction of the genre's capacity to count the Two as One, to anticipate the sum of the generic scission.

6. Hence also why Lyotard's polemic against the (Hegelian) subject, the *Selbst*, the self, of which modern history teaches us the fission, is incomplete. It affects only the subject of speculation, the *telos* of the result, the totalizing interiority. But 'subject' today designates something else completely. To be brief: a subject – that is, a subject-process – is what keeps open the gap of the Two of the occurrence, what insists in the interval between events. A subject is deduced from a dysfunction in the count-as-One of the event. Such a subject summons no whole, nor needs language (as being)

in order to be. Lyotard is justified in excluding that there exists such a thing as *the* language. But Lacan also excludes this, since for him what ex-sists is not 'the language' but language, non-all. And for me as well, 'history' does not exist, only historicity, in which the duplicity of events is the symptom for a vanished subject.

7. And, consequently, since the nineteenth century, we can name proletariat the series of singular events that politics maps as heterogeneous to capital. One will object that there is no reason to keep this name, 'proletariat'. I say that there is also no reason *not* to keep it. The truth is as follows: one has wrongly made 'proletariat' function as a juridico-historical name, the subject of responsibility in history. But 'proletariat' is a mathematico-political concept – it always has been, insofar as it refers to effective procedures. The subject here is that of the interval and the excess, in a history that in-exists, and an archipelagic, de-generated dispersion. If the name embarrasses you, take that of 'political capacity' ('communist' or 'heterogeneous'), or of 'non-domination' – whatever you want: the point will always be the putting into place of a strategy, here and now, in an a-generic discourse, of that which enjoins us to fidelity to an evental series. Politics always amounts to discovering that fidelity is the opposite of repetition.

One will have understood that my differend with *The Differend* is situated at the point from which I pronounce that, if for me Jean-François Lyotard, the philosopher, looks too much to the desert of the multiple, we must nevertheless admit that 'the shadow of a great bird falls on his face'.[5]

---

5   *Translator's Note*: Allusion to a line from one of Badiou's favorite poets, Saint-John Perse, in the long poem *Anabase* (*Anabasis*). See Saint-John Perse, *Selected Poems*, trans. Mary Ann Caws (Princeton: Princeton University Press, 1982), p. 37.

15

Gilles Deleuze, The Fold: Leibniz and the Baroque[1]

There is a book that proposes a concept (that of the Fold). The concept is seized within its history, varied within the fields of its application, ramified by its consequences. It is furthermore distributed in accordance with the *description* of the site where it is thought and the *narration* of its uses. It is inscribed as law, both of the place and of what takes place. It is *what matters*. These are the last words of the last page: 'What always matters is folding, unfolding, refolding' (p. 137).

An attentive and discerning exposition of Leibniz, leaving unexplored not even the subtlest detail, serves as a vector to Deleuze's conceptual proposition. The next to last statement of the book is: 'We remain Leibnizan' (p. 137). What is important is clearly not Leibniz, but that we – compelled to fold, unfold and refold – we moderns remain Leibnizian.

This raises the question as to what is meant by 'remain'. Are we going to open an academic discussion on Deleuze's historical exactitude (both exemplary and beautiful: he is a perfect reader)? Are we

---

1   Review of Gilles Deleuze, *Le Pli: Leibniʒ et le baroque* (Paris: Les Edition de Minuit, 1988). English translation is *The Fold: Leibniʒ and the Baroque*, trans. Tom Conley (Minneapolis: University of Minnesota Press, 1992). Page numbers in the body of the text refer to this translation.

going to oppose a wily and nominalist Leibniz, a shrewd eclectic, to the exquisitely profound and mobile Leibniz exhibited in Deleuze's paradigm? Do a survey of the texts? Engage in a genealogical quarrel?

Let us leave all that aside. This rare and admirable book offers us a vision and a conception of *our* world. We must address it as one philosopher to another: for its intellectual beatitude, the enjoyment of its style, the interlacing of writing and thought, the fold of the concept and the non-concept.

Perhaps there is also the need for a discussion, but it will be a very difficult one in that it would begin with a debate on discord, on the *being* of discord. Because for Deleuze, following Leibniz, this is not to be found between true and false, but between possible and possible. Leibniz justified this by some divine measure (the principle of the best). Deleuze, not at all. Our world, that of an 'enlarged chromatism', is an identical scene 'where Sextus will rape *and* not rape Lucretia' (p. 82). A discord is the 'and' of the accord. To perceive the harmony of this, we need only stay within the musical comparison of 'unresolved accords'.

If we wish to maintain the vigilant tension of the philosophical *disputatio*, we have no choice but follow the thread of the central concept, even if it means abandoning Deleuze's equanimous sinuosity. It is absolutely necessary to unfold the Fold, to force it into some immortal unfolding.

We shall operate within the yoke of a triplet, a triple loosening of the lasso Deleuze uses to capture us:

- The Fold is first of all an *anti-extensional* concept of the Multiple, a representation of the Multiple as a labyrinthine complexity, directly qualitative and irreducible to any elementary composition whatever.

- Next, the Fold is an *anti-dialectical* concept of the Event, or of singularity. It is an operator that permits thought and individuation to 'level' each other.

- The Fold is finally an *anti-Cartesian* (or anti-Lacanian) concept of the subject, a 'communicating' figure of absolute interiority, equivalent to the world, of which it is a point of view. Or again: the fold allows us to conceive of an enunciation without enunciated, or of a knowledge without an object. The world as such then will no longer be the fantasy of the All, but the pertinent hallucination of the Inside as pure Outside.

All these *anti*s are put forth with softness, the marvellous and captious softness of Deleuze's expository style. Always affirm, always refine. Dividing unto infinity in order to lead division itself astray. Enchanting the multiple, seducing the One, solidifying the implausible, citing the incongruous.

But we shall stop here. Stop short.

I. THE MULTIPLE, ORGANICITY

It is not by abruptly imposing an order that we might hope to get to the end of the Deleuzian dodge. An example: We need to read no farther than twenty lines in before coming across this: 'The multiple is not only what has many parts but also what is folded in many ways' (p. 3). One is immediately tempted to make an objection: to begin with, a multiple is not composed of its *parts*, but of its *elements*. Furthermore, the *thought* of a fold is its spread-as-multiple, its reduction to elementary belonging, even though the thought of a knot is given in its algebraic group. Finally, how can 'what is folded in many ways' be *exposed* to the folding, topologized into innumerable folds, if it was not innumerable to begin with in its pure multiple-being, its Cantorian being, its cardinality – indifferent to any fold, because containing within itself the being of the fold, as a multiple *without qualities*?

But what is the value of this punctuation in the terms, or parameters, of Leibniz-Deleuze? They reject a set-theoretical ontology of elements and belonging, and therein would lie a – classical – line of the *disputatio* on the One and the Multiple. Leibniz-Deleuze's thesis is that the point, or element, cannot have the value of a unit of matter: 'The unit of matter, the smallest element of the labyrinth, is the fold, not the point' (p. 6). Hence the constant ambivalence between 'belonging' (of an element) and 'inclusion' (of a part). We can say that Leibniz-Deleuze's ontology apprehends the multiple as a *point-part*, that is, as an extension (an unfolding) or a contraction (a fold), with neither atom nor vacuum. This is diametrically opposed to a resolute 'set-theoretical' orientation, which *weaves out of the void* the greatest complexities, and *reduces to pure belonging* the most entangled topologies.

And yet, this line of examination is hardly established before it is ramified, unfolded, and complicated. Deleuze-Leibniz's ruse is never to leave alone any pair of oppositions, never to be overtaken or taken over by any dialectical scheme. You spoke of a point, of an element? But we know very well that Leibniz-Deleuze distinguishes between three kinds: the *material* or *physical* point-fold, which is 'elastic or plastic'; the *mathematical* point, which is both pure convention (as extremity of the line) and 'a position, a site, a focus, a place, a point of conjunction of vectors of curvature'; and finally the *metaphysical* point, the mind, or subject, which occupies the point of view or position that the mathematical point designates at the conjunction of the point-folds. So that, Deleuze concludes, you must distinguish 'the point of inflection, the point of position, the point of inclusion' (p. 23). But he also concludes, as we have just seen, that it is impossible to think of them separately, each supposing the determination of the other two. What figure of the Multiple 'in–itself' can be opposed, without appearing foolish, to this ramified evasion of the point under the sign of the fold?

Now philosophy, according to Deleuze, is not an inference, but rather a *narration*. What he says about the Baroque can be applied admirably to his own style of thought, whereby 'description replaces the object, the concept becomes narrative, and the subject becomes point of view or subject of expression' (p. 127). What you will find then is not a case of the multiple, but a description of its figures, and, even more so, of the constant passage from one figure to another; you will not find a concept of the multiple, but the narration of its being-as-world, in the sense that Deleuze says very rightly that Leibniz's philosophy is the 'signature of the world' and not the 'symbol of a cosmos' (p. 127); and neither will you find a theory of the Subject, but an attentiveness to, a registering of the point of view into which every subject can be resolved, and which is itself the end term of a series that is likely to be divergent, or without Reason.

Thus, when Deleuze credits Leibniz with a 'new relation of the one and the multiple', it is principally for what is diagonal, subverted, indistinct in this relation, inasmuch as 'in the subjective sense' (and so the monadic), 'the one must also have a multiplicity "of" one and a unity "of" the multiple' (p. 126). Finally, the 'relation' One/Multiple is de-linked and undone to form the quasi-relations One/One and Multiple/Multiple. These quasi-relations, all subsumed under the concept-without-concept of the Fold, the One-Fold as reversal of the Multiple-Fold, are what is aimed at by description (which is what the theme of the Baroque is used for), narration (the play of the World), or enunciating position (Deleuze neither refutes nor argues, he states). They can neither be deduced, nor thought within the fidelity of any axiomatic lineage or any primary decision. Their function is to avoid distinction, opposition, fatal binarity. The maxim of their use is the chiaroscuro, which for Leibniz-Deleuze is the *tincture of the idea*: 'and so too clarity plunges into darkness, and continues to plunge deeper and deeper; it is natural chiaroscuro, a development out of obscurity, and it is *more or less* clear to the degree that sensibility reveals it as such' (p. 90).

The method is typical of Leibniz, Bergson, and Deleuze. It marks a position of (subjective or enunciative) hostility with respect to the ideal theme of clarity, which we find from Plato (the Idea-Sun) to Descartes (the clear Idea), and which is also the metaphor of a certain concept of the Multiple, the one that demands that the elements composing it can be exposed, by right, to thought *in full light* of the distinctiveness of their belonging. Leibniz-Bergson-Deleuze does not say that it is obscurity that is valued. He does not polemicize in such frontal manner. No, he *nuances*. Nuance is here the anti-dialectical operator par excellence. Nuance will be used to *dissolve* the latent opposition, of which clarity magnifies one of the terms. A continuity can then be established locally as an exchange of values at each real point, so that the couple clarity/obscurity can no longer be separated, and even less brought under a hierarchical scheme, except at the price of a global abstraction. This abstraction by itself will be foreign to the life of the World.

If the thought of the Multiple deployed by Deleuze-Leibniz is so fleeting, if it is the narration, without any lacuna or outside, of the folds and unfolds of the World, this is because it is neither in opposition to an other thought, nor set up on the outskirts of an other. Its aim is rather to *inseparate itself from all thoughts*, to multiply *within* the multiple all possible thoughts of the multiple. For 'the really distinct is neither necessarily separate nor separable', and 'nothing is either separable or separated, but everything conspires' (pp. 55–6).

This vision of the world as an intricate, folded, and inseparable totality such that any distinction is simply a local operation; this 'modern' conviction that the multiple is such that it cannot even be discerned as multiple, but only 'activated' as Fold; this culture of the divergence (in the serial sense), which compossibilizes the most radical heterogeneities; this 'opening' without counterpart, 'a world of captures instead of closures' (p. 81): all this is what founds Deleuze's fraternal and profound relationship to Leibniz. The multiple as a large animal made up of animals, the organic respiration inherent to one's own organicity, the multiple as *living tissue*, which folds as if under the effect of its vital upsurge – in perfect contradiction with the Cartesian concept of extension, which is punctual and regulated by the shock: Deleuze's philosophy, for its part, is the capture of a life that is both total and divergent. No wonder he pays tribute to Leibniz, who upholds, more than any other philosopher, 'the affirmation of a one and same world, and of the infinite difference or variety in this world' (p. 58). No wonder he defends this audacity, 'baroque' par excellence: 'a texturology that attests to a generalized organicism, or to a ubiquitous presence of organisms' (p. 115).

In fact, there have never been but two schemes, or paradigms, of the Multiple: the mathematical and the organicist, Plato or Aristotle. Opposing the Fold to the Set, or Leibniz to Descartes, reanimates the organicist scheme. Deleuze-Leibniz does not omit remarking that it must be separated from the mathematical scheme: 'In mathematics, individuation is what constitutes a determination; now the same does not hold for physical things or organic bodies' (p. 65).

Animal or Number? This is the cross of metaphysics, and the greatness of Deleuze-Leibniz, metaphysician of the divergent World of modernity, is to choose without hesitation for the animal. After all, 'this is not only an animal psychology, but also an animal monadology. The two are essential to Leibniz's system' (p. 109).

The real underlying question here is that of singularity: where and how does the singular meet up with the concept? What is the paradigm of such an encounter? If Deleuze likes the Stoics, Leibniz, or Whitehead, and if he does not much like Plato, Descartes, or Hegel, it is because, in the first series, the principle of individuation occupies a strategic place, which it is denied in the second. The 'Leibnizian revolution' will be greeted, with a stylistic enthusiasm that is rare in Deleuze's supple narration, as 'the honeymoon of singularity and the concept' (p. 67).

But to begin with, what is singular? For me this is the problem that dominates throughout Deleuze's book, and it is as a *witness for the singular* that Leibniz is summoned. He who has sharpened thought on the grindstone of the infinity of occurrences, inflections, species, and individuals.

II. THE EVENT, SINGULARITY

The chapter 'What is an event?' occupies the centre of the book (pp. 76–82), and it is more about Whitehead than Leibniz. But both in what precedes and what follows, the category of event is central, because it is the one that supports, envelops, dynamizes the category of singularity. Deleuze-Leibniz considers the world as 'a series of inflections or events: it is a *pure emission of singularities*' (p. 60).

Once again, the question central to the thought of the event attributed by Deleuze to Leibniz-Whitehead is intriguing and provoking. Let us quote: 'What are the conditions of an event for everything to be event?' (p. 76).[2]

The temptation is great to counter this with the following question: If 'everything is to be event', how can the event be distinguished from the *fact*, from what-happens-in-the-world according to its law of presentation? Should we not rather ask: 'What are the conditions of an event for *almost nothing* to be event?' Is what is presented really that singular just for being presented? It can be argued just as reasonably that the course of the world in general displays nothing but generality.

How then can Leibniz-Whitehead-Deleuze extract from the organicist scheme of the Multiple an *evental* theory of the singular, when 'event' means: everything that happens, inasmuch as everything happens?

This enigma can be expressed simply: while we often understand 'event' as the singularity of a rupture, Leibniz-Whitehead-Deleuze understands it as *what singularizes continuity in each of its local folds*. But on the other hand, for Leibniz-Whitehead-Deleuze, 'event' nonetheless designates the origin – always singular, or local – of a truth (a concept), or what Deleuze formulates as the 'subordination of the true to what is singular and remarkable' (p. 91). Thus, the event is both omnipresent and creative, structural and unprecedented.

---

2   Translation modified.

As a result, the series of notions related to the event are continually disseminated and contracted into the same point. Let us give three examples.

1. From the moment Leibniz-Deleuze thinks the event as an immanent inflection of the continuous, he must simultaneously suppose it is from the *point of this immanence* that we speak of the event (never 'before' nor 'from outside'); and yet, that an essential *pre-existence*, that of the global law of the world, *must* elude us if we are to speak of it:

> Leibniz's philosophy . . . requires this ideal pre-existence of the world, this silent and shaded part of the event. We can speak of the event only as already engaged in the soul that expresses it and in the body that carries it out, but we could be completely at a loss about how to speak of it without this part that is subtracted from it. (p. 106)[3]

This image of the 'silent and shaded part of the event' is admirable and adequate. Yet, we must see that what is excessive – shaded – in the event for Leibniz-Deleuze is *the All that pre-exists it.* This is because in an organicist ontology of the Multiple, the event is like a spontaneous gesture in the dark backdrop of an enveloping and global animality. Deleuze clearly explains that there are two aspects to Leibniz's 'mannerism', which opposes him to Cartesian classicism:

> The first is the spontaneity of manners that is opposed to the essentiality of the attribute. The second is the omnipresence of the dark backdrop which is opposed to the clarity of form, and without which manners would have no place to surge forth from. (p. 56)

For Leibniz-Deleuze, the pre-existence of the World as a 'dark backdrop' [*sombre fond*] signs the event as *manner*, and this is

---

3   Translation modified.

coherent with the organicity of the multiple. This conception authorizes us to say that it is from a combination of immanence and excessive infinity that proceeds our capacity to 'speak of' an event. Thinking the event, or making a concept of the singular, always requires that a commitment and a subtraction be conjoined, the world (or the situation) and the infinite.

2. The most highly dense chapter of Deleuze's book, and in my opinion the most accomplished, is chapter 4, which deals with 'sufficient reason'. Why is it that Deleuze is especially skilful (and faithful) in this passage? Because the version he gives of the principle, namely, 'the identity of the event and the predicate' – which is even better summarized when he states: 'Everything has a concept!' (p. 41) – is in reality the maxim of his own genius, the axiom without which he would be discouraged from philosophizing.

Once again, Deleuzian determination is constituted by blurring an established dialectic through the play of nuances: the principle of reason allows him to superimpose at each point Nominalism and Universalism. Here we find the most profound of Deleuze's programmes of thought:

> For some, the Nominalists, individuals would be the only existants, concepts being only carefully ordered words; for others, the Universalists, the concept has the power of being infinitely determinable, the individual referring only to accidental or extraconceptual determinations. But for Leibniz, at the same time only the individual exists, *and* it is by virtue of the power of the concept: monad or soul. Thus this power of the concept (to become subject) does not consist in determining a genre of infinity, but in condensing and in prolonging singularities. The latter are not generalities but events, or droplets of events. (p. 64)

We will grant the need to subvert the couple Universalism/ Nominalism. But can it be to the extent of the 'monadic' statement: 'Everything has a concept'?

In fact, Deleuze *reverses* the hidden axiom that is common to Nominalism and Universalism, an axiom that says that nothing *of the Multiple* has a concept.

For Nominalism, the Multiple exists, while the concept, and so the One, is nothing but language; for the Universalist, the One exists in accordance with the concept, and the Multiple is inessential. Leibniz-Deleuze says: the Multiple exists by concept, or: the Multiple exists in *the One*. This is precisely the function of the Monad: to carve out the One from within the Multiple so that there may be a concept of this multiple. This will establish a fertile equivocity between 'to be an element of' or 'belong to', which are ontological categories, and 'to possess a property', 'have a certain predicate', categories of knowledge. Deleuze expresses this with clarity: 'Finally, a monad has as its property, not an abstract attribute . . . but other monads' (p. 110).

Once we arrive at this point, thought is submitted to the most extreme tension:

- either the multiple is pure multiple of multiples, and there is no One from which it can be held that 'everything has a concept';

- or the multiple 'possesses' properties, and this cannot be only in the name of its elements, or its subordinate multiples: there must be conceptual inherence, and therefore essences.

Deleuze congratulates Gabriel Tarde for having spotted in Leibniz a sort of substitution of *having* for *being*: the being of the monad is the sum, the nuanced, hierarchized, and continuous inventory of what it 'possesses': 'what is new is that analysis bears upon species, degrees, relations and variables of possession in order to use it to fashion the content or the development of the notion of Being' (p. 109).

Of course, Deleuze knows that 'possession', 'having',

'belonging' are metaphorical operations here. But the analysis of being within the register of having (or domination) allows him to *slip* concepts into the plot of the multiple without having to take a clear position on the question of the One. The problem is even greater for Deleuze than for Leibniz, because for the latter there is a total language, an integrating series of *all* multiplicities, which is God. Without this stopping point, dissemination necessarily, for lack of the One, makes a fiction out of the concept (just as the crucial concept of vanishing quantity, or the infinitely small, is a fiction for Leibniz).

A solution probably does exist, and Deleuze borrows *segments* from it. It involves distinguishing the operations of knowledge (or *encyclopaedic* concepts) from the operations of truth (or *evental* concepts). From the point of the situation, and so in 'monadic' imma-nence, it is true that everything has an (encyclopaedic) concept, but *nothing* is event (there are only facts). From the point of the event, *there will have been* a truth (of the situation) that is *locally* 'forcible' as an encyclopaedic concept, but globally indiscernible.

At bottom, this distinction is what is at stake when Deleuze-Leibniz discerns the 'two floors' of the thought of the World: the level of *actualization* (monads), and the level of *realization* (bodies) (cf. p. 29). We might say that the monadic infinitely proceeds to the truth-verification of that of which the corporeal is the effectuation. Or that the monad is a functor of truth, whereas bodies are encyclo-paedic assemblages. Particularly since actualization corresponds to the mathematical metaphor of a 'curve with infinite inflection', and realization to 'coordinates that determine extrema' (p. 102). In this, we can without too much trouble recognize the 'open' trajectory of truth with regard to the stability 'in situation' of knowledges.

But *at the same time*, Deleuze will try to 'sew back up', or fold one onto the other, the two floors thus discerned. To keep the gap between them, the event would have to break up *at some point* the 'everything has a concept': there would have to be a break-down of meanings. But Leibniz-Deleuze thoroughly intends to establish that any apparent breakdown, any separate punctuality, is in fact a superior ruse of continuity.

Deleuze is at his most brilliant when he is devoted to 'repairing' the apparent gaps in Leibnizian logic.

People traditionally object to Leibniz that his monadology prohibits any thought of the relation? No, Deleuze shows that 'in a certain sense all Leibniz does is ponder relations' (p. 53). In passing he produces this stupefying definition of a relation: 'the unity of the nonrelation with matters of wholes-and-parts' (p. 46), which subjugates and persuades the reader – except that, in mathematical ontology, whole-parts would have to be replaced by multiple-void.

People have found an unsustainable contradiction between the principle of sufficient reason (which requires that everything possess a concept and the requisites of its activity, thus binding everything to everything else) and the principle of indiscernibles (which claims there is no real being identical to an other, thus unbinding everything from everything else)? Deleuze promptly answers: no, the connection of reasons and the interruption of indiscernibles only engender the best flux, a higher type of continuity: 'The principle of indiscernibles establishes divisions; but the divisions are not lacunae or ruptures of continuity; on the contrary, they redistribute continuity in such a fashion that there can be no holes, that is, in the "best" way' (p. 65). It is for the same reason that 'we cannot know *where the sensible finishes and the intelligible begins*' (p. 66).[4] It is clear that universal eventality *also* means universal continuity for Deleuze-Leibniz. Or again: for Leibniz-Deleuze, 'everything happens' means nothing is interrupted, and *therefore* everything has a concept – that of its inclusion in the continuity, as an inflection-division, or fold.

3. What a joy to see Deleuze so naturally mention Mallarmé as a poet-thinker, and to feel he places him among the greatest!

On page 30, Deleuze calls him 'a great Baroque poet'. Why?

---

4 Translation modified.

Because 'the fold is probably Mallarmé's most important . . . operative act'. And he mentions the fan, 'fold after fold': the leaves of the Book as 'folds of thought' . . . The fold would be 'the unity that creates being, a multiplicity that makes for inclusion, a collectivity having become consistent' (p. 31).

This topology of the fold is descriptively unchallengeable. Pushed to its logical consequences, it brings Deleuze to write: 'The Book, fold of the event' (p. 44).

On page 67, Mallarmé is evoked once more, in the company of Nietzsche, as 'the revelation of a Thought-world that emits a throw of dice'. The throw of dice, says Deleuze,

> is the power of affirming Chance, of thinking all of chance, which is above all not a principle, but the absence of all principle. Thus Mallarmé gives to absence or nothingness what issues from chance, what claims to escape it all the while limiting it by principle. (p. 67)

Deleuze's aim is clear: show that beyond the Leibnizian Baroque there is our world, where a play 'makes incompossibles enter into the same world, shattered' (p. 67).

It is paradoxical to summon Mallarmé in service of such an aim, but I shall come back to that. This paradoxical reference permits us, however, to understand why the list of thinkers of the event, according to Deleuze (the Stoics, Leibniz, Whitehead . . .), is only made up of names that could just as well be cited for their *opposition* to any concept of the event: declared adversaries of the void, of the clinamen, of chance, of disjunctive separation, of the radical break, of the Idea – in short, adversaries of everything that opens up thought to the event as rupture, and, to begin with, what has neither inside nor connection: a separated void.

Fundamentally, 'event' means just the contrary for Deleuze: an immanent activity against the backdrop of totality; a creation or novelty, certainly, but thinkable from within the interiority of the continuous. An *élan vital*. Or again: a complex of extensions, intensities, singularities, which is both punctually reflected and accomplished in a flux (p. 79). 'Event' is the gesture without end or fixed form that in innumerable points affects the one and only anarchic World-Animal. 'Event' names a predicate-gesture of the World: 'predicates or events', says Leibniz. 'Event' is only the linguistic pertinence of the subject-verb-complement system, as opposed to the essentialist and eternitarian judgement of attribution, with which Plato or Descartes are reproached: '*Leibnizian inclusion is based upon a scheme of subject-verb-complement that since antiquity has resisted the scheme of attribution.* Here we have a Baroque grammar in which the predicate is above all a relation and an event, and not an attribute' (p. 53).

Deleuze maintains immanence, excludes interruption or caesura, and only moves the qualification (or concept) of the judgement of attribution (and so of the One-being) to the active schema, which subjectivizes and complements.

This is because Deleuze-Leibniz, outside of the void, wants to read the 'what happens' in the flesh of the full, in the intimacy of the fold. The last key to his argumentation is thus: interiority.

III. THE SUBJECT, INTERIORITY

Deleuze intends to follow Leibniz in his most paradoxical undertaking: establish the monad as 'absolute interiority' and go on to the most rigorous analysis possible of the relations of exteriority (or possession), in particular the relation between soul and body. Treating the outside as an exact reversion, or 'membrane', of the inside, reading the world as a texture of the intimate, thinking the macroscopic (or the molar) as a torsion of the microscopic (or the molecular): these are undoubtedly the operations that constitute the true effectiveness of the concept of Fold. For example:

> The 'unilaterality' of the monad implies as its condition of closure a torsion of the world, an infinite fold, that can be unwrapped in

conformity with the condition only by recovering the other side, not as exterior to the monad, but as the exterior or outside *of* its own interiority: a partition, a supple and adherent membrane coextensive with everything inside. (p. 111)

We can see that with the Fold, Deleuze is searching for a figure of interiority (or of the subject) that is *neither* reflection (or the Cogito), *nor* the relation-to, the focus (or intentionality), *nor* the pure empty point (or eclipse). Neither Descartes, nor Husserl, nor Lacan. An absolute interiority, *but* 'reversed' in such a way that it disposes of a relation to the All, of 'an unlocalizable primary link that borders the absolute interior' (p. 111). Leibniz calls this primary relation, by which the absolute interiority is folded onto the total exterior, the *vinculum*, and this is what allows the monadic interior to subordinate to itself, or illuminate, the 'exterior' monads, without having to 'cross over' the boundaries of its interiority.

The analysis of the axial concept of vinculum proposed by Deleuze, in the light of the Fold, is pure wonder (all of chapter 8). His intelligence is visibly excited by the challenge, by the tracking down of an entirely new path: a subject *directly* articulating the classical closure of the reflexive Subject (but without reflexive clarity) and the baroque porosity of the empiricist Subject (but without mechanical passivity). An intimacy that is equal to the entire world, a soul folded everywhere within the body: what a happy surprise! This is how Deleuze recapitulates the requisites:

1) *Each* individual monad possesses *a* body that cannot be separated from it; 2) each one possesses *a* body insofar as it is the constant subject of the vinculum fixed to it (*its* vinculum); 3) for variables this vinculum has monads taken en masse; 4) these masses of monads are inseparable from infinities of material parts to which they belong; 5) these material parts make up the organic composition of *a* body, whose vinculum, envisioned in respect to the variables, assures its specific unity; 6) *this* body is the one that

belongs to the individual monad, it is *its* body, to the extent that it already avails itself of an individual unity (thanks to the vinculum now envisioned in relation to the constant). (p. 113)

This conception of the subject as interiority whose own exterior forms the primary link to the infinite Multiple or the world has three principal effects.

First, it de-links knowledge from any relation to an 'object'. Knowledge operates through the summoning up of immanent perceptions, it is an interior 'membrane' effect, a subsumption or domination, of multiplicities taken 'en masse'. To know is to unfold an interior complexity. In this sense, Leibniz-Deleuze is in agreement with what I have called the contemporary problem of an 'objectless subject': 'I am forever unfolding between two folds, and if to perceive means to unfold, then I am forever perceiving within the folds. *Every perception is hallucinatory because perception has no object*' (p. 93).

Second, Deleuze-Leibniz's conception makes of the Subject a series, or an unfolding of predicates, and not a substance, or a pure empty reflexive point, whether it be as an eclipse or as the transcendental correlate of an object $= x$. Leibniz-Deleuze's Subject is *directly multiple*, and this is its strength. For example: 'Everything real is a subject whose predicate is a character put into a series, the sum of predicates being the relation among the limits of these series' (p. 47). And in parentheses Deleuze adds: 'we shall avoid confusing limit and subject', which is far from being a simple statement of Leibnizian orthodoxy: contemporary humanism, the humanism of 'the rights of man', is literally poisoned by an unexpressed conception of the subject as limit. Now the subject is indeed, at best, what provides multiple supports for the relation between several serial limits.

Third, Leibniz-Deleuze's conception makes of the subject the point (of view) from which there is a truth, a *function of truth*. Not the source, or the constituent, or the guarantee of truth, but the point of view from which the truth is. Interiority is above all the occupation of such a point (of view). The vinculum is also the ordering of the cases of truth.

Deleuze is perfectly right in showing that if there is 'relativism' involved, it does not affect the truth. For it is not the truth that varies according to, or with, the point of view (the subject, the monad, interiority). It is the fact that *truth is variation* which demands that it can be so only *for* a point (of view): 'It is not a variation of truth according to the subject, but the condition in which the truth of a variation appears to the subject' (p. 20).

This conception of the truth as 'varying' (or undergoing a process) does demand that it always be ordered at one point, or from case to case. The true is only manifest in the trajectory that examines the variation that it is: 'In each area the point of view is a variation or *a power of arranging cases*, a condition for the manifestation of the true' (p. 21).[5]

The problem is undoubtedly that these considerations remain linked to an 'unseparated' vision of the event, and *therefore of the points (of view)*. Deleuze points this out with his customary perspicacity: 'certainly no void is given between two points of view' (20). But this lack of a void introduces a complete continuity between the points of view. The result is that the continuity, which stems from the whole, is opposed to the singularity of the variation. Now, a truth could very well be, on the contrary, the becoming-varied. And because this becoming is separated from any other by the void, a truth is a trajectory *delivered to Chance*. This is something to which neither Leibniz nor Deleuze can give his consent, in the end, because ontological organicism forecloses the void, according to the law (or desire, it is all the same) of the Great Animal Totality.

---

5   Translation corrected.

IV. NATURE AND TRUTH

The extreme amplitude of Deleuze's philosophical project contrasts with the modesty and receptivity of his prose. Deleuze is a great philosopher. He wants and he creates a real quantity of philosophical greatness.

Nature is the paradigm of this greatness. Deleuze wants and creates a philosophy 'of' Nature, or rather a philosophy-nature. By this we can understand a *description in thought of the life of the World,* such that the life thus described may include, as one of its living gestures, the description itself.

I do not use lightly the word *life.* Flux, desire, fold: these concepts are captors of life, descriptive traps that thought sets for the living world, for the present world. Deleuze likes the baroque, those for whom 'the principles of reason are veritable cries: Not everything is fish, but fish are teeming everywhere . . . Universality does not exist, but living things are ubiquitous' (p. 9).

A concept must undergo the trial of its biological evaluation, or its evaluation by biology. So for the Fold: 'The essential is elsewhere: basically, two conceptions [epigenesis and preformation] share the common trait of conceiving the organism as a fold, an originary folding or creasing (and biology has never rejected this determination of living matter, as shown nowadays with the fundamental pleating of globular protein)' (p. 10).

The question of the body, of the specific mode in which thought is affected by the body, is what is essential for Deleuze. The fold is an adequate image of the incomprehensible link between thought and body. The entire third part, which concludes Deleuze's book, is entitled 'Having a Body'. We read there that the fold

surely billows between the body and the soul, but already between the inorganic and the organic in the sense of bodies, and still between the 'species' of monads in the sense of souls. It is an extremely sinuous fold, a zigzag, a primal tie that cannot be located. (p. 120)

When Deleuze mentions 'modern mathematicians', he is of course talking about Thom or Mandelbrot, that is, those who (aside from being indeed great mathematicians in their own fields) have attempted the morphological, modelling, descriptive projection of certain mathematical concepts onto geological, organic, social, or other empirical data. Mathematics is only touched on or mentioned inasmuch as it claims to be included without mediation into a natural phenomenology (pp. 16–18).

Nor do I use lightly the term *description*. We saw that Deleuze requires the style of thought implicit in description and narration, in opposition to the essentialist argument or dialectic development. Deleuze lets thought roam through the labyrinth of the world; he lays down marks and lays out threads, sets mental traps for beasts and shadows. Monadology or nomadology: he proposes this literal permutation himself. He likes the question to be indirect and local, the mirror to be tinted. He likes there to be a tight-woven screen that forces us to squint to perceive the outline of being. The aim is to sharpen perception, to make hypothetical assurances move about and stray.

Finally, when you read Deleuze, you never know exactly who is speaking, nor who assures what is said, or declares himself to be certain of it. Is it Leibniz? Deleuze? The well-intentioned reader? The passing artist? The (really genial) matrix Deleuze gives of Henry James's novels is an allegory of the detours of his own philosophical work:

> What I am telling to you, *what* you are also thinking about, do you agree to tell *him* about *it*, provided that we know what to expect of *it*, about *her*, and that we also agree about who *he* is and who *she* is? (p. 22)

This is what I call a description *for thought*. What is important here is not so much to decide (he, she, it, etc.), but to be led to the point of capture or of focus where these determinations assemble a figure, a gesture, or an occurrence.

If Deleuze were less prudent, or more direct, perhaps he would have risked vast and accomplished descriptions in the style of Plato's *Timaeus*, Descartes' *World*, Hegel's *Philosophy of Nature*, or Bergson's *Creative Evolution*. This is a tradition. But he suggests, rather, the vain possibility (or the contemporary impossibility) of these attempts. He suggests this all the while presenting the concepts, the operations, the 'formatives' for it. The Fold might be the most important of all (after Difference, Repetition, Desire, Flux, the Molecular and the Molar, the Image, Movement, etc.). Deleuze submits it to us through partial descriptions, as that which possibly *describes* a Great Description, a general capture of the life of the World, which will never be accomplished.

V. FIVE PUNCTUATIONS

The author of the foregoing lines has made *the other ontological choice* – that of subtraction, of the empty set, and of the matheme. Belonging and inclusion play for me the role that Deleuze attributes to the Fold and the World.

However, for both of us the word 'event' signals an edge, or a border, of Being, such that the True is assigned to its singularity. For Deleuze as well as for myself, truth is neither adequation nor structure. It is an infinite process that has its aleatory origin *in a point*.

The result is a strange mixture of infinitesimal proximity and infinite distance. I shall only give here a few examples, which will also serve as a contrasting re-exposition of Deleuze's thought.

1. The Event

That there be excess (indifferently shadow or light) in the occurrence of the event, that it be creative, I readily agree. But my distribution of this excess goes against the grain of Deleuze's, who finds it in the inexhaustible fullness of the world.

For me, it is not from the world, even ideally, that the event gets its inexhaustible reserve, its silent (or indiscernible) excess, but *from its not being attached to it*, from its being separated, interrupted, or – as Mallarmé would say – 'pure'. And it is, on the contrary, what *afterwards* is named of it in souls or effectuated in bodies that brings about the global or ideal worldliness of the event (a suspended effect, that I call a truth). The excess of the event is never related to the situation as an organic 'dark backdrop', but as a multiple such that the event *is not counted for one in it*. The result is that its silent or subtracted part is an infinity *to come*, a post-existence that will bring back to the world the pure separated point of the eventual supplement, under the laborious and unachievable form of an infinite inclusion. Where Deleuze sees a 'manner' of being, I would say that the worldly post-existence of a truth signals the event as *separation*, and this is coherent with the mathematicity of the multiple (but effectively is not so, if we suppose its organicity).

'Event' means: there is some One, in the absence of continuity, in the suspension of significations, and *thus* there are some truths, which are chance trajectories subtracted – by fidelity to this supernumerary One – from the encyclopaedia of the concept.

2. Essence, Relation, All

In his war against essences, Deleuze promotes the active form of the verb, the operation of the complement, and sets this 'dynamism' – opposed to the judgement of attribution – against the inexhaustible activity of the All.

But is the relational primacy of the verb over the attributed adjective sufficient to save the singularity, to free us of essences? Must not the event rather be subtracted from any relation *just as* from any attribute, from the doing of the verb *just as* from the being of the copula? Can the taking-place of the event support being in continuity, or in intermittence, between the subject of the verb and its complement?

The great All annuls just as surely the local gesture of singularity, as the transcendent Essence crushes individuation. Singularity demands that the separating distance be absolute and thus that the void be a *point* of Being. It cannot support the internal pre-existence, whether of the One (essence), or of the All (world).

3. Mallarmé

Although descriptively exact, the phenomenology of the Fold cannot be used to think what is crucial to Mallarmé's poem. It is only the secondary moment, a local traversing, a descriptive stasis. If it is the case for Mallarmé that the world is folds, a folding, an unfolding, the aim of the poem is never the world-as-fan or the widowed stone. What must be counterpoised to the fold is the stellar point, the cold fire, which places the fold in absence and eternalizes that which, being precisely 'pure notion', counts no fold. Who can believe that the man of the 'calm block', of the constellation 'cold with forgetfulness and disuse', of the 'cold gems', of the severed head of Saint John, of Midnight, and so forth, has taken on the task of 'folding, unfolding, refolding'? The 'operative act' essential to Mallarmé is that of detaching, of separating, of the transcendent occurrence of the pure point, of the Idea that eliminates all chance – in short, it is the contrary of the fold, which metaphorizes the obstacle and the intricacy. The poem is the *scissor* of the fold.

The Book is not 'the fold of the event', it is the pure notion of eventality, or the poetic isolation of *what is absent from any event.* More generally, Mallarmé cannot be used for Deleuze's aim (to testify to the divergence of the series of the World, to enjoin us to fold, unfold, refold), for the following reasons:

1. Chance is not the *absence* of any principle, but 'the *negation* of any principle', and this 'nuance' separates Mallarmé from Deleuze by the entire distance that brings him closer to Hegel.

2. Chance, as a figure of the negative, is the principal support of a dialectic ('The Infinite is the result of chance, which you have denied') and not of a play (in the Nietzschean sense).

3. Chance is the *self-realization* of its Idea, in any act in which it is at stake, so that it is an affirmative, delimited power, and not at all a correlation of the world (the term 'world-thought' is totally inadequate).

4. The effectuation, by thought, of Chance, which is also the pure thought of the event, does not give rise to 'incompossibles' or whimsical chaos, but to 'a Constellation', an isolated Idea, whose scheme is a Number ('the only number which cannot be an other'). It is a question of matching the Hegelian dialectic and the Platonic Intelligible.

5. The question is not to reduce to nothingness whatever is opposed to Chance, but to get rid of nothingness so that the transcendent stellar isolation, which symbolizes the absolute separation of the event, might emerge. Mallarmé's key concept, which is certainly not the fold, might just be purity. And his central maxim, the conclusion of *Igitur*: 'Nothingness gone, the castle of purity remains.'

4. The Ruin of the Category of Object

One of Deleuze's strong points is to have thought with Leibniz an objectless knowledge. The ruin of the category of object is a major process of philosophical modernity. And yet, Pascal would say, Deleuze's strong point only holds 'up to a certain point'. Caught up in the twists and turns of the All and the denial of the void, Deleuze assigns the absence of object to (monadic) interiority. But the lack of object is a result of truth's being a process of making holes in what constitutes knowledge, rather than a process of unfolding. And also of the subject's being the differential of the perforating path, rather than the One of the primary link to worldly multiplicities.

Deleuze seems in fact to keep, if not the object, at least the *tracing of objectivity*, inasmuch as he keeps the couple activity/passivity (or fold/unfold) at the centre of the problem of knowledge. And he is forced to keep it there, because his doctrine of the Multiple is organicist, or vitalist. In a mathematized conception, the genericity (or the hole) of the True implies neither activity nor passivity, but rather *trajectories* and *encounters*.

5. The Subject

Deleuze is a thousand times right to think the Subject as 'relation-multiple', or as a 'relation of limits', and not as simple limit (which would reduce it to the Subject of humanism).

In the end, however, we cannot avoid formally distinguishing the subject as multiple configuration, from other 'relations of limits', which are constantly being inscribed in some situation or other, I have proposed a criterion for this, which is the *finite* fragment: a subject is a finite difference in the process of a truth. It is clear that in Leibniz what we have is on the contrary an interiority-One whose vinculum subordinates *infinite* multiplicities. Deleuze's subject, the subject-as-fold, has as its numeric formula $1/\infty$, which is the formula for the monad, even if its clear part is $1/n$ (p. 178). It articulates the One with the Infinite. My conviction is rather that *any finite formula* expresses a subject, if it is the local differential of a procedure of truth. We would then be referred back to the characteristic numbers of these procedures, and of their types. In any case, the formula $1/\infty$ certainly brings us within the toils of the Subject, the paradigm of which is God, or the One-infinite. This is the point where the One makes up for its excessive absence in the analytic of the Event: if the event can be reduced to the fact, if 'everything is to be event', *then* it is the Subject who must take on both the One and the Infinite. Leibniz-Deleuze cannot escape this rule.

Against the grain of all this, pure interiority must be abandoned, even if it is reversed into coextensive exteriority, in favour of the local differential of Chance, which has neither interior nor exterior, being the matching up of a finitude and a language (a language which 'forces' the infinite of the variation of the subject-point from its finite becoming-varied). There is still too much substance in Leibniz-Deleuze's subject, too much concave folding. There is only the point, and the name.

IN CONCLUSION

Deleuze cumulates the possibilities of a 'descriptive *mathesis*' whose performances he tests locally, without engaging its systematic value.

But can and must philosophy remain within the immanence of a description of the life of the World? Another road – which, it is true, must renounce the world – is that of the salvation of truths. It is subtractive and active, while Deleuze's is presentifying and ludic. To the fold, it opposes the motionless intricacy of the empty set. To the flux, the stellar separation of the event. To description, inference and axiom. To the gamble, to the experiment, it opposes the organization of fidelities, To creative continuity, it opposes the founding break. And finally, it does not join together, but separates, or opposes, the operations of life and the actions of truth.

Is it Deleuze or Leibniz who assumes the following: 'The soul is the principle of life through its presence and not through its action. *Force is presence and not action*' (p. 119)? In any case, this is the concentration of everything from which philosophy, in my eyes, must preserve us. It should be possible to say: 'A truth is the principle of a subject, through the void whose action it supports. A truth is action and not presence.'

Unfathomable proximity, within what bears the name

'philosophy', of its intimate Other, of its internal adversary, of its royal detour. Deleuze is right on one point: we cannot separate ourselves off from it without perishing. But should we merely content ourselves with it convivially, we shall nonetheless perish, because of it.

First translated by Thelma Sowley, revised by Bruno Bosteels

15

Objectivity and Objectality[6]

There is one central question for Monique David-Ménard. In a first approach, we could call it purely speculative, since it is a kind of variant of the ancient question: 'Why is there something rather than nothing?' However, this question rather cuts transversally across the double qualification of the author: both philosopher and psychoanalyst. For what is at stake is a problem of *encounter*: how do we encounter *the heterogeneous existent*? The fact is that there must be, for thought, a radical exteriority, and that thought must open up a mode of access to it. How? According to which protocols? And by taking which risks? Monique David-Ménard is passionate about deciphering this enigma, in the double register of what it discovers in terms of sense in the philosophical tradition and of the symptom in psychoanalysis. Or perhaps it is in terms of the symptom in philosophy, and of sense in the analytical construction of the Subject.

Monique David-Ménard's first axiom at bottom treats of the mystery of the 'there is'. It states – in a lexicon that is already Kantian, by its adoption of the category of the object: 'If the object is truly constituted as other than the subject, this heterogeneity implies that truth is the encounter of the heterogeneous for thinking' (p. 161).

---

6 Review of Monique David-Ménard, *La Folie dans la raison pure: Kant lecteur de Swedenborg* (Paris: Vrin, 1990).

There must be an encounter with the existent as such. And it is at this point of the subject's capacity for the encounter that the scene of truth plays itself out, truth about which the author will say that it is 'the cross of philosophy' (p. 161).

The very beautiful book *La Folie dans la raison pure* (Madness in Pure Reason) takes on the task of telling us — in a highly conceptual story that is also as suspenseful as a detective novel — how the philosopher Kant bore his cross.

I

The point of departure is, I think, doubly marked. There is first of all an observation typically guided by analytical flair, which in and of itself, by its illuminating force, is a veritable find: before patiently bearing his cross of truth in an infinite and cautious labour, Kant bore the cross of madness. David-Ménard will say, in lapidary style: 'thinker tempted by occultism'. Enlightened man put to the test by the temptation of delirious obscurantism. This temptation functions as symptom, to the point that the whole theoretical oeuvre constitutes its heavy therapeutics. This point justifies the subtitle, *Kant lecteur de Swedenborg* (Kant as Reader of Swedenborg). But it is clearly much more than as 'reader' that Kant relates to Swedenborg. What is terrible in this first encounter is that it indicates the possibility that the other and crucial encounter, that of the heterogeneous existent, may never take place. For in the speculative delirium of madness, which Swedenborg shows us can become the law of a subject, thinking never joins up with its Other. It moves within the homogeneous. The 'there is' is subtracted. It is a matter, says the author, 'of a pure universe of discourse in which thought never encounters anything but itself, in which it never manages to seize anything different from itself' (p. 176).

How to be sure that we are indeed in the encounter with a real existent? How not to confuse homogeneous immanence and its delirious productions with a legitimate knowledge of what is?

Monique David-Ménard will show that the Kantian category of the object, with its extraordinary system of guarantees, comes in as an obstacle, or a break, with regard to the risk that there would be nothing else for thought than thought itself. Kantian objectivity is the philosophical therapeutics of a terrible exposure to Swedenborg's speculative delirium. This exposure, at bottom, would tend to identify thought and desire within the subjective immanence. It would be the moment, both sickly and tempting, when thought is as if eaten away and dissolved by the mechanism of blind belief, or deregulated discourse. Starting form there, one imagines the particularly ambiguous resonance of Kant's famous declaration according to which, with regard to the supreme interests of reason, he had to substitute belief for knowledge! The fact is that, in order to extricate himself from the encounter with madness, he had first had to separate – and with what rigour! – knowledge from belief.

But the properly philosophical stroke of genius – a magnificent lesson in reading – consists in following the trace, or the trajectory, of the delirious temptation (of which Kant takes on the conceptual auto-analysis) *within* the architectonics of the *Critique*.

The first effect is that of a reversal. David-Ménard shows, I dare say demonstrates, that it is on the basis of the transcendental dialectic and the antinomies of reason that the aesthetic and the analytic take on meaning, even though the latter come first in the order of exposition. In effect, it is only from the point of view of reason at risk of falling prey to a discourse without escape, without 'exit', that the Kantian constitution of the object becomes clear.

Kant's Critique in fact goes *from negation to existence*. This is both and at the same time its therapeutic movement, with regard to the temptation of madness (which links the subject to the Nothing), and its movement of sublimation, which under the severe law of the heterogeneous object detaches thought from the constraints of desire.

One will observe the profound logic of this renunciation of the temptation of the homogeneous, of totally free thought, which deals with nothing except itself: it is indeed a matter of renouncing, in favour of alterity and the heterogeneous, the autonomous and desiring delights of the nothing of being. The renunciation, and this idea is admirable, *is not that there is nothing, it is that there is something*. At bottom, the human being *desires* for there to be nothing – nihilism is a structure of desire, of which the speculative madness is the symptom. The cure, the severe discipline, consists in holding that there is some existent.

The fundamental intuition will thus touch upon the relation between the something and the nothing, between the object and the void, between being and nothingness.

This is why the two strongest chapters in my eyes are the first, 'Negation and Object in the *Critique of Pure Reason*', and the fourth, 'The Position of Existence in Kant'.

II

I will retain two points from the first of these chapters. Monique David-Ménard shows very well that the Kantian dialectic seeks to flush out the presuppositions of existence within discourse that are masked by the apparent necessity of the concept. The general scheme – which amounts in sum to bar the path to the judgement of existence when one does not dispose of a universal property of the entity in question – inverts the desiring tendency of delirious madness. Since for the latter 'existence' is not itself anything but an attribute of thought and does not entail any encounter with the heterogeneous, it endlessly concludes by inferring 'existence' on the basis of universal predications: from the fact that I sense myself in all things, universally, the object of an all-powerfulness, I draw the conclusion of the existence of a persecutor. Kant, as Monique David-Ménard summarizes, will say on the contrary: '"God is all-powerful": this is necessary, if God is. But it is not contradictory for Him not to be. And if He is not, He is not all-powerful' (pp. 51–2).

It is in my eyes crucial to be clear about what is at stake in purely logical terms – that is, the relation of a universal proposition and an existential one. From the affirmation that 'every x has the property P' (for example, every God has the property of being all-powerful), the delirious thinker concludes in general that there exists in effect a being endowed with this property. For him, there is no desiring interest in universalizing except if an existent *case* of the universal concerns him personally. Formally, the thing can be written as follows (inference of an existential from a universal proposition):

$$(\forall x)\ P(x) \rightarrow (\exists x)\ P(x)$$

Kant forbids this inference which, because it does not undergo the test of any exteriority, makes existence into an immanent predicate of thought, and does not allow us to break with madness.

What is actually most curious is that pure logic vindicates the mad person rather than Kant. Indeed, the statement:

$$(\forall x)\ P(x) \rightarrow (\exists x)\ P(x)$$

is a theorem in most presentations of first-order predicate calculus.

But this bizarre fact will prove enlightening. Indeed, in this whole affair the point is not pure logic, but ontology. What is a non-delirious ontology? Such is the true question of the philosopher. If the logician admits that from the universal proposition an existential one can be drawn, *it is because he excludes all interpretations of his calculus in an empty universe.* In an empty universe, indeed, the statement in question could not be valid: you may well suppose that 'every' object has the property P; if there exists no object, none will have the property either. Consequently, if the universe is the empty set $\emptyset$, the statement is false. This means that first-order predicate logic *is not* a logic of the void. The logician implicitly decides in favour of heterogeneous existence, in that the theorems of pure logic that are his are valid *only* in non-empty universes (in which there exists at least one object).

Let us say then that what the antinomies of reason unveil for us is that, in spite of the desiring impulses tempted by empty universes, one could not have consistency in thought except by accepting the axiom: 'there is something, and not nothing', and by drawing from it all the consequences, which in fact are *already* at work in the aesthetic and the analytic, even though their subjective motif becomes clear only in the dialectic.

III

In her truly remarkable analysis of the categories of the nothing (pp. 60ff.), David-Ménard shows how, once it is freed from mere subjective vacuity, the nothing gives itself in the correlation between understanding (or concept) and sensibility (or intuition). At issue here is what I would like to call the *disciplined* nothing, such that the position of the object organizes its exercise, precisely in that such 'nothings' allow one to stake out the absence of any object.

There would be a nothing that is essentially logical, or corresponding to the understanding, which presents itself as concept without intuition; and an 'ontological' nothing, corresponding to sensibility, which presents itself as an intuition without a concept. In both cases, the experience is 'annihilating' in that it delivers no object. On the contrary, the heterogeneity of existence is signalled, in the form of the object, as *full* correlation of the concept and the intuition.

Existence takes off from the nothing by aligning experience upon the object, in the double avoidance of the logical nothing and the ontological nothing. Objectivity establishes itself at the very point where the un-chaining, and thus the un-leashing, of the faculties (understanding and sensibility) would deliver thought over to the delirious phantom of its self-sufficiency.

Thus, to be able to *think* the nothing (as disarticulation of the cognitive faculties) is a necessary mediation in the therapeutics of madness, whose mainspring is the constraining of the object.

But the price paid is then that *the object is a category of the phenomenal*. The noumenon, the transcendental 'object = x', will be posited *beyond*. As such, they will be subtracted from presentation. In this regard Kant organizes a logic of the empty place (the place of the unpresented) as the correlate without intuition of a subject that is itself empty. This double emptying out is required so that experience may be definitively pegged to heterogeneous existence.

The object is that which sustains thought *between two voids*. I would call this figure of the guaranteeing of existence: the encircling of the Other. David-Ménard clearly shows that it is a question of displacement:

> The theory of the negativity of the noumenon is mediately linked to the denegation of the rapport to Swedenborg, by virtue of the displacement by which the void of the hallucinated world becomes the void of the intelligible world. For a psychoanalytical reading, what we are dealing with here is indeed a displacement (*Entstellung*). (p. 148)

But by now we are already in the chapter on existence. The crucial question is the following: why is existence (*Dasein*) in Kant always the existence of objects, and never that of the subject?

The (subtle) response is that 'existence' does not designate presence to representation. If the object is *the* category of existence, it is because 'object' names precisely *that which* is heterogeneous to the subject. The result is that what exists must necessarily ex-sist to the subject.

From this point of view, David-Ménard organizes a very fine critique of Heidegger's reading of the twists and turns in the Kantian analytic. In substance, it appears that thanks to the emphasis placed on the transcendental imagination, Heidegger attempts an integrally subjective re-appropriation of *Dasein* and misses the radical dimension of Kant's claim with regard to existence. Contrary to what Heidegger thinks, Kant was right to 'draw back' before the abyss opened up by the subtleties of the imagination. For this abyss, in which the painstakingly conquered and cherished security of heterogeneous existence risked being lost, opened up once again the 'Swedenborgian' peril.

We must hold that existence is strictly ob-jective, that it objects to the solipsistic delirium. Whence, moreover, the paradigmatic value of the sciences as being strictly inhuman and in no way flattering to the subject's presumption.

The object establishes reality as the 'deconstruction of idealism as system of belief'. This is the whole point of the famous passage in the *Critique* on the refutation of idealism. David-Ménard will call this whole protocol of thinking 'the position of existence between conclusion and belief' (p. 168).

It is from this 'in-between' that psychoanalysis can be grasped. David-Ménard can thus conclude with a kind of baton passing from Kant to Freud: 'It is psychoanalysis that can assume the movement sketched out by Kant: that of inscribing the metaphysical question of reality into a problematic of belief' (p. 234).

IV

My questions, or punctuations, will be limited to three.

1. Aside from the empty concept without object and the empty object without concept, should we not suppose the empty or void object with concept, that is, *the concept of the void itself*? And is it not for lack of such a – let us say fully ontological – concept of the nothing that Kant finds himself constrained to contain the heterogeneous existent within the strict figure of the object? In effect, it may be that the nothing, rigorously (mathematically) subsumed under a concept, is precisely that which sustains the heterogeneous existent. This would mean that, given that the void is certainly not an object (even if perhaps it is a letter), we are not constrained, in order to avoid madness, to the phenomenal confinement of objectivity (since the void is not a phenomenon either).

One could then suppose that it is not so much under the effect of the temptation of madness that Kant grounds his doctrine of objectivity, as much as it is because his logic, too marked in this regard by the discovery of English empiricism, remains resolutely intuitionist. By 'intuitionist' let us understand the fact of requiring for all existence a constructive donation, that is, precisely, a mixture of intuition and concept. That all heterogeneous existence must be intuited and constructed is an empiricist dogma, rather than a necessary precaution against dogmatic fits. Besides, and to our very own day, this dogma turns out to be compatible, and first of all in Kant, with the 'reasonable' admission of all kinds of moral and religious chimeras. Which is something that the path carved out by Epicurus and Lucretius, for whom the void is the first name of the heterogeneous existent, splendidly indifferent to subjects as much as to gods, seems to exclude much more radically.

Let us say that the Kantian doctrine of the object is captive to a logic that, by the foreclosure of the void in its ontological sense, misses precisely the point of the heterogeneous and prepares the rehabilitation of the imperatives of religious morality.

2. Aside from the void, it is clear that Kant forecloses the infinite from all cognitive experience (which, here again, allows him to reserve it for religious postulates). The figure of the object as emblem of the heterogeneous is first and foremost a clause of finitude.

David-Ménard points at this in her rigorous analysis of the relation between 'object' and 'world':

> The object of knowledge is the solution of the problem posed by the idea of world, provided that it allows us slightly to modify the terms of the problem by constraining thought so as not to demand an infinite synthesis for the object (*Objekt*) that it thinks; the latter, by this restriction (*Beschrankung*), can become an object (*Gegenstand*). The object is that which, by slightly transforming the conditions of the synthesis in which the problem of the world consists, renders possible the – displaced – solution of the problem. (p. 48)

This 'restriction' is in reality quite drastic. What it obliterates is that it is not at all required that the infinite be given by way of synthesis. As Cantor has established, and as differential and integral calculus already required before him, the infinite can be given as literal materiality which founds a universe that is non-closed but consistent. This donation opens onto a multiple heterogeneity that no longer lets itself be folded back into the figure of the object, nor disposes a world. What Kant in the empiricist discipline of the object cannot see is that the infinite is precisely this field of the thinkable *that is neither object nor world.*

At bottom, the Kantian 'restriction' is once again comparable to the security restrictions with which intuitionism overburdens mathematics and for which, after the void, the infinite must pay the price.

3. David-Ménard has a nice formula to recapitulate the 'case' of Kant: 'A the junction of a post-Newtonian epistemology and a melancholic character' (p. 217).

The whole problem is summed up in what we can distribute along the two slopes of this 'junction':

- *Post-Newtonian?* Except that Kant does not really enter into the infinitesimal resources of the underlying mathematics. His logic remains experimental and numerical ($7 + 5 = 12$), his (induced) conception of time and space is not really *armed* with the science of his time. On these questions (everything that philosophy is meant to think of the 'labyrinth of the continuous'), we should have the courage to say that Kant falls short of Leibniz, and, moreover, well short of the otherwise laborious efforts expended by Hegel. The fact that the post-Galilean mental revolution first of all touches not upon the category of causality but upon the literal handling of the infinite does not seem to concern him at all. The equation 'existence = objectivity' is also the outcome of a view of mathematics that *in fact is still Greek.*

Kant is thus deprived of what constitutes the heart of the problem: the *immediately infinite* extension of the donation of existence, which Pascal had already grasped and understood as undermining the simply 'objective' view of the real.

- *Melancholic?* The philosophical melancholy of the *Critique* is certainly courageous enough to state what we must know how to lose, or rather know how to let be beyond all grasp (the suprasensible world). But this courage is also a step back. It is a question of developing some security mechanism, reinforced with a great deal of guarantees, against any renewal of the loss. From this point of view, what I see at work in the *Critique*'s subtle twists and endless reprises, in its vain distinctions and its forbidding legislations, is the labour of obsession, always exposed to denial.

Allow me, therefore, to counter-balance, rather than to contradict, Monique David-Ménard's diagnostic with the following one: the Kantian doctrine of phenomenal objectivity is the junction of a pre-Leibnizian mathematics and the locking mechanism of an obsessional.

16

On Françoise Proust,
Kant: The Tone of History[1]

No doubt this book itself presents first and foremost the singularity of a tone. To the tone, or the tonality, of history, such as Françoise Proust endeavours to restore them in the wake of Kant, there corresponds in her writing a kind of metaphorical vivaciousness, which is nevertheless compatible with an insistent solemnity.

Commenting on the sublime, as the occurrence of an insensible at the very heart of the sensible, Françoise Proust describes

> the movement by which nature is carried away by a kind of immobile displacement . . . that movement by which a given is violated, swept up, blasted by something undetermined, which does not present itself and yet possesses efficient force, irresistible power, liberty. (p. 21)

One will appreciate that the prose of Françoise Proust *does justice* to the sublime: in this book there is something carried away, its displacement is perceptible.

But also the paradox of a certain immobility, a certain harshness, which introduces the insensible in what could be pathos. For the

---

1   Review of Françoise Proust, *Kant: Le ton de l'histoire* (Paris: Payot, 1991).

movement of being carried away is cut short by the formulaic trenchancy, the daring theses, which perform a balancing act on top of the moving rigour of the analysis, as if riding the crest of a wave of thought.

Let us consider, for example, this strong definition of history: 'History is the collection or recollection of sublime experiences of liberty' (p. 21).

Almost everything is given in this definition: that history is not, cannot be, the heaviness of long-term structures and laws; and that liberty is not a faculty, a disposition, a nothingness lodged within being, but, always, the singularity of an experience.

What deserves to be called 'history' lies in the figure of the event, and not in that of the rational totality. History is constituted through the imposition of a discontinuity; and it delivers the aleatory unicity of a subject. Of this knot of the evental surrection, the discontinuous strike, and the free subject as singular advent, Françoise Proust proposes to establish how and under what conditions we can be taken [*pris*] by it, that is, always, over-taken by surprise [*sur-pris*].

And first of all, what is it that *begins?* How does 'it' begin, this being-free in (or by) history? Françoise Proust writes: 'To begin is a *declarative*: "I begin!" It states neither the object nor the mode of its operation. The decision does not precede the action. I dare, leave (the enclosure, the series), break (with the course of nature), begin' (p. 90). There is great political vigour in this assignment of the beginning to the declaration. I approve that Françoise Proust puts the declaration, the daring-to-declare, in which decision and action are indiscernible, at the source of any historical rupture. Thus conceived, 'historical' politics knows no protocol of operation, it is not transitive to the object and to the laws of its knowledge. What is more: it demands a de-position of the object, of objectivity. The force of this conviction lies in tearing the political decision away from all dialectics of the subjective and the objective. No, the point is not to raise consciousness of what there is, to change necessity, through reflection and action, into liberty. No passage from the in-itself to the for-itself. The beginning, under the injunction of an event, is pure declaration. In this regard, Françoise Proust agrees – *horresco referens!* – with Mao, for whom the subjective maxim of politics, independently of the heavy weight of the 'relations of force' and their prudent interiorization, was, in his own words: 'Dare to struggle.'

It is certain that this whole vision of history is suspended from the concept of the event, which, in the vocabulary borrowed from Kant, is reciprocal to the sublime. What can we say about the sublime? Françoise Proust's maxims display a solemn lucidity: 'The sublime is that something that *within* the thing de-thingifies the thing' (p. 163). Or again: 'The sublime is that which inappears within appearance, the point of the invisible within the visible' (p. 163).

One will indeed admit that the event, if it is not a pure 'fact', if it is not captive of objectifying legislation, must appear under a derogation of the law of appearance. It is therefore legitimate to affirm that the visibility of the event is indiscernible from an invisibility, since it is not adequate to the laws of visibility.

One will nevertheless observe that the insistence with which Françoise Proust underscores that the inapparent is *within* appearance, that the non-thing is internal to the thing, that the invisible is a point of the visible, leaves open the possibility that the event discovers for us the *bottom ground* [*fond*], or the real, of appearing, of the thing, or of the visible. It is for this reason that I prefer to talk about the event as a *supplement*. Certainly, we must retain the de-linking, the deposition of any figure linked to objectivity. But not in the sense that we would thereby have proof of some *reverse side* of linked visibility, of regulated appearing, and even less of its being, as if the inapparent were the 'heart' of appearing. Only in the sense that, in purely random fashion, there emerges some ultra-visible, some indiscernible between the visible and the in-visible, which happens upon the 'objective' situation, or upon the laws of objectivity, like an incalculable excess, at once separated, supernumerary, and disappearing.

And yet, we have to admit that the images with which Françoise Proust concludes her book go in this direction. Let us quote this beautiful passage:

> History is not solar (diurnal) but starry (nocturnal) . . . The events shine in the starry sky of history. Pure flashes of light, they have always already past, always already disappeared, and relive only when history wakes up from its dogmatic slumber. Then they sparkle and twinkle, they sent out some notes to indicate that beginnings and dawns are always possible and that history stands watch over them. (pp. 345–6)

From these lines I retain four themes with which I am in profound agreement:

1) The star-studded reference reminds me of Mallarmé, capital thinker of the pure 'upsurge', the undecidability of the event. He, too, taking exception to the sombre hypothesis that nothing will have taken place except the place, inscribes 'on a vacant and supreme surface', an exception reserved for empirical time (and it is this exception that Françoise Proust names history), a Constellation, 'cold with neglect and disuse'.[2] And it is true that the eventual, discontinuous, and multiple constellation of stars is like an immobile reserve from which one can name everything that *will begin* anew.

2) The 'always-already-disappeared' marks with precision that the event does not possess a measurable intrinsic duration. The fact that it supplements the appearing depends on it always being a disappearing.

---

2   *Translator's Note*: See Stéphane Mallarmé, 'A Dice Throw', *Collected Poems*, trans. E.H. and A.M. Blackmore (Oxford: Oxford University Press, 2006), p. 181.

3) However, this disappearing is not such that we would be dealing with a definitive loss. The star figures here, in its reserve, the available *trace* of a dawn of history. In its 'having-taking-place' it is what a new awakening requires and perceives to encourage its new beginning.

4) And thus, from one event to another, and even from all the events to a single one, there is a weaving of singular awakenings, a complicity of everything whose being has consisted in an excessive disappearing. This is what I myself have called 'evental recurrence'.

With great pertinence, Françoise Proust thus latches on to that which in the evental disappearance is nonetheless integrally affirmative: 'Each event gives rise, by its potential for actuality, to the Idea of a world, that is to say, it presents the time and space of its advent, the mirage of a maximal coexistence of singularities or of liberties' (p. 136).

In truth, this point is enormously complex. One clearly understands that the event is not simply a forgotten rupture, or a closing-in-upon itself, but that it frees up an *other situation*. Are we really dealing with another situation, or with a 'mirage', a simple 'Idea'? Therein lies the whole problem. Françoise Proust admits that we are dealing with an *augmentation of liberty*, in the guise of a 'maximum'. It is in this respect that the event contains indeed a radical potential for affirmation. And yet, for Françoise Proust, what is thus presented exists only in the time of the event's advent. And since this time is that of an 'always-already-disappeared', we should say that the affirmation contained in the event is at the same time integral and instantaneous: 'There is no eternity or historical accomplishment, there are only instants of eternity, instants of history' (p. 242).

Can one not say then that the event, as the raising of an Ideal, is only the fulguration of a promise? To which I would oppose that, in its very disappearance, the event hands us the imperative of *weaving* together a truth.

Françoise Proust declares: 'A public experience of liberty does not constitute a moment in a process of historical liberation, it exists for its own sake' (p. 22). This much is certain, and it sits well with the critique, formulated by Lyotard, of the philosophy of the 'result'. But what exactly is a 'public experience of liberty', under the radical supernumerary condition of an event? Françoise Proust seems to reduce it to the event itself, and thus to an ecstatic, or eternal, instant. I would rather think that the event itself, precisely because its entire being lies in disappearing, does not constitute the stake of any experience. Experience concerns the work-in-the-situation of the post-evental trajectory, the work of the nominal trace in which, sheltered for eternity by its name, the vanished upsurge endures. And this is what I call the singularity of a truth, which is the chance labour, the improbable becoming, of that which 'will have taken place', if one supposes that the situation has been integrally *affected* by the disappeared event. Or, to remain in close proximity to Françoise Proust's Kantian lexicon, if one follows the trajectory of the situation *as if the Idea handed down by the event were supplementing it*. This alone, I believe, configures an experience.

It is no doubt from this point that the questions that I have for this very beautiful book can be organized.

Françoise Proust makes almost no concessions to current opinions. One will therefore be surprised to see her so easily share the one that holds that the history of the twentieth century has been 'catastrophic'. Far be it from me, the idea that this history would be bright and shiny! But I will say that our century, like any other, distributes some astounding state horrors as well as some powerful evental upsurges from which proceed intense and lasting experiences of liberty. The sublime is recurrent in them: October 1917, the Chinese popular war, the Resistance, Gdansk 1980, the years 1967 to 1972 almost everywhere'. . . If history is evental, it is from this point of view that we must 'judge' a century, and not on the sole basis of the descriptions of uniform horror.

But perhaps the difficulty stems from the fact that, as she reduces history to a few instants of eternity, Françoise Proust is at pains when it comes to defining politics. What is a *political* event? Proust will say: 'The republic, the public, is the only problem against which political experiences must measure themselves' (p. 219).

I can see very well that the point is to find another orientation of thought than those that remit politics either to an analytic of the social (coupling of the State and of society) or to the metaphysics of the community. Politics is neither the composition of social forces, nor the sheltering of the ego in an organic totality. To designate the collective (public) dimension of politics, Françoise Proust proposes the term *alliance*. The alliance means local diffusion, fragmentary and a-substantial 'community', founded on the determinate recognition of an agreement. The point in politics is 'to weave together fragments or islands of agreement' (p. 221).

Françoise Proust's will to substitute agreement for belonging, and the local or fragmentary for the global, seems to me totally judicious. But it is also still insufficient even for just arriving at the political question.

It is my conviction that to designate politics philosophically, in a mode of thinking that does not tie it to the massive social History but solely to the precariousness of the event, requires that we take into account the following:

- The tracing of the alliance (to use Françoise Proust's word) *in its subtraction from the form of the State*. A post-evental politics is the experience of a fragmentary freedom that is no longer prescribed by the State, nor governed by the administration of its power. The event is also and always a putting at a distance of the State, a measuring and an assuming both of its exact power and of the Idea of its abolition.

- The declarative singularity of the agreement, which connects it to the event *in the form of a prescription*. We can also say: may every agreement be *militant*.

- The revelation of the *infinite* character of collective situations.

This last point is crucial, and it no doubt entails a discussion with Françoise Proust about the infinite.

Françoise Proust explicitly rejects – in this regard, she seems to me indeed far more rigorous than many interpreters – the idea according to which the Kantian sublime would signal, within the event, the coming of the infinite. No, the sublime is not the affect of the infinite, nor the infinite tearing apart of the time of finitude. Françoise Proust writes so with vigour: 'The sublime is not the infinite' (p. 162). Or again: 'The sublime is not the infinite time, nor the time *of* the infinite. It is on the contrary the time of the finite, or of the always already finished' (p. 164). Wherein we observe that *fini* plays on two possible meanings: finite caesura of time, or time always already seized in its ending.

Now, it seems to me that the question is more intricate. To sum up, I hold that a *complete* thinking of the event is not compatible with a philosophy of finitude.

Certainly, one will admit with Françoise Proust that the event is by no means the 'worldly' advent of a suprasensible infinity. We must combat this vision of the sublime, which surreptitiously renders it Christian. It is not true that the paradigm for every event is the Christic descent of the infinite into the appearance of finitude. It is not even true that an event is the finite symbol of such a descent. Let us say that an event, thought as haphazard supplementation of any situation whatsoever – or, in Françoise Proust's lexicon, as silent caesura – is simply a finite multiplicity. And Françoise Proust is totally right to underscore that the *vanishing* dimension of this finite multiple makes it into an emblem of sorts of the finite, an attestation of finitude as end, which is the meaning of her 'always already finished'.

But to pursue this path to the end, we must observe that the infinite is quite simply what is proper to *what is*, the non-evental banality par excellence, that which precisely has no need for any event in order to be immediately attested to. Or, in my language, that any *situation* is infinite. This alone completes the secularization of the infinite. The result is that the evental supplementation operates 'locally' (or according to a finite proposition) with regard to an ordinary infinite. The extra-ordinary is finite, inasmuch as the ordinary is infinite.

And, moreover, the *traced* (or named) disappearance of the event, the immanent stigma of its abolition, summons in its turn the haphazard becoming of a fidelity that is in principle infinite, quite simply because this becoming – what I call the truth procedure – could not have any interior limitation: it 'works' within a situation that, like any other, is infinite. To be sure, the infinite of a fidelity to the event is different from the infinity of the situation, in that the second weaves together predicable, classified, statified multiplicities, whereas the first – the one that 'will have been' in its unachievable infinity, and which I name 'truth' – is unpredicable, uncircumscribed, subtracted from the statist *construction* of the situation. This is why I say that it is a *generic* infinity.

But in the end, the integral thinking of evental finitude supposes that one localizes it *in between two infinites*. Besides, as always-already-disappeared, it is indeed nothing else than the summoning of the void of this 'in-between' (*entre*) or of this 'den' (*antre*): the den of truth as to-come. For this finitude cannot be retroactively thought except in between the ordinary infinity of the situation and the generic infinity of a truth.

One will then ask: what is the finite, or the vanishing, proper to this generic infinity? I mean: what is that which 'in' the infinite labour of a truth signals the fact that what initiates it – the evental finitude – is a vanishing multiplicity? The vanishing multiplicity that makes up a generic truth is what I call a *subject*. So that every subject presupposes an event, whereas it seems to me that – and this is, I believe, the price paid to Kant and to the transcendental logic – for Françoise Proust, every event presupposes a subject.

This question is undoubtedly complicated. We must first of all grant to Françoise Proust the enormous merit of seeking to 'read' the possibility of a thinking of the event, not only – as has become a commonplace over the past few years – in the *Critique of Judgement* and the analytic of the sublime, but, more radically, in the *Critique of Pure Reason*. This is one of the biases from which she is opposed, and rightly so, to the 'soft' exegeses of Kantian politics, to everything that seeks to accommodate the reigning democratism. Let us say that in so doing, she incarnates, in the conflict of readings of Kant to which current 'political philosophy' can increasingly be reduced, an abrupt new path where Jean-François Lyotard preceded her (not without some hesitation) and which contradicts everything that derives from Hannah Arendt. If we absolutely have to pass through Kant – something of which, for my part, I am not at all convinced – we will be firm in affirming that the only legitimate path today is the one that finds in Kant's texts the means to contradict Arendt's concept of political judgement and of politics as the 'being-together', the stakes of which would lie in the reasonable conflict of opinions. To this 'politics of the spectator', Françoise Proust opposes the politics of incalculable singularities, and at once bids farewell to the dull argument about the conflictual peace of opinions. And it is also true that, to do so, she goes 'back' all the way to the root of the difficulty: the event, the caesura, the origin of that which flashes up and disappears from the fabric of the world as usual and summons us *sometimes* to liberty.

What Françoise Proust asks of the *Critique of Pure Reason* is to ground in a universal manner the 'receptivity' to the event. She brings to light that underneath the activity of knowledge, there exists 'a power to be affected' (p. 71). There exists an originary or transcendental passivity which functions as *arkhè*, as principle, with regard to the activity of knowing such as it is given in the configuration of judgements. There is the transcendental aesthetic and its forms (space and time), and there is the transcendental analytic and its categories (causality, etc.); but more radically there is a *transcendental pathetic*. As Françoise Proust will say: 'What is first is a blow that affects' (p. 71).

Françoise Proust mobilizes this primary receptivity of the transcendental subject in order to think the 'stroke' of the event, so as to guarantee its address: 'An event of liberty is not a product of your free will, it is not an effect of your will; it is what comes, what arrives and affects *us*, what begins and promises' (p. 97).

One will then ask: *who* is this 'us' anterior to the evental stroke, and *for whom* is there a promise? What is this passive faculty that in some way – this is, after all, the function of the whole transcendental field, whether passive or active – *guarantees* that the event universally 'affects' a subject?

It is nonetheless empirically clear that the event does not universally affect its supposed 'subject'. The nominal recollection of its vanishing is inscribed in the situation only at the cost of a haphazard wager, and it is precisely *on the basis* of such a wager that some subject-effect eventually lets itself be discerned. As for universality, far from remitting to a transcendental *structure* of passivity, it is the retroactive result of a *process*, that of a generic truth, which *will have validated* in the situation that it was supplemented by a real event. The only thing that needs to be presupposed is that a truth let itself be recognized, or shown, as such, and this presupposition amounts to the axiom without which philosophy does not exist: there is some thought.

To suppose, on the contrary, that there is some transcendental 'guarantee' for the recognition of the event amounts in my eyes to a grave weakening of the constitutive trait of the event: its undecidability, or its subtraction from any rule of receptivity at work in the situation. The surprise of the event is tied precisely to the fact that no passive structure can accommodate it; and that no subject, no 'us', pre-exists before the effects of its disappearance.

We must therefore go farther than Françoise Proust along the path of the surprise, the precariousness, the undecidability. The subject, who is as it were downstream from the event, is not 'tied' to it, or cut into, by some primary stroke. (I am thinking of this beautiful sentence: 'The kind of alliance that ties a subject together with what will have cut into it, marked it, hollowed it out and at the same time elevated it.') Quite simply because a subject *does not exist*, not even as pure passivity, before the evental supplementation. It is only under the condition of such a supplementation that the singularity of a subject occurs in the situation.

But we must also go farther than Françoise Proust in the opposite direction: no, the event is not reduced to being a caesura over which the prior events hold watch like so many stars. It is on the contrary *averred* from the point of the non-statist consistency of a generic truth. And *this* truth, in its turn, lets itself be recognized as that which is at the same time the infinite matter of any finite subject, and that with regard to which there exists some thought.

So one could say that Françoise Proust – this is perhaps the pathos that is proper to her, and thus also the source of her vigour – concedes too much and too little.

She concedes too much by supposing the transcendental 'preparation' of the event in the alleged passive subject. This is a universality of the easy kind.

She concedes too little by reducing the event to its finite upsurge. This means that she does not open the path to the thought of an organic correlation between the undecidable surprise of the event and the recognizable constitution of a truth.

One could also say: Françoise Proust clearly sees that the event 'ends' or 'finishes' a time. She does not see with all clarity how it founds another. And how, in so doing, its disappearance opens up in the situation *the immanent gap* between the banal infinity of the situation and the generic infinity of a truth.

But I am being unfair, as one always is. For Françoise Proust states very well that, in its paradoxical temporality, the event is a 'hole between a not yet and a no longer' (p. 96). It suffices to add that the event is *also* the initiation of a procedure of truth, which, for its part, proceeds as the opening of a 'hole between a no longer (that of evental finitude) and a not yet (that of generic infinity)'.

17

The Imperative of Negation[1]

As rare as philosophical books are, there are plenty of books 'of philosophy'. Let us call books 'of philosophy' – some of them highly estimable – those that make philosophical texts and references into their *subject matter* by way of commentary, history, explanation, promotion or condemnation. Let us call a philosophical book one that proposes a philosophy. No less and no more.

Without philosophical books, books of philosophy would have nothing real to them. Let us understand that in philosophy there is a real only in the regimen of philosophical *theses*, which have the task of cutting into opinion, whereas books of philosophy most often try to make do with opinion. To sew back into the fabric of opinions, or into what Lacan calls the university discourse, a few philosophical theses that tried as best as they could to tear themselves free from it: such is the stubborn labour of books of philosophy. As Plato would say: to return to the cavern. And he claims, after all, that it is necessary to return to it.

Guy Lardreau's *La Véracité* (Veracity) is a philosophical book. We will thus salute, above all, its real dimension. Besides, Lardreau for a long time now has been settling accounts with the semblant, in the name of a real marked in his eyes by the Maoist revolt of the end

1 Review of Guy Lardreau, *La Véracité: Essai d'une philosophie négative* (Paris: Grasset, 1993).

of the 1960s. It is not for nothing that in the subtitle of *L'Ange* (The Angel), which he wrote with Christian Jambet in 1976, we find the slightly over-reaching expression 'Pour une cynégétique du semblant' (For a Cynegetics of the Semblant). We will see furthermore that the real of the theses, in the Lacanian discipline to which Lardreau was sensible from the beginning, implies certain theses on the real.

What are the distinctive features of the properly philosophical will? Since always, they synthesize the act by which a thought, on the one hand, disjoins itself violently from the sophistics of its time (today, essentially, so-called 'analytical philosophy' and its pragmatic outcomes) and, on the other hand, takes up the challenge coming from the antiphilosophy that is contemporary to it (today, centrally, the Wittgenstein of the *Tractatus* and the Lacan of the 1970s).

Guy Lardreau enjoins us right from the start of his book to recognize that a genuine philosophical project obeys two rules:

1. Against the praise of the fragment, the aphorism, or the poem, it does not give up on the desire for a system. I like that on page 15 of *La Véracité* the author declares almost naïvely: 'the philosophy of which one will here find the systematic exposé . . .'

2. More profoundly: against the Wittgensteinian theme according to which whereof one cannot speak, thereof one must remain silent, a philosophy will endeavour, according to Lardreau's beautiful programme, to assert the rights of the real unspeakable. With great precision, its imperative will be: 'One cannot not say that which one cannot say' [*On ne peut pas ne pas dire ce qu'on ne peut pas dire*] (p. 15).

At bottom, almost everything is, precisely, said. For the lifeblood of this book devoted to negation is this 'one cannot not'. Lardreau will be faithful to the *one cannot not* through the system of a negative philosophy.

I

The matrix of this system is a metaphysical reinterpretation of the Lacanian triplet of the symbolic, the imaginary and the real. This triplet will be related, filtered, disposed by the Kantian inspiration of the transcendental constitution of experience. The Subject, such as the symbolic, the imaginary and the real form a knot in it, can indeed be said either as constituent or as constituted subject.

In Lardreau there is a strong metaphysical numericity at work, the logic of which has its origin in a confrontation of the Lacanian triplet and the Kantian doublet. The articulation of the three of the *instances* and the two of transcendental *constitution* will dispose a powerful topology of the figures of the Subject. We could also say that the Lacanian topology (to be brief: language, representation, and object) is here traversed through and through by the dualism of activity and passivity.

Activity (constitution) envelops both the symbolic and the imaginary. Thus three figures are generated: Subject 1 is the non-constituted constituent (language as such). Subject 2 is the constituted constituent (the subject-effect by which the signifier sustains itself as chain). Subject 1 and subject 2 taken together establish the realm of the symbolic. Subject 3 is the non-constituent constituted, which establishes the imaginary, or representation, or the sensible.

The real, subjectively assigned, can be said as passivity, in the sense that it exceeds constitution as active regime. It should thus be thought not exactly as subject 4, even though we can inscribe it under this number in the topology, but as the '+ 1' of the three. It is the unnameable subject that is the non-constituent non-constituted.

The whole point of this 'procession' of figures of the subject from the pure constituent all the way to the absolutely unconstituted, a procession that goes from language to the unsayable real, is that Lardreau uses it to inscribe, under the Lacanian *dispositif* (as formalized by Jean-Claude Milner), a singular crossing between Kant and Neo-Platonism.

1. Kantian: the constitution of the field of experience in the subject.

2. Neo-Platonist: the metaphysical triad of constitution – that is, the first three figures of the subject (unconstituted constituent, constituted constituent, non-constituent constituted) – which clearly go from the uncreated intelligible (language) to the created sensible (the imaginary).

3. Kantian: the doctrine of the pure real, or noumenon, insofar as it is the *remainder* of constitution, that which falls out, as excessive 'plus-one', outside of the procedures initiated by the pure constituent of language.

4. Neo-Platonist: the alliance, in intellection and in discourse, between the negative and the imperative dimensions.

This last point gives Lardreau's book its true impulse, its dramatic tone. Indeed, what is veracity? It is the right of the real within discourse, or the duty of those who inhabit it to take up [*relever*] this right. Veracity is thus *affirmatively linked to the negative*. To the negative – since the real is the unsayable proper to any discourse. And affirmatively – since precisely because it is the unsayable that is *proper* to it, the real can never, by any discourse, be missed *absolutely*. The imperative of philosophy is then, within all discourses, to take up [*relever*] the real point that is its remainder. And this negative exercise makes of philosophy, in Lardreau's sense, the pure passion of veracity. Which will also be said as follows: Philosophy 'has as its definition to be that discourse that does not despise any' (p. 96).

II

The exercise of philosophy as passion of veracity thus finds its matter in the non-contempt of discourses, whatever they are; and its form in the theory of the four figures of the Subject. It will dispose itself according to the three successive examinations of its effects: the moral examination, the political examination, and the aesthetic examination.

In sum, the book follows the order of the three Kantian *Critiques*. The theory of constitution of the real proposes a negative theoretics, which is followed by a negative (moral and political) practice, and we conclude on a negative aesthetics.

There is a genuine question concerning this order, and I link the first two reasons for my reticence to this question.

The theoretical is purely speculative, or philosophical. Its result is that the position of scientific activity *in the real* is nearly unthinkable (as I would gladly claim is the case for Kant, prisoner of an empiricist conception of objectivity). That science, and first of all mathematics, would have no relation to the real is in fact a thesis of Lardreau's book:

> If human beings can so easily agree on mathematics, it is because nothing is at stake in them for anyone, at least no truth in the sense that it is ordinarily understood, and rightly so, of a relation to the real. (p. 17)

It is first of all not true that 'human beings' easily agree on mathematics. Since Plato, they have not ceased to argue with a rare violence over the position that mathematics occupies, or over the paradigm it constitutes, in all questions in which knowledge is at issue and in which there is a problem of education. And that from within mathematical thinking there is agreement on the statements and their demonstration could well mean – such is my position – not that we do not touch upon the real, but the exact opposite: that mathematics is the writing of being itself, so that thinking immediately and universally finds itself constrained to it. Finally, I would like for Guy Lardreau to take the measure of the concession he makes by adopting this classical sophistic thesis from a number of his principal adversaries – most notably from Wittgenstein, who abruptly states in the *Tractatus* that 'mathematics is not a thought'. Meanwhile, he distances himself too much from two of his masters: Plato, for whom it is far from being the case that there is nothing real in mathematics, and Lacan, who sustains that mathematics *alone* gives us access to the real.

Besides, let us note that the formal disjunction of the theoretical and the practical imposes the identification of a moral philosophy. Now, any identification of moral philosophy de-identifies politics as a procedure of truth, exactly in the same way that the strict assignation of the theoretical to philosophy alone de-identifies science.

Why? Because, from the bias of a general philosophy of morals in which practice is thought, or rejoins its imperative, there is inexorably a suture at work to a more or less sophistic form of pious discourse. It is, moreover, this suture that Lardreau and Jambet desperately sought to undo in *Le Monde* (1978) – even as, by adopting its then emerging and now hegemonic form, that of 'human rights', they could not help, alas, but consolidate it.[2]

Now politics – and I mean the politics of emancipation, the only one that interests Lardreau and me – is *defined* precisely by the singular break that it marks, in its prescriptions and the outline of its possibilities, with all conceivable forms of pious discourse, most notably its 'humanist' version. In this sense there is no politics that is not the putting into work, or the capture, of a superhuman, or immortal, dimension of humanity. And no general philosophy of morals is ever capable of subsuming that *singular* form adopted, when there is politics, by this capture of the mortal by the immortal.

The Kantian order adopted by Lardreau thus seems to me to expose his project to a double obliteration of the real: the one that leaves out the matheme and the one that takes the form, under a militant prescription, of the *possible* of politics.

---

2   *Translator's Note:* Badiou is referring to Guy Lardreau and Christian Jambet's follow-up to *L'Ange*, their book *Le Monde* (Paris: Grasset, 1978).

III

In the case of morals and politics, we should say that Lardreau's subtle effort consists entirely in distinguishing the first from pure formalism and in authorizing the second to claim the discourse of the revolt.

But what are the means for this operation of salvage?

On the side of morals, it is a question of making it 'concrete'. One will thus complement the categorical imperative with a transcendental pathetics, at the heart of which lies pity, as a priori recognition of the suffering of the other.

About this transcendental pathetics, I will say three unpleasant things:

- It is the common effort of a number of 'neo-Kantian' philosophers today. Why? Because they all admit that one must start from the supposition of some radical Evil, which would be, precisely, indifference to the suffering of the other. The backdrop for this negative determination (linking the imperative to 'not supporting the suffering of the other') is a sombre balance sheet of the century, in which this suffering has been inflicted without saving on any expenditure by those very same endeavours that laid claims on emancipation – most notably, Stalinism. But the idea that, for lack of a creative and affirmative rupture from that which, in the State, has come to *suppress* politics in a terrorist manner, we ought to arrive at this conception of morals based on victimhood, is something to which I cannot consent. It is not some Kant subverted by the pathological element of the 'relation to the other' who will save us from certain violent effects of Hegel.

- It re-establishes, against all progressive traditions, the connection of philosophy to the discourse of mercy.

- It disjoins practice and theory all the way into the order of judgement, since it articulates the imperative not on a thought but on an affect.

We must do justice to Lardreau for hesitating before the consequences of this reliance on the supposed universality of pathos:

> The pathological duty, indeed, forces us . . . to restore the instance of the faculty of judgement in the sphere of morals, to recognize the necessity of a casuistics, which we will probably never make into a doctrine but which lets each subject orient itself by itself. Yet no sooner do we restore its place than we must admit, between the two instances of reason that we have so radically separated, something like a contamination. (p. 184)

Lardreau clearly sees that the 'purity' of the imperative is tainted by the casuistics of sensibility. And that, moreover, the *negative* vigour of his philosophy, its subordination to the real alone, seriously runs the risk of growing feeble in the empirical realities of the representation afforded to us, most often on television, by the spectacle of humiliations that the other endures.

But finally, the general tone seems to me to compound the generic difficulties of Kantian formalism with the particular difficulties of a casuistics of the sensible, always open to some form of abjection.

As far as politics goes, Guy Lardreau tries to keep its concept in a purely negative fashion, with the supplementary difficulty that he must assure its compatibility with the intricacies of the 'pathological duty'.

In truth, one could suppose that Lardreau's logic, just as it denies mathematics any connection to the real (in favour of philosophy), ends up making politics into a pure instance of the semblant (in favour of morals). The rigorous theme would be that politics must stay clear of all veracity, except so as to become sublime, and thus absolutely barbaric (which means: indifferent to suffering, and, as a consequence, immorally subtracted from the pathological duty). This is clearly what Lardreau himself at first seems to indicate:

> One can draw a first consequence, which at first seems obligatory: politics is a region such that the real should not insist in it, such that veracity cannot exist in it; that no other position could lay claims on reason except the assent to the order such as we actually find it before us, there where fortune has inscribed us – at best we can limit its efficacy with a moral representation. (p. 246)

This referral of politics to the pure acceptance of the existing order (market economy and so on), or to opinion without any grasp of the real, and with the whole completed by a supplement of humanitarian soul, is obviously nothing other than contemporary abjection. One understands that Lardreau cannot be satisfied with this, even though the order of his concepts (and, I would say, his post-Maoist political passivity) seems to lead him to that point.

The surprising jolt will come from a chiasmus between morals and politics. We saw that in the philosophy of morals, the purely formal imperative, deprived of all intuition, should be doubled by a passive universal decision. In politics, it seems there exists no possible form of the concept – there is only the sensible, only the given situations. It will be necessary to double this general sensible, delivered over to pure opinion, or to the semblant, with an absolutely formal and negative imperative, concerning the pure and undetermined uprising against what exists. The name of this uprising is revolt. What pity is to the categorical imperative (its sensible double), the revolt is to political opinion (its intelligible double). Politics will therefore be concentrated in the following unique imperative: 'One has reason to revolt.' Contrary to pity, which gives morality its objects and its cases, this revolt must necessarily dim or limit any object. The passage deserves to be quoted in its entirety, including its truly litigious ending:

If the revolt that animates the subject can, in effect, represent itself to itself as having no end other than itself, it cannot, however, collectivize itself, except by choosing an object . . . But this object will have to be as evanescent as possible, if the real of the revolt, as finality without end, is not to be entirely obfuscated by it. The purest revolts will thus be, not those that parade the most 'sublime' ambitions, or that display the radical will to 'change the world', but those that, on the contrary, lower themselves to the most tenuous, the most humble, most transparent objects. Which gives us the secret lesson, attuned to the entire workers' tradition: *there is nothing truly sublime except the two-penny revolt.* (p. 249)

One would like for Lardreau here to give a fairer measure of what that workers' tradition and this two-penny sublimity really produced in our national history, aside from the pitiful dissolution of the Gauche Prolétarienne. What is striking, in any case, is that to the menacing abjection of the casuistics of the 'pathological duty' (whom should I make suffer, or whom should I kill with my paratroopers, so that this suffering that I see may no longer be there for me to see?) there corresponds a casuistics of objects of the revolt about which the least one can say is that it is hardly promising. Should the revolt be so disjoined from thought that it must adapt itself in what it says to the symbolic derision of anything real?

The fact is that Lardreau has locked himself into an abstract opposition: either politics wants to change the world, and engage in a 'final solution' – in which case it realizes itself in barbarian immorality; or else politics *wants* nothing, it is pure negation – and then only evanescent objects are appropriate for it. In this arrangement, one will have recognized the one, inherited from the New Philosophers, of Totalitarianism versus the pure and minute uprisings of the plebs.

But politics is something else altogether. It is a form of thinking. It is precisely that which, under a prescription manifested in statements, takes the State in its field in the mode of an absolute *distance*.

Thus conceived, politics escapes the alternative of the sublime barbarism and the non-objective revolt. Meanwhile, what is assured is that in order to hold onto its real purpose, it must give up all general morals.

Finally, as far as aesthetics is concerned, I would like to say that Lardreau's book contains some striking developments. I am thinking in particular of what is said about the true nature of the rapport to art in Plato and Aristotle, or of the analysis of the true thought of Kandinsky.

And yet, one is surprised by a nostalgic, even restorative note: 'Either, then, art again finds figuration, the sensible jubilation, the affirmation of the presence given to an entity . . . or else it will henceforth fail in its mission' (p. 314). I also think that this is related to the defiance towards the destructive capacities of veracity itself. In the end, Lardreau's whole problem lies in knowing how the 'negative philosophy' that he promotes is not going to extend into a terrorist and barbarian philosophy. Hence the moderating complements that are the immediate sense of suffering of the other (in morals), the humiliation of objects and statements (in politics). But is this to start from the top in order finally to preach prudence everywhere? This is a general question of our time: every thought that, openly or obscurely, finds its real motif in the fear of the barbarians, comes back via Kant to the triplet of the morality of rights, the politics of the lesser evil, and the realist aesthetic. Whence, after the admirable metaphysical thrust of the beginning, on the part of Lardreau himself – who, as we know, hardly compromises with what is – the feeling of a deception, or a muted misery.

IV

In the end, this very beautiful book seems to me to be torn by the fact that the world with which its theses declare themselves to be contemporary are not comparable to these theses themselves.

Lardreau's conceptual force is admirable and entirely original, but the world he describes is that of common opinion. Indeed, what is this world?

- A world in which it is assumed that science, and notably mathematics, has no part in taking up the rights of the real. This point puts him in a dialogue shared with Heidegger, with Wittgenstein, but also with the educational *koinè*.

- A world in which politics has witnessed the power of the return to radical evil. And in which, consequently, no political will can ever do justice to the real either. One knows that such is the key point of 'convictions' and of contemporary debasements.

- A world in which the sense of pity must be found again before the suffering of the other, and to protect its rights. Today nobody can appear on the public stage without this kind of declaration on his lips.

- A world in which art, except for abstraction, is in crisis or even absent, demanding a return to the mimetic procedure. This is what one hears proclaimed every day and what, in reality, constitutes the only true threat for the becoming of contemporary art.

Of course, Lardreau gives the loftiest version of all these themes, and often the conceptual high point ends up by unravelling them. If he connects with them, it is perhaps by way of a kind of theoretical melancholy, which prepares him to absolve all claims of prudence and consent. A beautiful passage from his conclusion will make clear what I mean (Lardreau has just declared that he has always known what he just said):

An 'I've always known', though, which by no means entails the beatitude of reminiscence if, in the clarity of the latter, I am given the touch of the Other to which, not only at the origin but rather always already, my soul secretly accorded its kiss – return to coincidence, to integrity, abolition of time as the principle of division; which repeats, on the contrary, the separation that unfolds time, which tells of the boredom of exile, the desolate certainty that the Other is lacking and that one is lacking to the Other. An 'I've always known' that would at best be translated as 'so it was only that', so it was only me. (p. 370)

What is this 'me' whose sadness lies in never escaping from itself, and what is this Other that is always lacking? Ah! I am not melancholic – and that is what, from the point of view of the world, separates me from Lardreau. Not because of the melancholy per se, but because of the consequences that he believes he has to draw from it philosophically speaking – consequences that entail a great amount of prudence with regard to desire. I hold that mathematics remains the surest guide to think that of which the real is the impasse. I hold that it is not politics that has turned back upon itself in utter barbarism, but that it is on the contrary the end of this or that political sequence that opens up the State to its rogue career. I am convinced that any conception of the human being in terms of victimhood is the ideology of an essential contempt. And that the humanitarian pathos ruins all thought. I affirm that contemporary art by no means has exhausted the resources of rupture. Our century has been sinister, like all the others; and admirable, like all the others. Philosophy will be living up to the high demand of drawing up a balance sheet of the century only if it renews its affirmations. It will not suffice to follow up on the Hegelian apology of the labour of the negative with a circumspect doctrine of negative thinking.

My severity, you will have understood, is that of someone who reads a way of thinking that is close to him, who admires it, and who becomes enraged by the distance that little by little marks it.

There are so many things to welcome in Lardreau's project! The desire of philosophy, the restored taste for the system, the central tenets of the Lacanian challenge, the theory of the unnameable real, the obligatory Platonism, even the apology of the revolt . . . That only sharpens my impatience when I see all this cluttered and clouded by a disenchanted world, a kind of post-romanticism tempted by exile. And as a result, the consent to certain deleterious forms of prudence.

The world is as always an untotalizable multiplicity, subtracted from meaning, and in which the duty of thought has not lost its intensity in any of the domains in which it is averred.

Or again: nothing, in the world as it is, obliges us to dissociate theoretical reason from practical reason. Plato, our common master, would not have admitted that one authorize this separation, no matter how grave the circumstances. Let us *really* be those Platonists of the multiple about whom Lardreau's point of departure gives us hope that he will be one of them. For nothing real demands of us that we agitate that infallible sign, in philosophy, of morbid and regressive times: the 'return to Kant'.

18

Logology Against Ontology [1]

To support her praise of sophistics, her savant joy in restoring to us those figures for whom, she says, 'the logos takes precedence over the object' (p. 211), Barbara Cassin has recourse to the contrast between two poets: Saint-John Perse, whose majestic poems of praise she thinks remain Judaeo-Christian and phenomenological; and Francis Ponge, much more sophisticated, since he calls for 'a rhetoric by way of object' and, like Gorgias, supposes that 'all description, all praise, is at the same time praise of the logos' (p. 213).

Let us therefore begin, since Barbara Cassin's book is a major book, by two forms of praise in these two styles.

Let us say first of all: 'O! Book disposed in its branches and its fruits! Entwinement, as one sees in palimpsests, in early printed books, and in the great papyruses in their stranded jars, of the scribe's patience and the prophet's high vision! Reversal of the tables of the Law by the implacable softness of the found fragment, the restored verse, the newly transcribed preface! Old metaphysics undermined by the autonymous joy of the logos! Daring scruple, like that of a strategist at the edge of the sea looking out for the ontological monster, with no weapons other than the debris of his machinations!'

---

1   Review of Barbara Cassin, *L'Effet sophistique* (Paris: Gallimard, 1995). All references with page numbers in the body of the text are to this edition.

And let us then say: 'The book of Barbara Cassin. Leafed through in advance. Strata of dust lifted up in sprinkles. Strata of exact calculations. Strata of words assembled to destroy. Electrical strata: short-circuit between what is older than the ancient and more recent than the modern. Strata of sewing between multiple bits that we thought had different colours and that the needle and thread no longer allow us to distinguish. Smell of resin, of herbs in the sun, of wine jars. Leafed-through novel. I read this book as someone who eats. In the tooth, the different strata bring out a mixed taste. Succulence from traversing the taste of joyous erudition and of thought, sadder than it seems.'

But now it so happens that after the praise I must compare the state of seizure in which I find myself, the sweet linguistic pleasure, anaesthesized, of the consensual sharing – for this is indeed what Barbara Cassin tells us: consensus is the art of homonymy – compare this consensus, then, to something else altogether. To my old conviction, Platonist and anti-sophistic, that this tender and harsh book comes both to put to sleep and to shatter.

The sophistic axiom, the one that for Barbara Cassin opens up thought by cancelling metaphysics, is given to us from the start: 'Being, in a radically critical way with regard to ontology, is not that which the word unveils, but that which discourse creates' (p. 13). The point is to substitute, in a gesture of return to the originary sophistics, logology (the power of being and non-being of the mastered discourse) for ontology (the linguistic capture of an ante-predicative 'there is').

The political consequence of this axiom is perfectly and powerfully prescribed: politics is constituted by the rhetorical bond. As a consequence, it is foreign to the Good and the True. Whatever the specific definition of the political may be, Barbara Cassin tells us, 'it will never be confused, by definition, with the ethical distinction between good and evil, nor with the theoretical distinction between true and false' (p. 269).

The discursive and aesthetic consequence is equally necessary. From the fact that being is a language artefact, it follows that what creates the most being is at once the most developed fiction. It is the novel that is the densest logology. The false that knows itself to be false is what takes the place of the terrorizing and extrinsic norm of the true. Let me cite, in order to be once again lulled and seduced:

> A *pseudos* that knows itself to be *pseudos* and offers itself as such in a freely consented *apatè*, a discourse that renounces all ontological adequation in order to follow its own demiurgy, *logou kharin* and not *semainein ti*, such indeed is the novelistic 'fiction'. (p. 497)

Now that puts me on the spot, I who think against the grain of all that! For I think the following:

- Being qua being is articulated as pure multiplicity in mathematics, which is precisely not a discourse, nor does it require a rhetorical arrangement.

- The politics of emancipation are distinguished from the politics of administration in that they have precisely an effect of truth regarding that which in the collective remains, without them, invisible and unthinkable. And, moreover, their central philosophical category is not liberty but equality, whereas for Barbara Cassin (as for Hannah Arendt) the politics of appearance and opinion, supported by sophistics, makes liberty into the non-philosophical category of the political.

- The great novel no doubt has a powerful truth effect, and a truth may certainly present itself in a structure of fiction: but then we are entirely outside what can be called 'philosophy'.

I who think, in sum, that precisely because it is only the ruse of homonymy, all consensus is the perdition of thought, I would naturally be inclined to become indignant when Barbara Cassin declares: 'Performance is the measure of the true' (p. 20). This praise of virtuosity troubles me.

But the reasons invoked by Barbara Cassin are so learned, so specious, so strong . . . In a word, they are so Greek . . . The temptation of blissful sleep on the bed of rhetoric once again gets the better of me. To speak and, in so doing, to give being; to have no other political imperative than freely consensual persuasion; to delight in the admirable prose of novels. What else could one ask for? My strength will go no further, I can sense it, than to ask Barbara Cassin a few connected questions.

First question: Plato. Barbara Cassin must debunk Plato, since it is Plato who has put forth the exclusion of sophistics from the philosophical corpus. But is this debunking, according to Cassin's own criteria, performative? Barbara Cassin's project consists in opposing the philosophical history of philosophy with a sophistic history: it is a grandiose historical 'shifting' [*bougé*]. Does Plato not end up equally excluded from the new figure as the sophists were from the old one? On this point, Barbara Cassin remains Heideggerian. She adopts a closed idea of ontology and of metaphysics. She adopts the theme of their closure. She even thinks that the entrance onto the stage of the sophists in the pre-Socratic thematics, which she constructs with sovereign artistry, will accomplish what Heidegger, still the captive of ontological authenticity, could only programme. I quote: 'Far from lapsing thereby into non-philosophy, I believe on the contrary that one is confronted with such a strong stance with regard to ontology and metaphysics in general that it could well turn out to be philosophically insurmountable' (p. 26).

My question is the following: Does this instruction of the definitive critique of metaphysics not come at the price of a mistreatment of Plato? A Plato reduced, so to speak, to the exclusion of sophistics, which Barbara Cassin can thus easily *invert*, just as Marx pretended to do for Hegel? Ah! Plato remains the touchstone of all philosophy. I mean: the readability, the *type of intellectuality* of your project depends almost always on the *gesture* (foundation, oblivion, frontier, disorientation…) that one attributes to Plato.

The inversion of an alleged gesture of exclusion involves us in the pursuit of an original. It is by no means assured, however, that Plato misrecognized this original to such an extent.

Barbara Cassin thinks that it is a specifically sophistic thesis, and thus one that Plato obliterated in favour of an ontological imperialism, to hold that 'only the case of non-being permits one to become conscious of discourse and of the difference normally inscribed in the enunciation of identity: the "is not" should become the rule of the "is"' (p. 43).

Now, is this not the most constant motif of anti-sophistic philosophy (Hegel here would be paradigmatic)? Even better: is this not an axiom that Plato himself stakes out, admittedly in a labour that in his own eyes was paradoxical and risky, as the necessary obliteration of the 'first' ontology, that of Parmenides? Three examples, with which Barbara Cassin is more familiar than anyone but which, precisely because she cannot grasp them in her gesture of inversion, she never decides to take up in her teaching, albeit by way of a *complication* of its apparatus (that is, in sum, the bringing to light of a properly 'sophistic' dimension in Plato):

- In the *Sophist*, the inscription of difference, as prerequisite for all ideality, happens precisely from the fact that being, here defined as one of the supreme genres, can be differentiated only insofar as non-being is. The rule of intelligibility of being *qua being* is precisely non-being. Let us understand that if it is a question of thinking being in its difference as being, and not as a simple 'part of being' of another supreme genre (as a part of the being of movement, of rest, or of the Same), then we must 'envelop' the seizing of being under its Other, which is properly non-being.

- In the *Parmenides*, the final hypothesis, the one that will give its positive impulse to all of Neo-Platonism, is that the One is not. The super-eminence of the One will be thinkable only under the sign of its non-being.

- In the *Republic*, the generic form of being is the Idea. When it is a question of designating the principle of intelligibility of the being of the Idea, of what makes it knowable, we must have recourse to the transcendence of the Good. Now, what does Plato tell us immediately afterwards? That the Good is not an Idea, and thus that with regard to the ontological disposition, what is the root of being and the thinkable stands in exception to being, in the form proper to non-being that is the non-Idea.

The heart of philosophy – of metaphysics, I am not afraid of the word – has never been the donation of what is given. On the contrary, it is and always will be a matter of a diagonal procedure: you construct an ontological constraint, a normed discourse – for example, that of the Idea, or that of the supreme genres. And then it appears that being, the real of this discourse, the real of this constraint, is what never submits to it. It is its reverse, its diagonal point of exception, and, consequently, the non-being proper to the whole discourse on being. If being were unveiling and donation, all philosophy would be intuitive and poetic, and not conceptual. The conceptual network of philosophy is precisely the one that is built only under the ultimate rule of its failure; and being, which does not give itself, is what subtracts itself.

My question is then: is sophistics not the simple rhetorical immediacy of this subtraction, the pretension to settle there while doing without the constraint? To imagine that all this is already there, in ordinary language?

One could say: sophistics (or logology) has an immoderate amount of confidence in language. Not because it deciphers therein the primacy of non-being and the seizing 'in fiction' of a created-being, since metaphysics has never stopped giving the strongest examples of this primacy and this seizing. Nor because sophistics posits a *technical* reversibility of being and non-being, a mere rhetorical (and transmissible) arrangement of the immediately natural that 'gives' us language, whereas metaphysics discovers that only by submitting language to axiomatized and constraining conceptual formalisms does one open up thought to the subtractive (to *thinkable* non-being), which arrives only at the point of failure, or in a process of limitation, of these invented formalisms.

What philosophy with Plato repudiates is not the paradox or the 'immoral' complexity of the primacy of non-being, or of the sovereignty of language. It is on the contrary the *easiness* of the sophistic 'solution' that philosophy rejects. That non-being constitutes the rule for being is something flaunted by the sophists. But the difficult thing to do is not to state this and cheerily deduce from it the rhetorician's 'democratic' legitimacy; it is to manage to *think* this and mathematically to deduce from it the laborious existence of *some* truths.

Barbara Cassin wants to lock us up in the alternative: either being is a donation anterior to the saying, and truth is normative for the discourse from the outside; or being is a creation of the saying, in which case truth is useless, given that performance and opinion suffice.

I call (with Plato) 'philosophy' that which is originally subtracted from this alternative, that which diagonalizes it, by situating being in a 'voided' point that is neither anterior to the saying nor created by it, since thought opens itself up only in the *constructed* interval, or the infinite procedural limit, of its own discursive apparatuses. Whence, moreover, the fact that it is not in discourse that being (that is, non-being) is sayable, but in the matheme, in the formula, in always written traces. Whence, too, that a truth is the contrary of a truth imposed from the outside: it is an immanent production.

Philosophy will call 'dogmatic' the position according to which being is given in an unassignable anteriority with regard to the saying. It will call 'sophistic' the symmetrical position that being is a product of the saying. It will identify itself as the regulated labour of a diagonal that subverts the coupling (and, in truth, the profound identity in nature) of dogmatism and sophistics.

My second question will bear on Lacan. Is it so certain that on the basis of a few texts one can easily subsume Lacan under the renewed conception that Barbara Cassin proposes for sophistics? It is true that Lacan – and here Barbara Cassin's textual referents are, as always, literal – grounds reality in discourse and indicates that the outside comes to reveal discourse, and not the other way around. We can grant this much. But neither reality nor the outside is the real. And as far as the real goes, in the sense of the Lacanian topology of instances, we must observe: first, that it is unsymbolizable, and thus subtracted from pure rhetorical production; second, that if it operates by way of speech, it is as absent cause of the consistency of this speech, and not as creation coextensive with its power – this is so true that Lacan maintains in the end that the real is 'what one encounters'; third, that the real is delivered, not by what Lacan calls a correct symbolization and what Barbara Cassin would call a performance, but by the act of a break in which it is averred as the leftover waste, or obverse, of discourse; fourth, that even in the case of formalization, which is a writing and not a discourse, the real is its impasse, and not its production; fifth – and above all – that this real, which is the extimate being of all knowledge, remains the guarantee of truth. Indeed, says Lacan, 'truth can be situated by supposing that which in the real functions in knowledge'.

To sophisticate the intricacies of the triplet truth/knowledge/real is much more difficult than to philosophize them.

For if the being of the philosophers is always the diagonal point of an argumentative constraint; and if it delivers itself as that which is lacking from this constraint, then Lacan with his real is closer to Plato than to Gorgias.

Also granted: Barbara Cassin notes Lacan's objection to Plato that the objet *a*, which is the literal name of the real, is that of which there is no Idea. But precisely: for Plato, the Good, the One, or the Other, are determined as ultimate nominations of being insofar as there is no Idea for them either. And of which, consequently, there is only either a poem, it is true – as in the image of the Sun in the *Republic* – or a matheme – as is the case both for the object *a* in Lacan and for the One-that-is-not in the ninth hypothesis of the *Parmenides*.

Poem or matheme – but certainly no rhetoric of opinions.

Which brings me to my third and final question.

If it is discourse that creates being, if therefore the language performance is the measure of all 'value', then two spaces are the most adequate for the creative deliverance of the maximum of being. So-called democratic politics on the one hand, in the sense of Hannah Arendt – free rhetorical spacing of judgements in the public arena, fruitful hypocrisy of opinions; and, on the other hand, the demiurge of novelistic fiction.

What should we then understand by 'philosophy', supposing that under the emblem of the sophists one wants to maintain and strengthen its motif (as is Barbara Cassin's idea), if not the pale adequation of a metapolitics of judgement to an aesthetics of fiction? And if such is the bastard fate of philosophy, was Plato not entirely right to exclude from it the sophistic principle, so as to found a fully independent discursivity in which the determination of being as non-being in actual fact serves as the rule for an irreducible diagonal of thought?

Barbara Cassin links sophistics to a consensual multiplicity of discursive games, which creates worlds. She roots this ludic Nietzscheanism in the science of the texts. But philosophy begins by destroying the very concept of the world; it knows, as does Lacan, that there only is a fantasy of the world, and that it is only in its defection, or its defeat, that one can subtractively think some real.

Philosophy legitimately constitutes itself as anti-sophistics because it disposes the origin of truths as the vanishing point of the whole mutual shock of discourses. This point is what I call 'event'; and of the event there can be no anterior or constituent rhetoric since precisely the question of its name remains largely suspended. The event is the name of the without-name, that which is encountered, that which arrives and calls up a truth *as novelty*. To believe that there is 'creation' only in the order of language means to confuse the inventive and diagonal search for a nomination of what surges forth with the inaugural vanishing of this 'surging forth' itself. It means to practice what Lacan called 'idealinguistery'.

At bottom, by denying both the event and the procedure by which its subtractive dimension is constrained to deliver itself, sophistics offers only the most inoffensive rhetorical protocols of creation and novelty. What we target in sophistics is the fact that, beneath its subversive appearance, in terms of thought it authorizes only a technical variant of the conservation of linguistic and political resources. Sophistics is not worth the effort. As Deleuze would have said, even though he did not believe in truth either, sophistics is not 'interesting' . . . Besides, this is the ultimate and principal argument for Plato. The sophist is not so much immoral as he is fastidious: 'if he . . . enjoys dragging the argument back and forth, then he's been carried away by something that's not worth much of anyone's attention'.[2]

Barbara Cassin, for her part, does not bore us for a second. But perhaps this is because her most intense strategy consists less in restoring sophistics to its pre-eminence than in saving Heidegger. Therein lies, in my eyes, the *contemporary* force of her argument.

What are the key operations in this salvaging?

1. Displace the centre of gravity from the pre-Socratic concept of Parmenides towards Gorgias. It is at this cost that one

2   Plato, *The Sophist* 259c, in *Complete Works*, ed. John M. Cooper (Indianapolis: Hackett, 1997), p. 283.

can, according to Barbara Cassin, make a certain fictional democratism hearken back to the origins, which cures us from the fascistoid temptations in the style of the 'great forester', while still keeping his anti-metaphysical historical montage.

2. Keep the diagnostic of Platonic closure. Not, however, as gesture of the oblivion of being, but rather, if I can say so, as oblivion of non-being, oblivion of the free *pseudos* inherent in language. As exclusion of sophistics, rather than as obliteration of Parmenides.

3. Replace Heideggerian authenticity, which maintains the jurisdiction of ontology over the political, with the democratic hypocrisy. Thus, the National Socialist misstep becomes a metaphysical sin, and Hannah Arendt becomes the true liberal Heideggerian, whose sophisticated Greeks keep us away from any judgement of truth about the political thing.

4. Give preference to the novel over the poem, since the latter is a pretext for donation, presence, and ontology, whereas the former rejoices in artefact, the false, and logology.

This de-poeticized, de-philosophized, democratized Heidegger makes for a good enough figure so that we may keep the historical arch, that is, the condemnation of metaphysics.

Thus, too, Barbara Cassin thinks that the final Heidegger is not so far removed from the sophistic redemption to which she invites him *post-mortem*: 'So it is not by mistake that one could propose, to characterize both the last Heidegger and sophistics, the common name of "logology" risked by Novalis' (p. 115).

One can of course conclude that this name, common to Heidegger and sophistics, confers upon the latter all the guarantees of modernity.

One can also conclude that what this name shows – and such would be for me the best-founded diagonal use of Barbara Cassin's beautiful book – is that philosophy, in order to renew the anti-sophistic gesture that grounds it, must exclude the last Heidegger. In other words, philosophy must affirm, against Barbara Cassin and against, it must be said, many others, that in the conditions of our time to think the real of being – that is, to think being as non-being, that is, the event as power of truth – we must break with the Heideggerian historical montage, restore Plato to his place, and construct, without the least bit of shame, a contemporary metaphysics.

Of such an 'intempestive' attempt, this book by way of inversion renews the paradoxical courage. It is typical of strong books to stimulate the desire to rise up against them.

19

The Subject Supposed to be a Christian[3]

Paul Ricoeur's discourse, always gracious and characterized by infinite patience, even a kind of academic courtesy, is nevertheless, as a general rule, a combative discourse, always in close proximity to the liveliest debates. This is certainly the case for those debates that divide, roughly speaking, the 'consensual' camp, that is the one which unquestioningly ratifies the conjoint values of representative democracy and juridical humanism.

What is Ricoeur's strategy concerning memory and history? In truth, it is a matter of subtracting history from what has come to be called the *devoir de mémoire* (the duty to remember). What does this 'duty' actually involve? The irreducibility of the extermination of the Jews of Europe (in the narrow version) or of the 'totalitarian' camps (in the broad one) to any ordinary rational conception of historical narrative. And therefore, the submission of history as a discipline to a trans-historical norm. Admittedly, the idea of such submission is not new. The use to which Bossuet put it, for example, is well known. The novelty resides in the fact that the norm which governs the 'duty to remember' does not as such have the character

---

3   Review of Paul Ricoeur, *La Mémoire, l'histoire, L'oubli* (Paris: Seuil, 2000). English translation is Paul Ricoeur, *Memory, History, Forgetting*, trans. K. Blamey and D. Pellauer (Chicago: University of Chicago Press, 2004). Page numbers in the body of the text refer to this translation.

of Providence, as is the case for traditional Christian historians. This 'duty' submits history to an ethical constraint whose origin lies not in a theory of salvation, but in an occurrence of Evil. It can also be said that the 'duty to remember' must, indefinitely, leave open an essential wound in the fabric of history, thereby contradicting the evangelical message of redemption, which asserts that a radical event (the coming of the Son) has forever after sublated the destiny of humanity. From this stems the fact that the contention necessarily involves a third term: forgetting as dialectical correlate of forgiveness. The 'duty to remember' forbids forgetting, whose absolute possibility Christian redemption instead allows. Whatever the scandal at stake (including that of the massacre of innocents), our power of judgement is nothing in the face of the infinity of sacrifice to which Christ consented for our sins.

Let us be succinct, even brutal. Without the stake ever being specified, wagering on the possibility of maintaining himself, all the way through, within the framework of the rules of academic discussion, what Ricoeur in fact seeks to obtain through the sophisticated means of conceptual analysis is nothing short of a full victory. The victory of the Christian vision of the historical subject against the one which today is gaining more and more ground, and which is mainly, although not exclusively, of Jewish origin. On the one hand, a saving event splits the history of the world in two and, by virtue of the narrative's sovereignty, dictates that nothing that ever happens can be allowed to subtract itself from forgiveness, from the remission of sins, from the absolution of crimes, from ethical forgetting. On the other hand, an immemorial Law, of which some think a people are the repository, authorizes absolute judgement and the eternal memory of the crime – the industrial massacre – through which the Nazis (in the narrow version) as well as the Stalinists (in the broad version) attempted to eradicate entire populations deemed unworthy of life as measured by a Promethean and perverse project to found a 'new man'.

Let us assume that one belongs, as is the case for any philosopher installed within the democratic consensus, to a spiritual tradition that claims to found the juridical humanism imposed by such a consensus. Then, it is necessary to choose between the subject of the Law, who confronts a tradition of persecution, and the subject of faith, for whom a sacrificial event opens the path of salvation. And as the current, crepuscular, times are devoted to historical reversal and selling the past, the battlefield is the discipline of history.

I will therefore argue that Ricoeur's great book, in all its subtlety and erudition, is no less than a muffled expression of a sort of abstract war which involves, via control over the practice of historians, the spiritual direction of the 'democratic' camp.

For those like me who do not make any claim to being part of that camp, nor of any of its components, the objective analysis of what is happening within it is nevertheless of great importance. All the more because a certain labour of clarification appears necessary: what I have just stated is not affirmed by Ricoeur in those same terms, nor by those who respond to him. What is truly at stake in this polemic remains concealed, as always when one deals with the boundaries of ideology and conjunctural choices. One can even say that just like Descartes, Ricoeur advances masked – although it is clearly necessary to invert the respective meanings, religious or unbelieving, of the face and the mask.[4]

My work of reading must thus consist in showing where and how – though his name is never stated – what we will call 'the Christian subject' enters the stage.

---

4 *Translator's Note*: In his *Cogitationes privatae*, Descartes writes: 'Actors taught not to let any embarrassment show on their faces, put on a mask. I will do the same . . . I have been a spectator in this theatre which is the world, but I am now about to mount the stage, and I come forward masked.' See *The Philosophical Writings of Descartes*, trans. John Cottingham et al. (Cambridge: Cambridge University Press, 1985), vol. 1, p. 2.

I. THE ENDEAVOUR

In order to construct history's independence in relation to memory, Ricoeur seeks to suppress all reference to operators that could force the unity of the two terms. This is why he declares explicitly that he does not presuppose either an identifiable psychological subject that as such would be the bearer of a 'memory', nor a determinate actor (class, race, nation…) destined to be the subject of History.

One can say that Ricoeur practices a kind of *epochè* – or rather, a differed entrance onto the stage – not of all that could be, as in Husserl, the thesis of the external existence of an object; but rather of what would present itself, on the stage of the dialectics between history and memory, as a thesis of identification of a subject. This is a central point of Ricoeur's strategy: to reach the topic of the subject as late as possible. Just as, I might add, God himself indeed took his time, with respect to the history of men and their sins, to organize the redemptive coming of his Son.

In fact, the moment of the subject is pushed to the very end of the book, when it is a matter of treating the delicate but conclusive question of forgiveness. That is, it must be pointed out, at the moment when it is necessary – since without it, no forgiveness is possible – to separate the essential subjective identity from the criminal act that may be imputed to it.

This question of the separation between the identity of the actor and the criminal nature of the act is obviously crucial. Indeed, what does it mean that the event of salvation has taken place, if not that our subjective nature is no longer intrinsically sinful and that as a result it can, for all intents and purposes, always be separated from its vilest acts?

But once again, this is not the way Ricoeur speaks. It is only at the very end that he comes to introduce, with elegance, the theme of the possible separation of a subjective identity, to authorize forgiveness and open the way for forgetting. The elegance goes so far as to present this end as a mere 'epilogue', concerned with a difficulty

('The Difficult Forgiveness'), and concluding . . . inconclusively. As attested by the last lines: 'Under history, memory and forgetting. Under memory and forgetting, life. But writing life is another matter. Incompletion.'

The epilogue takes up sixty-five pages out of a total of almost seven hundred . . . what elegance, indeed! That of the smart politician, who knows that the crucial text – the one which will really determine the distribution of votes and the orientation of the Party – is not to be found in the lengthy report written in political jargon and addressing 'the current situation and our tasks', which everyone applauds, but in the brief and secondary motion dealing with the election of the assistant treasurer.

'To write life is another matter' . . . But 'life', my dear Ricoeur, the life of the redeemed subject, is really that to which you silently destined the very long and very fine discussions on the phenomenology of memory, on the status of the archive or being-in-time. This is why the subject – be it of memory or of history – remains indeterminate over the course of six hundred pages. Yes, almost until the end, identity is neither separable nor identifiable. It is an attributive hypothesis: that of which the operations of memory and of historical propositions could be said. And as it is possible – Ricoeur tells us – to limit oneself to this 'could', so one will describe those operations and those propositions without having to assume an identifiable subject. This is really the *epochè* I spoke of earlier, and which Ricoeur renames 'reserving attribution'.

Such is the endeavour that this vast and beautiful book displays: to settle 'objectively', by 'reserving attribution', the examination of the regimes of memory and the propositions of history, so as to make the subject enter the stage only at the crucial moment of correlation between forgetting and forgiveness. Then the subject, no matter how anonymous he may remain, has no opportunity of escaping its Christian over-determination.

II. THE METHOD

We can call 'method' that which authorizes the 'objectivity' of the first six hundred pages of the book. That is, the operations through which we are asked to proceed so as not to have to assume, or identify, 'under' memory or 'under' history, a philosophically recognizable subject.

There are clearly three fundamental operations in this book: attribution, proposition, and unbinding. However, only the first two are methodical. The third, as we shall see, is apologetic.

1. Attribution

This operation consists in taking the view that the processes of memory are objectively intelligible, without having to suppose the existence of a subject. To this end, one has to articulate the core of the problem – the presence of absence – in terms of an ontology of time in a Heideggerian style. It is only in a second moment, once this 'pure' core of intelligibility has been extracted, that the processes of memory become attributable to this or that type of subject. It is really because this attribution can be relegated to a second moment that one can assert that the first moment holds it in reserve.

In essence, the processes of memory can be thought as predicates that one is free to then attribute to subjective types.

Ricoeur can then embark upon a long discussion of the possible types of subjects to which this type of 'memorial' predicate can be attributed. In a very classical manner, he distinguishes three such types: the self, collectives, and 'neighbours'. In other words, the givens of history (collectives) framed by the fundamental diptych of the self and the other, of the soul and its neighbour. Which goes in the same direction as Saint Paul's thinking: belonging to the collective is ideally secondary to what commands charity: 'You shall love your neighbour as yourself.' Let us add: you will remember this command all the more to the extent that you have no memory of yourself. Here we witness the preparation, between the lines, of the subordination of memory, as the supposition of a collective imperative, to the saving space of forgiveness that a self grants to others.

The flipside of reserving attribution is the mobility of this attribution between the three types in question. Let us draw attention to the rules of this mobility, such as Ricoeur finds them in Strawson:

> These predicates possess the capacity of being attributed to others than oneself from the moment they are attributable to oneself. This mobility of attribution implies three distinct operations: 1) that attribution be suspended or performed; 2) that these predicates retain the same meaning in two distinct situations of attribution; 3) that this multiple attribution preserve the asymmetrical relationship between ascription to oneself and ascription to the other. (p. 125)

Despite the final clause of asymmetry, the pair which is constituted, in relation to attribution, by its reserve and its mobility, seems really to forbid memory processes any singularity. Is not a memory that is in some manner averred precisely the kind that makes reserving attribution impossible? Are we not dealing here, against its purely predicative treatment, with all the real of memory, as the quilting point between a subject that cannot be evacuated and that which, in its happening, constituted it in time? When Strawson and Ricoeur declare that memory predicates must 'retain the same meaning in two distinct situations of attribution', they disregard the fact that the central question that one addresses to a memory is not that of its meaning, but that of its truth. And that unlike meaning, a truth cannot be predicated in identical fashion about two distinct subjects.

We must therefore entertain the hypothesis that attribution is an ad hoc operator which aims at granting memory only a predicative status, reserving subjective singularity for the economy of salvation.

2. The Proposition

It underpins the fundamental operation of historical representation. The proposition's axiom of use is formulated numerous times, for example: 'The fact is not the event, itself brought back to the life of a witnessing consciousness, but the content of a statement seeking to represent it' (pp. 178–9).

One sees how Ricoeur tries to follow a middle path. He opposes the confusion between historical fact, on the one hand, and remembered real event, on the other. But he opposes just as much the dissolution of the fact in normative rhetoric or in the laws of fiction. If, as Michelet believed, history is the 'integral resurrection of the past', there will be confusion between history and memory.

But if, as nominalists think, history is strictly speaking coextensive with narrative, without anything real being represented in it, then no historical event can ever be certified. In particular, I would add (but Ricoeur would not), the Christ-event will never ever be anything else but the effect of one discursive regime among others. Consequently, all that one might suppose as real will be subjected to the vagaries of memory.

In actual fact, Ricoeur's middle path obstinately aims at maintaining the prerogatives of history over memory, without having to suppose, at this stage, any historical subject. Hence a kind of positivism of representation, which is certainly the riskiest part of his undertaking.

Indeed, what does it mean for history to be a set of propositions? That one has to write 'the fact that this or that happened', and not directly 'this or that'. This is what allows us to debate truth in history, not as the truth of a fact, which does not mean anything, but as the truth of a proposition.

This is positivism, in so far as everything in the end depends on the correspondence between the signifying aim of a proposition and a factual referent.

But can a proposition represent without implying in the

representation a subjective adherence to the proposition as such? Is it really possible to escape a maxim that one could draw from Lacan, a maxim that would stipulate that it is only for a subject that a proposition represents a historical content?

This is clearly what is at stake in the enormous passage on 'historical representation' (pp. 234–80), which alone would be worthy of detailed technical analysis. In it, one re-encounters Lacan, inasmuch as the capacity of the proposition to stand 'there' where the historical fact has taken place is christened a 'lieutenancy' in a way that echoes the psychoanalytical doctrine of the 'place-holder' of unconscious representation. One can nevertheless note that Ricoeur ends up throwing in the towel, since at the end he simply speaks of an 'enigma' which he presents as the enigma of a 'refiguration'. In short, it is a feature of the being of history to be able to be represented in propositions. The enigma is one of nature; it must be shifted, so says Ricoeur, towards an ontology of historical being: historical being is the being to which it can happen that it is refigured as such in propositions.

It seems to me that there could be a different way of lifting the enigma than this rather dormitive virtue of the historical opiate. One would need to suppose that the historical proposition only exists as such once it has to configure the fact for a subject in the present. There would thus not be one historical representation, but a partition originally distributed among immediately active subjective types. This does not mean that there would be no historical real, far from it.

Rather, this real would be averred as representation only in a field where all becoming-represented (any lieutenancy or place-holding, if you like) confronts a multiple.

This can be said more simply: history is well represented in propositions. But the genesis and destiny of these propositions are subordinated to the present multiplicity of political subjects.

Ricoeur cannot accept this subordination, because he wishes to preserve, to his own (political?) ends, the univocal existence of some historical representations. Moreover, he is also not willing to accept that the subjective adherence to representations is a constitutive phenomenon, because he wishes to engineer the stage entrance of the subject only when the identity of this subject will be practically constrained.

This is taken care of by the third great operation of his *dispositif*: unbinding.

III. UNBINDING AND REDEMPTION: THE CHRISTIAN SUBJECT

When all of Ricoeur's effort, through the operations of attribution and proposition, is directed to safeguarding a kind of phenomenological objectivity on the side of memory, and a 'narrative' objectivity on the side of history, without letting the two be confused, the process of unbinding seeks to organize forgiveness – and forgetting – into a completely new subjective element. Up to this point, we had temporalized predicates whose attribution was suspended. We now have a completely new register, that of power and possibility. Identity, hitherto suspended, proves impossible to find on the side of the substance, the bearer or the predicates attributed to it. All subjective identity is the relation between a capacity and its possibilities.

Was this not in a way what I suggested, when I said that memory and history become activated only from the point of view of a subject in the present? Should we not understand by this that history itself in the end is a representation that depends on the new possibilities that a subject inscribes in the future of the past, its to-come? It is clearly at the point where, through unbinding, the author engineers the stage entrance of a flexible and active subjective identity that I feel closest to him, without all the same being able to agree with him. For the path adopted by Ricoeur avoids having to consider history from the perspective of politics, his goal being to entrust morality if not with history's narrative, at least with its judgement. Let us suppose that his starting point is a juridical question broadly understood: Can one separate a criminal act from the identity of the culprit? For example, can one separate the extermination of the Jews of Europe from the Nazi group, or from the German people, or even from a given identified executioner? We have seen that one can separate attributions from the process of memory and the representative propositions of history from any pre-constituted subject. But when culpability is at stake, the subject is required, precisely as a subject whose entire being is either guilt or innocence. Put differently: the question of the subject, of his identity and of the separability of this identity, only emerges – and this is good old post-Kantian logic – with moral judgement.

To be more precise, only a third separation, after that of memory and that of history, summons in advance the theme of subjective identity: the separation between the identity of a subject and the moral or juridical qualification of his act. This separation is the one that is at work in forgiveness and whose way of operating is unbinding.

Those pages, precisely entitled 'Unbinding the actor from his act', which propose 'an act of unbinding', to my mind, contain the ultimate meaning of the book as a whole.

The fact that these pages spar with Jacques Derrida is not irrelevant. This is a very short but incisive confrontation, very different from the peaceful quibbling with American academics as regards historical narrative, or even from the good-natured reference to the positions of Vladimir Jankélévitch regarding the forgiveness granted (or un-grantable) to the Germans. Here we encounter, in a flash, the real adversary, the other spiritual virtuality of the democratic camp.

Jacques Derrida indeed contends, in a 1999 text entitled *Le Siècle et le pardon* (The Century and the Pardon), in accordance with his ontology of difference, that if one separates the culprit from his act, one in fact grants forgiveness to a subject other than the one who has committed the act – or, to quote him, that as consequence of this unbinding, 'it is no longer the culprit as such that one forgives'.[5]

Ricoeur, as can be expected, responds with a doctrine of possibilities which originated in Aristotle. There is the act, it is clear, but the act does not exhaust what the subject potentially is, or what he is capable of. Now, the identity of the subject resides precisely in this capacity. This is why Ricoeur in the end rejects Derrida's objection. The subject one forgives is really, says Ricoeur, 'the same, but potentially other, not another'.

In fact, it is necessary to engage in an even more radical decoupling than that of act and power or potentiality. It is necessary to distinguish, within the very power of action, between the capacity and its effectuation. Here lies the true foundation of unbinding:

> This intimate dissociation means that the moral subject's capacity for commitment is not exhausted by its various inscriptions in the way of the world. This dissociation expresses an act of faith, a credit addressed to the self's resources of regeneration. (p. 490)

One can see the force of such a gesture, just as one can read its provenance: there is a fundamental asymmetry between the capacity and the act, between the criminal, even abominable, effectuations, and the credit that can be accorded to the possibilities of subjective redemption.

Under the sign of forgiveness, the culprit would be deemed capable of something else than his offences and his faults. He would be restored to his capacity to act, and the action to that of continuing. It is this capacity that would be saluted in the minor acts of consideration where we have recognized the incognito of forgiveness played

---

5   *Translator's Note*: See Jacques Derrida's interview with Michel Wiervorka, 'Le Siècle et le pardon', originally published in *Le Monde des Débats* 9 (December 1999) and subsequently included in Derrida's book, *Foi et savoir / Le Siècle et le pardon* (Paris: Le Seuil, 2001), p. 110. English translation is 'The Century and the Pardon', available at fixion.sytes.net/pardonEng.

out on the public scene. Finally, this restored capacity would be invested with the promise that projects action into the future. The expression of this liberating discourse, abandoned to its naked enunciation, would be: you are worth more than your actions (pp. 502–3).

How indeed could it be any different for a Christian? If the moral economy of a subject does not reside in the power to act and if it is not this power as such that is sublated by God's sacrifice, of what worth is the immense forgiveness granted by the Saviour to a generic humanity?

It all comes down to the fact that it is indeed necessary that the subject may always be saved, no matter what his action has been, for Christ's economy of salvation to prevail eternally and universally. 'Let him who has not sinned cast the first stone.' Yes, of course. Even if it is Himmler or Eichmann? The law of men, admittedly, must be carried out. So says, so demands Ricoeur: this however has virtually nothing to do with the 'true' judgement, the aptly named 'last judgement'.

But then why does Ricoeur remain so silent on the evidently Christian pre-formation of a subject who – being substantially separable from memory and history – is identically exposed to the immeasurable resource of forgiveness and forgetfulness? Fundamentally, my main criticism bears on what I consider to be not so much hypocrisy as a lack of civility, a lack of civility common to so many Christian proponents of phenomenology: the absurd concealment of the true source of conceptual constructions and philosophical polemics. As if it were possible that as radical a choice, especially today, as the one of a specific religion could, at any time, erase its adherence to the effects of discourse!

This is to offend Christ – so Pascal would have thought.

But it does not dispense us from the need to examine the form of the argument.

At a very abstract level, one can simply point out that the pure power to act, in its very indetermination, even if it is not that of an other – as Derrida objects – is not correlated to the identity of the subject either. Strictly speaking, it identifies neither the same nor the other. It is, to adopt the Hegelian vocabulary, the share of non-identity in identity. Therefore, if, to put forward this part of the subject, one forgives the act, one may as well say that one does not forgive anybody in particular, which means that any form of forgiveness is aimed at the generic humanity in each of us. This is really the case of Christ's manoeuvre, which welcomes each and every one only in so far as their gesture relieves them of an 'original' sin, therefore of a fault which, having in effect been committed by all, will be seen as committed by none. This is a supposition, it must be said, which exceeds the resources of philosophy and which hands the baton over 'to the ultimate paradox proposed by religions of the Book', as Ricoeur alludes on one occasion alone (p. 278).

Why not reverse the perspective and start from the act as the unique real point of subjective identity? If the apparatus of Aristotelian thought here proves necessary, is it not ultimately because the correlation between the power and the act is fully intelligible only through a pre-comprehension of objective ends of subjects? In reality, for Aristotle and all the successors attributed to him – or invented – by Ricoeur (Leibniz, Spinoza, Schelling, Bergson, Freud, and Kant himself: see p. 491), capacity (power) is directed to its own good, and in the end to the Good.

If the act diverts it from the Good, it is only an accident, perhaps one of extreme gravity, but inessential when it comes to the always-available resource of good action. This is the decisive point for a Christian, because it alone allows the logic of redemption to be comprehensible also philosophically. All that will have to be done is to rename as 'the subordination of power to the essential positive dimension of the act' what, for the believer, has historically been the consequence of the Saviour's effective coming (it is here that all the themes connect up): the universal establishment of all souls in the possibility of salvation.

Fundamentally, Ricoeur has to distinguish history from memory carefully because the Saviour has really come, and this could not possibly be shielded from the historical facticity of which the New Testament and its erudite commentaries provided representative propositions. And because, for that matter, there is no need to remember it, nobody remembers it. He must also criticize the idea of a 'duty to remember', because Christ's sacrifice, breaking as it does the history of the world in two, is the exemplar of a pure projection which re-absorbs time in an eternal sublation and imposes a sole duty of belief and fidelity, always in the present. In terms of the 'duty to remember', it is soon only a matter of 'letting the dead bury the dead'. And ultimately, Ricoeur must connect the motif of subjective identity to pure power, to potentialities, to capacity, because this path, and this path alone, allows an apparent synthesis of the evangelical message (left in the shadows, although it constitutes the main engine of the argument) and of a philosophical theory of responsibility. As always: *Fides quaerens intellectum.* Even if in the book, with its almost theatrical imbalance between discursive quantities, it is as if the maxim was: *Intellectus quarens fidem.*

My sole ambition in this text was to clarify things. I for one believe that there only exist human animals whose generic soul has never been sublated by any sacrifice, bar those sacrifices they themselves have performed so that some truths could exist. It is permissible for those animals to become subjects, in always singular circumstances. But it is only their action, or the mode in which they persevere in the consequences of such action, that qualifies them as subjects. So that it is decidedly impossible to say, as does Ricoeur: 'You are worth more than your acts.' It is the very opposite that must be affirmed: 'It can happen, rarely, that your acts are worth more than you.'

This is why the only path leading to subjective identity is that of misrecognition.

As Lacan said, in a point that François Regnault has commented on so well: 'God is unconscious.'[6]

Translated by Natalie Doyle and Alberto Toscano,
revised by Bruno Bosteels

---

6 *Translator's Note*: See Lacan's statement: 'For the true formula of atheism is not *God is dead* – even by basing the origin of the function of the father upon his murder, Freud protects the father – the true formula of atheism Is *God is unconscious*', in *The Four Fundamental Concepts of Psychoanalysis* (The Seminar of Jacques Lacan, book XI), ed. Jacques-Alain Miller, trans. Alan Sheridan (New York: W.W. Norton, 1998), p. 59. See also François Regnault, *Dieu est inconscient: Études lacaniennes autour de saint Thomas d'Aquin* (Paris: Navarin, 1986).

PART III. NOTICES

20

For a Tomb of Gilles Deleuze

WHAT IS THINKING?

He liked to say that 'philosopher' was something that he was naïvely, since he put his efforts, without worry or regret, into describing thinking as a component of life. Naïve, but prudent and rigorous. He did not identify, as others do, 'philosophy' and 'thinking'. For him, there were not one but three registers of thinking: philosophy, to be sure, but also science and art.

What do these three endeavours share in common, for them to deserve this same name, 'thinking'? For Gilles, 'to think' means: to make a section in the chaos. To be as close as possible to chaos, and nonetheless to shelter oneself from it. The power of a thought is its capacity to stay as close as possible to the infinite with the minimum thickness for shelter. A thought is all the more creative, the less sheltering it needs. A powerful thought stands, almost naked, in the fiery midst of the virtual.

PHILOSOPHY

Philosophy emerges from the double peril of the absorption back into chaos and the oblivion of chaos in the premature production of transcendence. As subjective tension, philosophy only appears to be defined in purely affirmative terms (creation of concepts). It is much more profoundly defined under a negative command: resist the ineluctable temptation of transcendence, endure the proximity of chaos, victoriously traverse the Acheron.

THE INHUMAN

Against the return of humanitarianism and the conservative philosophy of right, one never ceases to rejoice in the force with which he affirms that the inhuman is the measure of all 'human' creation. But what are the just names of the inhuman? For him, the first and the simplest of these names is the animal. Art is the creation of a becoming-animal (or plant, or ocean, or Cosmos . . .) of the human. And this becoming is monumental. The work is like a tree planted on the horizon, a picked-up heap – unique, dishevelled, and consistent – of sensations that are available forever.

POLITICS

Four important principles:

- The value judgement brought to bear upon a historico-political episode must be immanent. The point is to recapture the intensity that was there, in the moment. We must never refer to some faraway result. Gorbachev does not teach us anything about October 1917. Consequences and lessons lead thinking astray.

- The temporal succession does not count. Historiography, too, leads us astray. The multiplicity of circumstances must be traversed, if possible, at infinite speed, and not according to a single story line. The point is to understand which eternal proposition was created in the flash of the political moment.

- The three figures that singularize artistic creation can be found again in politics: vibration, embrace, opening. Politics creates intensity, gathers and moulds, separates and ventilates. Therein lies its only interest for thought.

- If politics is comparable to a work of art, it is because it creates, in the instant, some moving novelty. What does it create? 'New links among people.'

Gilles Deleuze: creator, by way of concepts, of new links, of hitherto impossible connections. He wove thought like a piece of cloth – with its folds and all.

21

Jullien the Apostate

What I like about François Jullien is that he is not a sinologist. Now there is a strange way of defending him, people will say, against the attacks from some of his colleagues, who accuse him precisely of not conforming to the canons of their discipline.[1]

Hic Rhodus, hic salta, as . . . Marx said.

What is a sinologist? It is a connoisseur of a closed field, of which he is the intellectual owner. And why so adamant on this point? Why here more than elsewhere does a mentality of experts impose itself? Against this mentality, surely, it is not enough of a counterweight to invoke the 'leftist' slogan from the Cultural Revolution, which pretended that, before being an expert, one had to be communist. 'Red and expert'? Certainly not. Expert and colourless, most often. One will object that this is the case of all academic specialists – including, let us say it, the philosophers enclosed in their history, their fetish-authors or, in the case of analytical scholasticism, their stuffy grammarian exercises. To diagonalize knowledges has never been the strength of the Sorbonne types, in spite of the 'interdisciplinary' fad, which immediately squares them by turning diagonals into disciplines.

---

1 *Translator's Note*: Badiou is responding to a series of attacks against the work of François Jullien, most notably in books such as *Contre François Jullien* by Jean-François Billeter (Paris: Allia, 2006). For a discussion of this polemic, see Henry Zhao, 'Contesting Confucius', *New Left Review* 44 (2007): 134–42.

Yes. But to the amateur that I am it seems that the sinologists overdo it, for a fairly simple reason that is at once material and metaphysical: the Chinese language and Chinese writing – mysteries on a white page that surround knowledge with an almost sacred aura. Specialists from all disciplines love to seek shelter behind the old destroyed Babel. Who has not heard the objection that, not knowing the language – from Greek to formal logic via German or Hebrew – they could not hope to understand anything whatever of what was said therein? Only to be followed by organizing an interdisciplinary conference on translation, without in any way moving the lines. Once again, though: sinology goes to extremes in this, as the Chinese language functions like a Great Wall behind which practices or ideas are hidden, of which only the sinologist penetrates the meaning, albeit the most superficial one.

So then, let us go to the heart of the polemic as I see it. One sometimes imputes to François Jullien, in veiled terms, that he is not as much of a sinologist as he says he is. Let us speak clearly in the place of the masked slanderers: that he is not as strongly interior to Chinese language and thought as is ordinarily supposed. Evidently, these insinuations dishonour those who propagate them. It is of interest to objective reason, however, to clarify what renders them possible – just as it is of interest, if I may be allowed this personal comment, to clarify what renders possible the unlikely, the unimaginable suspicion of anti-Semitism that some believe they can spread about me. The slander is no less irrational than what it tries to affect, or to infect.

I believe that, precisely, what renders possible the attacks on Jullien with the tone that we all know is the fact that he puts his immense science as a sinologist at the service of an aim in thinking that does not close the domain in question but exceeds it. Everyone can see that Jullien's work deploys a Difference between Chinese thinking and philosophy in general – that is, philosophy insofar as it contains certainly ontology, but also questions of strategy, moral wisdom, aesthetics, erotics . . . But this difference by no means aims to isolate China, to make it into a counter-paradigm, or to claim that, endowed with such a cultural transcendental, it communicates with nothing. For what interests Jullien in this Difference is neither difference nor identity. What interests him is the universal space in which this different can be thought, so that one finds oneself neither on this side nor on the other, but in the paradoxical trajectory that makes and will continue to make a single intelligible world of the insuperable difference itself.

This aim is evidently heterogeneous to sinology proper, which is the description of the differential elements of the difference in question. It is nonetheless crucial to observe that it is equally heterogeneous to that contemporary form of imperialism that is the certainty of the dismantling of differences under the homogeneity of Capital. Here the names should not mislead us. When one declares that Jullien, by exaggerating the differences between Chinese thinking and philosophy, hinders the great progress of modernization of China, or forbids the latter to rejoin, in a self-evident humanist finality, the unified world of representative democracy and the free market, one speaks of a single space that is totally different from the one that Jullien proposes. Let us say it: one makes oneself the harbinger, once again, of the claims of the West.

It is here that one understands that Jullien must battle on two fronts. Whence, parenthetically, the fact that he has twice as many enemies. On one side, to academic sinology, he opposes a process of thinking that lays out the logic of differences and identities only in order to dis-enclose the space where it operates. Which is what turns sinology towards its outside. On the other side, to the 'democratic' propaganda that wants to incorporate China without delay into our crepuscular ruminations, he opposes a process of thinking that surmounts the differences and identities only in order to render intelligible their irreducibility. And this time, the point is to turn the overcoming of sinology towards its inside.

Jullien's paradoxical trajectory sheds light on each border of a given difference by the separation of identities, and then sheds light on the identities by traversing the differences. In the end, his gift to thought is a hypothesis that is fundamental today: there is a single world, it is true, but this world is structured by different modes of thought. Fiercely opposed to this hypothesis are the tenants of the new democratic world order as well as the culturalists of multiplicity. There is nothing surprising, therefore, in the fact that Jullien is forced to do battle. Guard yourself on your right, guard yourself on your left – but you have no chance whatever in the centre, your idea is too strong.

This combat is both masterly and risky. As Spinoza said, everything true is as difficult as it is rare. I myself have my disputes with François Jullien. Partly political, because I believe that the disenclosure of the Chinese universe includes the universality of certain aspects of the Maoist adventure – Cultural Revolution and all – and no matter how 'Chinese' this adventure may well be, for better or for worse. Partly philosophical as well, because I believe that the Chinese difference is less exterior to philosophy than interior by default: of the axioms that found philosophy, it only picks up some and in the end suppresses some others. But these disputes presuppose precisely that one recognize the extreme importance, the novelty and the fecundity of Jullien's diagonal investigations.

When one is a philosopher of the post-dialectical dialectic (this is how, forgive me, I would like to define myself), one must sustain at the same time that adversity is a natural milieu and that it is without much importance. Yes, François Jullien: your enemies are legion and well-installed, but they are also without importance. Let us forget them, let us move forward.

A Note on the Texts

The information about the original sources and previous translations of the texts is as follows:

1. 'The Adventure of French Philosophy' was first published in English in *New Left Review* 35 (2005): 67–77. The author's original typescript, as yet unpublished in French, is titled 'Panorama de la philosophie française contemporaine' and dated June 2004.

2. 'The Current Situation on the Philosophical Front' first appeared in French as 'État de front', serving as the introduction to the collection *La Situation actuelle sur le front de la philosophie* (Paris: François Maspero, 1977), pp. 5–19. The text is signed collectively by the Yenan Philosophy Group, a section of Badiou's Maoist formation at the time, the Union des Communistes de France Marxiste-Léniniste (UCFML). Three other contributions by Badiou to *La Situation actuelle* are translated below, in Part II.

3. 'Hegel in France' first appeared in French as 'Hegel en France', in *Le Noyau rationnel de la dialectique hégélienne* (Paris: François Maspero, 1978), pp. 11–17. This small booklet, containing two prefaces and a series of thirteen footnotes annotating the translation of Zhang Shiying's reading of the Hegelian dialectic, was authored by Badiou in collaboration with Joël Bellassen and Louis Mossot. For

the full English, see Alain Badiou, *The Rational Kernel of the Hegelian Dialectic*, ed. and trans. Tzuchien Tho (Melbourne: re.press, 2011).

4. 'Commitment, Detachment, Fidelity' first appeared in French under the title 'Saisissement, dessaisie, fidélité', *Les Temps modernes* 531–33 (1990): 14–22. The first two terms in this title are somewhat difficult to translate, but they are meant to indicate Badiou's changing attitude towards the figure whom he often calls his 'absolute master', Jean-Paul Sartre – from being gripped, when Badiou was still an adolescent, to a later sense of distance or detachment, but always with a deep and unwavering fidelity to the author of the *Critique of Dialectical Reason*.

5. 'Is There a Theory of the Subject in the Work of Georges Canguilhem?' originally appeared in French as 'Y a-t-il une doctrine du sujet dans l'œuvre de Georges Canguilhem?' in the commemorative volume *Georges Canguilhem: Philosophe, historien des sciences. Actes du colloque, 6-7-8 décembre 1990* (Paris: Albin Michel, 1993), pp. 295–304. The English translation by Graham Burchell appeared in *Economy and Society* 27.2–3 (1998): 225–33.

6. 'The Caesura of Nihilism', which deals with the work of Jean-Luc Nancy, is a lecture that Badiou presented at the University of Cardiff on 25 May 2002.

7. 'The Reserved Offering', presented at the colloquium devoted to Jean-Luc Nancy on 18–19 January 2002, at the Collège International de Philosophie, was first published in French as 'L'offrande réservée', in *Sens en tous sens: Autour des travaux de Jean-Luc Nancy*, ed. Francis Guibal and Jean-Clet Martin (Paris: Galilée, 2004), pp. 13–24.

8. 'Foucault: Continuity and Discontinuity' is the translation of the author's typescript 'Foucault: continuité et discontinuité', which is dated 2003. It was published the following year in the psychoanalytical journal *Le Célibataire* 9 (2004): 55–68.

9. 'Jacques Rancière's Lessons: Knowledge and Power After the Storm' was first published in French as 'Les leçons de Jacques Rancière: Savoir et pouvoir après la tempête', in *La Philosophie déplacée: Autour de Jacques Rancière*, ed. Laurence Cornu and Patrice Vermeren (Paris: Editions Horlieu, 2006), pp. 131–54. The English version, translated by Tzuchien Tho, was published in the collection of essays *Jacques Rancière: History, Politics, Aesthetics*, ed. Gabriel Rockhill and Philip Watts (Durham, NC: Duke University Press, 2009), pp. 30–54.

10. 'The (Re)commencement of Dialectical Materialism' first appeared in French as 'Le (Re)commencement du matérialisme dialectique', *Critique* 240 (May 1967): 438–67.

11. 'The Flux and the Party: In the Margins of *Anti-Oedipus*' appeared in French as 'Le flux et le parti (dans les marges de l'*Anti-Œdipe*)', in *La Situation actuelle sur le front de la philosophie* (Paris: François Maspero, 1977), pp. 24–41. An earlier version had appeared in the journal *Théorie et politique* (March 1976): 3–13. The English translation by Laura Balladur and Simon Krysl, with a rich apparatus of annotations, has been published in *Polygraph* 15–16 (2004): 75–92.

12. 'The Fascism of the Potato' first appeared in French as 'Le fascisme de la pomme de terre', in *La Situation actuelle sur le front de la philosophie* (Paris: François Maspero, 1977), pp. 42–52. Badiou signed this text under the pseudonym

Georges Peyrol, which he frequently used for publications of the UCFML, not so much to hide his identity as to disguise the fact that these publications were often the work of just two or three authors.

13. 'An Angel Has Passed' also appeared in *La Situation actuelle sur le front de la philosophie* (Paris: François Maspero, 1977), pp. 63–82. The title is a pun on the French expression *un ange passe*, which is commonly used when a sudden silence or lull interrupts the conversation, as a way to break the awkwardness or spell. This text was also signed with Badiou's pseudonym, Georges Peyrol.

14. 'Custos, quid noctis?' originally appeared in *Critique* 450 (November 1984): 851–63. The title is a biblical expression (*Isaiah* 21.11), taken here from the Vulgate; in the King James it simply reads: 'Watchman, what of the night?'

15. 'Gilles Deleuze, *The Fold: Leibniz and the Baroque*' first appeared in *Annuaire philosophique: 1988–1989* (Paris: Seuil, 1989), pp. 161–84. The first English translation, by Thelma Sowley, appeared in *Deleuze and the Theater of Philosophy*, ed. Constantin Boundas and Dorethea Olkowski (New York: Columbia University Press, 1994), pp. 51–69.

16. 'Objectivity and Objectality' translates Badiou's unpublished French typescript dated 1991 and entitled 'Objectivité et objectalité'. The difference between these two terms derives from the 'double reading' proposed by the author under review, Monique David-Ménard, according to which 'objectivity' refers to the philosophical constitution of the object after Kant and 'objectality' to the psychoanalytical interpretation after Freud and Lacan.

17. 'On Françoise Proust, *Kant: The Tone of History*' first appeared in French as 'Sur le livre de Françoise Proust, *Le Ton de l'histoire*', *Les Temps modernes* 565–566 (1993): 238–48. Kant's name is mistakenly omitted from the title of Proust's book in Badiou's review.

18. 'The Imperative of Negation' is the translation of Badiou's unpublished typescript 'L'Impératif de la négation', dated 1995.

19. 'Logology Against Ontology' was first published as 'Logologie contre ontologie', in the journal *Po&sie* 78 (December 1996): 111–16.

20. 'The Subject Supposed to be a Christian' first appeared in French as 'Le Sujet supposé chrétien de Paul Ricœur: à propos de Ricœur, *La Mémoire, l'histoire, l'oubli*', in the psychoanalytical journal *Élucidations* 4 (March 2003). The English translation by Natalie Doyle and Alberto Toscano was published in the journal *The Bible and Critical Theory* 2.3 (October 2006): 27.1–9. Badiou's title is implicitly modelled on Jacques Lacan's formulation *le sujet supposé savoir* ('the subject supposed to know').

21. 'For a Tomb of Gilles Deleuze' appeared under the title 'Pour un tombeau' in the section 'Deleuze, hommage au philosophe disparu' of the French newspaper *Le Monde* (10 November 1995).

22. 'Jullien the Apostate' originally appeared in French under the title 'Jullien l'apostat', in the collective volume *Oser construire. Pour François Jullien* (Paris: Les Empêcheurs de penser en rond, 2007), pp. 147–51. Badiou's title is a double pun: on the name of the Roman Emperor Julian the

Apostate, also known as Julian the Philosopher, who restored Hellenistic paganism as the state religion; and more obliquely, on the frequent cases of apostasy or renegacy found among French Maoists such as Guy Lardreau and Christian Jambet, whom Badiou discussed in reviews included earlier in this collection.

Index

(handwritten margin notes: "No Buber Camus? marcel?")